S4P183

The biology of religion

the history of religion

In Usukuma, Tanzania, in 1962, several women were killed by mobs of male villagers on the grounds that they were witches. Personal misfortunes are attributed to witchcraft and spirit diviners are approached to ascertain the witch's identity. Once the witch has been found a special cry is used to alert others to her presence. When sufficient men have gathered, they strip off her clothes, chase her to the edge of the village with freshly cut sticks, and beat her severely, sometimes to death (Tanner 1970).

The biology
of religion

V. Reynolds
R. E. S. Tanner

with illustrations by Penelope Dell

Longman
London and New York

Longman Group Limited
Longman House
Burnt Mill, Harlow, Essex CM20 2JE, England
and associated companies throughout the world

Published in the United States of America
by Longman Inc., New York

© V. Reynolds and R. E. S. Tanner 1983

First published 1983

British Library Cataloguing in Publication Data
Reynolds, Vernon
  The biology of religion.
  1. Religions
  I. Title   II. Tanner, R.E.S.
  306'.6 (expanded)   BL802
  ISBN 0-582-30021-5

Library of Congress Cataloging in Publication Data
Reynolds, Vernon.
  The biology of religion.
  Bibliography: p.
  Includes index.
  1. Religion and science—1946–   2. Socio-
biology.   3. Human evolution.   4. Religion.
I. Tanner, R.E.S. (Ralph E.S.), 1921–
II. Title.
BL256.R49   306'.6   82–6573
ISBN 0-582-30021-5   AACR2

Set in 10/11 pt Linotron 202 Bembo
by Syarikat Seng Teik Sdn. Bhd. Kuala Lumpur.
Printed in Singapore by
Kyodo Shing Loong Printing Industries Pte Ltd

Contents

Acknowledgements

We should like to thank the following people for their help, in various ways, with the preparation of this book: Mr B. A. L. Cranstone allowed us to make illustrations from material from the Pitt-Rivers Museum, Oxford; Prof. S. Fukushima obtained a number of Japanese charms for us to draw; Prof. C. Geertz helped in some early discussions; Prof. E. Hulmes made helpful comments on aspects of Islam; Prof. G. A. Harrison generously allowed the time and facilities for the book's preparation; Dr A. J. Boyce helped with correlation statistics for the final chapter; Dr J. Krebs and Dr G. Parker helped to clarify issues relating to r and K selection; Dr T. Raychaudhuri provided some information on suttee; Dr and Mrs H. Kawakatsu provided a superb series of 'Fiery Horse' symbols. We also had useful discussions with Prof. M. Cullen, Mr D. Dickins, and our estimable publisher, Dr W. I. Stevenson. We have been helped by the staff of the Radcliffe Science Library, the Tylor Library, and the North Oxford Mobile County Library. We could not have managed without the interpreting and typing skills of Mrs G. Naish and Mrs A. Thorpe. Many other colleagues, friends and relatives have helped – we thank them all. Finally, we wish to make it clear that we take full responsibility for all the statements, ideas and illustrations in the book.

V.R.
R.T.
P.D.

We are grateful to the following for permission to reproduce copyright material:

Academic Press Inc for extracts from 'Religion & Health' by K. Vaux *Preventive Medicine* (1976); George Allen & Unwin Ltd for an extract by C. D. Darlington from *Evolution of Man & Society* (1969); American Public Health Association for our Fig 2.1 from pp 1101–64 *Am. J. Public Health* (1962); The American Anthropological Association & the author for our Table 7.6 (Dorjahn 1958); The American Sociological Association & the authors for our Table 5.5 (Haney et al 1972); Armand Colin Editeur for our Table 3.4 (Lachiver & Dupaquier 1969); Cambridge University Press for our Table 3.1 & Fig 3.1 (Laslett 1977), & our Figs 7.1 & 7.2 (Flandrin 1979); Human Relations Area Files Press for our Tables 9.1 & 9.2 (Nag 1962); Holt Rinehart & Winston Inc, CBS Publishing for an extract from pp 75–76 (Chagnon 1977); Indian Journal of Medical Research for our Table 12.2 (Singh et al 1962); Israel Medical Association for our Table 2.3 (McKusick 1973); Kinsey Institute for Sex Research for our Fig 6.1 from Fig 56 p 306 (Kinsey et al 1953); Lippincott/Harper & Row for our Table 14.8 (Wynder et al 1959); National Council on Family Relations for our Table 3.6 (Ukaegbu 1977); Oxford University Press for our Fig 13.1 by D. C. Gajdusek *Tropical Neurology* ed. J. D. Spillane (1973); Pergamon Press Inc for our Table 11.1 (Maddison & Viola 1968), & our Table 14.1 (Comstock et al 1972); Society for the Study of Social Biology for our Table 10.2 (Cross & McCusick 1970); University of Chicago Press for our Table 1.1 (Pianka 1970); Wayne State University Press for our Tables 2.1 & 2.2 (Schull et al 1962); John Wiley & Sons Inc for our Fig 10.1 (Dublin 1963).

Though every effort has been made, we are unable to trace the copyright holder of our Table 3.5 from p 224 *Annales de Demographie Historique* (1969), and would appreciate any information which would enable us to do so.

To
Frankie and Penelope

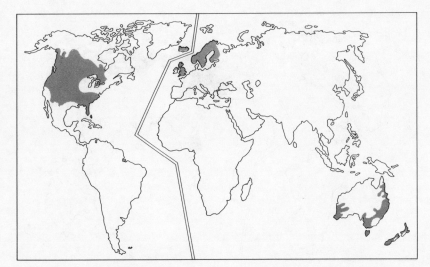

Distribution of the major world religions

Christianity:
Protestant

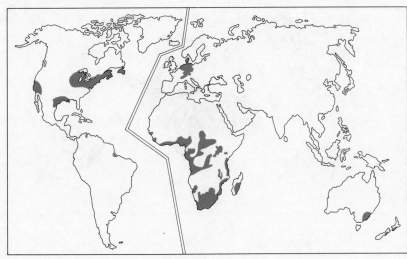

Christianity: mixed
Protestant and
Roman Catholic

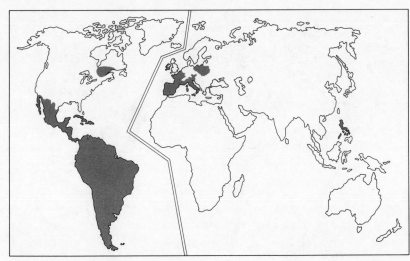

Christianity:
Roman Catholic

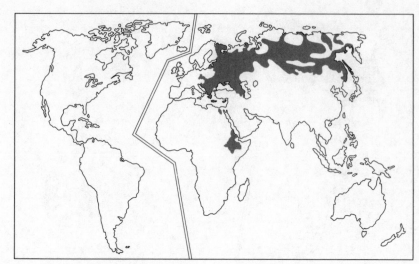

Christianity:
Orthodox

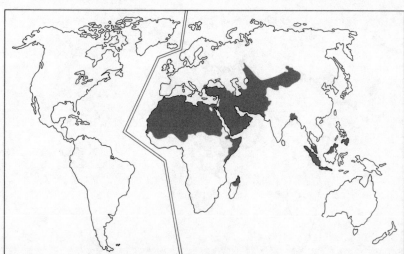

Islam

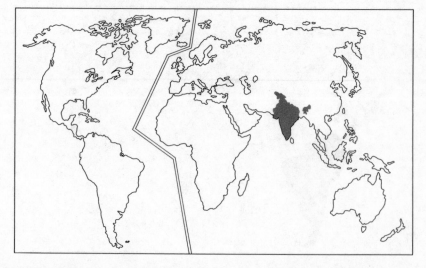

Hinduism

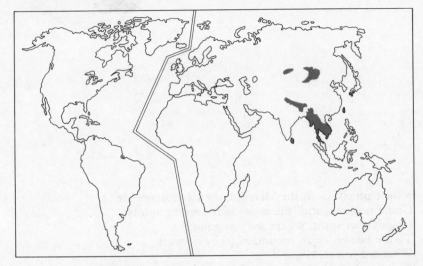

Buddhism

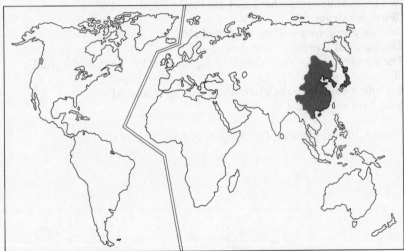

Confucianism, Taoism
Shinto and Buddhism

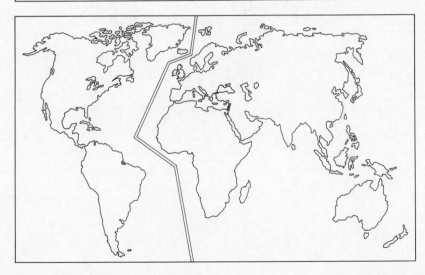

Judaism

In the name of God, the Merciful, the Compassionate!
'Grandmother spirit' [the *ḍukun* addresses the spirits],
'Grandfather spirit, where are you going?'
'To the Purwosedjati mountain' [they answer].
'What are you seeking?'
'We're seeking dringo herb and onions.'
'Why, whatever for!'
'We are going to medicate the little baby.'
The harmful worms – may they all die.
The good worms – may they stay for the whole length of the child's life.
Ah, the medicine looks black [the *ḍukun* spits into it] –
Yes, I am medicating the child.

(from Clifford Geertz, *The Religion of Java*, page 93)

Part One

Introduction

1 Religion and sociobiology

Kotsu Anzen, Kaiun Yakuyoke Goshugo from Kinkajuji Fudoson (a Buddhist temple in Kyoto). This type of lucky charm is found in Shinto contexts in Japan. It is often stuck on the windscreen of cars and taxis as a guard against accidents.

The question we shall be asking throughout this book is 'How does membership of a religious group,* or belief in a religious faith, affect individuals' chances of survival and their reproductive success?' This question has never been properly answered before, and has rarely been formulated in the precise way we have put it above. It raises a number of issues about the relationship between culture and nature, or more exactly between the way human beings organize their social arrangements and beliefs on the one hand, and the processes of natural selection on the other. For it is often pointed out that man is an animal species which needs to survive physically and reproduce in typical mammalian fashion if it is to continue in existence; and it is equally often pointed out that man is unique among all animal species in that he alone is a true language user, a true thinking and speaking being, who creates his own social world and his own existence. He enters at birth into a largely man-made way of life, bringing to it his own particular genetic endowment. What happens to his genes is a question for biology, and this depends largely on his ability to survive and produce fertile offspring who will reproduce in their turn. If, for religious reasons, an individual is subject to infanticide or attracted to a celibate way of life, or if by following a religious practice he or she contracts a disease and dies, the results in biological terms are fairly clear-cut. If, on the other hand, he or she follows religious practices that are conducive to health and hygiene, ending up with a big healthy family all of whom go on to reproduce in their turn, the results for his genes are again clear, at least in the short term. But as Malthus saw in the human demographic field and Darwin in the biological one, successful reproduction leads to overpopulation, shortage of resources, and differential survival according to how well individuals can manage in the ensuing competition.

There arise questions of whether and how religions can be seen as developments arising out of human efforts to deal with long-term survival prospects. Animals, it is now being understood, have come to deal with long-term survival problems in a very complex way. It is a fact that only those creatures are alive today whose ancestors have behaved in ways that have led to their own survival and that of their

* For a suitable working definition we can use the same one as is used by Rappaport (1968), which is taken from Durkheim as follows 'a society whose members are united by the fact that they think in the same way in regard to the sacred world and its relations with the profane world, and by the fact that they translate these common ideas into common practices' (Durkheim 1961: 59).

offspring. Thus genes have been selected which enabled both competitive and co-operative strategies to be combined in ways that were appropriate to their survival in the short and long term. In every generation throughout evolutionary history certain genes have been weeded out, and they continue to be weeded out, by the criterion of reproductive success. Sometimes the process is dramatic and whole species are weeded out, or whole orders even, because their genes cease to produce viable results. Sometimes the process is one of population expansion followed by reduction when resources get tight, by the process of starvation. In many species overproduction is associated with an increase in numbers of predators and in this case the predators select genes.

'Individual selection' is the norm in animals rather than 'group selection' even though most animals live in groups and it is groups that normally survive through time. It is in the context of group life that the genes of individuals are selected for or against. Group life itself, in animals, is largely the product of individual selection. From this fact arises a set of theories about the genetic transmission of co-operative behaviours which together constitute the subject of sociobiology. The subject is summarized in E. O. Wilson's *Sociobiology* (1975), a useful discussion of theory and facts.

That is our starting point. Wilson's book takes us from insects to primates. But when it comes to applying its perspectives to man it meets with a whole series of complex problems, most of which still remain to be sorted out, and some of which this book, by way of examples, casts light on. Man is an exception to many (but not all) rules of animal life. Food is a scarce resource for him, as with other species, but he can by his own conscious efforts increase its variability and supply, which few other species can do except by storage as in the case of bees or squirrels. Man can plan ahead, ration resources, distribute food in one way or another. Human reproduction is likewise subject to all manner of rules and taboos, prescriptions and proscriptions, and only man can engage in sexual activity while employing mechanical means to avoid the production of offspring. Man can conceive of his own personal death, or transition to another world, or return in another form; he can speculate on the future course of events, however hazily, and plan accordingly. He knows there will be future generations, who will have problems akin to his. He may make a mess of his planning, and a bad mess may mean loss of life, but he does have the brain-power, the conceptual equipment, to foresee and construct ways of life that he hopes will survive and prosper beyond his own lifetime, and he has the memory and oral or written traditions, embodied in his cultures and their precepts, to help him to solve problems and try to deal with the unpredictability of the environment.

Nothing could be more different from the animal situation at this, the group level. In animals it is only individuals that transmit genes, and it is in part at the genetic level that socially relevant instructions are passed from generation to generation. In man, by contrast, it is more often at the level of ideas of appropriate action, by the transmission of institutions with roles meshed into social structures, that social action and organization continue down the generations.

It has become fashionable of late to decry the man/animal dichotomy, to state that it is outmoded, against the evidence, and to seek for unifying processes between man and nature. This is all to the good, but should not blind us to such differences as exist. We seek a balanced theory, avoiding bias either way. Though accepting the different mode of inheritance of social patterns in man and animals, we recognize that man nevertheless has to survive and has to reproduce in sufficient numbers to go on surviving as a species. Given his partial emancipation from short-term ecological and genetic controls, his survival nevertheless depends on his genetic potentials, genetic limitations, and above all on the environmental possibilities of wherever he happens to live. He is not altogether free; far from it. We can expect the powerful forces of natural selection to eliminate both individuals and groups if they do not arrange things properly. To this extent we are in the same situation as all other species of animal life. The difference is entirely that we have far more room to manoeuvre, we can do so far more quickly and can act far more appropriately to new kinds of crises than they can.

Here we begin to see the significance of asking the question 'How does membership of a religious group affect individuals' chances of survival and reproduction?' Man has used culture to facilitate his occupation of all sorts of environments and in doing so has had to adapt to different climates, kinds of food, and so on. To some extent (e.g. in skin colour) we know his adaptations have been genetic, but by and large this has not been the case. Any other species that had succeeded in colonizing the whole planet would have had to make many more genetic adjustments than man has done, and would undoubtedly have speciated. In man's case, curiously, genetic studies have shown a remarkable uniformity from one population to another. Differences between populations, for most genes studied, are of frequency only; the genes themselves tend to be the same in population after population from the equator to the arctic circle. Despite years of intensive study, the number of human genes whose selective advantage is actually understood can be numbered on the fingers of one hand. The 'sickle-cell gene' is one such, giving some resistance to malarial infection. But in nearly all other cases, gene distributions have not been successfully correlated with environmental factors. Some human population geneticists are now coming to the conclusion that most human genes may well be selectively 'neutral', and their distribution is due to genetic drift rather than natural selection. Others prefer the 'selectionist' view and emphasize past selection and the known fact that in many cases single genes do not act alone but are linked to others, or play a part in developmental processes that are important with respect to survival and hence natural selection.

Culturally, however, man is very diverse. He does not share a common culture, differences being of kind rather than of frequency. It has thus been argued that culture is man's method of adapting to all the subtle and complex differences he has had to deal with as he colonized the earth. The genetic argument that follows this is 'neutralist': owing to man's cultural adaptability, his genes have been transmitted at rates based on mating frequency and the elimination of pathological mutations, but without much interference in this process from environmental factors. Those genes continue to exist whose properties lead to the production of individuals whose brains and bodies are capable of incorporating the prevailing cultural inputs of their societies. A great variety of polymorphisms and gene combinations can do this.

At the level of social action, we no longer have to deal with genetic

substrates in any causative or programmatic sense, but with enabling
mechanisms that allow the cultural instructions to emerge in praxis. As
a colleague, John Gillman once put it (personal comment): the genes provide the tools, but the tools themselves don't tell as much about the
machines those tools are engaged in making, repairing and modifying.

Cultures, and their ingredients like religions, are thus largely independent of genetic causal mechanisms. But they are nonetheless at the
ecological interface; it is they that determine how biologically successful, in terms of survival and reproduction, individuals and their groups
will be. Thus while religions cannot be understood as caused by natural
selection working on genes, they nevertheless have implications for
natural selection. They are part of the social environment in which the
gene frequencies work themselves out. This states in the clearest terms
how human cultures and their ingredients are related to genes. Our cultures are not like the social organizations, or even the so-called 'cultures',
of other animals. The latter are often very flexible and responsive to
changes in ecological circumstances or social factors such as population
density. This responsiveness arises because individual animals have
evolved responses to adjust behaviourally to a range of situations.

This is not to deny that the behavioural adjustments of animals can
be innovative, such as the learning of blue tits to peck holes in milk bot-
tle tops, or the use of sticks to obtain termites by chimpanzees. But
such kinds of learning, which mark the pinnacle of wild animals' flexibility, fall far short of human cultural processes because the latter are
not just 'adjustments' to environmental factors. Human cultures are
actually recreated environments. The culture brings about a new situation for its members, a network or grid or mesh between them and the
real world. Animals perceive the real world with their senses, which
order it for them, but man, besides doing this, actually re-structures it
through his ideas and mechanical devices. He builds not only objects
but intangible institutions with rules which become totally real for him,
as anyone who ignores or disobeys them finds out.

Now we can see man's curious situation. He has built up these cultures, these rules of do and don't, can and can't, should and shouldn't.
There are good reasons for their existence. Some of the reasons are connected with his genetically and physiologically determined body processes, such as the endocrine changes at puberty. Some are connected with
his psychological 'needs', both biogenic and sociogenic in origin. Some
of the reasons for religions or religious practices are to be understood as
adaptations to a 'real' world of environmental pressures and constraints.
Others arise out of the logic of the mind in its cultural and social context.

The question of 'adaptation' is a particularly intriguing one. What
makes it so is that religions nearly always go far beyond any simple
adaptation to environment in the sense that one adapts one's clothing to
the prevailing temperature, or cultures 'adapt' their houses to the climate. Religions re-state and then reveal to people the 'true' nature of
Nature. By 'true' here is meant 'culturally true'. Thus religion may tell
a person that a certain kind of animal is sacred and must not be killed or
eaten; or, as in parts of South America, it may insist that good crops
occur only when the spirits of the ancestors so wish it, and the spirits
have to be approached with reverence and ritual before planting seeds.
Malinowski (1935) described how Trobrianders used magic in their

I. A rice seedling planting-out
ceremony (Mibu Ohana-Taue)
directed at the deity
Sanbai-Sama in modern
Japan. This Shinto rite involves
a flautist and a number of
drummers who attend the first
planting-out by the women of
the community.

II. Among the Sukuma of
Tanzania, rainmakers carry
out ceremonies at the end of
the dry season in waterless
stream beds. They sacrifice a
black goat and throw 'thunder'
stones on to the ground.

gardening, not just as an 'extra' but as deeply ingrained understanding of the art of horticulture. The same is true of Japan (Plate I), and rain-makers are known to everybody (Plate II). Christianity sets man above all the 'beasts'; Buddhism sets him among all living things as an equal; Hindus elevate the cow; Muslims and Jews denigrate the pig.

Here we are coming to a more adequate understanding of what it is that religions really are, which we need to discuss before we can broach the question of religion and biology. It would be a mistake of omission not to see clearly at the outset the phenomenon of religion as it appears to those individuals practising it (that is its 'emic' aspect) and its appearance to an outsider (its 'etic' aspect). For example, the Islamic practice of *wudū'*, a minor ritual ablution that gets rid of minor ritual impurity, is prescribed in the Koran to be performed before each *ṣalāt*, or act of prayer. The essential elements of the *wudū'* vary somewhat according to the sect concerned, but according to the Shāfi doctrine they are (in order): washing the face, washing the hands and forearms up to the elbows, rubbing the wet hands on the head, and washing the feet. Other sects include beard, nose and mouth in the ablutions. All sects allow the use of sand instead of water if the latter is unavailable. Finally, there is the major ritual ablution, *ghusl*, for major ritual impurity; this involves washing all over the body and hair.

The emic reasons for these activities are the Koranic injunctions, commands that carry the full weight of Islamic belief, to ignore which could constitute sin. Etically, to an observer with biological or medical interest, one reason for washing could be that it promotes hygiene and reduces the incidence of infectious disease, or conversely that it actually spreads disease. The etic comprehension is quite separate from the emic one. It is the same in the case of the Christian shared communion cup or the Muslim pilgrim kissing the Kaaba stone: both practices might very well meet with almost any Western doctor's disapproval.

We see here the complexity of the field of study we have embarked on. Reproduction requires many years' survival. Survival depends on adequate health up to the time of reproduction. Adequate health depends on avoiding serious disease. All societies have developed ways and means of disease control, depending on their local disease environment and population density factors that affect possibilities of spread of infective agents. Religion sometimes but not always concerns itself directly with disease control. Its prescriptions may harmonize with other ideas of hygiene or they may not. In emic terms, religious acts may be thought so sacred that disease transmission is just not a factor to be reckoned with. The water of the Ganges is so pure in the minds of pilgrims that its enormous bacterial content, even if suspected, is an irreverent irrelevance. Religions are not by and large 'about' health and disease; they are about sanctity, the purification of sin, good and evil, rather than medical ideas of clean and dirty. They are, everywhere, embedded at many points, in many curious and subtle ways, in the cultures of which they form part. They transcend the world of nature in the same way all culture does. Just as living matter had new properties that were not present in the inorganic world – the ability to reproduce, to vary, to compete for scarce resources, to evolve – so culture has properties not found in the organic world – arbitrariness, symbolic content, linguistic representation.

Just as we need a different theory to explain the evolution of life from the one appropriate for the evolution of the inorganic world, so we need yet a third theory for the evolution of culture. In the inorganic world our theory involves processes such as entropy, cooling and the organization and reorganization of atoms and molecules into a variety of complex integrated forms.

In the case of life, our theory involves the process of natural selection, enabling only certain genes to proceed forward from one generation to the next, again leading to the production of variety as selection takes different paths in the many different environments of our planet.

In the case of cultures, our theory involves the processes of representation, explanation and social reorganization, yet again producing an infinite variety of forms according to the particular ecological and historical circumstances faced by human societies since man became intelligent enough to devise cultures, and perpetuate them, some two or three million years ago.

This book will only marginally be concerned with the inorganic level of phenomena – with non-living, physical matter and the theories involved in accounting for its construction, its forms and its processes of change over time. This book is concerned with the two remaining levels, the natural world and the cultural world, and especially with the problem of explaining the complex relationship between them.

We shall be constantly on the lookout for any general relationship that may become apparent between these two levels, but we shall be careful to let the data speak for themselves, rather than selecting data and fit one particular idea. In particular there exists one idea we shall keep in mind as a possible link between these two levels. This is the idea of 'functionality' or 'adaptation'. In this idea, the events and processes that occur at the cultural level have three distinct relations to the natural world.

First, cultural processes may serve the bodily needs of individual humans, as in the 'functional' theory of Malinowski (1944). Second, they may be in some way functional with respect to the reproductive success of individuals, a Darwinian approach favoured by E. O. Wilson, N. Chagnon, W. Irons, M. Dickemann and others. Third, cultures may in some respects be adaptive to the environment i.e. they improve the access of people to the scarce resources around them in the physical world, as in the theories of M. Harris, R. Rappaport, A. Vayda, and others.

There is value in each of these different approaches; each plays its part and sheds its particular light. They should not be seen as exclusive of each other. The differences between them, great though they are, pale into insignificance against a perspective that comes from another quarter. There exists a school of thought in social anthropology that holds that much, perhaps most of what we can properly call 'culture' is not functional or adaptive in any of the above senses; it has a life of its own, rules unto itself that were first brought into existence by the imaginations of our ancestors, and have ever since been subject to interpretation and modification by other people down the ages, a process that we see going on apace today, wherever we look, and that we ourselves contribute to, each in his or her own particular ways.

A very interesting range of explanations thus exists at the present, between those who hold that cultures exist as second-order, dependent variables, the primary determinants being biological or ecological; and those who hold that cultures are *sui generis*, being different expressions of a common human capacity, the capacity for culture, which, though doubtless evolving in the organic world as part of our biology, has since given rise to a great variety of forms that cannot be explained in terms of their functions or adaptivity to the natural world.

It must certainly be true that cultures are not wholly free to vary, at least not if they are to survive. Many, of course, have failed to survive. Is it by chance that others have survived? Or have they adapted and evolved in ways we can discover by studying them? We can only see what *has* survived, and we never can be sure what *will* survive. What does it take for a culture to survive? It is an old dilemma. There is no easy way out, such as a general law. Such laws have been formulated. 'Social Darwinism' was one such; 'society-as-an-organism' was another. Let us look briefly at these.

'Social Darwinism' is something of a misnomer, but it is by now too firmly attached to a particular theory to do much about it. This theory held that evolution had led to the emergence of higher forms of culture and civilizations from lower ones. The 'higher–lower' distinction here was also value-laden: higher meant 'better'. Existing societies around the world were seen as representatives of particular levels of cultural evolution. Higher societies (the highest were those of western Europe) were better in all respects. They had more advanced technology, better brains, better ideas, better music, more advanced religions, and so on. But in one respect they were at risk – they did not always reproduce their numbers faster and so were in danger of being over-run by 'savages'; also owing to miscegenation they were in racial danger from peoples with less excellent 'blood' (or genes). The above sketch runs together the thinking of many European writers on the subject, from Gobineau, via Spencer, to Rudi Lenz and other psycho-racialists of pre-Nazi Germany.

The idea of 'society-as-an-organism' was another effort to bring order to the social world by linking it with the natural. This view was particularly widespread in early twentieth-century Germany. The idea was that just as a body is made up of many cells, each kind of cell having its particular function, so society is made of social 'cells'. It is the harmonious working together of these cells that produces an efficient and capable society that can prosper and evolve through time (see Weindling 1981).

The first type of theory was both mistaken and politically malicious. It was mistaken in that there is no evidence for any evolutionary pathway such as the exponents proposed. Modern anthropologists well-nigh universally reject any value-laden scale of societies, seeing them as equals, however different they are. And although one can suggest scales of development for certain aspects of culture, e.g. technology, those societies with 'primitive' technologies do not always have simple religious ideas or simple kinship systems, indeed they may be more complex than our own. The political implications of Social Darwinism need no spelling out.

The second 'cell-state' kind of theory was also mistaken. It seems to have been based on a more fundamental belief by its proponents, who were middle and upper-class academicians mostly of a scientific and often of a medical bent, that societies can only survive if they run 'efficiently'. One problem with such theories is that the pace of change in societies is so rapid at times that survival can be dependent on a large amount of incomprehension between generations, rapid changes of function by 'cells', development of new kinds of 'cells' and the disappearance of outmoded ones. The theory is, in other words, too static. Politically it cannot be described as 'malicious' though it can be seen as a useful scientific basis for constructing authoritarian ideologies, so that dissidents or unco-operative groups can be weeded out, and thus used as an aid to control by the exercise of power.

Cultures, then, do not evolve like organisms, and are not built like organisms. Today, we are searching in new directions for links between nature and culture. On the one hand there is the demonstration by ecological anthropology that cultures provide *Homo sapiens* with a newer and faster way of getting to grips with his environment than can be achieved by the organic evolution of new behavioural strategies and adaptations of other sorts. On the other hand there is the emphasis placed by sociobiology on the more strictly Darwinian idea that it is those individuals who are most successful at surviving, reproducing and rearing their offspring to reproductive age who do in fact pass on their characteristics to the next generation. Hence the process of transmission of cultural characteristics through time is somehow part of the more basic neo-Darwinian ('neo' =new, because it includes genetic ideas of which Darwin was not aware) process of evolution by 'natural selection'.

This last viewpoint is the one we find most intriguing, perhaps because it seems inherently improbable; also because it does seem possible to test it against some of the facts already recorded in scientific journals and other places by observers unbiased one way or the other since they had no interest in sociobiology as such, and mostly ante-dated it anyway.

Why, it may be asked, have we chosen to focus on the religious activities of people and groups? This may seem an odd, even a bad place to start, but we have not found it to be so. Religions are very concerned with matters biological – with sex, with reproduction, with contraception, with birth and child-rearing. Indeed, it may be that no other aspect of cultural life is so influential in determining how people conduct their day-to-day doings as their beliefs, and these are nearly always deeply ingrained in the religions of their cultures. We have found that a life-cycle approach, taking religions as they concern themselves with all the natural stages of human life from conception to death, comes quite naturally, so we have made it the main basis of our method in this book, taking up the whole of Part 2.

Apart from the life-cycle, there seemed to be two other essential considerations in a biological approach: the effects of religions on human genetical systems; and on the distribution of diseases. With regard to genetics, the evidence we found was convincing that religious can lead to changes in the gene frequencies of their adherents, mainly through closure of gene pools. How this relates to survival will remain unclear until more is known of the advantages and disadvantages of the genes concerned, a currently very hazy area in human biology.

Regarding diseases, again, it became clear that different religious groups tend to differ, often markedly, with regard to their proneness to particular diseases. Sometimes this remains a puzzle, but at other times there are indications of causal factors. For instance, where a religion forbids smoking its adherents largely avoid lung cancer.

But, and this is an important but, even though we have used medical sources to a great extent, our primary orientation is not medical but biological. In other words, it is interesting that lung cancer can be avoided by following a religion that forbids smoking, but if, as often happens, lung cancer occurs late in life, then avoiding it may not necessarily have much effect on a person's reproductive success and ability to rear children, and those are the important questions as far as biology is concerned. So we are only concerned with the health and sickness of religious populations in so far as their long-term biology is affected: what they die of is less important to our analysis than *when* they die.

'Religion' is, quite clearly, a vast topic. No single work can do anything like justice to the range of ideas and phenomena involved in any *one* religion, let alone all the religions of the world. We make no pretensions to being comprehensive. Whole religions are omitted, others barely mentioned. Some social anthropologists, Egyptologists and other specialists will be disappointed at the poor coverage. We are aware of this. We are also aware how easy it is to falsify religious ideas, or distort them. These are dangers we have been well aware of. We have done our best, of course, to avoid pitfalls. But in the main, because of our very subject matter and orientation, we have allowed ourselves to be led by the existing literature on our subject, rather than forcing it into a preconceived shape. This literature consists in the main of two kinds: first, as referred to above, journal papers, chapters and books in the fields of genetics, medicine, biology, etc.; second, the prescriptions and taboos of religious kinds to be found in religious works such as the Bible, the Koran, the Torah and the Talmud, or in commentaries written by clerics and theologians, or by students of religion.

It always occurs where two sets of ideas are being juxtaposed, that those who are most interested in the fine-grain details of the phenomena studied (here the religious ideas), tend to find them out of context or oversimplified, while those who seek generalizations (here the biological ideas of survival, and reproductive fitness) need to group and lump and classify. It is hard to see both the wood and the trees, but this we have consistently tried to do, by alternating between the specific and the general.

Thus our model of the relation between cultural rules and the laws of the natural world has been what could be called an 'open-interaction' model. It is open in the sense that we do not adopt a firm one-way causal argument. Two such arguments exist: first, that natural laws have cultural consequences; second, that cultural rules have natural consequences. We accept both of these, and see them as part of a single process, akin to Durham's idea of 'co-evolution' (Durham 1978).

In relation to sociobiology, especially as it abuts on to ecological anthropology, there is an intriguing idea which initially seemed useful in our examination of biology and religion. This is the idea of K and r selection (MacArthur and Wilson 1967). K stands for the carrying capacity of the environment, r stands for the maximal intrinsic reproductive rate. The idea is that natural selection acts differently on species in two ways according to ecological conditions. Where resources are more or less continuously 'tight' throughout the year, a condition found mostly in the rather seasonless tropics, natural selection has pro-

Religion and sociobiology

duced species with behavioural strategies that produce relatively few young, together with a lot of parental care, often bringing in the male as well as the female, so as to assure the survival of those few who are born; this is *K* selection. By contrast, where resources are plentiful at one time of the year but scarce at another, a condition found mostly in the seasonal temperate zones, evolution has resulted in species with social and behavioural strategies that produce an abundance of young at the good time, and there is a great thinning out later. In this case parental investment by the male is not prolonged; his activities are geared to moving from one mate to another. This kind of selection is *r* selection. Pianka (1970) developed these ideas and we have included a summary of them (see Table 1.1).

	r *Selection*	K *Selection*
Climate	Variable and/or unpredictable: uncertain	Fairly constant and/or predictable: more certain
Mortality	Often catastrophic, nondirected, density-independent	More directed, density-dependent
Population size	Variable in time, nonequilibrium; usually well below carrying capacity of environment; unsaturated communities or portions thereof; ecologic vacuums; recolonization each year	Fairly constant in time, equilibrium; at or near carrying capacity of the environment;. saturated communities; no recolonization necessary
Intra- and interspecific competition	Variable, often lax	Usually keen
Selection favours	1. Rapid development 2. High r_{max} 3. Early reproduction 4. Small body size 5. Semelparity: single reproduction	1. Slower development, greater competitive ability 2. Lower resource thresholds 3. Delayed reproduction 4. Larger body size 5. Iteroparity: repeated reproductions
Length of life	Short, usually less than 1 year	Longer, usually more than 1 year
Leads to	Productivity	Efficiency

Table 1.1 Some of the correlates of *r* and *K* selection (After: Pianka 1970)

Using these ideas as a starting point, it was possible to set up some predictions, or hypotheses, about cultural processes, purely in order to see whether they acted in ways analogous to those of natural selection in relation to the organic evolution of species. If we found that they did, this would be of the greatest interest, since it might point the way to the discovery of general laws embracing both biology and cultural processes. As one of us had already written:

Sociobiology is the study of society in which emphasis is laid on genetic transmission mechanisms in relations to ecological adaptation. As such it cannot account for the patterns of human cultures because these are not based on genes, and the extent to which they can be understood in terms of ecological adaptation is very variable. Of interest for the future is a possible link-up of sociobiology with ecological anthropology (perhaps via games theory or cybernetics) since this may provide the basis for a general theory of society linking both the social worlds of non-human species and those of man (Reynolds 1980: 41–42).

In actual fact, we eventually determined not to follow the parallel of r versus K selection, but to focus on r and exclude K. One reason for not using the r/K dichotomy as rendered by Pianka (see Table 1.1) was that we should only be confusing matters concerning the evolution of species by natural selection with matters concerning the evolution of religious rules by cultural selection. This, however, could be overcome by the simple expedient of using K^c and r^c instead of K and r. A second reason was rather more complex. In the case of K selection, constancy of food supply is generally linked to the relatively seasonless tropical conditions, while on the other hand r selection and a fluctuatating food supply (plus other fluctuations) are found in the seasonal temperate zones. In the case of man, this set of linkages has been transformed by the increasingly thorough management of food supply through agriculture and pastoralism in the temperate zones, so that today it is in these regions, not the tropics, that man has gone furthest in assuring himself an adequate food supply throughout the year. Because of man's interference with the food supply, the relation between ecology and selection processes has thus been changed, but again we did not need to abandon the idea of a K/r dimension because of this. We could still have argued that where food resources are stable all the year round (i.e. for man mainly in the temperate zones) social rules are geared to the production of a relatively small number of young per family, and that the husband is brought in extensively to contribute to family care: this would, then, be a K^c dependent process. By contrast, where food resources remain subject to fluctuations, owing to inadequate human controls, floods, and droughts, (i.e. in the so-called 'Third World', 'South', or 'developing' countries) social rules are geared to the production of larger numbers of young per family, and parents would distribute their energies accordingly: this would be an r^c dependent process.

A third and major reason, however, became clear to us when we looked carefully through the data in our own book. It became clear that, from our life-cycle approach, the resulting religious prescriptions and taboos were nearly all concerned with the extent of reproduction, and not with the carrying capacity of the environment. Our approach led to the emergence of a contrast between religions that were actively 'pro-natalist' and those that were 'anti-natalist' or concerned in various ways to limit the production of young. We had not studied or intended to study the way religious rules related to the 'carrying capacity' of the land. Indeed, this would seem to be a very difficult task indeed in the case of man, because the idea of K (carrying capacity of the environment) is not straightforward, for two reasons. First, peoples the world over can and do import highly variable amounts of food from other areas to support their populations, which affects any idea or measure of 'carrying capacity'. Second, the variable use of fertilizers and insecticides by man again produces effects on the carrying capacity of his land. Neither of these processes occur in the animal world.

The final reason, however, arose from the biological critique of r and K selection (Stearns 1977). Stearns contrasts two types of explanation for the correlations associated with r and K selection, which he calls 'deterministic' and 'stochastic'. Both are concerned, though in different ways, with establishing life history strategies from environmental data. The two methods do, in fact, differ with regard to their predictions. But more importantly, Stearns found that when he tried to test either method empirically (in a number of fish species) he found it impossible to get clear results because of a large number of ambiguities in the results. Most of the ambiguities stemmed from the large, and unknown, number of steps between the genetic and phenotypic levels of analysis. Stearns concluded:

In short, the theory of r and K selection contains a serious, and to my way of thinking fatal, flaw: A population that has a life history thought to result from r selection is called 'r selected'; a population with the opposite traits is called 'K selected' in the absence of either evidence or deductive logic indicating that such traits have been molded by density-dependent effects. Such traits may eventually be shown to result from density-dependence, but the connection has yet to be demonstrated. (Stearns 1977: 155).

In view of the fact that this comprehensive review of the relevant studies is inconclusive, we felt that to base our analysis of cultural selection on what appears to be a rather tentative hypothesis regarding natural selection would be a mistake.

We have thus considered the matter of reproductive strategies as such in relation to the environment and its properties, seeing religious ideas

The Life Cycle		r^c- selection	r^c+ selection
Ch. 3	Conception	Few better	Many better
Ch. 4	Infanticide and abortion	Approved of	Disapproved of
Ch. 5	Birth and childhood	Few births, more care	Many births, less care
Ch. 6	Adolescence	Delayed reproduction	Early reproduction
Ch. 7	Marriage	Late marriage	Early marriage
Ch. 8	Celibacy	Approved of	Disapproved of
Ch. 9	Divorce and widowhood	Remarriage disapproved of	Remarriage preferred
Ch. 10	Middle and old age	Refrain from reproduction	Reproduction continued
Ch. 11	Death and disposal of the dead	Shock, separation, denial	Acceptance as routine
Ch. 12	Concepts of disease	More hygiene conscious	Less hygiene conscious
Ch. 13	Infectious diseases	Intervention and cure	Resignation, passivity
Ch. 14	Non-infectious diseases		

Table 1.2 Predictions for religious rules based on r^c- and r^c+ selection

and rules as an intervening variable. We have not been concerned with the K/r dichotomy (or continuum, or distinction), but with what could be called the $r-/r+$ distinction. If religious rules seem to be favouring high levels of reproductive activity we can think of these rules as pro-natalist or $r+$, and vice versa. In order to distinguish the cultural version of r from the biological one, we shall call it r^c throughout. The distinction involved is thus between r^c+ for pro-natalist rules and r^c- for anti-natalist rules of culture. On the basis of this distinction we can draw up some predictions (see Table 1.2) concerning the topics of our various chapters, against which we shall check our findings in the final part of the book.

We can end this preliminary consideration of theoretical arguments by frankly acknowledging that religions can be auto-destructive and thus run counter to any evolutionary tendency to survive and reproduce. The inhabitants of Jonestown, Guyana, were a breakaway sect of white and black Americans. They had vowed to kill themselves if ever the authorities tried to destroy their way of life. The founder of the sect was the Rev. Jim Jones, his church was called the Christian Assembly of God. According to reports in the mid-1970s, this sect, both before and after the move to Guyana, lived under a regime based on physical force, and there is evidence that some church members were wanted men. Many however were not and were simply attracted to the faith, it seems. In any event, a visiting US congressman, Leo Ryan, sent there

III. The scene after the mass suicide by members of the Christian Assembly of God at Jonestown, Guyana, in 1978. Cyanide was prepared in orange juice and drunk by adults who sprayed it into the throats of children using syringes.

to report on the sect, together with two cameramen and a journalist, were ambushed and killed by sect members, after which the majority of the people on the 2,700 acre settlement gathered together and committed mass suicide by cyanide poisoning. The number of bodies found was given as 383, including that of Jim Jones himself, his wife and son. These events took place in mid-November 1978. (Plate III.)

The example of Jonestown is of relevance to the present argument because of the clear evidence it provides (as have other religious acts of mass self-destruction) of the power of ideology to take over and control human life. Considerations of survival, resource control, defence of self and group, family size, etc. can all be abandoned in favour of self-destruction. No other species does anything truly comparable (not even the famous lemming). Other species certainly act or even adapt in ways that lead to their extinction, but the parallel is not a close one.

Clearly, the complex case of the events at Jonestown should not lead us to hasty generalisations. It was an exceptional event, though not a unique one. We should not conclude that Christian teaching, or indeed the teaching of any of the major religions, contains instructions for suicide. The opposite is the case. What we can draw from this and allied examples is the demonstration that when a set of religious beliefs is firmly integrated into a group's general ideology and the group's existence is threatened, it may turn on itself rather than surrender. The religion, perhaps, gives the unity needed for concerted action, even though that action may be against its principles.

Our next concern is the life cycle. Before beginning it, however, we can introduce it with a kind of prologue concerning religion, fertility and genetics. For if religion is having biological effects we should expect to see them reflected in patterns of fertility and gene distribution.

Conclusions

In this first chapter we have presented the main ideas relevant to our field of interest. The primary question we shall be asking is 'How does membership of a religious group, or belief in a religious faith, affect individuals' chances of survival and their reproductive success?' We contrasted two modes of explanation of social processes in animals and man: the natural and the cultural. We examined the various kinds of selection processes that can be distinguished: natural selection, cultural selection, group selection and individual selection. We then considered the question of whether cultures could be seen as 'adaptive' responses to ecological conditions. Animal learning (including animal 'culture') was contrasted with the human equivalents, in terms of the tendency of human cultures to re-fashion the environment (by the use of value-labels etc.). Emic and etic approaches to the understanding of religious ideas were contrasted for instance in relation to medical matters, where religions sometimes appear to favour practices that seem medically disadvantageous.

The issue of adaptation was seen as both central and complicated. We distinguished three kinds of adaptation: one relating to the needs of the body; another relating to reproductive success; and a third relating to the environment. Each of these, when used as a background for the explanation of features of religions, produced functional answers. However, it was by no means clear that religious ideas and practices could necessarily be understood in functional terms. Religions might be, and doubtless are, to a great extent *sui generis*, with their own predicates, logics, rules and structural principles relating to other aspects of social organization and the history of particular situations.

Nevertheless we set ourselves to search for any rules that might exist relating religions to biological processes. We looked at two earlier attempts, both of which can now be seen as failures: that of Social Darwinism, and that of the cell-state. Our search for new directions brought us again to sociobiology. Religions, clearly, were much concerned with the regulation of biologically relevant actions of individuals at all stages of the life-cycle, and we focused in particular on two contrasting kinds of cultural selection, namely $r+$ selection and $r-$ selection, and we found it possible to set up some predictions about the kinds of religious rules we would expect to find in human societies.

2 Fertility and genetics

Introduction

In the first chapter we laid out the general outline of the arguments that concern us, arguments about culture and nature, genes and survival, individuals and groups, adaptation and idiosyncrasy.

This second chapter represents a first step in the investigation itself. It is an intermediate step before beginning a series of investigations into the human life-span, and how religions bear on the biologically important stages of man's passage through life, from birth to death. Before plunging into that, there is some preliminary spadework to be done. For it could be said that even though religions have rules and convey ideas relating to the biological side of man's existence, the effects of those rules can only be guessed or hypothesized about. This is in large part true. Where a religion bans the use of a certain kind of food, as for instance when Islam and orthodox Judaism ban the pig regarding it as unclean, polluted and unfit for human consumption, we can suggest that this is, or was, functional – it has saved, or does save, more lives than it has lost, hence those groups which have practised this rule have survived, while others have not. Evidence for such arguments is in general not to be found; they are thus weak in any scientific sense, being little more than reasonable conjectures. The question thus arises: What evidence is there that religion has any biological effects? Could it not be that religions are of no biological consequence at all?

Genetic evidence

It is with that sceptical question in mind that we come now, first and

Some religions condone occasions of licence before periods of austerity. In this imagined scene, a pre-Lenten fancy dress party is being held. Endogamous groups at such times relax their barriers and genes flow across normally closed frontiers.

foremost, to the matter of genetics. We shall show that some groups held together by common religious beliefs, because they tend to keep apart from people of other religions, often do develop or maintain characteristic genetic features. The importance of this first step is to demonstrate that some groups that are distinct in the religious sense are also genetically distinct. This is nearly always because they form endogamous units, and there is thus every reason to suppose that they are genetically distinct because of the so-called 'founder effect' – the result of their ancestors having had certain genes or certain frequencies of certain genes – together with the process of genetic drift occurring thereafter.

But we should be unwise to conclude that a founder effect, together with the process of genetic drift occurring thereafter, can explain the whole of such differences as we find. It is always possible, and indeed likely, though immensely hard to demonstrate, that natural selection has played or is playing a part. The reason it is so difficult to prove this is that with a very few exceptions we do not know the selective advantages of single genes and it is the frequency of single genes we have to use in order to demonstrate genetic differences between religious groups. Those single genes whose selective advantage we do know about are mainly anti-malarial genes, such as gene S (sickle-cell) and the gene for haptoglobin, G6PD. In such cases we can naturally expect the genes concerned to be present and spread in malarial zones, and where we find them elsewhere we can safely attribute this to migration; if their population frequency differs according to religion this would not be due to natural selection unless there is some aspect of religious activity that renders some groups more liable to contract malaria than others. In fact, such an occurrence does exist: the Parsees of Bombay are a distinct group both by virtue of their beliefs and their considerable wealth. This latter enables them to have private pools in their gardens. Mosquitoes breed in these pools and thus transmit the malarial agent, *Plasmodium*, to Parsees, who have responded as a group with an unusually high frequency of the gene G6PD (Mourant 1954).

Such clear cause and effect relations between religion and genetics are very rare and await further research. But much work has been done to show that religious groups do differ genetically, and in such cases we can never assume that natural selection may not be at work. For example, where there is a taboo on eating pork, any genes conferring resistance to the specific diseases conveyed by eating this meat will have no advantage and their frequency ought therefore to be lower than in groups that do eat pork. The only snag is that we do not know of any such genes! Again, sexual selection can and probably does operate through religion, as follows. Say the concept of physical attractiveness of either men or women differs between different religious groups; those features that are favoured by a particular group will cause their possessors to find marriage partners more easily and will very possibly lead them to produce more children (assuming that not everyone marries). This effect remains a speculation, however, because not only is it hard to find physical characters that are fostered by religious doctrines, but we do not know the genetics of such characters anyway.

Most of our knowledge of genetic factors is derived from medical studies, and we do in fact know of many genetically controlled diseases. Some of these are the result of mutations and others are the result of the transmission of deleterious genes from parents, who are termed 'carriers'. In such cases, endogamy within religious groups will tend to build up the frequency both of the genes themselves and their associated disease phenotypes in the groups concerned. Because many cases of disease-associated genes are known, we are able to see their association with religions most clearly, but we should not therefore assume that religious (or any other) endogamy is a 'bad thing'; if it were so it would not be so common as it is. We simply do not know enough about its genetic advantages in particular cultures and their physical environments.

As we shall see, religious groups are often genetically distinct. This disproves the objection that religions have nothing to do with biology, or that religious beliefs have no biological consequences. On the contrary, they do. It follows that in most cases, where we have religious continuity down the generations, we also have biological continuity.

This is not always true, however. For instance, a monastery of celibate monks can continue down the centuries without physical reproduction, simply by taking its new members from the surrounding community. Orphans have provided the life-blood of monasteries in Sicily for centuries in just this way. Such cases prove the essential separateness of social and physical continuity. But they are the exception, and most religious belief systems are in part transmitted biologically, by sexual reproduction among belief-sharing members. In such systems we find distinctive genetic markers of religiously defined social groups.

This may all sound very straightforward but it has nevertheless to be stressed, as there are all sorts of other arguments we might be presenting, but are not. We are not arguing that genetic or ecological factors determine social (religious) forms. Just the opposite: religious ideas bring about different relations between man and his environment, and between man and man, and hence have biological consequences. Is there a feedback? Do the biological consequences of the rules and ideas affect those rules and, perhaps, 'steer' them, or bring about changes in them or eliminate some and strengthen others? Quite possibly they do: there is endless room for conjecture, and indeed there is endless conjecture in books and papers on socio-ecology and sociobiology. But what is there in the way of solid evidence? We have already shown how difficult it is to find hard evidence as to how genetic differences arise in the first place. So let us focus on the question of how gene frequencies can be maintained or exaggerated in religious groups.

Marriage rules: Japan

Religions organize marriage and hence mating arrangements by indicating to people the range of individuals who are possible or preferred mates. The fact that another person shares the same religion can be seen as a prerequisite for marriage and in some cases an injunction to reproduce. These prerequisites and injunctions may be in a positive or negative form; there may be precise injunctions about marriage partners, certain degrees of close kin such as brothers and sisters may be tabooed, while other more distant kin such as second or first cousins may be preferred. Such details often fall within the religious doctrine itself and are sanctioned by the deity. It is a sin to disobey them.

Details of just such a distinction come from Japan. In the history of

Japan neither common law, Buddhism nor Shintoism prohibit consanguineous marriages whereas the Catholic Church has banned marriages of siblings, half siblings, first cousins, first cousins once removed, and second cousins. The incidence of cousin consanguinity found in Catholic marriages (which would have required an ecclesiastical dispensation) in Nagasaki has been shown to be 4.92 per cent of all marriages (Schull 1953). The incidence of this degree of consanguinity in the marriages of the surrounding non-Christian community was 8.2 per cent. Allowing for errors, the difference between these two rates probably lay between 6.6 per cent and 3.37 per cent. It was also concluded that this difference in marital consanguinity rates had existed for some centuries.

More detailed studies have been carried out on the island of Kuroshima in the Nagasaki Prefecture. This island contains some 2,250 people who have been either Buddhist or Roman Catholic since the original occupation in the seventeenth century (Schull *et al.* 1962). While the Roman Catholics may not have practised their religion during the long period between the expulsion of the original missionaries and their reappearance in the nineteenth century, they do appear to have followed injunctions against consanguineous marriages. This distinguishes them clearly from the Buddhists on the island, with whom they have, apparently, always lived in harmony. Comparing sub-parishes of roughly equal size it was found that in the Buddhist marriages the mean coefficient of inbreeding was 0.01809 while in the Roman Catholic sample it was 0.005778. Consanguineous marriages thus occurred more frequently among Buddhists with the average coefficient of inbreeding differing three-fold between these two small communities.

	Buddhists			Catholics			Grand Total
	Related	Unrelated	Total	Related	Unrelated	Total	
Number of families	14	21	35	22	118	140	175
Number of childless couples	1	2	3	0	8	8	11
Number of children ever born	74	101	175	140	676	825	1,000
Number of children dying before 20 years of age	10	11	21	20	61	81	102
Per cent childless couples	7.14	9.52	8.57	0.00	6.78	5.71	6.28
Per cent mortality	13.51	10.89	12.00	13.42	9.02	9.82	10.20
Mean children ever born	5.29	4.81	5.00	6.77	5.73	5.89	5.71
Variance children ever born	7.60	9.56	8.59	9.33	8.93	9.07	9.06
Mean children surviving to 20 years of age	4.57	4.29	4.40	5.86	5.21	5.31	5.13

This pattern of mating was associated with other differences. Firstly, within each community, the reproductive performance of related parents produced more children than that of unrelated ones. Second, again within communities, the mean number of children surviving to the age of 20 years was slightly greater in the families of more closely related than among the less closely related parents. However, between the two communities, the less closely related Catholics produced a greater mean number of children than did the Buddhists. The data are given in Table 2.1.

Table 2.1 A summarization of the reproductive performances of Buddhists and Catholics, related and unrelated, married in the years 1920–39 (From: Schull *et al.* 1962)

Fertility and genetics

Also, the data show a considerably higher death rate of children in related marriages than in unrelated ones, 13.51 per cent as compared to 10.89 per cent among Buddhists, and 13.42 per cent as compared to 9.02 per cent among Catholics. The mean number of children per family surviving to 20 years of age in the Catholic community was 5.31 and in the Buddhist 4.40.

What do these data signify? They tell us that, whichever religious group we take, the fertility of the more closely related couples, and the viability of their children, is somewhat greater among the more closely related parents than the unrelated ones. But at the same time more children, on average, are produced by the Catholic parents who are less closely related in general than are the Buddhists. The answer to this apparent conundrum is not hard to imagine, knowing as we do that Catholicism forbids mechanical forms of contraception. Thus we probably have here evidence of the effect of religious rules on reproductive performance at group level. And since the two groups do not differ significantly with regard to child mortality, the Catholics must be expanding their population relative to the Buddhists. Two factors complicate this picture however. First, some 3–5 per cent of Catholic women become celibate nuns, and second there is a certain amount of emigration from the island each year.

The above data concern rates of fertility and mortality, the primary determinants of evolution. Both of these are to some extent the cause of gene frequencies whether the genes are selective or neutral, and the outcome of gene frequencies for genes that are selective. Schull *et al.* do indeed give data for these communities in respect of a number of genes. The frequency of red–green colour blindness, a genetic trait, was 0.0417 for Buddhists and twice that, 0.0923, for Catholics. The distribution of ABO genes among the heads of households and their spouses is shown in Table 2.2

As this table shows, Buddhists and Catholics have a very similar frequency of blood groups A and AB. But for group B the Catholic frequency is three times as high as that of the Buddhists, while for group O the Buddhist frequency is twice that of the Catholics. The gene fre-

Buraku	*Phenotypes*				*Gene frequencies**		
	A	*B*	*O*	*AB*	*p*	*q*	*r*
Motomura							
Buddhists	35	5	21	5	0.36950	0.07826	0.55224
Furusato							
Buddhists	12	5	24	3	0.18606	0.09440	0.71952
Catholics	12	8	4	1	0.32114	0.20913	0.46973
Todobira							
Catholics	37	27	20	6	0.28383	0.20895	0.50722
Total							
Buddhists	47	10	45	8	0.29026	0.08470	0.62504
Catholics	49	35	24	7	0.29162	0.20893	0.49945

Table 2.2 The distribution of ABO blood groups among heads of households and their spouses by buraku and religion (From: Schull *et al.* 1962)

* The frequencies are maximum likelihood estimates, with *p* estimating the frequency of the gene, I^A, *q*, the gene I^B, and *r* the gene I^O.

quencies themselves, *p* (gene A), *q* (gene B) and *r* (gene O), are also shown in this table. No anthropometric (i.e. gross morphological) differences were found between the two groups.

The authors conclude: 'Whether these differences have arisen as a consequence of or merely been maintained by religion is moot since the two communities do not have a common origin in the recent past. The important consideration, however, is the occurrence of demonstrable differences between individuals of a common race isolated from one another only by religion' (Schull *et al.* 1962: 297).

The Amish

The members of the Amish sect of Protestants who came to the United States in the early eighteenth century have remained socially isolated since then and constitute a 'genetic isolate'. A study of the Amish in Homes County, Ohio (Cross & McKusick 1970) has revealed distinctive differences between them and their surrounding non-Amish neighbours. The sect is strictly endogamous and marriage partners are taken mostly from within the home community (accounting for 86.1 per cent of partners); marriage with members of other Amish communities is in proportion to the number of social and genealogical ties. The Amish are very conscientiously endogamous, as was shown by a study of blood groups that indicated that there were no paternal exclusions even for premaritally conceived children, despite the fact that some Amish girls prior to marriage worked outside the community as domestic servants (Jackson *et al.* 1968).

Let us consider first some non-genetic features of this group. The adult sex ratio in this community of 9,724 was 1.003 males per female as compared with 0.971 for the entire US population and 1.043 for rural regions alone. The ♂:♀ sex ratio over the age of 55 years was 1.216, a much higher male figure than for the general US population which in 1960 was 97.1 (US Dept of Commerce 1979).

The Amish crude birth rate was 33.3 as compared with 21.1 for the entire US. They thus had an intrinsic rate of natural increase of 3.019 per cent which would double their number every 23 years. They marry later than their peers outside the community, average age at marriage being 23.0 years for females and 24.1 years for males as against 20.6 and 22.8 years respectively in the US as a whole. Birth control in any form was and is strictly forbidden and the only restriction on eventual family size is the delayed age of marriage for women, often encouraged by their mothers, which accounts for the unusually high proportion of wives who are older than their husbands (34.7%) whereas for the whole US population in 1977 it was 14.4 per cent (US Dept of Commerce 1979).

Only 3.8 per cent of Amish women who had lived with their husbands up to the age of 45 years had never been pregnant, which is a little below the 4–5 per cent of married American women who are thought to be unable to become pregnant due to involuntary causes. The community had a twin birth rate of 15.3 per 1,000 live births, higher than the highest known non-Amish twinning rates of 14.5 for US non-whites and 14.3 for the Norwegian population, while the Amish of northern Indiana have an even higher twinning rate of 21.1.

The importance of the Amish for genetic studies is that, as far as one can tell, few new genes have come into the community by immigration or conversion since they arrived in the United States 150 to 250 years ago (McKusick 1973). Several normally rare recessive gene diseases regularly occur among them. Some 50 to 52 cases of the Ellis–van Crefeld syndrome, a form of dwarfism with relatively greater shortening of the distal part of the extremities, polydactyly, and dysplasia of the fingernails, have been found in one Amish group. This is about equal to the total number reported for the whole of the rest of the world up to that time (McKusick *et al.* 1964a). Similarly, Amish groups show high frequencies of pyruvate kinase deficiency anaemia (Bowman *et al.* 1965), haemophilia B (Wall, *et al.* 1967), limb-girdle muscular dystrophy (Jackson and Carey 1961) and cartilage–hair hypoplasia (Plate IV), a short-limbed form of dwarfism with sparse fine hair (McKusick *et al.* 1965). All these conditions are much rarer in non-Amish communities. McKusick (1973) lists 12 genetic disorders first identified among the Amish and a further 18 which have been studied among them (Table 2.3).

The Dunkers

Parallel studies of the Old Order Dunkers (Glass *et al.* 1952 and Glass 1953) show a similar demographic isolate but one which has experi-

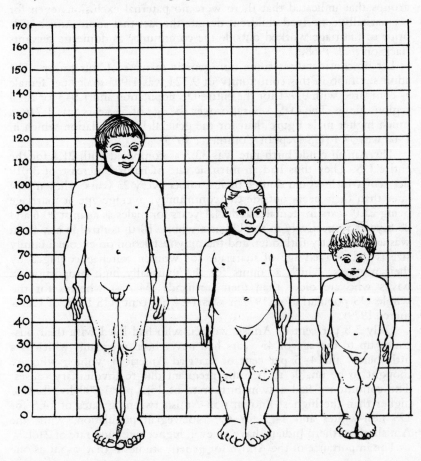

IV. Cartilage–hair hypoplasia in Old Order Amish children. This is a form of dwarfism. On left is a normal child of 7 years. Centre and right are affected children aged 9½ and 5½ years respectively. (McKusick *et al.* 1965)

Some 'new' genetic disorders first identified among the Amish
Troyer syndrome (multisystem disease)
Mast syndrome (spastic paraplegia with dementia)
Cartilage–hair hypoplasia
Pseudo-mongolism (autosomal recessive)
Byler disease (fatal intrahepatic cholestasis)
Hypertrichosis cubiti (? autosomal dominant)
Cross oculocerebral syndrome with hypopigmentation
Short leg and cataract
Albinism, 'yellow mutant'
Hershberger syndrome
Deafness–myopia–oligophrenia
Adducted thumbs syndrome

Other genetic disorders studied among the Amish
Agoitrous cretinism
Amyotrophic lateral sclerosis (autosomal recessive)
Ataxia telangiectasia
Biedl–Bardet syndrome
Craniosynostosis
Cystic fibrosis
Dominant spastic paraplegia
Ellis-van Creveld syndrome
Epidermolysis bullosa
Haemophilia B
Hydrometrocolpos
Limb-girdle muscular dystrophy
Phenylketonuria
Pyruvate kinase deficiency haemolytic anaemia
Reno-retinal dysplasia
Swiss-type agammaglobulinaemia
Symphalangism
Weill–Marchesani syndrome

Table 2.3 Genetic disorders among the Amish (From: McKusick 1973)

enced a drastic reduction in the size of the endogamous group from some 70 years ago when these German Baptists split into three groups that have remained separate. Since 1850 about 64 per cent of Dunkers have married other members of their group.

Comparison of Dunkers' ABO blood groups with those of their US neighbours and those of their ancestors in Germany showed that group O had typical US frequency, whereas group B had a lower frequency than both the general US population and the West German one from which they had originated, while group A was significantly higher. For MN blood groups, M was approximately 10 per cent higher than West German and general US population levels. Rh frequencies conformed closely to the US average.

Mid-digital hair, a character under close genetic control, showed a significantly higher frequency of fingers without hair on the mid-digital segment, this being in many cases absent on three out of four fingers. Another such character, distal hyper-extensibility of the thumb, was significantly lower in this isolate than in the Baltimore white population with which it was compared. The Dunkers had 74.7 per cent un-attached ear lobes as opposed to 59.5 per cent in the Baltimore sample, while left-handedness and ambidexterity did not differ from the general US population.

Jewish sects

Since the creation of the modern state of Israel, considerable work has been done on the genetic composition of the Jews (see Goodman 1979 and Mourant *et al.* 1978). This has confirmed their heterogeneity as between Ashkenazi, Sephardi and Oriental Jewish communities. The separation of these groups probably began with the first dispersal of the Jews deported to Babylon in 586 BC and continued with a long series of subsequent dispersals. These three groups, of which 80 per cent are Ashkenazim, have been geographically separate for some 1,500 years and have developed different profiles of genetic diseases and disorders (Adam 1973; Krikler 1970; Sheba *et al* 1962).

Groups of Ashkenazi have unusually high frequencies of some autosomal recessive diseases, particularly essential pentosauria (pentose in the urine), adult type Gaucher (a form of enlarged spleen), Tay-Sachs (infantile idiocy) and familial dysautonomia, which have frequencies of 0.020, 0.020, 0.013 and 0.010 respectively, as well as other rarer recessive conditions such as Niemann–Pick, Factor XI deficiency, spongy. degeneration of the central nervous system, and torsion dystonia. Ashkenazi groups have been found to lack some diseases such as phenylketonuria, which has a non-Jewish European rate of nearly 0.01.

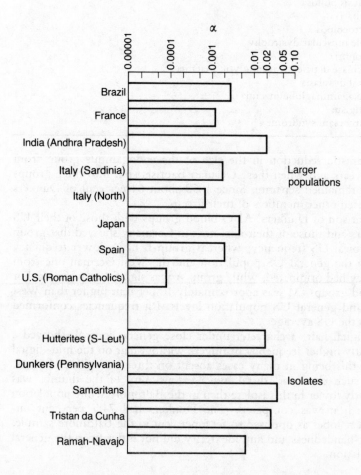

Fig. 2.1 Average inbreeding coefficient (α) in some larger populations, and in some isolates. Note that α is given on a logarithmic scale. (From: Bodmer and Cavalli–Sforza, 1976)

Bonnè (1965), Sheba *et al.* (1962) and others have made special studies of the Samaritans, a self-conscious and self-distinguishing Jewish sect
living in two communities, Nabulus and Holon, in Israel. The whole
sect has 460 members and dates its existence back to the first/second
centuries AD, though this is disputed. It is wholly endogamous and
claims always to have been so. In some respects it can rightly be regarded as one of the most inbred groups in the world. It has a very high
degree of inter-relatedness, α, the average logarithmic coefficient of inbreeding being 0.0519 for the whole population (see Fig. 2.1). First
cross-cousin marriage is the preferred form, up to 40 per cent of marriages being of this kind.

No fewer than 13 deaf-mutes, a genetic, probably recessive condition, were found in a study of this sect, all of them first cousins or
nearer relatives of each other, and the disease has been traced back to a
single individual born in 1783.

Their blood group frequencies are mostly as expected (i.e. conform
to those of neighbouring populations) except that they are very low on
gene B ($q = 0.06$), and in the case of the MN system, a significant excess
of MN heterozygotes occurs, indicating the possibility of a selective
advantage for this condition. A number of Hl^A histocompatibility
alleles are completely absent from the Samaritans – these make some of
the antibodies concerned with the body's immune response system.
Their absence could imply gene loss, through failure of those ancestors
with these genes to reproduce, coupled with lack of introduction of the
genes from outside because of the strict practice of endogamy. Or the
missing alleles could simply be the result of 'founder effect', i.e. no such
genes were present in the original founders of the sect and have never
entered it. The same applies to the G6PD gene: common among their
Ashkenazi neighbours, it is absent in the Samaritans.

The Sephardim have one genetic disease of known high frequency:
the semi-lethal 'familial Mediterranean fever' affecting one out of 600
persons among Libyan Jews. This disease is transmitted by an autosomal
recessive gene. It appears as a periodic syndrome with recurrent fever
and pain in the abdomen, chest and joints. This disease is also relatively
prevalent among Iraq Jews and Christian Armenians but does not occur
at all among Iranian, Yemenite and Indian Jews. Some rare recessive
diseases have been found in specific Sephardic sub-groups: Tunisian Jews
have selective B_{12} malabsorption, and a high proteinuria frequency of
0.02; while Moroccan Jews have glycogen-storage disease Type III and
ataxia telangiectasia in high frequencies.

The Oriental Jews are a heterogeneous group of communities with
no common denominator but most of them, particularly the Babylo-
nian group, are characterized by high frequencies of favism and the
thalassemias.

A cautionary note

In assessing the results of some genetic surveys, we should take due
note of the caveat sounded by Karlin *et al.* (1979) who point out:

*The usual frequencies quoted are averages of large Ashkenazi populations . . . It
should be emphasized that systematic screening programs on these diseases for
other populations are lacking. Bloom syndrome, once considered a 'Jewish*

genetic disease' can no longer be placed in this category according to recent studies (German 1979). In our opinion 'Jewish genetic diseases' can be largely an artifact of the intensive data collection among Jewish populations. As more population groups and/or isolates are researched, the concept of 'Jewish genetic diseases' will probably disappear.

This warning note is well taken. Where detailed research focuses on particular groups, more curious findings will be made in those groups and could mistakenly be thought to be characteristic of them. An analogy can be made with crime rates: as more police are brought into an area its 'paper' crime rate goes up because more crimes are discovered.

We should not, however, make the mistake of throwing the baby out with the bath water. Depending on the degree of isolation of the group in question, some true genetic distinctness can be expected. But in regard to an entire, enormously dispersed group such as 'the Jews' or even 'the Ashkenazi Jews' no such general statements are likely to be valid except within well-defined limits.

Those limits themselves need close scrutiny. How, for instance, do we know whether the boundaries of gene pools are as closed as they appear to be? People of a given sect may claim never to marry outsiders, but they may have sexual relations with them for a number of reasons, producing children who, from a genetic standpoint, are not their parents', but only half so. One way in which this can occur is, of course, as a result of illicit liaisons. Another is as a result of the violations of all rules that occur in times of war: conquerors rape their captive women or turn them into prostitutes for a while. Third, there is the well-known occurrence of 'saturnalia', or ritualized orgies in which conventional barriers to sex are broken down and gene flow crosses the normal boundaries.

Despite the existence of specified periods of sexual laxity just described, a number of religious sects do create gene pool closure to a greater or lesser extent among their members. We cannot generalize from this about religions of all kinds. Some religions, especially those that proselytize, emphasize the idea of conquest and out-mating, the conversion of marriage partners from outside groups, or simply the bringing of more and more people into the religion. Therefore they are constantly dispersing any characteristic genes or changing gene frequencies they might have. In such cases no gene pool closure could occur though the existence of marker genes derived from the original population might be expected along the lines of conquest (*Hebrew Encyc.* 1953: 45).

What, then, do the data from genetics show? It seems clear enough that they do substantiate the idea we set out to examine, namely that if religious rules had any real impact on human biology this should show up in differential gene frequencies. It evidently does so (see Table 2.4). Religions indicate to individuals whom they should marry and thus with whom they should reproduce and this affects the content of gene pools.

But they do much more than this. They transmit important beliefs that affect the reproductive fitness of individuals. This they do by propounding 'proper' methods of food preparation, personal and community cleanliness, child care and other such processes; also by promoting and tabooing actions which could be advantageous or disadvantageous

Japanese (Schull *et al*. 1962)	Blood groups: Catholics high B, low MN; cf. Buddhists low B, high MN
Dunkers (Glass *et al*. 1952)	High-mid-digital hair; Low distal hyper-extensibility of the thumb; low blood groups B and N, high A and M.
Amish (McKusick *et al*. 1964)	High Ellis–van Creveld syndrome; pyruvate kinase deficient haemolytic anaemia; haemophilia B; limb-girdle muscular dystrophy.
Ashkenazi Jews (*Meals* 1971)	High Tay–Sachs disease; Gaucher's disease; familial dysautonomia (Riley–Day syndrome); essential pentosauria.
Samaritans (Sheba *et al*. 1962; Bonnè 1965)	Absence of some Hl^A alleles; absence of Glucose-6-phosphate dehydrogenase; low blood group B, M and N; high deaf-mutism
Hindus (Das 1978; Tiwari *et al*. 1968)	Significant differences between castes for blood groups O, MN, Rh and P.
Muslim Kurds (Lightman *et al*. 1970)	Low on deuteranomaly, high PTC non-tasters
Muslim Israelis (Adam *et al*. 1967)	High red–green vision defect
Sephardi Jews	High familial Mediterranean fever
Yemeni Jews	High phenylketonuria; A-thalassemia
Iraqi Jews	High B-thalassemia
Iranian Jews (Adam 1973)	High oriental Dubin–Johnson syndrome.

Table 2.4 Some gene frequency differences shown in religiously differentiated populations

to the survival or inclusive fitness of the individuals concerned. We shall look at details of such processes in the following chapters.

Conclusions

The question this chapter addresses is a preliminary one, namely to enquire whether there is any solid evidence (rather than reasonable conjecture) for biological effects of religion. We have argued that the 'hardest' evidence is genetic, and we have shown a number of cases where religious rules have brought about different gene frequencies between religious sects. These we have attributed to a number of processes: founder effect, genetic drift, natural selection, dietary (taboo-related) rules – nearly always augmented by the working of endogamous marriage rules.

These marriage rules are mostly concerned with the degree of affinity tolerated or encouraged by the religion or sect concerned. We noted, for instance, that in some Japanese communities there were both Buddhists and Catholics. The former allowed much closer inbreeding than the latter and more cousin marriages did, in fact, occur. We noted the results with respects to fertility: the more closely related couples being, apparently, more fertile than the less so. However, contrary to expectations, the Catholics had larger families than the Buddhists, a result attributed to widespread observance of a particular religious rule: the ban on use of mechanical contraceptives in Catholicism. We noted, also, a number of genetic differences between the two religious communities, while morphologically they are indistinguishable.

Other examples of endogamous religious groups we looked at were the Amish, the Dunkers, and a number of Jewish sects (notably the Samaritans). We found it possible to distinguish all of them genetically from their neighbours or host communities. We took due note of the need for caution, arising from the possibility that intensive study of particular groups can give rise to misleading ideas about their genetic distinctiveness. Nevertheless we concluded that there exists good evidence of genetic differences between religious isolates, and were able to see a number of mechanisms that would tend to bring them about. Such genetic differences as do exist have no discernible effects on cultural selection; in no sense should they be seen as causing the rules, ideas and actions that give rise to them. They are mostly differences of frequency arising from cultural practices, based on religious affiliations, causing homogamy and consequent gene pool closure.

Part Two

Religion
and the life-cycle

3 Conception

Introduction

How do religious rules affect biologically significant action? The method we have adopted in Part 2 to answer this question is to use a life-cycle approach. There are other possibilities, but we have found that the life-cycle approach enables us to see the effects of religion on human biology in the clearest possible way. We shall therefore take the various parts of the human life cycle from conception to death and at each point ask the question: 'How do a person's chances of survival and (when appropriate) of reproduction become affected, channelled or controlled by the fact that he or she belongs to a particular faith or religious group with particular beliefs and practices?'

So, to begin at the beginning, we start with conception of the individual and ask the question: How does membership of a religious group affect the chances of conception? Any pair of parents may have a religion and in so far as they do, this religion will provide them with information about how and when it is appropriate, correct and moral to conceive. These rules will affect the biological chances of conception actually occurring, and therefore will affect the coming into existence of a new individual.

Age of marriage and conception

The age at which marriages may be contracted and consummated is laid down by various religions. No age limits have been fixed for the mar-

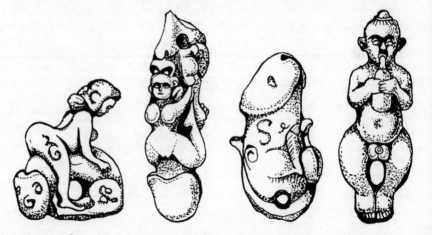

Small Buddhist fertility charms purchased in 1980 at the Rachanata temple in Bangkok. They are worn round the neck by women wishing to conceive.

riage of Muslims and quite young children may be married. There is the well-known example of Muhammad's wife Aisha who was married to him when still a nine-year-old child playing with toys (Glubb 1970). It is the custom not to hand over the girl to her husband until she has menstruated, rather than going by age alone. The tendency for girls to be married at the earliest possible time continues to be the norm in some Muslim village communities (Monteil 1952) unless such marriages are controlled by other considerations (Levy 1969). Naturally, pre-pubertal marriage cannot produce conception, and hence the overall rate of marital conceptions will be reduced.

Hindus relate the age of the prospective bride to the age of her husband. An eight-year-old bride is regarded as suitable for a man of 24 years (Laws of Manu 1969) and even younger wives are allowed for distinguished suitors (Philippe 1974). Jewish law recommends 12 years as a minimum age for the marriage of a girl and 13 years for a man but such minimum ages have been modified in most Western countries by civil law, which in Israel has raised the minimum age for a girl to 17 years, while giving no minimum age for a man (Israeli Marriage Age Law 1950, as amended 1960).

In Christianity the minimum age for marriage has varied from time to time and place to place but has never been as low as in Muslim and Hindu countries. As a result, biological maturity precedes age of marriage and we have the phenomenon of premarital conceptions. To see whether Christianity in Britain has had any noticeable effect on restraining premarital sexual intercourse we can compare the dates of weddings and the dates of baptisms of the first child in parish registers. In seven parishes for which records are available from 1550 to 1849 (Table 3.1), premarital pregnancies, shown by baptisms recorded within nine months of marriage, fell during the sixteenth and seventeenth centuries but rose again during the eighteenth and nineteenth (Laslett 1977).

	1550–99		1600–49		1650–99		1700–49		1750–99		1800–49	
	A	B	A	B	A	B	A	B	A	B	A	B
Aldenham (Herts)	6	27	12	75	8	48	9	45	17	51	25	63
Colyton (Devon)	31	79	41	163	14	64	15	50	41	128	53	121
Hartland (Devon)	13	48	32	138	43	176	48	153	95	207	56	132
Easingwold (Yorks.)	0	—	5	26	4	41	8	62	32	108	11	38
Alcester (War.)	1	6	18	75	7	80	16	89	19	82	14	73
Banbury (Oxon)	10	33	23	140	8	81	43	162	73	237	0	5
Hawkshead (Lancs.)	0	—	25	116	19	95	16	70	44	97	44	95
Total	61	193	156	733	103	585	155	631	321	910	203	527
Percentage of live births less than 9 months after marriage		31.6		21.3		17.6		24.6		35.2		38.5	

A = Baptisms before 9 months. B = Total baptisms.

Table 3.1 Pre-nuptial pregnancy in seven parishes, by period (From: Laslett 1977)

A further study concluded that more than one sixth of all brides in English rural and semi-rural parishes between the late sixteenth and early nineteenth century were pregnant at marriage. Further, the proportion of pregnant brides increased after 1700 (Table 3.2).

It was during the seventeenth century that the influence of the new, more puritanical form of Christianity appears to have brought down

Period	Births			Baptisms	
	Area	No.	%★	No.	%★
Pre–1700	South			84	15
	Central	85	27	158	16
	North			116	30
Post–1700	South	176	47	141	38
	Central	135	37	299	32
	North	289	44	372	38
Total		685	41	1,170	31

Table 3.2 Births and baptisms registered in parish records within nine months of marriage (After: Hair 1966)

★ = Percentage of all births and baptisms recorded in parish records.

the premarital pregnancy rate substantially (Fig 3.1). It is only then that it can be postulated that religion had much effect on restraining premarital sexual intercourse and thus the level of conceptions.

Data from other areas show quite different patterns. In a Swiss valley with a strong Catholic tradition dictating premarital chastity for both men and women despite long engagements, there appears to have been virtually no premarital impregnation (Friedl *et al.* 1976).

A study in Indiana, USA (Christensen 1953) found that 9.9 per cent of religiously celebrated marriages and 21 per cent of civil weddings were followed by the birth of a live child within seven calendar months of the marriage.

A more detailed comparative study (Christensen 1960) has examined premarital conception rates in Utah, where religion is a motivating force in the lives of many people and premarital sexual intercourse is regarded by them as an extremely grievous sin, in Indiana where chastity norms are prescribed by a variety of denominations but less often observed in practice, and in Denmark which has a long tradition of sexual intercourse during the engagement going back several centuries despite the Lutheran Church's efforts to establish a chastity code. The data (Table 3.3(a)) show the lowest incidence of premarital pregnancy to

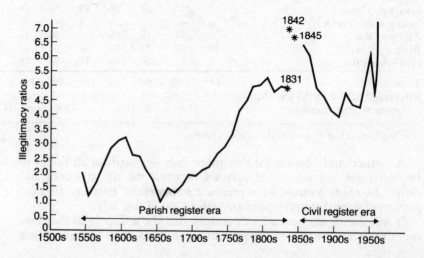

Fig. 3.1 Illegitimacy ratios in England, 1540s to 1960s. (From: Laslett 1977)

Indices	USA		Denmark	
	Utah County, Utah	Tippecanoe County, Indiana	City of Copenhagen	Entire country
I. Illegitimacy rate	0.9	2.9	11.2	6.6
II. Premarital conception rates				
(a) Child born within first six months of marriage	9.0	9.7	24.2	32.9
(b) Child born within first nine months of marriage	30.9	23.9	30.5	44.3

Table 3.3 (a) Comparative rates of premarital conception (From: Christensen 1960)

Type of ceremony	Utah County, Utah %	Tippecanoe County, Indiana %	Copenhagen, Denmark %
Civil	16.6	21.0	37.0
Religious	1.1	9.9	13.5

Table 3.3 (b) Factors associated with premarital conception (From: Christensen 1960)

have been in Utah. In all three places, a far higher proportion of pre-marital pregnancy occurred among those who had civil weddings (Table 3.3(b)).

Obligation to have marital intercourse

Most religions, certainly the major ones, require a husband to have in-tercourse with his wife. The Laws of Manu state of Hindus that 'rep-rehensible is the husband who approaches not his wife in due season' (Laws of Manu 1969) and the Jewish code (Ganzfried 1927) states that the wife cannot be deprived of her rights to coitus except by her con-sent and that it is forbidden to force her. The Roman Catholic code (Arregui 1927) states that each spouse is bound to render marital dues to the other, while the Koran states 'your women are to you as cultivated land; come then to your cultivated land as ye wish' (Koran, Sura 3.223). Buddhism is less verbally specific but can be seen in other ways to favour marital intercourse and the production of children. For example young Thai Buddhist wives pray for fertility in front of a spirit shrine surrounded by tin penises (Plate v). The concern for fertility was suf-ficiently strong in nineteenth-century Japan for itinerant Buddhist monks to be fully occupied in carrying portable fertility shrines round the countryside on their backs (Plate vi). Finally, we know that Austra-lian Aborigine wives visit sacred sites and perform certain fertility rituals (Kaberry 1939; Berndt and Berndt 1964).

The timing of sexual intercourse

One of the most important ways in which religions can affect the fertil-

V. In this scene at a Buddhist fertility shrine in Bangkok, a woman is praying that she will conceive. In front of her are a number of small spirit shrines and red tin penises.

ity of sexual intercourse is by making statements about times at which sexual intercourse is preferred and times at which it is forbidden.

Biologically ovulation occurs around the mid-point between two successive menstruations. In order for a mating to be fertile, the sperm needs to meet the egg after its emergence from the ovary during its passage down the Fallopian tube. In order for a mating to be fertile the sperm has to be present in the Fallopian tube between the tenth and the fifteenth days of the menstrual cycle. Only if it is present at that time can fertilization take place and the subsequent process of implantation and embryonic development follow.

These biological facts have never been precisely understood by those who, in bygone ages, formulated religious rules pertaining to times of sexual intercourse. However, ordinary observation is enough to show that certain times in the menstrual cycle are more fertile than others. Thus without understanding the detailed biology of reproduction, religions have in fact been able to produce rules relating to the preferred times for fertile reproduction, and for 'safe' periods.

If a religion has a rule that sexual intercourse must occur during the period in which we know that matings are likely to be fertile, then this religion is clearly promoting reproduction. Correspondingly if a religion has a rule that matings should not occur during that period then this religion is decreasing the chances of reproduction. In fact many re-

VI. An itinerant Buddhist monk in nineteenth-century Japan with a portable fertility shrine on his back.

ligions seem to encourage sexual intercourse in the fertile period by forbidding or restricting it during menstruation.

The Jewish code forbids coitus for seven days following the cessation of the menstrual flow and for a short period before to a minimum total period of monthly abstinence of 12 days (Leviticus 18:19 and 20:18; *Encyc. Judaica* 1971). The Muhammadan taboo on coitus is limited to the period of the menstrual flow and this must be followed by a ritual cleansing (Koran, Sura 2.222). There have been no recent re-statements of the Roman Catholic view which has traditionally been that there is no official objection to coitus during menstruation (Davis 1946). Hindus state that the four days after the appearance of the menses are unfit for intercourse as are the eleventh and thirteenth days (Chadrasekaran 1952).

Further restrictions on intercourse relate to religious festivals wherein sexual activity is prohibited. During the Middle Ages, devout Christians were forbidden intercourse for three 40-day periods in the year, on Saturdays and Sundays, and on major feast days as well as for three days before taking Communion, so for such people marital intercourse was only possible on some 160 days in the year (Bieler 1963). Restriction on Sunday intercourse was probably widespread to a much later date (May 1931) and in relation to the taking of Communion it is certainly present today (Puzo 1972). Lent is still a period in which no religious weddings are celebrated and in which there is abstinence from marital relations among the devout; there is traditionally self-denial of various kinds during Lent among both Protestants and Catholics in

Europe and the timing of births has been related to this religious event (Nurge 1970). Such customs are clearly $r-$ in our scheme.

There are no such restrictions during the Muslim, holy month of Ramadhan when men are encouraged to have intercourse with their wives at night (Koran, Sura 2.183) as a comfort from the daytime fasting. Hindus however are reported to avoid coitus during some religious festivals and fast days as well as on new and full moon days, the eleventh day after the full moon and often on specific days of the week such as Saturday, Sunday and Monday. Restrictions have also been reported for days when the husband shaves and has a bath, days of sowing in the fields and when there are solar and lunar eclipses. A couple may avoid intercourse on as many as 120 days in the year outside any restriction imposed by menstruation (Chandrasekaran 1952).

Subsequent conceptions

We would expect logically that religious rules concerned with promoting fertility would favour intercourse for newly married women whereas there might be rules which tended to restrict the occurrence of intercourse in the case of women who had already had a certain number of children or perhaps in the case of those women who had just given birth to a child. Such rules would make good sense because even though, on the one hand, it is important for reproduction to occur, on the other hand too much reproduction lessens the chances of survival of offspring already born. However, we have not found explicit rules to restrict intercourse by women who already have a number of children, although even among some of the most intensely religious Amish, who are enjoined to have as many children as they can, some sort of restriction tacitly occurs (Resseguie 1974).

By what other means, then have religions devised rules to slow down the overproduction of children? Islam lays down clearly that children should be nursed for two full years (Koran, Sura 2.233), and contemporary data show that ordinary Muslims (and also Hindus) in Pakistan and India nurse continuously for an average of 21 months (Potter *et al.* 1964). There is little contemporary information on any Western association between Christian values and prolonged nursing.

Christian pressure for the use of wet-nurses
However, in seventeenth-century France, it was generally held that sexual relations could 'corrupt the milk of the nursing mother, reduce the supply and even make it disappear if she had the misfortune to conceive again' (Flandrin 1979). Some non-Christian societies (e.g. Muslims) have overcome the restrictions on a husband's sexual relations while the mother is nursing by allowing the husband to marry more than one wife. The Jews in the first centuries AD obliged the husband to practise *coitus interruptus* during the entire period of nursing (Noonan 1966). The seventeenth-century Christian Church for doctrinal reasons was unable to accept *coitus interruptus* as a solution, let alone authorize the husband to have intercourse with other women, and it found a convenient solution to the husband's sexual needs by encouraging the practice of 'putting babies out to nurse' thus permitting the resumption of sexual relations.

Biologically, nursing the child can hold back ovulation and hence the

	Women's Age groups (yrs)						
	15–19	20–24	25–29	30–34	35–39	40–44	45–49
Not putting children out to nurse	0.429	0.530	0.490	0.421	0.300	0.132	0.016
Putting children out to nurse	0.545	0.589	0.603	0.501	0.417	0.116	0.023

Table 3.4 Average number of births per annum for married women, depending on whether or not they put their children out to nurse (From: Lachiver and Dupaquier 1969)

conception of a further child. Data from seventeenth-century France show that women who put their children out to nurse had higher fertility rates than those who did not (Table 3.4). Also, the interval between births was shorter for those whose nursing was terminated by the deaths of their children than those who were not (Table 3.5).

It also seems likely, to complicate matters further, that the practice of wet-nursing increased or even doubled infant mortality among urban families (Bardet n.d.). The Church gave support for this practice, advising that 'the wife should, if she can, put her children out to nurse, in order to provide for the frailty of her husband by paying the conjugal due, for fear that he may lapse into some sin against conjugal purity' (Fromageau 1733).

Thus, in biological terms, two contrary effects resulted from the implementation of the Church's moral rulings. First, because, presumably, the environment of the wet-nurse was less favourable than the home environment (as has been reported more recently for Uganda and Jamaica), infant mortality was increased; and secondly, there was an increase in fertility because of the earlier resumption of ovulation and sexual relations.

In Islamic cultures suckling wives tend not to engage in sexual intercourse with their husbands until their children have been weaned. The net effect of this sexual avoidance is to increase the coitus rate per menstruating wife (Dorjahn 1958) which should increase fertility. Is polygyny a fertility-increasing mechanism? Islam has always allowed and encouraged polygyny. The origin of plurality of wives came after the battle of Badr (AD 624) in which some 60 Muslim men died. These men and their wives had left their families in order to follow Muhammad to Mecca. They had changed their religion and as a result the widows could not go home. The small community of Muslims now had to create a means of coping with a sudden problem of the large number of unattached women (Watt 1968). This, at least, is the historical basis for polygyny in Islam, and clearly it increases fertility where there is a short-

	Intervals (in months)					
Parity	1st–2nd	2nd–3rd	3rd–4th	4th–5th	5th–6th	6th–7th
Normal	18.3	22.7	23.3	24.9	23.4	24.2
After death	15.7	17.6	19.1	17.7	19.5	22.5

Table 3.5 Intervals between births after deaths in infancy at Bléré (From: Lachiver 1969)

Age groups (years)	Age specific fertility rates per 1,000 women		Mean live births per woman	
	Monogamous wives	Polygynous wives	Monogamous wives	Polygynous wives
15–19	93.5	69.8	0.198	0.128
20–24	331.4	246.3	1.442	0.902
25–29	363.4	270.0	2.954	1.986
30–34	364.0	257.8	5.239	2.773
35–39	273.7	149.1	6.947	5.579
40–44	181.8	158.3	6.642	5.292
45–49	82.6	26.8	7.716	5.741

Table 3.6 Age specific fertility rates and mean live births by type of marital union and age group of women — Ngwa Igbo, Nigeria 1974 (From: Ukaegbu 1977)

age of men. But in other situations polygyny has been shown to produce lower fertility (Ukaegbu 1977). (Table 3.6.) Why should this be so?

One reason could be the relative ease and speed of divorce. This is carried out by the husband by a mere statement of repudiation (Aghababian 1951); since divorce is preceded by marital strain, intercourse for the wife in question is likely to have been infrequent. A divorced wife cannot marry again immediately because three menstrual periods have to pass before remarriage is legal (Koran, Sura 2.228). A second reason for lowered fertility relates to age. To have multiple wives is certainly prestigious but is also expensive in the time and effort involved in negotiations and their maintenance. Nowadays specific cash outlays are involved. Polygynists thus tend to be old. This should tend to lower fertility owing to low coital frequency, low sperm count and low sperm mobility (Davidson 1948). Third, polygyny has the effect of preventing younger men from having legitimate access to women. Nevertheless (see below) Muslim communities appear in some areas to have higher fertility than their non-Muslim neighbours.

By contrast, Hindu marriage is indissoluble and a wife is not released from her marriage even when sold or repudiated by her husband (Laws of Manu ix:46) and there are no arrangements for an impotent husband to be divorced (Laws of Manu ix:70). But there are arrangements for the male line to be continued either by fertilizing the wife through a relative of the husband or by the marrying of an additional wife should the first prove infertile. On the failure of a wife to conceive by her husband, she can be authorized to have intercourse with a brother-in-law or another member of her husband's caste (Laws of Manu ix:59) but only to the extent of begetting one son. The same arrangement applies if a husband-to-be dies before the consummation of the marriage (Laws of Manu ix:69–70). Hinduism also allows for a barren wife to be superceded after 8 years of marriage, one whose children have died after 10 years and one who bears only daughters after 11 years (Laws of Manu ix:81). All these features seem pro-reproductive (r^c+).

Judaism allows divorce by mutual consent (*Encyc. Judaica*, 1971, ii:1052) though not until there has been much effort to save the marriage. Arrangements can be made for the annulment of a marriage which cannot be consummated. This is also the case in Christianity, which in addition allows for the annulment of a marriage in which either partner refuses or is incapable by some new situation of having marital intercourse. More importantly Judaism can invoke the 'levirate' which requires a marriage between the widow whose husband has died without offspring and the brother of the deceased, or the giving of a formal release by his family so that she can remarry (*Encyc. Judaica* 1971, II:122–31). All these measures would tend to increase women's fertility rates by increasing the likelihood of conception (r^c+).

Hindu restrictions on the remarriage of widows

The Hindu scriptures state (Laws of Manu IX:94) that the bride must be considerably younger than the bridegroom and that all women must eventually marry, the bride being a virgin. There is a restriction on the remarriage of widows but not of widowers, which results in a high proportion (up to 28.8%) of married women becoming husbandless before the end of their procreative lifespan (India, Government of 1964). (Table 3.7)

Years of age	Married (%)	Widowed and not remarried (%)
15–19	69.5	0.5
20–24	91.8	1.83
25–29	94.2	2.9
30–34	91.4	6.4
35–39	87.0	11.1
40–44	77.7	20.7
45–49	69.7	28.8

Table 3.7 Married and widowed women – distribution, India, 1961 (From: Indian Ministry of Information and Broadcasting 1964)

The Laws of Manu state that a virtuous wife who remains chaste after the death of her husband reaches heaven even if she has no son (Laws of Manu V:160). The idea that widows cannot remarry as a general rule probably derives in part from the older practice of widows of royal castes and sometimes Brahmins who sacrificed themselves on their husbands' funeral pure (suttee), a practice which was made illegal by the British in 1829.

However this religious ban on the remarriage of widows applies less strictly to low-caste Hindus and the majority of younger widows remarry (Dandekar 1959). Nevertheless a large proportion of widows remain 'socially sterile' for religious reasons. This religious restriction on the remarriage of widows has long been the object of reform in India. It was particularly abhorrent to Mahatma Gandhi who wrote that 'widowhood imposed by religion or custom is an unbearable yoke and defiles the home by secret vice and degrades religion' (Gandhi 1926).

The current relaxation of widow remarriage rules is associated with a declining trend in mortality so that husbands are less likely to die during their wives' reproductive lives. Widow remarriage also decreases the demand for young girls in the marriage market. Thus it seems that this relaxing of religiously based restrictions may well lead to an increase in the conception rate.

Contraception

Besides affecting the chances of conception by rules about birth spacing, frequency of intercourse and remarriage, a potent and frequent topic of religious ideas is contraception. Contraceptive rules may exist, for example, for mothers with young babies, unmarried teenagers, or people who are not in a social position to be able to rear offspring successfully such as, in some societies, adult men and women who are not married to each other. What are the rules in different religions?

Much Hindu teaching is strongly pro-natalist. The begetting of a son has always been regarded as a primary religious duty (Laws of Manu II:28) and ensures the salvation of the father (Laws of Manu IX:137–8). Hinduism has no explicit teachings on contraception and no centralized institutions through which to make such declarations. However, the rules imply that Hindus should not practise contraception until a son has been born *and prospered*, a clearly $r+$ exhortation.

Buddhism is as quiet about contraception as it is about the whole question of marriage. An enquiry among Sinhalese Buddhist monks (Ryan 1953) showed that those who were well educated found no inconsistency between Buddhist ideology and contraceptive practices and indeed did not view the issue as a matter of intense religious concern. However, less well educated priests in village monasteries were in almost complete agreement that contraception was wrong according to Buddhist teachings on the grounds that prevention of birth was tantamount to killing, but their conviction was not strongly expressed. A further aspect of Buddhist anti-contraception belief is that a prevented potential birth is the prevention of a rebirth, the working out of dead person's religious destiny and should not be interfered with (Ling 1969; Ryan 1952).

Islam has a strong procreative orientation which comes from a belief in the active providence of Allah. The number of children that should or should not be born is in Allah's dispensation (Koran, Sura 42.48–9). Certainly marriage is recommended and the unmarried are told to restrain themselves (Koran, Sura 24.32–3), while husbands are as already stated enjoined to use their wives as 'land to be cultivated' (Koran, Sura 2.223). Islam has no contraceptive tradition of wide currency. Abstinence was no part of the Sufi ascetic's life, of whom many including al-Ghazali were married. A traditional view would be that any restriction of the number of potential children would show a lack of piety, but modern views have supported contraception based on the tradition that Muhammed did not oppose *coitus interruptus* (as stated by the Mufti of Egypt in 1937).

The Christian attitude to procreation is largely unstated as the New Testament has none of the procreative directness of the Koran. It has exerted a moral force towards the stability of marriage and has heightened the importance of children as immortal souls received by their parents in sacred trust.

This stress on the nuclear family, the involvement of a few people in a predominantly permanent relationship, has led to an emphasis on respect for the individual personality and on affection as the most important ingredients in personal relations. Since the early Christians could not have had the assurance of the support of their extended families because of their conversion to a new religion, their need for intimate personal relations was intensified; personal security came from the religiously supported nuclear family and to a lesser extent the Christian community. Children came to be more directly important as filling out the couple's experience of a full life as well as providing them with economic support in later life; this was an important basis for children being cared for and wanted (Lorimer 1954: 189–91). Though this may have been the approved and accepted way of helping ageing parents in the past, it appears to be less of a perceived obligation than it was. A study in the USA (Dinkle 1944) showed that this obligation was felt more strongly by Catholics and rural people than by Protestants and city dwellers, and much depended on the degree of family hardship.

The early Christian Church (Fagley 1965) was ambivalent towards sexuality, increasingly stressing abstinence in relation to religious vocations while affirming the goodness of procreation within marriage, and the sinfulness of 'fornication'. The Orthodox Church still condemns non-procreative sex but does apply its doctrines in a more flexible manner than the Roman Catholic Church. The latter holds procreation to be an obligation in marriage involving 'heroic' marital abstinence when there are medical, psychological or social objections to impregnation. In general, Christianity does not actively promote contraception because of its concern with family and children. Catholicism actively forbids it in mechanical forms; other sects are more or less opposed to it.

Catholic theology holds a fundamental premise concerning the nature of marriage. Marriage is the lawful contract between man and woman in which the primary purpose is the generation and education of offspring, and the secondary purpose is mutual help and the allaying of concupiscence. St Augustine, who might perhaps be described as the founder of Christian moral teaching about marriage, held that any deliberate avoidance of conception made a wife into a prostitute and destroyed thereby the idea of marriage itself (*De moribus manichaeorum* II: 189n.). This approach to the relationship between men and women will tend to increase fertility or maintain it at high levels, if unchecked by other ideas. The Catholic Church backs up this ruling on the nature of marriage by asserting that the moral obligation of man corresponds to the precepts of natural law, firstly to preserve life and secondly to perpetuate mankind (Davis 1946, I: 126).

Even when Catholic doctrine allows the planned limitation of marital intercourse to the supposed non-fertile period in the wife's menstrual cycle, it should not be indulged in for any pleasurable purpose. Any such restriction of intercourse can only be lawful under an overriding moral consideration of a medical, social or economic nature. So this limited acceptance of a form of contraception is no way out for those Catholics who want to have sexual relations for reasons of mutual pleasure. At the same time there is nothing in Catholic moral doctrine by which the faithful have an obligation to procreate, and some moral theologians state that 'it seems much more important to make sure that their consent (to periodic continence) is truly mutual and that they are able to practise it without serious danger to chastity or marital harmony and family welfare...Married people are almost always the best judges of the reasons they may have for spacing children or limiting their family by these means.' (Ford and Kelly 1963, II: 430). This more moderate view was certainly not that of earlier Catholic moral theologians which is shown in the Encyclical *Casti Connubii* (Pius XI 1931) and which is quite clear that 'every attempt on the part of the married couple during the conjugal act or during the development of its natural consequences, to deprive it of its inherent power and to hinder the procreation of a new life is immoral'. Catholic doctrine does not, however, support the mere multiplication of children as the result of heedless over-indulgence of married couples' sensual appetites. Parents are expected to apply their natural rationality to the necessity of restraint, an *r*— exhortation.

This seems to be a 'counsel of perfection' and it has undoubtedly been applied by numbers of intelligent, well-disciplined and believing Catholics. But where a culture, in which Catholicism is the major religion, favours a continuing and active sexuality and expects a high fertility, these doctrines scarcely determine the actions of any but the smallest minority, for instance in such countries as Brazil and Guatamala. Disobeying these religious rulings is seen as part of human frailty while on the other hand any interference with its consequences is seen as a wilful defiance of divine law. Certainly these attitudes have contributed to the failure of most attempts to reduce the population growth of many Catholic Third World countries.

Fertility differentials between Christian denominations

The fertility of one denomination cannot be compared with that of another unless the influence of other social factors that could be associated with differentials has been controlled in some way. Where this has been attempted in an American city (Whelpton and Kiser 1943), there was not much difference in fertility between Catholics and Protestants who had only elementary schooling. But with higher education, differences appeared so that with college education the Catholics had a standardized birth rate of 134 per thousand to the Protestants' 99. In Holland (Dirksen 1954) it was found, as elsewhere (Eaton and Mayer 1953), that Christian orthodoxy of any type was associated with higher fertility. Possibly only where there is a special relationship between the Roman Catholic Church and particular social conditions, as in parts of the Irish Republic, can there be a clearly identifiable negative effect on fertility, mainly through the delay of marriage or its avoidance altogether by such means as entering religious celibacy or simply staying unmarried (Arensberg and Kimball 1940).

Considerable work has been done (Population Council 1968) on Roman Catholic attitudes to contraception and it is possible to reach certain conclusions. Firstly the more devout Western Catholics have and desire smaller families than do the marginal Catholics or non-Catholics in less developed countries, such as those of South and Central America. In such countries it is impossible to differentiate a Catholic from a non-Catholic fertility pattern. A study (Alvirez 1973) of Mexican American fertility showed that actual religiosity of women had slight effect on desired family size and there was no discernible effect at all in the case of their husbands; nor did Catholicism affect the use or non-use of effective means of contraception. Within developed countries the procreative impact of Catholicism is greater, as shown in the consistent excess of Catholic over Protestant completed family size and family size ideals.

The Roman Catholic Church continues to condemn the use of any physical or chemical barrier to conception but it allows periodic continence as contraception by the avoidance of the fertile period. Thus Roman Catholics in developed countries practise contraception widely but probably rely more than non-Catholics on the 'rhythm' method. There

Most recent method	1955	1960	1965*	1970
None	43	30	21	18
Rhythm	27	31	28	14
Other	30	38	51	68
Percentage total	100	100	100	100
Number of women	787	668	846	1,035

Table 3.8 Percentage of U.S. white Catholic women aged 18 to 39 who have never used any method of contraception, or who most recently used the rhythm or some other method (From: Westoff and Ryder 1977)

* Data for 1965 differ from earlier data because 'sterilization for contraceptive reasons' was not previously included as a form of contraception.

	Age of women				
Year of birth	20–24	25–29	30–34	35–39	40–44
1916–20				28	45
1921–25			30	46	43
1926–30		37	40	52	50
1931–35	30	40	50	50	
1936–40	43	54	68		
1941–45	51	74			
1946–50	78				

Table 3.9 Percentage of U.S. white Catholic women not conforming to Church teaching on birth control (From Westoff and Ryder 1977)

In the 1955 and 1960 studies (on the top and second diagonals respectively), a woman is classified as not conforming to Church teaching if she had *ever* used any method of contraception other than rhythm. In the 1965 and 1970 data (third and bottom diagonals, respectively) the classification relates to the method *most recently* used.

is a well-documented increasing trend in the USA for Catholic women to use unapproved methods of contraception (see Tables 3.8 and 3.9). Much of this deviation has been among the more educated Catholics (Westoff and Ryder 1977).

Religion, population density and the control of fertility

How do religious rules on contraception tie in with population density? How can we understand, from a biological standpoint, the encouraging of births by Catholicism in the slum conditions of Rio de Janeiro? Or Islam's similar indifference to the slums of Karachi, Bandung and Cairo, or the Hindu lack of sexual controls in Calcutta and Benares? These religious views or tendencies seem to foster high infant mortality rates and inadequate living conditions for their followers. However, it may be unreasonable to imagine that the Roman Catholic Church has much influence in such countries as Brazil and Mexico, or to take its negative attitude to contraception in isolation from its equally well-known views on the permanence of marriage and the virtues of chastity. These countries have taken early marriage and high fertility rates for granted for centuries. It is difficult for a centralized religious system such as Roman Catholicism to divide its moral doctrines so that it permits contraception in some areas and prohibits it in others. Adjustments have to take place in other ways, e.g. in age at marriage. There is also, as we have seen, a lot of variation in how individuals choose to interpret the central dogmas. As Davis (1967) has shown, people tend to have the number of children they think appropriate and then in one way or another cease reproduction.

Thus Roman Catholic encouragement of fertility and its record in effectively influencing its members to this end has been most uneven. In some countries such as the Netherlands and Britain, Catholics have a low birth rate and in others such as Guatemala, the rate is very high. If Roman Catholicism has any influence it is certainly obscured by economic, personal and social influences.

Conclusions

In summary, we can see that the subject of conception in relation to religious rules and practices is a complex matter. Marriages may be encouraged before as well as after puberty; if the latter, one result is a greater or lesser number of premarital or extra-marital or 'illegitimate' conceptions, and this we see especially in Christianity. Religions that emphasize chastity and/or Puritanical forms of Christianity tend to have low rates of illegitimate conceptions despite later marriage.

Rules concerning the timing of sexual intercourse must affect conception rates. If religions ban sex during periods of menstruation they increase the likelihood of conception. In some cases, sexual intercourse is banned during certain periods of austerity, as during Lent in Christianity. Hinduism too has periods of abstinence. Muslims however do not forbid sex during their religious festivals.

Hindus and Muslims restrict the chances of rapid re-conception after a birth by rules emphasizing prolonged nursing. The Christian invention of 'putting babies out to nurse' in the seventeenth century increased female fertility and reduced the inter-child interval, but at the same time seems to have been associated with increased child mortality.

Regarding polygyny, we can readily ask how this would affect fertility, but the answer is complex. In early Islam it seems to have been designed for, and to have succeeded in, increasing the fertility rate. But other data show a decline in fertility where Islamic polygyny is also associated with easy divorce and older age of husband.

Remarriage rules occur in Judaism and Christianity, in cases where the marriage is not consummated. Judaism also has special arrangements for the remarriage of widows. Hinduism is strongly pro-reproductive for younger wives but does not allow the remarriage of widows. Recent opposition to this, however, together with lower mortality rates in all age groups, increases the likely conception rate.

Contraceptive rules vary both between and within religions. Hinduism is pro-natalist for sons, and therefore must be anti-contraceptive in the early stages of marriage. Buddhism is anti-contraceptive to the extent that this is believed to interfere with the rebirth of human souls in their progressive reincarnations. Islam is traditionally pro-creative but *coitus interruptus* was never tabooed and may be practised whenever this is felt to be appropriate. Christianity is emphatic on the virtues of limited reproduction and tends to lay emphasis on the need for inter-parental love as expressed in sexual activity; where it opposes contraception this is because the practice divorces sex from its true purpose. This is most clearly seen in the Catholic taboo on mechanical means of contraception, but there is no taboo on the 'rhythm method'. Nevertheless, sex is not for pleasure as such, and people wishing to restrict their family size should, if Christian, refrain from sex. At the present, however, we noted evidence that Catholics, and doubtless all other

Christian denominations, are less and less influenced by centralized dogmas and are tending to act in breach of these. We concluded that religious rules have to be viewed very much in their social contexts and not given too much weight in determining actual outcomes in the matter of sexual activity and consequent conception rates.

4 Infanticide and abortion

Introduction

In Chapter 3 we saw how religious rules about such things as chastity, virginity, or time and frequency of intercourse, all affect the possibility and probability of conception taking place. Not only are there rules that favour the occurrence of conception, for instance by tabooing intercourse during the period of menstruation, but there are rules that reduce the chance of conception taking place, for instance the religious sanction of the so-called rhythm method, which involves abstaining from intercourse during the period of ovulation when conception is most likely to occur. In general, then, we could not say that religion either definitely promotes or restricts the biological process of conception. It has rules for both. If we want to know about the adaptiveness of the religious rules in force at any one time, we need to know whether they are likely to increase the chances of survival in relation to other, secular rules and prevailing economic circumstances.

In this chapter we move on a step in the life cycle, to the point where conception has occurred and a new life has begun. Life is regarded in all societies as a precious commodity – often the most precious. Many cultural rules are concerned with the preservation of human life. There are additionally, at the start of life when the infant is helpless, strong biological mechanisms by which most mammals, especially primates, protect and nurture their infants. The mother–infant relationship is

A Japanese Buddhist–Shinto belief holds that girls born in the Year of the Horse will be difficult to marry off. Early neonatal mortality in 1906 and 1966, which were such years, was significantly higher for girls.

THE YEAR OF THE HORSE

based on a set of powerful biological patterns of behaviour which normally ensure that the infant does not starve, or get lost or injured. Not only mothers, but other females and also males show protective responses to infants in animal societies.

It is against this background that we now consider the following question: Why do rules exist permitting or even exhorting infanticide and abortion in human societies? The simplest, 'armchair' answer would be that humans plan their families according to their needs and resources. This uses a 'rational' model of man: he takes nature into his own hands rather than being subject to natural forces. Biologists, however, may wish to look for other reasons than this. Is there in fact a positive relationship between the purposeful destruction of new viable human life and the survival or reproductive chances of those already in existence, or of future children, planned but as yet unconceived?

Again, in animals we do find cases where baby-killing occurs. In overcrowded mouse colonies babies have been observed to die because their mothers kept moving them to new sites (Mackintosh 1978). In rats, the mother, under a variety of pressures including overpopulation, may eat her young. In langur monkeys (Sugiyama 1965) and lions (Schaller 1972) it is males who sometimes kill infants; a male who takes over a new group kills all young infants and mates with their mothers. While not, it would seem, in the immediate interests of group survival, this mechanism can be understood in terms of the 'selfish gene' theory and must, presumably, have advantages in the long term or it could not have evolved.

In man, however, we are not dealing with genetic but with cultural prescriptions, and we should not prejudge the issue of adaptiveness. We must ask: Why is new life sometimes killed? When does this happen? Who is selected? Is there any evidence relating this to individual, kin-group or whole group survival? What are the rules and how does religion in particular make them effective?

Infanticide in small-scale hunting and gathering societies

There is some evidence from small hunting and gathering communities to indicate that people only keep the children they can rear without damaging their own survival. The Australian Aborigines have a record of widespread infanticide and moreover they have on occasions articulated reasons for their practices: 'Me bin keepem one boy and one girl, no good keepem mob, him too much wantem tuckout' (Willshire 1895) and 'too much young fellow, no good two fellow pickaninny' (Smyth 1878). The Aborigine belief in reincarnation, according to Malinowski (presenting the data of others who wrote earlier than him) served as an excuse for the practice of infanticide (Malinowski 1913). For these nomadic people, living often in very uncertain conditions, a mother could only carry a single child and would kill or arrange to have killed any subsequent children until the first one was able to fend for itself. There is plentiful evidence of the extent of this practice (Krzywicki 1934). In Aborigine society there does not appear to be any distinction between male and female babies as regards infanticide. It is a matter of birth spacing and the main consideration is the effect on the mother's mobility.

Even after a period of relative security, the possibility of famine and enforced long migration would make any attempt to save the life of a baby born very soon after its predecessor a danger to the more valuable life of its mother. In these circumstances infanticide is (or was) seen by the Aborigines as functionally advantageous. It even carried with it 'a certain natural propriety... often regarded as a moral action, and, to some extent, compulsory, although it is clear that it caused much sorrow at least to the mothers involved' (Fisher 1930: 200).

While it produced sorrow, it was at least socially sanctioned and involved no danger to the mother, who had already survived childbirth. Abortion would have been less certain to succeed and would have involved danger to the mother. Also, abortion might terminate a pregnancy which might produce a needed child should earlier children have died by the time of this birth. These may be the factors promoting infanticide rather than abortion in the Aborigines.

Other hunting societies have also been shown to practise infanticide. Only rarely, however, do we have quantitative data. One in which we do, however, is that of the Netsilik Eskimos in the early part of this century. The figures in Table 4.1 are given by Rasmussen (1931).

Current age of mother	Total children born to her	Children killed
60	12	7 girls
45	4	0
26	3	0
65	11	4 girls
29	4	2 girls
50	10	4 girls
40	6	2 girls
30	3	2 girls
20	1	0
40	5	1 girl
60	7	1 girl
65	7	1 girl
45	11	7 girls
29	5	1 boy, 1 girl
35	7	2 girls
55	10	3 girls
26	4	1 girl, 1 boy
Totals	108	40 (= 27% of those born)

Table 4.1 Infanticide among the Netsilik c. 1920 (From: Rasmussen 1931)

Finally let us quote from Chagnon's study of the Yanomamö Indians of South America. A long quotation is given because of its unusual clarity and detail. The Yanomamö hunt and gather food, and in addition they grow crops.

As is apparent, there are more males in the Yanomamö population than females. This demographic fact results from the practice of selectively killing female babies: female infanticide. The Yanomamö also practice male infanticide, but because of the preference to have a male as their first child, they unknowingly kill more females than males. The Yanomamö have only three

numbers: *one, two, and more-than-two. They are accordingly, poor
statisticians. They are quite unaware of the fact that they do kill more female
babies, and every time I questioned them about it, they insisted that they killed
both kinds – 'more-than-two' of both kinds.*

*A child is killed at birth, irrespective of its sex, if the mother already has a
nursing baby. They rationalize the practice by asserting that the new infant
would probably die anyway, since its older sibling would drink most of the
milk. They are most reluctant to jeopardize the health and safety of a nursing
child by weaning it before it is three years old or so, preferring to kill the
competitor instead. Kaobawä's wife, Bahimi, killed a new-born male shortly
after I began my fieldwork. She later told me, quite tearfully, that it would
have taken milk away from Ariwari, Kaobawä's favorite child. Ariwari at the
time was over two years old, but Bahimi refused to wean him. Sometimes a
child is killed simply because the mother doesn't feel that she can care for it
properly and that it would be an inconvenience to have to tend a baby. I once
saw a plump, well-fed, young mother eating a large quantity of food that would
have been suitable to give to an older infant. Her emaciated, filthy, and nearly
starved child – about two years old – kept reaching out for the food. The mother
explained that the baby had gotten a bad case of diarrhea some time ago and had
stopped eating. As a consequence, her milk had dried up. She refused to attempt
to feed it other foods because 'it did not know how to eat other foods'. When I
insisted that she share her food with the child, he ate it ravenously. In short, she
was letting the baby die slowly of starvation. I have similar accounts from
missionaries who have also witnessed cases such as this.*

*Male babies are preferred because they will grow up to be warriors and
hunters. Most men make known their wishes to have a son – even to the point
of insinuating that the wife ought to deliver a male or suffer the consequences.
This is always done in a subtle way, usually by displaying signs of anger or
resentment at the thought of having a daughter that constantly eats without
being potentially an economic asset or guardian of the village. Many women
will kill a female baby just to avoid disappointing their husbands. The
Yanomamö also practise abortion in a very crude but effective way. The
pregnant woman will lie on her back and have a friend jump on her belly to
rupture the amnion. Sometimes abortions are effected because the woman does
not want to kill the baby after it is born. In other cases a man will order his wife
to abort if he suspects that somebody else conceived the child.*

*Several techniques are used to kill a newborn child. The most common
method is to strangle it with a vine so as not to touch it physically. Another
common method is to place a stick across the child's neck and stand on both ends
of it until it chokes. In some cases the child is not given the stimulus to breathe
and is simply abandoned. Finally, some women throw the child against a tree or
on the ground and just abandon it without checking to see if it was killed by the
injuries sustained. One of the New Tribes Missionaries discovered a female
baby in 1964 that had been discarded in this fashion and brought her home with
him. The baby's face was badly bruised on one side, but she survived. The
missionary subsequently adopted her legally and is raising her in England.*
(Chagnon 1977: 75–6).

Infanticide in pastoral societies

A somewhat different picture appears in pastoral societies such as the
pre-Islamic Arabs, who tended to kill girl children. Their own ('emic')
justification for this was not the hardship of transporting babies in de-

sert conditions since they could carry young children on their camels and donkeys. In their patrilineal societies daughters married into other lineages and were lost in an economic sense to their parental families. Marriage did involve the acquisition of bride wealth in the form of livestock, and decisions to kill girl children thus involved consideration of the loss of a one-off capital increase, set against the long term cost of rearing a girl to marriageable age. Lost too would be the social bonds she could create by the marriage she would one day make.

Whereas hunters and gatherers have little property, agnatic (patrilineal) nomads have disposable herds necessitating the survival of male relatives for inheritance; as property increases, the need for sons increases with it. The early Arabs are recorded as having a religious reverence for their patri-clans in which a kinsman's blood was of great importance. All the duties of kinship were part of their religion with a clan god maintaining the enduring sanctity of the clan bond (Smith 1901: 47). Religion thus sanctioned the male-centred organization of these societies and by regarding women as second-class it also sanctioned female infanticide.

The killing of male and female babies can be interpreted against this male-dominated background. We should note in this example that female infanticide is clearly tied up with cultural arrangements concerning marriage and property. In other words, female infanticide in this context is, proximately at least, an adaptation to a cultural system not a natural one. Ultimately, the cultural system may be an adaptation to the natural environment but this cannot be assumed and has to be demonstrated.

Muhammad and the prohibition of infanticide

The Islamic view of female infanticide is quite clear: the practice is forbidden. Muhammad made several straightforward statements that the care of daughters is a cause for glorifying Allah and referred to them in the Koran as 'Allah's daughters'. He accompanied this by stating in the Koran that 'the female child buried alive shall be asked for what sin she was put to death' (Koran 6.141 and 152). This has been taken by some Islamic theologians as specific disapproval of female infanticide (Watt 1967).

This change in attitude towards female infanticide enforced by Muhammad cannot obviously be explained in terms of any prospective advantages to the new Muslims from an expansion in the female population. Muhammad's institution of this change occurred before the migration to Medina in AD 622 and the establishment of a settled Muslim community. The First Pledge of allegiance to the Prophet from his Meccan nucleus of 12 men that they should not steal, commit fornication, nor kill their offspring (Ibn Ishaq 1970: 199) occurred when the future was far from clear. It was not the result of any clearly evident economic factors. It was initiated by the Prophet for other reasons, and later became part of the dogma of Islam.

Muhammad himself was an orphan and possibly he was influenced by this personal experience. He knew that his own life was an act of God's providence. His father had died before he was born; if his father had died a few months earlier, the Prophet knew that he himself would not have been conceived (Cragg 1971: 28). He believed he was born fatherless by God's grace, and this shaped his thinking. Muhammad repeatedly refers to the wonder of procreation as one of the awesome signs of God: 'We have created man of an extract of clay . . . Blessed by Allah, the best of creators' (Koran 23. 12–24) so it is not surprising that he initiated this change of attitude towards a custom which was common in his day.

While no doubt he was a man who showed considerable and considered violence at times when it served his purpose, he also showed a consistent trait of compassion based on his own experiences as an orphan. He took part in some twenty raids or battles (Watt 1968) among which was the battle of Uhud in which he was wounded. He ordered the execution of all the men of the Jewish Qurayzah clan, and of two popular singers after the surrender of Mecca, who had presumably satirized his activities. And he organized the treacherous killing of some Khaybar Jews under the cover of an embassy (Ibn Ishaq 1955). But such behaviour was less out of keeping with the times than his concern for orphans. Orphans are mentioned 23 times in the Koran as against some 30 times in the very much longer Old Testament and not at all in the New Testament (Cruden 1769). Effective Christian concern for orphans occurs later as a result of the Church's insistence on legitimacy.

After the establishment of the Islamic community as a religious state, the avoidance of infanticide meant more mouths to feed in difficult economic circumstances. This was particularly so as the people had cut themselves off from their own lineages and clans by becoming members of the new religion and so had lost the possibility of getting food and labour and other support in the traditional ways. This was certainly a difficult period, and when the Muslims had reached the limits of their first expansion out of Arabia, the ruling class reintroduced female infanticide for a time because of the high male death rate from war and murder. This had left a surplus of high-born but unmarriageable women who could not by law be married to men from their recently conquered dominions (Darlington 1969: 350).

It is always necessary to remember that, for Muslims, Muhammad's words written down in the Koran are not merely his own, but the literal words of God and as such have had power to modify Muslim behaviour down the centuries. Though there have been times of neglect, there has also been a constant tendency for leaders to go back to 'the word of Allah'. Today there is little evidence that there is serious neglect of girl babies. Data from Algeria suggests a certain degree of failure to register the births of females (Breil 1959: 74*ff*) with much the same position in Egypt (Mboria 1938) and Jordan (*Statistical Yearbook 1960*). So it seems that in modern times Islamic law has been effective in preventing any neglect of female infants.

These changes of attitude and practice can probably be interpreted best as a result of several factors. Initially, Muhammad's own ideas arose from the special circumstances of his life, in part as a reaction against the old rules of kinship. Later thinking attributed to the Prophet may have been concerned with promoting marriage and the family, and stimulating growth of the Muslim community from within, by increasing the birth rate as much as possible.

Carthaginian sacrificial infanticide

In the latter half of the fourth century BC not only were the priests at Carthage sacrificing children but these were preferentially first-born ones. Diodorus Siculus (xx,14: 5–6) records that some nobles had sub-stituted bought children for their own with the result that the priests, to punish them, had demanded an offering of 500 infants of registered no-ble birth to be sacrificed to Baal Hammon, their chief god. Sacrifices by the aristocracy appear to have been a regular feature of their religious practices and from archaeological evidence it has been estimated (Weyl 1968) that 20 per cent of the first-born children of the wealthy were sacrificed.

It is known that the Carthaginians had comparatively small agri-cultural resources on which to base their economy and its trading expansion, and that these had been reduced by progressive soil erosion, possibly resulting in malarial undrained swamps and the decline of the timber forests which sustained their trading fleets. Other societies have killed infants as a means of population control but in the case of Carth-age it is hard to see the phenomenon purely as an effort at restitution of demographic or ecological balance.

The Carthaginians did not just kill off 'spare' children, they killed off the 'best' ones. First-borns tend to be more successful when compared with later children, who have increased tendencies to chromosomal abnormalities, pernicious anaemia resulting from mother–infant Rh blood group incompatibility, and mutations in general. Weyl (1968) makes the point that if the policy of killing first-born were applied to contemporary USA it would strike down a disproportionately large number of the most gifted progeny as well as thinning the ranks of the ruling class. Other religions have had the idea of a jealous god that has to be placated but have sacrificed animals; not so the Carthaginians. There can be little doubt that this religiously induced practice was mal-adaptive in a biological sense. Perhaps the reason for it may lie in the internal instability of Carthage. The city depended on a mercenary army and a priesthood not recruited from the nobility (contrast Rome and Greece), hence potentially at least at odds with the ruling class. At times of crisis the rulers may have been unable to resist outrageous de-mands by the priests, and may have been forced to shed their very life-blood in the supposed interest of their state, though definite evidence on this point is lacking.

Nevertheless, we have to note that, whether first-borns or no, the effects of infant killing are the same; and the link with reduced resources of food and timber must not be ignored.

This is not an isolated example of sacrifice of first-borns. The Nayars of southern India are reported at one time to have sacrificed their first-born sons to the goddess of smallpox (Sherring 1872: 81). Extreme measures doubtless arise from economic, political or social crises, and religions can act as intermediary agencies formalizing the necessary unpalatable action. Biologically such action often seems maladaptive: individuals lose the children in whom they have invested months or years of effort. In certain conditions, however, the increase in birth spacing and decrease in family size resulting from these measures could make sense, and these events are, we have seen, associated with rather abrupt changes in ecological circumstances, for the worse.

Infanticide and religiously supported status

Some societies have developed complicated systems of status differentiation supported by religious myths; the Hindu caste system is the most conspicuous example. Written into Hindu religious belief and practice is the caste structure: an ancient hierarchy of endogamous groups related to each other by social interdependence.

Sub-caste members endeavour to better their socio-religious positions by arranging up-caste marriages for their daughters. It has been understood for some time that such a system can result in a surplus of women in the top part of any of these sub-caste systems, and this has frequently been overcome by female infanticide (Dumont 1970; Dickemann 1979) together with polygyny among the powerful, while the men at the lower end of a sub-caste, as a result, tend to marry women of sub-castes inferior to their own. The surplus of high-born unmarried women cannot be married to men of lower castes than themselves without involving their families in complicated issues of religious pollution and there are few roles in Hindu society which unmarried women can perform.

The importance of caste in restricting marriage appears to have been particularly strong in Rajputana, resulting in large-scale infanticide of female babies, as early British administrators noted when the first censuses showed, in some cases, double the number of men to women. The 1852 census of Mysore showed, for instance, that the Thakoor caste had 10,695 male and 5,865 female children and that out of every thousand of the Thakoor population, there were at least 42 girls less than boys below the age of 12. A census for some villages in Kathiawar made in 1845 shows that the ratio of males to females was more than two to one in many cases.

The methods used were starvation, poisoning, strangling, exposure, burial alive or drowning in milk after a prayer had been offered that they might be reborn in the form of a boy. This in itself indicates that any simple population reduction was not the object of the exercise: births *were* wanted but they had to be male. However, we should note that infanticide will always increase birth *spacing,* and as such conforms with $r-$ selection expectations if environmental resources are 'tight'.

A Victorian study of Hinduism (Wilkins 1975: 167–8) shows that Bengali Brahmins had daughters who never lived with their husbands, and often had annual abortions. Abortions were also induced by young widows, who were not allowed to remarry. Astrologers professed to be able to state the sex of the unborn child and abortion followed female diagnoses since the advent of a female was regarded as a curse and a misfortune.

The British administration waged a long campaign against these practices based on the Christian premise that they were no less than murder, without really understanding the Hindu preference for sons, let alone the overpopulation problem. Some figures related to the government's campaign are included in Table 4.2. While it took many years for these practices to be reduced so that they were at least no longer so obvious, some measures were immediately successful. A police detail quartered in one village in which there was a massive imbalance between girls and boys was apparently responsible for 10 out of 13 girls born in the next year surviving (Chevers 1870: 752,759). While the de-

(a) *Census figures on which the government campaign against female infanticide was based*

Year	Children under 10 years	
	male	*female*
1834	979	394
1837	968	264
1841	1,650	826

(b) *Census figures after the government campaign against female infanticide*

Year	Persons under 20 years	
	male	*female*
1850	3,844	3,423
1851	3,901	3,598
1852	3,919	3,686

Table 4.2 Kathiawar population census for various districts (From: Pakrasi 1970)

liberate killing of female babies may have been stopped (Government of India Census Report 1891) one report has commented that 'many a girl is allowed to die unattended when medical aid would be at once called in if the son were attacked' (Dubois 1972: 606).

Although there is a cultural preference for boys among Hindus, it is also true that at the practical level girls are more likely to be in the family kitchen and therefore have access to greater food supplies. Seen in terms of India's agricultural productivity and population pressure, it is possible that female infanticide arose as an effective means of keeping the population within reasonable limits and that Hinduism with its emphasis on male heirs was the religious sanction for doing this.

Abortion and the human soul

Both Hinduism and Buddhism, with their beliefs in an almost endless succession of lives, have every reason to oppose the idea of aborting a potential human being already started on another turn on the Wheel of Existence. The teachings of the Gautama Buddha state that 'rebirth takes place when a father and a mother come together, and the one to be born is present' (Suriyabongse 1954).

In Thailand a Buddhist who induced abortion was seen as not only impeding an individual's rebirth but also disobeying the prohibition against the taking of life (Hanks 1968: 16).

A modern study in Sri Lankha (Ryan 1953) quotes a Buddhist as saying: 'If a dead "soul" wishes to be born into your family, it would be a terrible sin to prevent its birth. We will pay for such acts in our next life. Children that are to be born to you must be allowed to be born. That is how life goes on. We cannot and should not prevent this.'

Both these religions have the concept of the cycle of rebirth by which humans can achieve release from suffering. To prevent a foetus coming to term by abortion would be to interfere with this process, to injure a living creature, and thus to commit a sin for which one would in due course have to suffer in turn. However in Buddhism there exists also an idea of divorcing oneself from sexual activities altogether, so that there is often a pronounced reluctance to marry. Abortions are sometimes obtained by young girls who have conceived, in preference to a forced marriage (Nash and Nash 1963).

Ancient Greece

Abortion was accepted in ancient Greece (Monpin 1918) in the fourth and fifth centuries BC when it was not only legitimate but even recommended. It was accepted not only in Sparta but also in Athens, that weak and crippled infants were to be destroyed for the good of the state. There was also no moral objection to the destruction of the foetus for reasons of the common good.

Aristotle wrote (*Politics* vii, xvi) not only that deformed children should be disposed of but that children born to unsuitably matched parents, particularly those over age for optimum breeding and those surplus to the needs of the state, should be destroyed as well. That he was thinking within the accepted margins of contemporary religious ideas is shown by the fact that he recommended daily visits by pregnant women to the shrines of the deities controlling childbirth. In his own words:

With regard to the choice between abandoning an infant or rearing it let it be lawful that no crippled child be reared. But since the ordinance of custom forbids the exposure of infants merely in order to reduce numbers, there must be a limit to the production of children. If contrary to these arrangements a copulation takes place and a child is conceived, abortion should be procured before the embryo has acquired life and sensation; the presence of life and sensation will be the mark of division between right and wrong here. (Aristotle, Politics vii, xiv).

In other words, he was calling for slower reproduction but, failing that, for early abortion, a programme that would constitute a case of r-selection.

The Greek ideal of health was the Platonic ideal of perfect physical and mental balance (Plato, *Republic* v). The sick, the crippled and weaklings were inferior people and attention should only be given to them if their condition was likely to improve. If a man's condition was hopeless, or his disease incurable, the physician should not touch him. Treatment would be senseless since the goal, the restoration of health, was unattainable (Plato, *Republic* III:408). Thus the chronically ill Greek patient was burdened with odium as well as sickness.

The Hippocratic oath, sworn by Apollo the Physician and his students, stated that a physician would not involve himself in abortion or give a deadly drug to anyone (Hippocrates: 299). There thus appears to be a contradiction in Greek thinking, although the oath may in fact have been composed and used only in later times as there is no record of it being used in the pre-Christian era (Scribonius Largus 1887) even though Hippocrates himself lived in the fifth century BC. It may have been a statement of reforms aimed at by Orphic and Pythagorean philosopher-physicians who objected to the callousness of the Greek ideal of health.

Japan: abortion and astrology

While wholesale abortion for secular economic and health reasons is a common experience in modern Japan, this is still a country in which fertility can be markedly influenced by astrological assumptions. It was widely held for instance that girls born in 1906 and 1966, both the Year of the Horse, would grow up to be bad natured and hence difficult to marry. This idea is reflected in birth statistics. In the earlier of these two years (1906) the sex ratio of officially reported births was 107.6 males to 100 females compared with a long constant sex ratio ranging between 104 and 105 males to 100 females (van der Tak 1974). While it is possible that some parents, anxious to avoid the Horse stigma, 'adjusted' the birth dates of their female children in that year, this difference may have been caused in part by the conscious neglect of girl babies.

In the latter year (1966) the overall birth rate dropped precipitously from an expected 18.7 per thousand population to an actual 13.7 per thousand. At the same time the induced abortion rate rose from an expected 30.6 per thousand births to 43.1 per thousand births. Early neo-natal mortality of girls (including accidents, poisoning and violence) rose from 5.17 per 100,000 live births in 1965, to 7.78 in 1966. No such massive increase occurred in boys, for whom the comparable figures are 6.20 (1965) and 6.94 (1966) (Data from Kaku 1975; see Tables 4.3(a) and (b)).

Table 4.3(a) Induced abortion rates in Japan 1965–67 (From: Kaku 1975b)

	Observed	Expected (per 1,000 births)
1965	33.8	33.0
1966	43.1	30.6
1967	28.0	28.8

Table 4.3(b) Early neo-natal mortality rates in Japan 1965–67 as result of accidents, poisoning and violence (From: Kaku 1975a)

	Boys	Girls	Total (per 100,000 live births)
1965	6.20	5.17	5.70
1966	6.94	7.78	7.34
1967	4.33	4.13	4.23

Japan, a country with Buddhism as one of its two principal religions (the other being Shintoism), became after the Second World War the most officially permissive country in the world for abortions. The 1952 Amendments to the 1948 Eugenic Protection Law authorized abortions for economic as well as health reasons, but researchers (Potts *et al.* 1973) have inferred from comparing the Ryukyu Islands, where abortion remained illegal, with Japan proper that the decline in fertility would have occurred from illegal abortions even if it had not been permitted through doctors specializing in legal abortions.

The Buddhist attitudes to abortion in Thailand and Sri Lankha noted earlier, with their traditional concern for human life and the concept of rebirth might, one would expect, have made themselves felt on the Japanese abortion issue. There is little evidence, however, of effective concern. In the case of Shintoism there would be few moral difficulties, as Shintoists believe that the foetus does not have a spirit until it has seen the light, so that the technique of abortion is considered to be sending 'from darkness into darkness' (Calderone 1958: 149). In any case, it seems that the modern Japanese have no effective religious or ethical attitudes that abortion is improper, judging by the ease with which abortion has become a regular feature of contemporary life and become institutionally legalized (Goode 1973: 340).

The infanticide of the abnormal and deviant

No society living at or close to the level of subsistence agriculture can afford to carry more than a very few individuals who are so physically and mentally abnormal that they cannot contribute to the community's needs. Their presence in contemporary industrialized society in such numbers as to be a considerable social and economic burden on both families and the state is due to ethical abhorrence of infanticide against a background of general affluence. In the Christian West, it is particularly among the more religiously motivated that survival of an abnormal child is more easily accepted. A study in Pennsylvania (Zuk et al. 1961) showed Catholic mothers were more acceptant of retarded children than non–Catholics. It was concluded that this was because Catholic belief gives explicit absolution from any feeling of personal guilt by its insistence that every child is a special gift of God bestowed on the parents. Also, a retarded child may be seen as a unique test of religious faith.

In less affluent societies abnormal children are at best regarded as inauspicious, at worst as a sign of their mothers' involvement with sorcery (Buxton 1973: 250). This is the case in some African societies, for example the Sukuma of Tanzania, who seek to find out which of their ancestors is displeased enough to cause such a birth (personal observation R. Tanner). Traditional societies are unlikely to see such a birth as a chance happening and have of course no knowledge of chromosomes or genes. In such cases, religious procedures exist to determine the cause of the misfortune. This can include the killing of infants born in an abnormal way, or who later develop in what is considered to be an abnormal way. The Sukuma are recorded (Cory 1951, 1953) as having killed children born by breech presentation and those who cut their upper teeth first. The African Kgatla killed children born by breech presentation by smothering them with manure immediately after birth, as they were regarded as evil omens (Schapera 1966: 223 and 225). The Mandari (Buxton 1973: 250) kill babies born with extensively marked bodies, and in the past males born with one or no testicles were abandoned on ant hills. There are numerous further examples of such practices (Krzywicki 1934).

Twins have received special treatment in the religious practices of a wide variety of peoples (Lagercrantz 1941) either because they are seen as assets or because they represent dangerous powers or forces. The Nupe of Nigeria (Nadel 1954: 26) consider that twins are lucky and a sign of divine benevolence, representing a special incarnation, a concen-

tration of the 'kinship soul'. There are annual sacrifices on their birth-
day and their homes have a twin-shrine. The Mandari of the Sudan
(Buxton 1973: 144–9) welcome twins but recognize that their delivery
presents a greater danger for the mother and children than a single birth
and that their life expectancy is lower. As they are seen to be signs of
the 'Spirit of the Above' and in a precarious position, special rituals are
performed. In these cases twins receive above average care throughout
their lives. The sickness of one may result in similar medical treatment
of the other. Among the Nuer (Evans-Pritchard 1956: 131) they are regarded as having a single soul which survives if one of them dies.

In other cases twins are regarded as dangerous. Among the
Kavirondo of Kenya (Wagner 1949: 194 and 325–9) anyone looking at
young twins may be afflicted with eye disease, giving rise to prolonged
avoidance and to their ritual seclusion in their mother's hut for several
years during which period even the rubbish may not be removed from
inside the hut. At the same time, paradoxically it would seem, their
birth is a blessing of fertility which must be celebrated and communi-
cated to other people through the performance of specific rituals.

Among the Tallensi of Ghana (Fortes 1949: 271) twins are not
greeted with joy but they are not destroyed, nor regarded as sacred, nor
is the mother subject to moral censure or ritual penalties. No woman
wants to bear twins as it is believed that twins may not be completely
social beings at birth and this view is supported by the expectation that
at least one of a pair of twins will die.

The Sukuma of Tanzania are recorded (Cory 1951: 58) as having
killed twins. Symbolic representations of the dead children were used in
ceremonies for purifying their parents, such ceremonies being carried
out by the chief or headman. It is doubtful however, whether this practice was as widespread or institutionalized as Cory suggests since there
exists, even now, a secret society which devotes itself only to twin
rituals involving the presence of twins (Millroth 1965: 165).

We can consider the possibility that where fertile land or other
necessary scarce resources are available, twins are accepted and reared;
they may even be regarded as having special religious significance. On
the other hand where it is difficult enough for parents to rear singletons
because of food shortages, lack of house space and so on, religious
sanctions may exist for killing one or both of them. This kind of 'ecological determinism' of religious attitudes is not, however, adequately
documented with the necessary facts. In particular we need to be aware
that the decision to keep twins does not necessarily depend on the ability to supply double the amount of food, etc. needed for singletons. If
the food supply is fixed, and if their existence is regarded as a gift of the
gods, great extra efforts may be made, and resources made available to
keep them alive. In man, the food supply is far more flexible than in
animals – a fact that makes any simple explanation impossible.

R. A. Fisher has written that there is a 'natural tendency, wherever
infanticide is practised without the pressure of the severest hardship, to
strengthen the feelings of tenderness and compassion towards the newly
born child, by the natural elimination of those who are the most willing
to murder their offspring, for the sake of an easier or a freer life' (Fisher
1930: 200). This idea is of great interest. What Fisher seems to imply is
that selection can work in either of two opposite directions depending
on the level of (economic) 'hardship' families face. Where hardship is

severe, those families practising some infanticide do best because they rear their few remaining young successfully to an age when they in turn can reproduce. But where there is food a-plenty, families practising infanticide deplete their numbers relative to the rest, and so their line tends to die out. These ideas can be seen in relation to the ideas of $r-$ and $r+$ selection respectively; what is curious is Fisher's approach through the psychological characteristics of parents, which he regards as genetically transmissible to their offspring. In animals such as rats, lions or langurs, all of which practise infant killing in certain circumstances when population density is high, we can see how Fisher's process would work in terms of the transmission or elimination of certain kinds of genes or gene-controlled mechanisms. But in man, given the power of forethought, one and the same mother, pair of parents, group or society can 'change its mind' about infanticide rules from time to time depending on assessment of the circumstances, and so the process is less likely to depend on a gene-controlled psychological mechanism.

The ancient Jews and modern Jewish thought

The early Israelis before they became a settled people may have practised infanticide in order to help the survival of the family. The Old Testament makes occasional references to the practice (II Chronicles 28:3; Leviticus 19:21) as a form of sacrifice. Abraham's exchange of Isaac for an animal in Genesis 22 is of interest: killing potential food instead of infants could be seen as a move from $r-$ to $r+$ selection if it were shown to be associated with an improvement in resource reliability. The practice of killing children must have been very real for it to have provoked the Biblical writers Ezekiel and Isaiah to speak out so strongly against it.

At least by Biblical times a monetary penalty was laid down for causing an abortion in the course of a quarrel and the penalty became death if the woman's own death resulted, for which there is a parallel in Assyrian law (Code of Hammurabi).

From early Talmudic times, abortion was not considered a transgression unless the foetus was viable, whereas the infanticide of a child at birth made the killer guilty of murder. Talmudic scholars held to the view that Biblical references to all kinds of harm referred to the woman and not to the foetus, basing their conclusion on the idea that murder could only occur to a live human being.

However, all abortion was subsequently prohibited when Talmudic scholars argued from the laws concerning abstention from sexual relations with one's wife. These were forbidden when they were likely to hurt the foetus, and the perpetrator was 'a shedder of blood'. The great Jewish writer Josephus stated that 'the Law has commanded us to raise all children and prohibited women from aborting or destroying seed; a woman who does so shall be judged a murderess of children for she has caused a soul to be lost and the family of man to be diminished'. Such words would be in line with an $r+$ selection trend.

In present day matters such as the probability of mental or physical defect of the child because of the mother's illness, or the after-effects of drugs such as thalidomide, the general tendency among Jewish liberals in Christian countries like Britain, is that abortion can be justified in the interests of the mother's mental health, but much depends on the stage of the pregnancy. The state of Israel prohibits abortion on pain of imprisonment, but an amendment has relieved the mother of criminal responsibility for self-inflicted abortion (Criminal Law Ord., 1936, as amended 1966). The liberal Jewish viewpoint extends therapeutic abortion to a wide range of circumstances, including excessive mental anguish (Levine 1968). Israel's prohibition of abortion unless the mother's health is in danger, highlights the fact that in classical rabbinic Judaism, medicine is essentially prophylaxis and not therapy (Wolf 1976). However outside Israel, contemporary Jewish women are often the most liberal of all religious groups on the subject of abortion (Westoff et al. 1969) largely accepting abortion as justified in a range of circumstances beyond that of the health of the mother. Much may depend, it seems, on the prevailing attitude to population level. Israel itself has long sought immigrants, seeking to expand its numbers, its strength and its army. This would not apply elsewhere. It is thus to be expected that attitudes to abortion will be along $r+$ lines in Israel itself and along $r-$ lines elsewhere, at least in affluent countries where $r-$ attitudes are prevalent generally and the resource base is tight, but reliable.

Islam and abortion

Islam, in line with its generally strong procreative orientation (Hathout 1972) regards abortion as entailing the loss of a life. Thus it is not reasonable to perform it for any less pressing need than the saving of a life; there is in such attitudes no more than the continuation of the same themes which have already been described for Judaism and Christianity, and they have come out of the same cultural environment.

While Islamic jurisprudence regards the foetus as a person, there has been some divergence of opinion. The most prolific and perhaps the most famous of Islamic philosopher–theologians, Al-Ghazali, a married man who attempted to become a Sufi mystic, considered abortion at any time to be a crime becoming graver and graver as the pregnancy advanced. However, most Islamic scholars have defined two phases of intra-uterine existence, before and after the instillation of life, normally occurring at four months.

In Islamic law abortion is an offence punishable by the payment of compensation. The actual rules, are as follows: when a man marries a woman, he 'buys' the future contents of her womb. He is entitled to the equivalent of full adult compensation after four months for wilful abortion. Up to four months he is entitled to one tenth of the full sum (Hathout 1972). Similarly a share of the property of a father who dies while his wife is pregnant is kept aside until his widow's pregnancy is completed so that her child can inherit. Perhaps only Islamic law in practice does really regard the foetus as a human being by giving the unborn child such economic rights.

However, in Islam, as in other religions, abortion becomes more common with Western-style education. A modern study in the Lebanon showed (Yaukey 1961: 31) that almost no traditionally educated Muslims had abortions but the numbers rose proportionately with Western education, and the number of Western-educated Muslims having had abortions in the Islamic community studied actually exceeded the numbers for Western-educated Christians. Economic security thus does seem to go along with a shift towards r – oriented beliefs and practices, and a Western-style education can be seen as a link in the chain of events by which this comes about.

The Christian community and abortion

Since Christianity sprang from a Judaic background, it is not surprising that it followed Judaic lines of thought. The destruction of the foetus was considered sinful from the start since Christians considered all forms of human life to be sacred. So it was ruled early that intercourse during pregnancy could be a sin partly because of the danger of causing abortion (Clifford 1942), and partly because the object of coitus was to procreate and conception had already taken place (Augustine). These views were generally held at least until the eighteenth century (Amort 1752). Tertullian argued that abortion was synonymous with murder because of the presence of a soul in the foetus (Tertullian 1884, 1 (9):71) but Augustine made a distinction between a formed and an unformed foetus (Augustine 1847: 137).

Abortion was made punishable according to canon law in the West by the Council of Elvira (c. AD 300) and in the East by the Council of Ancyra in AD 314. The canon law penalty for anyone procuring abortion, automatic excommunication, dates from the legislation of Popes Sixtus V and Gregory XIV in the late sixteenth century.

Early Christian thought also held to the Judaic view that the life of the mother had priority over that of the unborn child. Tertullian (*De Anima* III:470) wrote 'sometimes by a cruel necessity, whilst yet in the womb, an infant is put to death when, lying in the orifice of the womb, he impedes parturition and would kill his mother if he is not to die himself . . . of the necessity of such harsh treatment I have no doubt'.

The Christian attitude to abortion can be seen against the need to maintain the community's population growth, dating from the original small but expansionist Christian groups isolated in either hostile or indifferent societies. This was combined with high losses from war and disease and emigration related to missionary movements. This attitude is still maintained in new Christian communities in Africa and in those small, closed Christian sects in the New World such as the Amish, the Hutterites and the Doukhobours, and to a lesser extent the Mormons at least until they became the dominant culture in the state of Utah.

The contemporary African feeling in the independent churches is against abortion. Longmore (1959: 136–7) describes a case in which the minister of an African church was forced to resign because his daughter had procured an abortion with the help of his wife but without his knowledge. His own proven non-involvement in his daughter's abortion was insufficient for his congregation not to demand his excommunication. Abortion would generally be regarded as wholly repugnant to African Christians of all denominations, though it is certainly resorted to particularly in urban areas among women who cannot afford to remain pregnant.

This type of situation highlights the particular difficulties for any religious guidance over abortion. In general terms Christian populations have caught up with or overtaken local food resources, and overpopulation is now seen as a personal and collective misfortune (besides being a major threat to the survival of the human species). But the early

Christian view of the sanctity of life, even when unborn, soon became part of the Church's written dogma, making decisions on such matters as individual, rather than community, responsibility, still less conceding that the state has any moral right to legislate on abortion.

So increasingly the Christian, and especially the Roman Catholic Church became not only the repository of a moral doctrine which was unsuitable for any situation of overpopulation either familial or communal, but also in the forefront of opposition to the legal availability of medically safe abortions in whatever country it was the dominant church, aided by other religious groups that shared the same view.

This has meant that abortion has to be resorted to illicitly by practising Catholics. The situation is made worse by the Catholic ban on most forms of contraception. It has been estimated that bungled abortions account for more than 40 per cent of female hospital admissions in Santiago, Chile, and that one-third of all pregnancies end in abortion (Ehrlich and Ehrlich 1972: 291).

In the Roman Catholic view any induced abortion is the equivalent of murder irrespective of duration of the pregnancy. In contrast, many Protestant theologians have made a distinction between the period when the foetus is unable to survive independently (abortion allowed) and when the foetus could survive on its own (abortion not allowed).

In most developed countries religious opposition to the legalizing of abortion seems only to have been a delaying factor but opposition will continue to come from vociferous pressure groups of Christians in terms of the Biblical injunction to 'be fruitful and multiply', leaving the consequences quite deliberately and willingly to God.

To Catholics, abortion is seen not only as another aspect of the contraception question but more specifically is also the directly intended and totally indefensible destruction of innocent human life, whether the foetus has attained independent viability or not, irrespective of any civil law on the subject and regardless of the method used or particular situation.

The background to this attitude is the same as the Judaic view that a soul is lost, that it is a violation of the fundamental human right to life itself, and that the age of the foetus cannot affect matters since 'it is probable that embryonic life is human from the first moment of its "existence"' (New Catholic Encyc. 1967: 1,29).

A number of surveys have shown this view to have been widely questioned. Christian conservatives are more likely than liberals to oppose abortion (Plate VII). Frequent church attendance is correlated with disapproval of abortion even among nurses and social workers (Hertel et al. 1974). A study in Canada concluded that more than any other factor, a decline in religious values and beliefs would contribute to liberalized attitudes towards abortion and that socio-economic characteristics were more important in shaping a woman's attitudes towards abortion than situational variables, such as accidental pregnancy, contraceptive practice, and desired or expected number of children (Balakrishnan et al. 1972).

A study among clergymen (Price-Bonham et al. 1975) found that a more liberal attitude to abortion was correlated with a more liberal attitude to sex and women generally. A more recent study (Westoff et al. 1969) in the USA showed that Catholic women were more opposed to abortion than Protestants, among whom fundamentalists were the least in favour, although there was less opposition to abortion if the reasons were that the woman was not married, could not afford another child or simply did not want any more children. Non-white women were consistently less in favour of abortion than white women and except for Catholics, the higher the level of education the more favourable the attitude to abortion. All categories overwhelmingly favoured abortion if the mother's health was threatened. The more active the woman was in religious affairs the more opposed to abortion she was likely to be.

A study of abortion in Louisiana, in a predominantly Catholic community (Schneider 1974) shows a high degree of conservatism towards abortion. Louisiana still has a statutory criminal law prohibiting abortion and a Medical Practice Act which prohibits abortion except after consultations when the mother's life is in danger.

A study in Northern Ireland (Compton *et al*, 1974) showed that Roman Catholics were less likely to have abortions than Protestants, and that for both religious communities abortion was primarily a middle-class phenomenon. Roman Catholic women however were more likely to be left without adequate social support during this time of great personal stress because of the hostile attitude of their Church; this influenced the willingness of community members to assist them, as well as deterring them from asking for their help.

Religious and other dilemmas

If we take the view that survival of the species is the most important issue currently facing mankind, abortion and infanticide may be seen as benign solutions to the population problem. But individual feelings are

VII. A Christian anti-abortion rally in modern USA.

also involved, and mothers may be deeply upset either by abortion, or infanticide, or both. Men too are deeply implicated, often being the agents who conduct the abortions or condone and perhaps arrange for infanticide.

Small Christian communities tend to oppose abortion and at the same time they appear able to cope with any children that are born. The Amish have a high birth rate but it tails off before the end of fecundity, so one suspects that abortion, *coitus interruptus* or abstention come into practice. The Hutterites who have the same fundamentalist beliefs, care for children on a more centralized community basis than the Amish. There is not quite such a drop in the birth rate in older Hutterite mothers, perhaps related to the fact that part of the burden of rearing their babies is borne communally.

These are biologically significant religious and social attitudes. Children are born into communities which can cater for them only so long as there are land and resources enough for them to take up when they are adult. This was the position for the early Amish, but they have been so reproductive that they have run out of vacant land. Now the community has become less geographically integrated and it can no longer provide the total service to its members which it used to do. Thus the previously successful high reproductive rate is gradually becoming disadvantageous (Hostetler 1970). It is a situation in which we would predict the emergence of a 'modern' or 'liberal' group of pro-abortionist Amish youth. Will one emerge?

This kind of process must be common to other religious groups as they spread into host communities. Their ideas diffuse with their general expansion but some of the ideas themselves become unworkable as distances between members increase, or numbers become too great. Then various social adaptations, or processes of fission and fusion occur. New 'liberal' ideas replace old orthodoxies, not only in response to prevailing economic resources but also in relation to the social and political climate. Thus if abortion is tabooed by a small group which then, as a result of expansion, infiltrates a larger one practising it, what was advantageous in an earlier generation becomes disadvantageous in the next. Various internal (intra-familial) and external pressures (from the community) come into play to reduce completed family size. These pressures reach individuals in the form of ideas concerning the 'best thing to do'. We could call them 'optimization strategies' without undue distortion, and can try to subsume them under the $r+/r-$ continuum.

Dilemmas now arise. Say 'optimal' family size is two or three children but to achieve this means adopting sinful measures, what is to be the actual day-to-day practice? This kind of dilemma currently affects millions of people. Here and there, all over the world, individuals, parents, small groups, states, nations and even world religions are considering their attitudes in the light of modern conditions. The trend in more affluent countries has been in general one of r selection, especially selection for smaller family size and more permissiveness concerning abortion (not, however, concerning infanticide). Infanticide seems abhorrent to all the major religions (except perhaps Hinduism) and to the secular states in which they exist. The widespread practice of adoption has indeed all but eliminated infanticide in many countries.

We should note that the changes that have taken place, and are taking place, are doing so because of changes in ways of thinking that begin with a few breakaway individuals who then bring about debates and discussion. Finally they can lead to changes in norms and laws. There may be long periods of agonizing personal choice, but choice there is at times of change. This is the process by which cultural change comes about where it is not the imposed result of external conquest or internal oppression. To ignore the complex interplay of choices and dilemmas is to fail to understand how existing cultural features can modify and be modified by prevailing economic and other trends. Ultimately some groups thrive and others decline. Some expand in wealth, others in numbers, still others in both. Some get poorer, smaller, and eventually vanish. Relative wealth has declined in China, India, Greece, Egypt, Italy, South America and Middle America, having shifted to Western Europe, North America, and Australia. Religions have contributed to and accommodated to new conditions to a greater extent in some places than in others. In India, Hinduism goes on; in Greece and Italy the ancient classical pantheons and their ideas have vanished. Whatever priests have said, conquests have taken place, and individuals have had to wrestle with the contradictions between rival religions, and between the sacred and the secular. The simple idea that 'cultures represent adaptations to prevailing ecological circumstances' is not enough. The gradual, or sudden, changes that occur in cultures are, to some extent, linked to ecological circumstances. But the study of abortion and infanticide shows that religious attitudes may not keep pace with other aspects of culture and may have more or less success in thwarting secular ideas of 'progress'. To the extent that modern states combine new secular ideas with older religious ones, they present people with moral dilemmas about how to act in decisions that have major biological consequences. Nowhere is this clearer than in the matter of how to decide on abortion in modern, overpopulated, industrialized, Christian societies. Except in the most centralized and dogmatic religions, the results of the changes in attitudes and actions of individuals can lead, over time, to changes in the religious beliefs themselves.

Conclusions

We began this chapter by noticing that infanticide and a number of related processes occur in animals, where they can be readily understood as adaptive, the outcome of the processes of natural selection. In man, the question of adaptiveness of cultural processes is not an *a priori*, but has to be investigated very carefully.

Hunter-gatherers, we noticed, do or did practice infanticide; both sexes were killed among the Australian Aborigines; the Netsilik Eskimos preferentially killed girl babies; likewise the Yanomamö people (who combine agriculture with hunting) preferably kill girls but also some boys.

The pre-Islamic, pastoral Arabs practised female infanticide. In that agnatic society we saw how this strategy involved a calculation of the cost of loss of new social ties and the bride-wealth she would bring in against the cost of rearing the girl. Against this background, Islam developed the contrary principle of safeguarding all babies; Muhammad, himself an orphan, disapproved of infanticide of any kind, and Allah, in the Koran, forbids it. We can see the change as away from $r-$ and towards r+ selection in a newly emergent religious minority with a felt need for greater numbers and a perceived sufficiency of scarce resources to manage this.

We examined the case of killing first-borns in ancient Carthage. Why, we asked, kill off the 'best' children, rather than, say the sick, or other categories? Is this not biological nonsense? The Nayars provided another such case study. We saw that abrupt changes in social and economic circumstances underlay such extreme responses, and we can look at first-born killing as an immediate form of massive birth-spacing on a population scale – a quick response to a sudden crisis.

In Hindu India, as we saw, boys were wanted more than girls, and widespread female infanticide was accompanied by prayers that a boy would be born. Nonetheless, such a practice can be seen to increase birth-spacing, even though it may not reduce the final number of children reared in a family. Both Buddhist and Hindu beliefs stress the rebirth process, and tend to oppose abortion; Buddhism prefers non-marriage; Hinduism used to favour female infanticide.

A surprisingly clear population programme is to be found in the writings of Aristotle and the practices of pre-Christian Greece, focusing on the elimination of the sick and the weak along the lines of some modern eugenics programmes. The 'Hippocratic oath' was seen to be a later, post-Christian development.

Ancient Judaism was against abortion and infanticide; in modern times we have seen a continuance of this in Israel, whereas outside Israel abortion (not infanticide) is often condoned by 'liberal' Jews. Again, in Christian groups we can contrast 'liberal' versus 'conservative' elements in the religious community. And again, Islamic beliefs show this dichotomy well, pointing to a Western-style education as a link in the chain of ideas from traditional–conservative–orthodoxy to modern–liberal–permissiveness. The dichotomy can be seen as a case of cultural selection from r+ towards r−. We ended the chapter with a general discussion of the points at issue.

Birth and childhood 5

In the preceding two chapters we looked at conception and then abortion and infanticide with respect to the role that religion played in organizing these events or affecting the survival chances of individuals in the very earliest phases of the life cycle. Assuming that conception has been successful and that neither abortion nor infanticide are being practised, we now come on to the event of birth itself and the subsequent years up to adolescence.

The new infant is of great importance to its family and the social group; this importance is generally very well understood and in most societies the arrival of the new infant is regarded with great interest and joy. It is also a matter of great social interest to others apart from the child's family itself; it is of interest to the whole community in small-scale societies and it is of interest to the widely ramifying branches of the family and its friends in larger ones.

In biological terms the new infant has the genetic potentials of its parents and its kinship lines, and it also has the reproductive potential for those genes to continue their existence into ensuing generations. At the same time birth is a dangerous period even in advanced societies; early infancy is often the period when mortality achieves its highest levels before old age.

From a biological point of view, given our interest in reproductive success, the health of the infant and child is particularly important because at this stage of the life cycle reproduction has not yet occurred.

A Christian child's prayer, accompanied by wooden angels, manufactured in the Philippines.

Biologically speaking the infant and child are more important than the post-reproductive individual. Thus, in so far as religions have rules pertaining to the health and welfare of infants and children, these rules are of more relevance to human biology than those concerning older people who are past the reproductive period.

Do religions always have rules to cover the events of birth? It seems that the major religions and tribal religions all do. It is in terms of these rules that decisions are made at this crucial period of the life cycle, decisions that have biological effects. We cannot therefore, as might be possible in animals, assume that natural selection will work consistently to produce mothers who are best fitted to bear and rear their children, nor can we assume that those infants will be favoured by natural selection who are best fitted to look after themselves during the birth process and afterwards. In the case of humanity we have to look at these matters through the prevailing cultural screen, and it will always be the case that natural selection will favour those mothers who are best fitted to produce more offspring in terms of the rule structures and other cultural features pertaining to births in the society concerned. Likewise natural selection will favour those infants who are able to nourish themselves in ways which the community itself stresses as appropriate. To give a hypothetical example, let us take an infant whose own mother's milk supply was insufficient for him to live, but who was perfectly capable of nourishing himself on cow's milk. Cow's milk, however, was taboo in the society concerned. That infant would be weeded out by natural selection if no adequate alternative was available. In actual fact, among the Sukuma of Tanzania, newborn infants receive sheep's milk, the only occasion it is used for human consumption, possibly because sheep are associated with female ancestors (personal observation, R. Tanner). Survival thus depends on the ability to digest this milk. Another example: in rural Thailand and parts of India the mother does not nurse the baby until several days after birth, giving it honey, banana mash and water or other mixtures instead. Such infants must be able to digest this diet in order to survive.

We thus need to bear in mind that right from the act of birth itself the child is born into a cultural world in which the attitudes, rules and practices prevailing in the society make up the social world which will lead to its survival or otherwise.

Life and death choices during parturition

In any birth there may be complications during labour and there may be such difficulties that decisions have to be made whether the mother's or the infant's life is to be saved. What do religions have to say about this matter? If the infant is allowed to die and the mother is saved, her more immediately available genetic potential is saved. Assuming the mother can have further infants, the loss can soon be put right.

On the other hand if the mother is sacrificed in favour of the infant, then the potential is lost for further infants to be born through that particular female and, unless there are rules for replacing the lost female with other females who would not otherwise be involved in the reproductive process, there will be a reproductive delay until the baby reaches puberty, and a loss of overall reproductive potential. This could be seen as a bit of r – social engineering. Replacing a dead mother by an unmarried sister is a widespread solution to the problem of maternal loss in small-scale societies, but that sister might later have married another man, so there is still a loss, though a lesser one. By contrast, a celibate woman who marries the husband of her dead sister in order to take care of their children and subsequently has children of her own would constitute a complete recovery of the group's reproductive potential as long as her fertility was equal to that of the lost mother.

What do in fact religions have to say about these things? Let us start by examining the extent to which those present at the birth, midwives or others can legitimately interfere with the birth process by making and following through religiously sanctioned decisions about survival. Judaism holds that when there is a question of saving the mother or the child, the latter should be destroyed on the grounds that it is the most viable life that gets preference if a choice has to be made (Levine 1968). Islam holds to the same view stating 'only if conservation of the pregnancy entails a definite danger to the life of the mother is the foetus sacrificed, for the mother is the "root" and the foetus is the "branch"' (Hathout 1972). Buddhists, too, consider that abortion is permitted when it is necessary to save the life of the mother (Ling 1969), and it is probable that Hindus take the same view. The Catholic view is that both mother and child have a right to life, neither has a better right than the other (Davis 1946, 2: 166–7) and that it is morally indefensible to sacrifice the child in order to save the life of the mother, even when this sacrifice is judged to be the only means of doing so; there have been a series of decrees from the Holy Office to this effect (1884, 1889, 1895, 1898, 1902).

Giving birth and religious influences

Religious rituals connected with childbirth and the protection of infants are known from Egypt as far back as the sixteenth century BC, involving incantations and the use of protective amulets (Erman 1901); the former were probably used as lullabies when the child was sick or listless and thus felt to be threatened by evil forces.

In Buddhist Thailand (Hanks 1968: 92) prior to a birth, offerings are made to the family's protecting spirit and to the ancestors. The husband prepares a ceremonial gift for the midwife to ensure the use of her private magic. She may string a holy thread round the house from which she hangs magical signs. Delivery should take place in a favourable astrological alignment during which the midwife says magical words.

The Hutterites use their own lay midwives in accordance with their belief in Christian communal self-sufficiency; the infant mortality rate in such cases is not significantly different from births delivered by physicians inside or outside the community (Converse 1973) probably because midwives detect and refer a large number of complicated pregnancies to physicians in time.

Midwifery in many cultures has technical and magico-religious aspects corresponding respectively to the natural and supernatural worlds of knowledge and experience. In Thailand, Buddhists, according to Hanks (1968), believe the resources of the supernatural world are freely and easily accessible to everyone. He writes 'the closer an enterprise was to the margin of life and death, the larger the supernatural element'. Thus in Thailand a professional midwife can develop a large clientele as a result of success, which is thought to be a combination of her skill in physical matters and her detailed astrological knowledge, brought into play to help the delivery.

In Hinduism confinement is considered to be ritually unclean; thus it follows that the lying-in room is often badly appointed, commonly a closet or an outside shed with as much air as possible excluded to prevent impurities escaping.

Hindu midwives, since they are in contact with impurity, are of low caste; the idea of impurity together with poverty leads to the use of dirty or old clothes and towels during the delivery, because such items must be thrown away afterwards. Indeed a midwife is likely to change into dirty clothes prior to delivering a child (Bose 1912). It is not surprising that the Western medical opinion of the Hindu midwife, who is often both illiterate and ignorant, is a poor one; a Western observer has written that the midwife is 'dirty in habits, careless in work and often callous to suffering, bold in treatment with the courage born of gross ignorance . . . which causes untold mischief to her patients' (Lankester 1924: 5), never using water to cleanse her hands and performing an hereditary function, impervious to the medical implications of her work.

Religious concern for the newborn baby and its mother

In all cultures there is concern for the newborn child, and any danger or anxiety is often accompanied by religious rituals. The child in danger of death is quickly baptized in Christianity, not to cure it but to ensure its membership of the Christian community; the newborn baby in Burma is often wrapped in a monk's orange robe as a protection against misfortune (Spiro 1971: 236).

Many cultures isolate the mother at the birth of her child as well as for a period afterwards in order to protect them from malevolent forces and to prevent them contaminating others. In Hinduism, the house in which the woman has been delivered and those in it are unclean for 10 days, during which time they do not have contact with those outside; then the room is cleaned to purify it and all clothes used during that period are thrown away. The mother does not become completely pure until after a further ceremony of ritual purification 40 days after delivery for a girl baby and 30 days for a boy; this period is shorter for lower castes (Rose 1907).

Some Muslim societies not only segregate mother and child but subject them to constant heat as well as washing them night and morning for 40 days (Smith 1954: 142). This heating of the mother and child is also found in Hinduism, where it is specifically related to ritual uncleanness; a fire is kept burning all the time in the closed room so that there may even be a shortage of oxygen (Lankester 1924: 5). It can be seen that some of these ceremonies have positive health implications, others negative, since they either bring in hygienic elements, or prevent the mother and child from being exposed to outside infections, or bring in germs and provide them with ideal conditions of spread.

In traditional societies, the mother, child, or both are likely to have a number of potions to drink and charms to wear which are thought to be protective against known and unknown dangers (Plate VIII). Even if the mother-to-be is taken to a Western-type maternity hospital in a de-

VIII An Afro-Arab father and children from the East African coast. Each of them is wearing amulets containing quotations from the Koran.

veloping country, it is still likely that she will be given such potions and amulets; even if she does not have them prior to the birth, they will be brought in by visitors at the first opportunity. In some modern African hospitals the systems of Western medicine and traditional magico-religious practices often run parallel, so that they are combining with or even competing with each other. After a birth the traditional system is most likely to get the credit for success from the family, as well as the mother herself, because they understand the purpose and the means of the traditional procedures best (personal observation R. Tanner). Even in the maternity ward of a modern European hospital the new baby is occasionally still given a crucifix to wear, both as a lucky charm and a Christian symbol.

There are interesting parallels between the ostensible indifference of contemporary Western society to directly employed 'magical' protection and the attitude of the Mbuti pygmies of Zaire who show similar indifference; neither feel much need for special ritual protection of infants and both are concerned very much with the present rather than the future as regards physical health. Among the Mbuti 'there is no apparent concern for any supernatural dangers and no precautionary steps taken' (Turnbull 1966: 57–8). Perhaps life in communities which are constantly changing membership, or where families rarely stay together for any length of time, as happens to greater or lesser extent among nomadic pygmies and in the West, go with the absence of the prolonged magico-religious rituals which are so often found when the child will be a member of a ramifying and deeply entrenched local kinship system.

The concept of illegitimacy and infant mortality

The principle of legitimacy in any society creates a social bond between the child and the rest of society through its family or clan. The rules of legitimacy are written into most religious rule systems and wherever they are strongly enforced, those who violate them, as well as their illegitimate children, suffer punishment.

Hindu Indian society has such strong concepts of legitimacy that the Laws of Manu contain no reference to illegitimacy even as a possibility to be legislated against. Enormous social difficulties ensue if there are such occurrences in the higher castes where neither premarital sexual relations nor adultery are tolerated; degradation of status and excommunication from one's caste, the be-all and end-all of Hindu social existence, almost certainly follow. Much depends in such cases on the relative status of the caste and whether it is isolated from castes of adjoining status. Dumont (1970: 115) states that it is 'a universal principle that the illegitimate child has a status markedly inferior to that of legitimate children' and Hinduism certainly shows itself to be the extreme example of this situation. We should note that here we are not describing the situation of a deserted unmarried woman and her child, but the offspring of less than legal unions that contravene sub-caste endogamy and the ideas of ritual purity involved in this. Such unions are, or were, common enough to create sub-castes which had distinct but inferior status (O'Malley 1932: 94–5). In one known case of cross-caste marriage the way out of the situation was for the whole family to leave their castes and become Christians (Archer 1974: 168).

There are further situations in which a girl conceives a child outside the common range of illegal and illegitimate unions. For a Hindu to conceive a child by a Muslim may be seen as beyond any possibility of legitimation. Such cases have resulted in the killing of the child and the subsequent suicide of the woman involved (Archer 1974). It is very probable that many Hindu women abducted by Muslims during the 1948 partition disturbances were unwilling to seek repatriation as their ritual impurity could not be removed in such a way that they could ever be legitimately married within their own sub-castes.

In Islam things are very different. It is sufficient for the father to acknowledge cohabitation with a wife or concubine to establish the legitimacy of the child (Levy 1969: 136). Since concubinage is lawful in Islam, it is not necessary for the mother of a child to be married to its father for it to be declared legitimate. But there is a distinction short of illegitimacy between the children of wives and those of concubines, the former having more rights within the family structure, such as inheritance of property, than the latter (Levy 1969: 79–80).

The principle that a child born in wedlock is legitimate if the mother's husband acknowledges paternity clearly indicates the socio-cultural rather than socio-biological definition of the word. In the Islamic Shafi and Maliki schools of law, a man can acknowledge as legitimate a child conceived before his marriage, and one conceived up to four years after his marriage has been terminated. In Hanifi law the period is two years provided that his wife has not remarried. Thus the stigma of illegitimacy is largely absent in Islam and it can be legally substantiated in very few cases; the general procreational atmosphere of Islam makes it unlikely that a father or mother will deny responsibility for a child.

In difficult cases interesting anomalies can occur. In one case, a Catholic Sukuma chief of Urima in Tanzania had a daughter only. Being a woman, she could not succeed to his position. To solve the problem, she bore a son in a love affair, and this son was then regarded as the lawful heir to the chiefdomship. The fact that the chief was a Catholic with a monogamous church marriage made him unwilling to follow the traditional practice of taking a second wife or wives in the hope of begetting a son (personal observation, R. Tanner).

In general, Christianity imposes penalties on unmarried mothers and their children. Often an unmarried mother-to-be does not have adequate social support during her pregnancy and the same often still applies to mothers without husbands after the birth. Even if the material aspects are catered for, in many areas in Christian countries a stigma remains. In some such countries the death rate of illegitimate infants is or has been higher than that of legitimate children.

Table 5.1 gives relevant data for Montreal during the eighteenth century; the death rate is a staggering 92.1 per cent. A present-day study in New York (Pakter 1961) found the death rate per thousand deliveries to be 24.9 for the unmarried, as opposed to 13.2 for the married. A study in Italy (see Table 5.2) showed that over a series of years the death rate for illegitimate children born alive was substantially higher than for legitimate children. A study in North Carolina (Table 5.3) showed that in the white community both the perinatal and post-neo-natal mortality

Year	Received	Died
1760	17	12
1761	28	28
1762	37	36
1763	20	17
1764	26	24
1765	20	20
1766	31	27
1767	28	25
1768	30	29
1769	25	21
1770	29	27
1771	24	24
Total	315	290

Table 5.1 Mortality of illegitimate children received as foundlings into Montreal General Hospital 1760–71 (From: Fortier 1963)

Year-	Legitimate	Illegitimate
1950	62.3	107.8
1955	49.9	81.0
1960	43.2	69.7
1965	36.0	36.2

Table 5.2 Legitimate and illegitimate child mortality, Italian mortality per thousand live births (From: Nodari and Pirovane 1970)

Colour	1957–61		1962–66	
	Perinatal	Post-neo-natal	Perinatal	Post-neo-natal
White				
Legitimate	30.7	5.5	29.2	5.1
Illegitimate	49.5	9.5	43.0	7.5
Non-white				
Legitimate	54.1	20.3	50.7	19.6
Illegitimate	60.0	28.9	57.9	27.7

Table 5.3 Perinatal and post-neo-natal mortality rates by colour and legitimacy, North Carolina, 1957–66 (From: Scurletis *et al.* 1969)

Cause of death	Legitimate (%)	Illegitimate (%)
Prematurity	26.8	37.3
Inborn factors and malformation	18.9	14.5
Birth injuries	9.4	7.0
Other causes	44.9	41.2
Total (%)	100.0	100.0
N	15,419	2,534

Table 5.4 Comparative death rates of legitimate and illegitimate children aged up to 12 months, Bavaria, 1960–62 (From: Steichele and Herschlein, 1964)

rates for illegitimate children were substantially higher than for legitimate ones, but the differences were not so marked for perinatal births. Among non-white illegitimate children there was a marked increase in the postnatal mortality rate (Scurletis *et al.* 1969). A German study (Table 5.4 and see also Maier 1964) showed that in a large sample of deaths between birth and one year of age, more deaths due to prematurity occurred among illegitimate children (37.3%) than among legitimate ones (26.8%).

A study in California (Berkman 1969) comparing the health of spouseless and married mothers currently raising children, found the spouseless substantially worse for both chronic conditions and functional disability as well as in their self-evaluation of their own health. Both mother and child can be seen to be at risk in this study.

However, when illegitimacy is common and does not carry a social stigma, as among blacks in N. Carolina it has been found (Haney 1972) that illegitimate conceptions reach term at a slightly higher rate than legitimate ones (see Table 5.5).

In societies where the social system does not provide any advantages for the male to marry, and apparently religious injunctions are few or ineffective, illegitimacy is so common that few specific disadvantages accrue to such children or their mothers. Caribbean rates of illegitimacy often exceed 50 per cent (Goode 1960), neither the man nor the woman having much, if anything, to gain from any formal arrangement going beyond the culturally sanctioned consensual union (Smith 1962 and Clarke 1957), at any rate until late in life after the child-rearing years are over.

The survival of the child and religious inferiority

Hindus, even including those of Hindu origin who have later been con-

Variable	Number of Women	Conceptions*		% Births/Conceptions		Ratio A/B
		Legitimate	Illegitimate	Legitimate (A)	Illegitimate (B)	
Total	990	2,256	1,534	86.9[†]	89.7[†]	0.97
Economic Status						
Poverty level	775	1,928	1,336	87.1	89.4	0.97
Lower middle income	215	336	198	83.6	91.4	0.91
Education						
8 years or less	147	426	326	84.5	86.2	0.98
9–11 years	483	1,106	786	87.2	90.5	0.96
12 years	268	569	317	88.2	90.2	0.98
13 + years	92	155	105	87.1	93.3	0.93
Age						
15–19	190	49	230	95.9	94.3	1.02
20–24	294	392	387	92.3	92.0	1.00
25–29	190	478	374	87.4	88.8	0.98
30–34	181	676	328	86.7	86.0	1.01
35–39	135	661	215	82.9	88.0	0.94
Parity‡						
One	250	61	239	67.2	88.7	0.76
Two	176	146	265	84.9	88.3	0.94
Three	160	320	230	85.3	87.4	0.98
Four	123	340	230	87.9	87.4	1.01
Five	86	365	164	82.5	87.8	0.94
Six or more	189	1,018	399	92.9	96.2	0.97
Marital status §						
Married, spouse present	354	1,187	300	87.4	90.3	0.98
Other married	258	1,059	263	87.8	90.9	0.97

* Conceptions not yet brought to term have been eliminated.
[†] These percentages are interpreted as follows: 86.9 percent of the reported legitimate conceptions resulted in a live birth, and 89.7 percent of the reported illegitimate conceptions resulted in a live birth.
‡ Six women had zero parity, accounting for 6 illegitimate and 7 legitimate conceptions.
§ No comparison is possible for never-married women.

Table 5.5 Outcome of illegitimate and legitimate conceptions by selected control variables (From: Haney 1972)

verted from Hinduism to Islam, Buddhism or Christianity, are much concerned with matters of purity and pollution. In the caste structure, those who are the most polluting and least pure are members of the lower castes and are allocated jobs which often put them into biologically unhygienic conditions.

On the other hand, the higher Hindu castes pay considerably more attention to regular, even perhaps compulsive cleanliness. Brahmin women bathe and put on clean clothes before cooking food; their kitchens are regularly cleaned for them and contact with refuse is reduced to a minimum, and if it occurs, followed by a thorough cleansing. However, in villages all cleaning jobs are relegated to the untouchables so that the more 'clean' a person aspires to be, the less will he handle dirt, even to remove it. As a result the floors of the moderately but not very rich (who can rarely afford domestic help) are sometimes actually dirtier than the homes of the despised poor (Myrdal 1968, III: 1607). Thus we cannot assume that the concern of all the higher castes for purity means that they will in fact inevitably be cleaner in biological terms than those in lower castes. But since the lower castes are obliged to

Period	Hindus (lower castes)	Hindus (upper castes)	Muslims	Indian Christians	Parsees	Europeans
1938–39	332	272	247	236	111	174
1939–40	257	217	182	197	100	68
1940–41	232	209	187	169	95	39
1942–43	245	196	179	190	92	55
1943–44	261	193	181	193	84	53
1944–45	253	204	199	189	68	47
1945–46	286	186	166	164	80	26
1946–47	308	185	189	179	72	37
Average rate	272	208	191	190	88	62

Table 5.6 Infant mortality rates (per 1000 population) by communities in Bombay city, 1938–47 (From: Chandrasekhar 1959)

undertake occupations such as lavatory cleaners, grave diggers, dung collectors and so on, they are overexposed to infections. The data on death rates show that the lower castes have higher rates of infant mortality. From 1938 to 1946 in Bombay the lower castes had an average infant mortality rate of 272 per thousand, as against 208 for the higher castes (Chandrasekhar 1959: 105; see Table 5.6).

The survival of unwanted or orphaned children

Christianity and Judaism have always been concerned about the survival of all children. The Old Testament shows some concern about orphans (Psalm 68, Deuteronomy 16 and 26) and the Talmud shows concern in particular for the rights of female orphans, who have a clearly stated claim for support (*Encyc. Judaica* 1971). In Jewish law, if there is no parental estate, the community has the obligation to support orphans by providing communal funds for a boy to rent and furnish a house and for a girl to be given clothing and the minimum dowry necessary for marriage. The Christian archpriest Datheus is recorded as having started a foundling hospital in Milan in AD 787, the earliest record of such an institution. Early Christians adopted unwanted infants into their families and provision was often made for abandoned infants to be left at church doors from the earliest times. In this approach Judaeo-Christianity is deliberately involved in saving the lives of children who would otherwise frequently have fallen sick and died from lack of care.

From the earliest days, Christian institutions for foundlings have often been run by religious orders created for that purpose (Plate IX). Many foundling homes were established during the Middle Ages but the most successful organization of this work was started by St Vincent de Paul who established the Paris Hospice des Enfants Trouvés about 1640. Although these institutions were designed for aiding the survival of unwanted children, their record of doing so was occasionally very poor (Fortier 1963).

The taking of another's child as one's own is clearly shown as having occurred in ancient Israel (see the stories of Abram and Hagar (Genesis: 16:2) and of Jacob and Bilhah (Genesis 30:3). But adoption was not a legal arrangement in old Judaic law. There was no recognized way of creating a kin relationship artificially by a legal act or fiction but the law did allow for guardianship under conditions which were parallel to those of adoption except for inheritance, which required a specific tes-

IX. A foundling wheel on the outside wall of a Roman Catholic orphanage at Bahia, Brazil. The mother is depositing her child together with a note to the orphanage about the child, some clothes and money on a revolving shelf. When she turns it the baby will enter the orphanage and she herself will not be seen.

tamentary disposition (*Encyc. Judaica* 1971). Thus guardianship appears to have been an individual act óf charity or self-interest in Jewish religious tradition and did not involve any institutions specifically catering for unwanted children.

However the state of Israel does now have provision for legal adoption (Adoption of Children Law 1960) which states 'an order under this act does not affect the consequences of the blood relationship between adoptee and his natural parents so that the prohibitions and permissions of marriage and divorce continue to apply. On the other hand, adoption as such does not create new such prohibitions and permissions between the adopted and the adoptive family.' This law thus has the effect of creating those ties between the adopters and the child which are usually recognized as existing between natural parents and their child, thus allowing for intestate succession. And it permits marriage between an adopted child and a member of the adopting family (see also *Encyc. Judaica* 2:302).

Hindu religious law makes it imperative for a man to adopt a son if he has no natural children 'because a son delivers his father from the hell called Put' (The Laws of Manu) and such an adopted child inherits from his adoptive father, even being cut out of any religious obligations to his natural parents. The ceremony of adoption consists of the transfer of paternal dominion over the child. However there does not appear to be any provision in Hindu law for the adoption of, or provision for, foundlings in a more general context.

Both Greek and Roman law allowed for adoption in order to continue the family line and it was possible for foundlings to be incorporated into families; there were no provisions for the care of unwanted children by the city state or religious institutions.

Adoption of a kind seems to have existed in pre-Islamic Arabia. When a man married the chief woman in a household he automatically became 'father' of any sons or daughters living with her (Watt 1968: 282). Muhammad may have thus 'adopted' Zaid bin Harithah, a slave, when he married the latter's owner Khadija, rather than later, as is sometimes assumed, when Zaid refused to return with his natural father who had come to Mecca to ransom him. Although Zaid was regarded as 'ibn Muhammad', he was not regarded as a legitimate, inheriting son. Thus it happened that Muhammad at his death was survived by three daughters only.

Islamic law seems to favour non-adoptive relationships, for adoption gives no right of inheritance. Certain verses from the Koran are regarded as grounds by the orthodox for refusing to recognize adoption as having any binding legal consequences. This is especially so in regard to property transmission:

> To orphans restore their property
> (When they reach their age),
> Nor substitute (your) worthless things
> For their good ones; and devour not
> Their substance (by mixing it up)
> With your own. For this is
> Indeed a great sin.   (Koran 4.2)

> Let those (disposing of an estate)
> Have the same fear in their minds
> As they would have for their own
> If they had left a helpless family behind.
> Let them fear Allah, and speak
> Words of appropriate (comfort).   (Koran 4.9)

> Those who unjustly
> Eat up the property
> of orphans, eat up
> a Fire into their own
> Bodies: they will soon
> Be enduring a blazing Fire.   (Koran 4.10)

Therefore, despite the form of adoption referred to above, the particular Muslim view of paternity has meant that there are few instances in which an adopted child can be called wholly legitimate (Levy 1969: 138).

Muslim canon lawyers have given considerable attention to the care of orphans when widows are left without sufficient means to keep themselves and their children. The Koran gives a general injunction about the care of orphans (Koran, Sura 2.218, 4.2, 93.6 and 9) perhaps deriving from Muhammad's own childhood difficulties. These arose out of contemporary social conditions in which the care of orphans fell upon the head of the clan who might be unwilling or unable to support them. As soon as Muhammad's followers moved to Medina and formed an independent community, this responsibility would have fallen on the Prophet himself as their head. There were a great many widows with children, because the sect had suffered high losses of men at the battle of Badr. Muhammad's strong feelings about the care of orphans are shown in the Koran, stating (Sura 4.11) that those who misuse the property of orphans go to Hell. In addition, since the giving of charity is one of the Five Pillars of Islam, there are pious institutions (*waqf*) in most Muslim communities which provide for the poor, including orphans.

In general, then, we can see that some major world religions actively become involved with children who have no parents or whose parents cannot or will not look after them, usually increasing their immediate, and in many cases long-term, chances of survival. Foundling homes represent one way in which religiously motivated groups may take over responsibility for these children and look after them. This is a clear example of how humans can do something which other species cannot do: we can set up *institutions* to rear infants whose survival would otherwise be threatened. In such cases as this, we can really talk about the *group* itself being the unit which looks after its own survival. What matters here is the way in which prevailing ethical and moral ideas, conveyed by religions from generation to generation, evaluate the life of children and instruct their adherents accordingly.

Religion and the education of children

Religious ideas may have dominated in the rearing of children more in the past than nowadays, in Western society at least, but they still play a major role in countries which have not yet fully accepted or been affected by the secularizing effects of much contemporary social change. Thus in the mid-twentieth century the Saudi Arabian government was approached by the United Nations with the proposition that child welfare advisers should visit the country, to which it replied that the Koran was completely adequate as a guide to child rearing and that no further advice was needed (*Annual Report*, UN Secretariat, Department of Social Affairs 1949).

In Islam the mother has a particular responsibility for the child during its early years. The length of this period varies between the different schools of law, but it is often until the child is seven years old, when the father takes over responsibility; even if there has been a divorce, children usually stay with the mother until this age. In the early years, therefore, Muslim children are assured of not being separated from their mothers by divorce. In Islam, too, the child may well not be born into a nuclear family in which he or she is closely related only to mother, father and siblings. For instance, the extended family of the well-to-do Hausa Muslim provides the child with a wide variety of relationships beyond his parents and thus any change resulting from divorce is somewhat mitigated.

In traditional Judaism the young child is an incomplete member of society and as such gets relatively less attention from the father than from the mother, as in Islam. As soon as the baby starts to talk his mother teaches him religious blessings and some simple Hebrew words so that from the earliest years he is steeped in the atmosphere and spirit of Judaic learning.

Formal education begins between the ages of three and five when the boy is first taken to the Jewish Torah teacher where he is taught respect for the Book, to hold it in awe and to aspire to be a rabbi. The child learns by mechanical repetition and memorizing which does not demand any understanding of the text, and in this respect Judaism is very similar to Islam with its village Koranic schools.

In both these religions the basis of the correct life is taken to be knowledge but not necessarily understanding of the scriptures. It is on this forcible feeding of dogmatic facts into young minds that future obedience to the dictates of the Torah and Koran are based. Thus any biologically relevant requirements are thoroughly ingrained into young minds. These ideas will tend to remain as positive inducements to compliance even after those children are grown up, and even when they may have lapsed from the practices of their faiths or are unable to follow them.

Certainly in the past there has been in most Christian communities some compulsory learning of the catechism as an essential basis for living, but it has never had the intensity and exclusiveness of Judaic and Islamic teaching, nor presumably the effect of causing people to follow a particularly detailed set of religious injunctions.

Only in small, socially and biologically exclusive sects such as the Amish and Hutterites has the learning of the Bible some degree of the same intensity. Even there, however, any biologically important injunctions in the Bible are not assimilated to the depth experienced by Muslims, whose relatively short holy book with its specific injunctions can be learnt very thoroughly by most children exposed to the traditional type of teaching. Among the Amish there is rather a shared use of the Bible as an important source of knowledge and belief.

It is difficult to obtain evidence of the effects of specific religious differences in upbringing on morbidity or mortality, but such differences probably do exist. A study in German cities (Wendt 1965) showed that Roman Catholics were more likely than Protestants to purchase playpens and harnesses for restricting the mobility of their children. It is possible to speculate that this would lead to Catholic children experiencing fewer accidents, but no data are available. In the case of Navaho infants, it has been suggested that the great extent of religious ritual and physical restraint affects the personality as well as reducing the chances of accidents happening (see Plate x).

If we can assume that culture is transmitted by education in the widest sense of the word, then religions have been responsible for a large part of the educational process in all societies. While much of this education was related to religious issues, matters outside religion were commonly taught within a religious framework. Until comparatively recently most people have looked at the world through religiously tinted spectacles acquired during childhood. Once formal education begins, even today, it is often at first largely religious. The level of religious indoctrination of the young depends on the level of religious interpretation of everyday life within the school. It provides a formal scheme of reasoning for what people are doing; it governs the child's outlook in a general fashion in line with the way of life of the surrounding society.

So the rearing of children in general terms involves hammering into their heads their religious duties and obligations as part of their cultural heritage. By this means the Hindu child comes to accept the ideas of ritual purity and impurity through which the caste system operates and hence the biological consequences of this are perpetuated. The Muslim child learns similar biologically advantageous and disadvantageous Islamic practices concerning matters such as personal hygiene, especially washing, and the Jewish child learns such things as the dietary and menstrual restrictions of the Talmudic code. These matters will be pursued in following chapters.

X. A Navaho child in its cradle board. The father chants: 'I have made a baby board for you. May you grow to a great old age. Of the sun's rays I have made the back, of the black clouds I have made the blanket, of the rainbow have I made the bow, of sunbeams have I made the side loops, of lightning have I made the lacings, of sun dogs have I made the footboard, of dawn have I made the covering, of black fog have I made the bed.'

Rearing the child away from the family

If we accept that the family is usually the best environment for the young child to develop in, then religions have in many cases taken the young child away from the parental home in order to rear it to a particular attitude to life. The idea of 'boarding' schools as a preferred type of education appears to have arisen in Christian countries, notably England, though not necessarily for religious purposes. Missionary schools are a good example of formally and forcefully depriving the growing child of his home environment for most of the year.

Catholic missions among the Yanomamö Indians of Venezuela have taken six- to seven-year-old children into schools where they cannot be visited by their parents. It has been commented that the 'emotional shock of living away from parents in such an exotic and insensitive environment will lead to serious developmental and emotional problems, crises of identity and personality disturbance that could be avoided' (Chagnon 1977: 159–61) even if the change-over from primitive isolation to being incorporated into the periphery of Latin-American society is more or less inevitable. The Wai-Wai of Guyana provide a very similar case (Guppy 1958).

Removal of children from their families is not, in such cases, an unfortunate accident; it is foreseen and planned. The Father Divine movement in the eastern cities of the United States taught a denial of family ties and responsibility towards the family (Bender and Spalding 1940) which resulted in the physical and emotional neglect of children by their parents leading to considerable insecurity and behavioural disorders in some children. The degree of emotional disturbance when children are reared away from home may well have biological consequences unless it is very well managed. It can lead to a loss of personal security which in turn can affect general health and impair reproductive capacity in later life unless self-confidence is restored. The so-called 'Moonies' provide a further example (Bromley and Shupe 1979).

Childhood behaviour and supernatural sanctions

The growing child in every society is taught not only how to 'behave' itself properly but the moral justifications for this, which are often expressed in religious terms. The idea that sin, disease and misfortune are connected has a long history as well as a wide-ranging contemporary usage.

It is during childhood that the moral ideas which have a biological bearing on survival are instilled. The Christian child is taught to honour his mother and father and, later, that he should not steal or covet the property of others. The first injunction is biologically advantageous at least while the child is dependent, but what about the latter injunctions that teach him to modify his own interests in favour of others to whom he may not be in any way related? Say the child is starving: should he not steal food? Should he risk undernourishment, when he could do better nutritionally by a bit of thieving here and there?

The concern for others which is instilled into children by a number of religions in regard to their families is a real killer if situations develop in which one individual can survive only at the expense of abandoning someone else to whom they have a moral and religious commitment.

The 1942 retreat of Indian refugees from Burma involved thousands of people attempting to struggle over the mountains to India; in many cases, as their skeletons testified, families had decided to stay and ultimately die together, rather than disperse so that at least one of them might survive (Stone 1969: 118–19). Any religion that inculcates this type of concern provides adequately for the normal and anticipated stresses and strains of community life, but fails to provide the means for the individual to survive in disasters. Certainly the stark injunction for Christians 'Thou shalt not kill' must act against the biological interests of the individual, his family, and even the religious community itself when sheer survival is at stake. In practice, Christians have tended to fight and kill readily at such times, both as organized armies and as individuals. In doing so, however, they have acted against Christian teaching however they may have rationalized their actions.

For Muslims, the Koran as the literal word of God obliges the growing child to follow a wide range of social practices divinely laid down. Muslim mothers in Java (Geertz 1960: 179) tell their children stories from the Muslim tradition, informing them that God created the world and will punish them if they misbehave. All Muslims base their lives on the necessity of fulfilling the Five Pillars: firstly, the affirmation of faith in God and Muhammad his Prophet; second, praying in the prescribed way five times per day; third, going on a pilgrimage to the holy places at Mecca once in a lifetime; fourth, fasting during the holy lunar month of Ramadhan; and finally the giving of alms.

By the time a boy is eight he will accompany his father to the mosque, learning a system of prayers involving drill-like movements which can, from a biological viewpoint, be seen as valuable physical exercise. He will see his elders practising daylight fasting during the holy month of Ramadhan (increasing their susceptibility to disease), and learn about the pilgrimage to Mecca (but not that it can be biologically disadvantageous since it brings people together and enables diseases to spread more rapidly). By adolescence the Muslim child will have accepted these rules of fasting and migrating as being basic premises around which his life should revolve.

The Hindu code of Manu is quite explicit in connecting disease with sinful acts and this remains the basis of contemporary Hindu law, although with not quite the same divine authority as the Koran holds in Islamic law. A wide range of disorders, minor ailments as well as major diseases, is explained in terms of punishment for crime, such as dyspepsia for the theft of cooked food and consumption for killing a Brahmin (The Laws of Manu XI: 49–53). Clearly this giving of reasons is a very different matter from the causation of disease by religious practices, but there is a biological aspect to such explanations since they may deflect attention away from discovery of means of cure.

Such details are embodied in the total social setting, however. The Buddhist, Hindu or Muslim child is brought up in a world in which religious events are the high points not only of the yearly cycle but also of his or her own life as well. The injunctions to wash, to avoid certain foods, etc. which, without religious trappings, would have little force on the growing child, are tied to many socio-religious events which are largely good fun for both adults and children.

Christmas and the end of the holy month of Ramadhan are marked by the giving of presents among Christians and Muslims respectively;

pagoda fairs for Buddhists are happy and popular occasions and the water festival of Holi for Hindus allows the excitement of public misbehaviour which at any other time of the year would be heavily censured. The Buddhist boy is the centre of complicated ceremonials when he is initiated into the order of monks, the Brahmin boy receives the sacred thread and the Jewish boy has his Bar Mitzvah. Only in main-line Western Christianity is the child often no longer the centre of public interest, although the ceremonies of Baptism and Confirmation retain some such features for the Christian community concerned.

Thus the child learns at an early age that the social order in its day-to-day workings is supported by religious sanctions. In many cases he will envisage God and the spirits arrayed against dissenters and disturbers of the moral balance of society. The Sukuma in Tanzania see the misfortunes of the family as necessitating divination to find a cause which can be put right and hence normality resumed; the child sees these processes in action. Many Christians, at least in their prayers, try and find the reason for their misfortunes, and seek help, or forgiveness; no one prays more fervently than an unhappy Christian child.

Even when society's overall moral pattern cannot be seen as related to a particular religion, the behaviour of children is often controlled by their recognition of an informal implied contract with God. Some Western parents are quite explicit in using this as a moral control. For example one American mother stated that her daughter was 'deathly afraid of being punished – not by me, but we've always told her that any little girl who tells a lie, God always does something terrible to them and she's deathly afraid of that' (Sears *et al*. 1957: 380).

A study in Tennessee among white Americans (Nunn 1964) showed that this use of religious sanctions occurred with some frequency and with evident effects on the child's behaviour and personality. These Tennessee parents were generally ineffectual and somewhat powerless persons who used this method to gain some control over their children. Another study in the Bahamas (Otterbein and Otterbein 1973) suggested that those parents who feared the supernatural inflicted more physical pain on their children, or the children in their charge, than those who did not have this fear.

Where children are brought up in the exclusive Protestant environment of a sect such as the Mennonites (Kurokawa 1969) this alliance with God is the accepted approach to life in general and in no way can threats of divine punishment be seen as an abnormal reaction. The authority of God figures powerfully in Mennonite life and parents see themselves, and are seen, as intermediaries between God and their children. Such attitudes are of importance biologically because they shape the future actions of individuals, when they come on to adolescence, marriage, and the rearing, this time as parents, of the next generation.

The circumcision of boys

The circumcision of boys is carried out as a religious ritual by both Muslims and Jews. There is no mention of circumcision in the Koran, and it was probably adopted without question by Muhammad from an existing Arab custom; there are several traditions giving his support to the practice. It is generally regarded as an essential part of the Islamic faith. It is usually performed with elaborate ceremonial by a religious specialist but often under conditions which are far from hygienic. A mass Muslim ceremony seen (by R. Tanner) in Pangani, Tanzania, in 1956, involved the use of a used razor blade in unwashed hands. No dressings were used, the air was dusty and the ceremony drew in large numbers of flies. Islamic laws provide no guidance as to how and when the ceremony should be carried out, or whether any children may be excused on the grounds of ill-health. Muslims appear to have given less attention than Jews to the medical complications of circumcision. The dangers of an unsterile knife used in ritual circumcision have been amply illustrated in a case in Cyprus in which there were 5 deaths from tetanus in 23 boys circumcised by a non-medical operator (Gosden 1935). There are great variations in the age at which circumcision is carried out in Islam. Perhaps the orthodox view is that it should be performed in the tenth year, just before the age when the boy can be punished for neglecting his prayers. Sometimes it is delayed so that expense can be saved by circumcising a group of boys together. In Dahomey it has been performed as early as the seventh day and among the Bosnians as late as the thirteenth year.

Judaism, on the other hand, offers specific guidance, defining when this operation must be performed or altogether abandoned. It is forbidden to circumcise a sick child before its recovery, or before the child is seven days old and 'gains some strength'. There is apparently Talmudic recognition of what may be haemophilia since it is forbidden to circumcise a child if the two previous children have died from bleeding after their circumcisions (Jakobovits 1961). The obligatory sucking of the wound by the circumcisor, which has now been mostly replaced by a number of glass or rubber suction appliances together with the use of swabs, was in part an attempt to reduce the danger of infection. Modern Judaism has paid considerable attention to the medical complications of circumcision, not only arising from inept ritual operators (Shulman 1964), but also by providing sterile environments in which it is performed. One US hospital provides a special operating theatre with communication links to an adjoining visitors' room so the relatives can see and hear the ritual operation and its prayers (Weiss 1964).

So both Judaism and Islam pay considerable attention to circumcision as a necessary rite and of the two, the former seems to pay more attention to the biological issue of cleanliness. We can presume that the Jewish mortality from circumcision has always been lower than for Islam, especially in tribal Islam.

While Christianity has no direct religious interest in circumcision, it has certainly been forced to recognize the importance of the ritual as part of African initiation rituals when such people convert to Christianity. It may be a block to conversion if the young men do not feel truly adult without this ceremony. The Universities Mission to Central Africa in southern Tanzania tried to Christianize this local initiation rite by introducing a form of circumcision under hygienic conditions by a hospital dresser, but with little success.

Despite its infective dangers, there is the further consideration that circumcision may be a prophylaxis against penile carcinoma. There is evidence that this disease is very rare in Jews (Wolbarst 1932) and there is a low incidence among Muslims as compared with Hindus (Bleich 1950). A recent study in Macedonia (Kmet et al. 1963) comparing non-Muslims with Muslims showed an incidence of 11.0 per thousand for the former and 2.7 per thousand for the latter. It has been suggested that circumcision has also resulted in a lower incidence of cervical carcinoma in women, but it is possible that the incidence of this disease is also related to other factors, such as ritual washing of the genitals and frequency of intercourse (Wahi 1972; Terris and Oalmann 1960; Mitra 1958; Sorsby 1931). In some parts of Africa there is evidence of a higher incidence of penile and cervical carcinoma among uncircumcised Ugandans than among circumcised Kenyans (Dodge *et al.* 1963).

A study of the epidemiology of cervical carcinoma in Lebanese Christians and Muslims (Abou-Daoud 1967) showed that cervical cancer was relatively as frequent in Muslim wives as in Christians, notwithstanding the different circumcision status of their husbands. In this study, 97.6 per cent of Muslim men, but only 1.9 per cent of Christian men were circumcised. Case history study of 140 women with cervical cancer and 140 controls revealed association of the disease with the married state, early age at first marriage, low socio-economic status, and no association with age at menarche or menopause. The author concluded that there was no reason to believe that in these populations any disease factor related differentially to either religion.

A further study of uterine cancer in relation to male circumcision was made in Ethiopia (Huber 1960). Comparing the rate of uterine cancer in an Ethiopian (Muslim) hospital sample with the rate in Europe, Huber found the two rates were the same (50 per 100,000 women) in the two areas, despite the fact that almost every male in the Ethiopian region studied was circumcised in early life. Evidence was, however, obtained that circumcision is a useful prophylactic against penile carcinoma. We return to this topic in Chapter 13.

Female circumcision

Female circumcision has been performed at various times and places throughout the world but particularly in areas under Muslim influence in Africa and in many indigenous African societies. There is no evidence that it occurred in early Egypt, but there is written evidence from Strabo (1950: 14,4,9) and Herodotus (1952: 2,104) that it occurred there in later times.

This operation has been wrongly attributed to Islam for it antedates any possibility of Islamic origin and does not occur in the key Islamic countries of Saudi Arabia, Yemen, Iraq, Iran and Turkey. It is not mentioned in the Koran but there are traditions, based on alleged remarks of the Prophet, that it was an embellishment for a woman, while it was obligatory for a man. According to Trimingham (1949: 182) the Muslim view is that female circumcision should consist of cutting off part of the clitoris and that any further mutilation is forbidden. The justification for female circumcision is that it reduces sexual desire in girls and protects their morals by removing erogenous parts; it can also lead to constriction of the vaginal opening, which is considered more pleasurable for the husband. University students in Khartoum (Nordenstam 1968: 95–6 and 205–6) regarded the practice of infibulation (closing of the entrance to the vagina by cutting and healing together) as unjustified but they continued to be in favour of clitoridectomy, or 'sunna' circumcision, suggesting that its justification was the protection that it gave from untimely pregnancy.

Once this rite has been performed there may be complications beyond those connected with the actual operation, such as infections, injury to adjacent structures and haemorrhage (Mustafa 1966). A Sudanese doctor (Hathout 1963) refers to the frantic struggling of girls who are forcibly held in the lithotomy position, so that what is actually cut and the extent of the operation can sometimes be uncontrolled.

The operation can result in complications for both marital partners later in life arising from difficulties over the consummation of the marriage if the vaginal opening is too small. As a result coital injuries occur, and rectal intercourse, prohibited by Islam, not infrequently occurs in error or by default as the vaginal opening is inadequate. Later there can be obstetric complications and the circumcised mother requires expert assistance in dividing the circumcision scar.

Circumcision: conclusions

From the biological point of view, the whole process of circumcision, for boys and girls, is very perplexing. Apart perhaps from the beneficial effects on penile and possibly cervical carcinoma, this cutting away of the skin around sensitive erogenous zones intimately concerned in the primary reproductive process seems to make biological sense. It is hard, also, to come to terms with the possibilities it brings of infection and subsequent difficulties in sexual behaviour and childbirth. Why then circumcision? Other religions manage without it, and do not necessarily have alternative scarifications. The foreskin of the male cannot be biologically disadvantageous or it would have been lost in the course of human evolution, eliminated by natural selection. The clitoris, arguably, makes reproduction more efficient by making sex more enjoyable for the woman. Why cut off or damage either of them? As often, clear answers are not to be found although speculative reasons can be adduced, e.g. that reduced fertility can be advantageous in conditions where there is a need for increased birth spacing. For a while, no doubt, cultural rules can continue to operate (in this case literally) on the basis of traditional ideas, the adaptiveness or functionality of which may relate to bygone times. Or once-adaptive actions can come to serve new purposes. Just as face or body scars can be used as tribal markers indicating membership of the community, so can circumcision. In this case, it does also seem that part of the aim is to reduce the intensity of immediate sensual pleasure arising from genital stimulation. A population control device? The explanation seems too facile to accept. There is no evidence that circumcised peoples have lower reproductive rates than uncircumcised ones, indeed the opposite seems to be the case. Perhaps the big advantage is still in relation to reduction of genital diseases. We return to this in Chapter 13.

Conclusions

This chapter has documented some of the many ways religions can affect the biologically important events of birth and the years following, up to adolescence. Though normally an event of rejoicing, a birth with complications is a difficult and even tragic event. In such cases, religious rules indicate whether priorities for survival are with the mother or the child. Such rules tend to be phrased in terms of a 'right to life' or other such dogmatic assertions, rather than on the more pragmatic conclusions that might arise were decisions to be left to those attending the birth and taken solely on biological considerations. Their implications for rates of reproduction were considered.

We saw in Chapter 3 that religions are of importance to women seeking conception, and seeking to avoid it. In Chapter 4 we saw how they affected the survival chances of unwanted children, both during pregnancy and after birth. The present chapter, once again, illustrates how religions are brought in around the time of birth, to ensure a safe delivery and afterwards to ensure the child's safety. Religious rules affect permissible diets and hence the child's intake of essential vitamins, carbohydrates, proteins and fats. They also dictate who may be present at a birth and how the delivery should be made, with notable effects on hygiene in the case of Hinduism.

Once accomplished, the human child, unlike an animal offspring, is either legitimate or illegitimate, and some religions, if they cannot be said actually to create this widely ramifying social distinction, certainly take a great interest in it and lay down rules for stigmatizing, excluding, or even (in some Hindu cases) killing the illegitimate child. Here these religions seem to be supporting the vital social institution of marriage, but from a biological viewpoint they are bringing about a set of difficulties for healthy children and reducing or eliminating their survival chances. There are no fixed universal rules, however, for other religions have institutions to care for such children with more or less success, thus saving them at least temporarily and quite possibly giving them survival prospects equal to those of legitimate children.

The same, in general, applies to orphans. Care from religious quarters may be appalling or excellent; they may be stigmatized or helped to overcome stigma. In some cases they are co-opted into religious colleges, e.g. as young monks, and so provide religions with a great return for the investment of time and effort put into their education.

As always, we have tried to stress the need to look into the 'small print' – the details of the rules of definition of who is legitimate, etc., precisely what this means in any society, and what this is likely to mean in biological terms.

During childhood the majority of social learning takes place, and this is when religions are most active, dinning their traditional wisdoms into the sensitive minds of children, who will one day repeat them to their own children in turn. For the most part such messages have to do with the prevailing moral code, but there is much besides, especially concerning ways of living to avoid 'impurity'. It is during the childhood years, then, that religions can hope to achieve their greatest impact in relation to matters of biological concern: control of diet, sex, anger, hate, jealousy; and the liberation of these latter emotions on to appropriate targets. In short, attitudes are set up that can lead to life-or-death outcomes in later life.

The chapter ended with a section on circumcision. Religion is often involved, ruling whether or not male or female circumcision should occur. And again, the biological interpretation was difficult. From the available evidence, however, we concluded that this act could be a 'social marking' device, with a variety of biological effects.

6 Adolescence

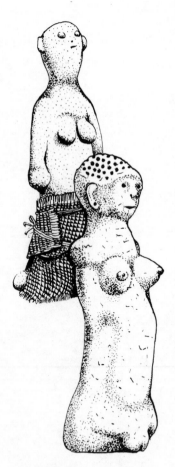

Zigua figurines from eastern Tanzania used in girls' puberty ceremonies as part of the instruction in their future wifely duties.

In the previous chapter we considered the period from birth through childhood up to the point of adolescence to see what effects religious beliefs and organizations had on the chances of the survival and health of the child. The question we asked was: How does membership of a particular religious group with its special rules restrict or help any given youngster to succumb to, or overcome, the environmental hazards, health problems and so on, of childhood, hence to reach reproductive age and be able to pass on his or her genes to the next generation? As we pointed out, any advantage that religious groups can give is going to be important biologically at this stage in life, far more important than any advantage with regard to health or survival after the reproductive period is over.

We can now consider the period of adolescence itself, that is the period during which the individual reaches and maintains reproductive maturity but is not yet wholly adult physically because certain aspects of the growth process (e.g. fusion of some bony epyphyses) are not finished, and also because some parts of the socialization process are not yet completed. So an adolescent is a person who is reproductively mature but socially and to some extent physically immature.

This is an interesting period with regard to the transmission of genes. By definition these young people are able to reproduce. One might suppose, therefore, that the best thing for their genes would be to get them reproducing straight away at top speed. There are good reasons for supposing this. The process of ageing is known to affect ova deleteriously and young eggs are probably less likely to contain mutations, chromosome anomalies and other defects which would lead to the production of infertile or inadequate young.

These facts suggest that reproduction should occur as early as possible. However there are also counterbalancing forces on the biological side. Firstly, as we have said, adolescents are not fully grown; they may still be several inches short of full height and in females the pelvis may not have fully developed, thus providing less than optimal birth space for babies. Social immaturity means that the adolescent has not yet become a full participant in society. Social status is not fully established and access to scarce resources is not yet secure, so a younger person is rarely in as good a position as an older one to rear young successfully, though this aspect does vary greatly from one culture to another. There is no advantage biologically in producing young unless they can be successfully reared to maturity; in fact it is better to wait.

For these reasons adolescence, from the biological standpoint, is best seen as a transition zone. During this period, how does belonging to a religious group affect the chances that an individual will eventually reproduce successfully? This is the question we want to look at in this chapter.

Firstly let us go over very briefly the physical and other processes of adolescence and remind ourselves of what these are. There is an end of the slow and rather stready period of body growth which takes place in childhood and there begins a rather sudden burst of growth called the adolescent spurt. It takes place earlier in the case of girls than boys. Most of the children who form the groups on which these statements are based are in fact white children, but the same process may well be true of peoples in most parts of the world. There may be up to two years' difference in average age of the adolescent spurt between boys and girls in one and the same population, though this does vary from country to country. Also the actual age at which the adolescent spurt takes place varies, not only from place to place but from one time to another, depending very much, it seems, on levels of nutrition. For instance, it is known that in the course of the present century, the adolescent spurt has occurred earlier each decade in most of the countries of Europe, in North America and in other areas where nutritional standards and health services have been improving.

Thus it is quite likely that anything religion could do to improve nutritional standards, hygiene or medical services would be reflected in earlier adolescence. This would in turn effectively expand the period available for reproduction and, in theory, produce conditions for the production of more offspring, healthier offspring and offspring more likely to survive. In the last chapter we saw that in countries where health is poor, religious attention often focuses on the production of many children. Our discussion in this chapter will enquire whether religions, and the moralities they engender, are responsible for promoting or delaying the onset of reproduction by those individuals who have survived the rigours of childhood in unhygienic communities with poor nutrition, and in hygienic communities with good nutrition. This will enable us to see religious practices and ideas in relation to hypothetical 'optimal rates' of reproduction, or other such ideas relevant to the problem of whether cultural features are biologically adaptive or not, and whether they could be considered as results of r^c- or r^c+ selection.

A number of biological alterations occur at adolescence: endocrine changes (increased oestrogen production in females and testosterone production in males) result in the development of changes in the primary and secondary sexual characteristics, with the start of menstrual cycles and breast development in females and the production of sperm in males, voice 'breaking', pubic hair etc. One of the chief characteristics of puberty is the development of new interests by the individuals concerned: an increasing social orientation towards members of the other sex and increased interest in sexual behaviour which, if unchecked, leads to the production of offspring. If religions are concerned with promoting or delaying reproduction processes, it is from this biological background of individual development they must work.

Initiation rites for adolescents

In small-scale societies studied by social anthropologists the change to adolescence is usually marked by rituals of one kind or another whereby designated elders formally bring children out of the state of childhood by what van Gennep (1960) called 'rites de passage' and bring them into the adult world, where new rules apply, new forms of dress are used and new kinds of behaviour patterns are expected. In nearly all such cases, religions play a major role in reorienting the child to his or her new status.

Where these rites occur they often concern themselves with both physical puberty and social status and recognize the movement from what is considered to be a pre-sexual world in which individuals are considered to be incapable of complete sexual relations (although they may in many cases have already indulged in sex play), to the sexual world of adolescence in which sexual relations of certain kinds are expected to occur and are, in fact, actively promoted by the teaching of sexual techniques by older men and women.

For both boys and girls these rituals are often followed by a period of segregation in which the initiates learn the proper approach to teenage sex and also details of the adult society towards which they are now moving. Boys may be shown sacred objects (such as Australian bull-roarers); taught the names of the gods and shown how humans impersonate them – as among the Hopi with their Kachina gods; toughened up by tribal scarification marking as in the Nuer of the Sudan, or among the Iatmul of New Guinea (Plate XI); or led to seek for personal visions, often in ways involving self-torture as among the now extinct Mandan Indians (Plate XII). Thus religions are very involved in the process of puberty rituals. The solemnity of the occasion as well as its in-

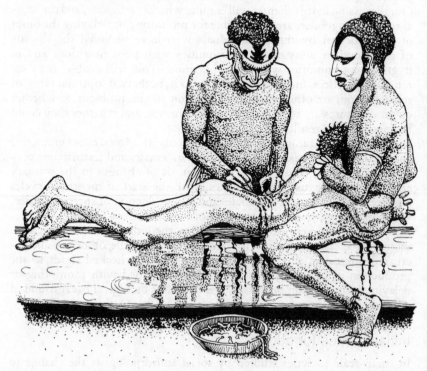

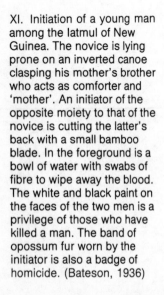

XI. Initiation of a young man among the Iatmul of New Guinea. The novice is lying prone on an inverted canoe clasping his mother's brother who acts as comforter and 'mother'. An initiator of the opposite moiety to that of the novice is cutting the latter's back with a small bamboo blade. In the foreground is a bowl of water with swabs of fibre to wipe away the blood. The white and black paint on the faces of the two men is a privilege of those who have killed a man. The band of opossum fur worn by the initiator is also a badge of homicide. (Bateson, 1936)

XII. A scene from life drawn by G. Catlin among the now extinct Mandan Indians. In the Okipa ceremony the warriors sought a personal vision through self-torture. They were hung from thongs inserted through their flesh and were turned until they fainted. (Catlin, 1841)

structional formality and learning processes impinge on the minds of all the participants; elaborate rituals and complicated symbols figure largely, justifying tribal myths, adult or masculine dominance, and other cultural features.

Regardless of the exact age at which these rituals occur, the aim is to produce 'proper' young adults, able to enter social maturity together with their age-mates, as the new and ascending generation of young adults. Thus what in our own society tends to be a shambles is handled by small-scale societies in a sensible way, inducing feelings of pride and social responsibility.

Puberty rituals for adolescent girls

These ceremonies may occur before or after menarche and in some societies have the purpose of preparing girls for marriage, which follows soon afterwards. Thus among the Bemba (Richards 1956) the primary purpose was to make the girls marriageable – to make them grow and become women. In the opinion of the adult women involved in the Chisungu ceremony it was designed to change the course of nature by supernatural means. Thus the initiates received the magic associated with growth and nubility and obtained supernatural protection from the dangers associated with the physical onset of puberty, to make it easy for them to have intercourse safely with their future husbands, and to be safely delivered of their future children. The whole lengthy ceremony makes the girl nubile in the eyes of the society and thus potentially fertile in a socially acceptable setting.

Although the initiators referred to 'teaching' the initiates, Richards says that no direct instruction was given and that initiation neither gives additional knowledge and skill nor the right to use them. It is likely that the girls already know about sex since families live in a small huts and they will already have learned by observation and participation the elements of sex, the birth process and child care.

What they do learn at puberty is the secret language of marriage, its etiquette, the rules and taboos of married life that a husband expects his wife to know. Richards writes that 'a girl may have little intellectual understanding of what is being done at the time of her (initiation), although she may be in a highly emotional state in which she is likely to be suggestible to the general emphasis laid on the importance of marriage and childbirth'. Secondly it teaches not so much the technical activities of marriage but the socially approved attitudes towards them and thus 'the rite not only consecrates the woman's duties in the sense of making them seem honourable, but it is an occasion for the public affirmation of the legal obligations of marriage'. The protracted Chisungu ceremonies make little use of supplications to or worship of supernatural beings, but they make great use of the exact performance of ritual acts and much use of elaborate symbolism and magic formulae; the girls are surrounded as they pass through these rituals with the penumbra of their community's religious understandings and practices.

Puberty rituals for adolescent boys

East African boys are initiated around the onset of puberty with the main purpose of inculcating tribal and religious values, economic skills and sexual techniques. The initiates may well be segregated for a long period during which they receive intermittent instruction in the form of aphorisms and songs which are sometimes complicated and difficult to understand. Boys' initiations parallel those of girls since they are intended to prepare the ground for the assumption of adult roles.

We may examine these rituals among the Zaramo of Tanzania (Swantz 1970) where they are associated with circumcision and Islamic roles. There, and among the neighbouring Zigua, the boys are segregated for three months during which they learn approved behaviour through a number of couplets learned by rote, connected with roughly made, temporary clay figurines illustrating them, all of which are combined as teaching aids made for this purpose and have no sacred or secretive connotations (personal observation, R. Tanner; see also illustration at head of this chapter).

The instruction places considerable emphasis on sexuality, but stresses sexuality in the context of society and social obligation, the etiquette of sexual behaviour in marriage rather than male pleasure *per se*. It also deals with the boy's changed relationship to his mother and the relationship he can anticipate with his future wife and in-laws. The rituals and their symbolism presuppose that the boys are of an age when both sexual and social maturity are about to be reached.

Swantz (1970) writes that 'it [the three-month puberty ceremony] is not the actual transition, biologically or socially; it is a form of preparation which emphasizes the male qualities of the growing boys'. The rituals make the boys 'clean' in their own eyes and in the eyes of society. That they are psychologically important is shown by the fact that it was

XIII. In this Jewish family scene, children are growing up in a setting in which the family atmosphere is combined with readings from sacred literature and the consumption of alcohol on a modest scale.

found that boys who had their initiations delayed had become emotionally disturbed.

In any society where religion is tightly bound up with the culture there is no need for any formal training for the growing young to know what the religion is and how to support it. As the child grows and passes through adolescence, the religion is learned casually and concretely through following out examples set by others (see Plate XIII) and 'it persists on the basis of a constant rehearsal of its complicated dramas, woven as they are into the whole rhythm of social and cultural life' (Geertz 1960: 177). Thus it is not correct to think of an adolescent being 'taught' a traditional religion in any formal sense. A Sukuma youth in Tanzania will see adults consulting diviners and discussing the results; some of his relatives will wear amulets and others will have spirit shrines in their house compounds – no teaching is involved. Others will see sacrifices being performed and be involved as curious spectators on the edge of the family groups.

Over the years adolescents learn the framework of religious and magical thinking which they will use for the remainder of their lives – not as an optional, unimportant system broken down into a series of obligatory performances but as something into which most of the circumstances of their lives will fit. Among the most important ideas they will gain is that of causation. What are the effects that particular modes of thought may have on biological processes? The Azande of the Sudan provide a useful example since their ideas have been studied with great care (Evans-Pritchard 1937). Evans-Pritchard has shown that they believe that every event has an ascertainable cause but that this cause is only the proximate one. The Western-trained mind usually accepts this as sufficient, but for a Zande there are more distant events which also act in a causal way, but which we would consider to be irrelevant.

The Azande adolescent grows up to accept that there are certain individuals who, by means of spells and psychic emanations can cause injury to the health and property of others, and that there are objects (usually vegetable) which have the power, when used in combination with spells, to affect life and health. A Sukuma hospital dresser brought up with similar beliefs did not dispute that he had caught dysentery from drinking dirty water; his questioning over causation went on to considering *who* had caused him to drink that water (personal observation, R. Tanner).

Where there are ideas of causation which relate malevolent forces to the occurrence of sickness and death it is not surprising that magico-religious means are sought to counteract them. Among the Azande, the local spirit diviner is contacted and, by killing a chicken and seeing how it runs as it dies, he interprets how best to approach the problem, both socially and medicinally. While it is not possible to state that the physical materials used in counteractions have no physiological or psychological effects, the adolescent is certainly trained to seek in his illnesses and misfortunes a very roundabout cure, at least in terms of Western science.

These magico-religious ideas can carry on long after this earlier conditioning has been superseded. For instance, the concept of witchcraft can survive even prolonged university training in the sciences (Jahoda 1968); however, students of the social sciences appear to change their beliefs more radically and Jahoda concludes that possibly these disciplines attract more sceptical students who are in the process of changing their ideas anyway.

The Santals of Bihar and the Muria of Orissa (north-east India) permit premarital sexual relationships. The Santals (Archer 1974: Chapters 5 and 9) from puberty enjoy a period which lasts until marriage in which boys and girls are under some obligation to pair off, but the pairs are not necessarily expected to develop into marriages.

In their relationships Santal adolescents are said to have few anxieties. The idea of contraception in any form is treated with derision. Pregnancy usually leads to marriage with the boy concerned if he acknowledges paternity and agrees to the marriage. If this does not happen and the girl's parents are not able to arrange a marriage by 'purchasing' a husband, village elders sometimes enforce marriage with an old man as it would be unthinkable for the child to have no guardian clan spirit, apart from the fact that such a birth would defile the village spirits. Thus here religious sanctions ensure that no premaritally conceived child is without a social father. A considerable amount of premarital sexual intercourse does take place among the Santals but premarital pregnancy does not constitute a social problem.

The Muria (Elwin 1947: Chapter 4) not only have semi-permanent sexual relationships between adolescents but have village dormitories in which teenagers cohabit with one another over a period of five years on average. This has the approval of the community and that of the tribal gods as well. Yet here things are very different. Premarital conception is seen as a social disaster bringing disgrace on the girl and financial penalty on the boy's parents. How then is conception avoided? The Muria themselves allege that conception is prevented by the supernatural protection of the tribal gods over the village dormitories; they have a number of folk ideas to achieve contraception, such as the need for frequent change of partners and they believe it helps to restrict intercourse to once or twice a week. There is no widespread use of *coitus interruptus*. They wrongly assume that conception is most likely to take place shortly after menstruation. Yet Elwin (1947) gives details of 1,738 fertile marriages of which only 92 involved a definite premarital pregnancy; the reason for this shortfall is hard to discover except for the known fact that the female reproductive physiology may take some years to function properly (Ashley-Montagu 1957: Chapter 5). Low adolescent birth rates have been reported for a number of societies in which teenage coitus is widespread, e.g. in Timbuctoo (Miner 1953: 177); this point is well discussed by Elwin (1947) with regard to a number of small-scale societies.

In the last two or three centuries, small rural communities in Western Europe allowed adolescents considerable but specified sexual freedoms, under a custom known as 'bundling'. This was not a situation of culturally endorsed general promiscuity as the relationships between these boys and girls were guided by both peer group and adult norms (Stiles 1869). Religiously endorsed marriage was the almost inevitable culmination of such relationships, certainly if the girl conceived. The local church allowed or tolerated such liaisons on the grounds that no permanent harm was done if the girls did not become pregnant, and that it was probably better to have this period of sexual experimentation quasi-legitimized than wholly secretive. In these rural villages if a pregnancy occurred, the biological father was not likely to be in doubt or to disclaim responsibility and the families concerned would probably give their tentative approval to the relationship. The local Christian community, family and church were interested in getting the couple married eventually even if the bride should be pregnant, or had given birth already, but typically the couple got married before the first child was born.

Religious teaching to adolescents in large-scale societies

The main world religions, in contrast with small-scale tribal forms, all give specific teaching to their growing children. Islam has long had village schools teaching children the Koran and Traditions of the Prophet by rote. Islam is a doctrinal faith and any such religion must be to a greater or lesser extent in conflict with the day to day process of living; its universalism makes this inevitable. Geertz (1960: 179) has described the Muslim adolescent student or 'santri' in Java as 'merely a young man becoming adult in a religious environment, grown to maturity with the droning chants of Islam echoing in his ears'.

Such a student could not have failed to learn the Five Pillars of Islam, of which four can be seen to have consequences of biological interest: the obligation to go on the Pilgrimage to Mecca (on which he may catch a communicable disease); the obligation to fast during daylight hours for one lunar month in the year (which may lead to lowering of disease resistance); the obligation to pray five times every day (involving a repetitive quasi-gymnastic activity); and lastly the obligation to give alms to help the poor and the crippled (leading to at least some self-impoverishment).

The Buddhist system of teaching is also formalized in some areas, where each boy is initiated at least for a time into the Buddhist order of monks as a 'novice' (Spiro 1971: 234–47). A three-day ceremony, carried out with considerable pomp if his parents' finances allow, usually occurs when the boy has reached puberty. A few initiates stay in the monastery for a few days only, but some stay for more than a year. They should all stay there for three wet seasons as postulants, according to the Patimokkha (rules for the Buddhist monkhood, derived from Buddha the Gautama's teaching and the needs of the monasteries which developed in the centuries after his death).

The Buddhist novice learns the religious superiority of the male since only males are eligible as novices. Even if he does not stay very long, he will certainly have learnt the Five Precepts as the minimum requirements for anyone calling himself a Buddhist. The Five Precepts are abstention from killing (a prohibition which applies to all creatures including insects), stealing, illicit sexual relations, lying, and imbibing any intoxicant conducive to slothfulness. Further Precepts add abstention from all sexual relations, taking food after midday, watching or participating in any theatrical entertainment, wearing jewellery or using perfume, sleeping on a high or ornate bed and handling money. These further Precepts are the periodic (and if possible the permanent) aim of every Buddhist. The Precepts are repeated on the occasion of any prayer. Some of them have even more direct biological consequences than the obligations of Islam, for example abstention from all intoxicants, the obligation to abstain from all sexual relations, and not to eat after midday. These monastic obligations go far beyond those required of all but the strictest Christian orders.

The influence of religion in multi-denominational societies

Membership of a community dedicated to a particular religion carries with it a characteristic pattern of belief so that members tend to support their religion's stand on moral issues. We have already shown how, in tribal societies and small communities, this influences patterns of thought if only because the growing child is exposed to little beyond the one approved pattern of living and thinking. To some extent this remains true of larger-scale Muslim, Hindu and Buddhist societies. The same cannot be said of Western societies, which have wide alternative systems of thinking and acting available for adolescents to choose between. How much does religious training influence the actions of adolescents in Western 'Christian' societies?

There is little doubt that the usual adolescent processes of learning are augmented in religious matters if they are educated in a clearly demarcated denominational school. Such students may be favourably disposed to religion anyway (Remmers 1951). Some results tend to show that these schools, whatever their denomination, produce more than their proportional share of students having the characteristics of closed-mindedness (Quin 1965).

Christianity is unusual among the religions of the world in that adolescents are often among the most active members of their denominations. A study in Greece showed that Christian activity peaked during adolescence and that this peak was not reached again later in life (Sakellariou 1938). Other studies in the USA have, however, shown an overall increase in religiosity with age, despite a general decline in orthodoxy (Zaenglein et al. 1975).

But things can go the other way. Just as adolescence is found in some studies to be a time for increased Christian activity, it is also a pivotal time in which adolescents can become less favourably disposed to religion than they were as children (Moreton 1944). That they cease to practise and/or believe then seems (Horton 1940) to be attributable to conflicts between them and other members of their particular denomination, and also in their homes (Gosse's *Father and Son* (1970) is eloquent on this subject).

It has been suggested that the religious enthusiasms of Christian adolescents are related to the anxieties caused by their ambivalent position in society. However, a study of US Southern Baptist youths who responded to a religious appeal to come forward for conversion, rededication and special service did not show any predisposing anxiety in these youths as compared with those who did not respond, nor did such anxiety as they had show any reduction as the result of this coming forward (Cooley and Hutton 1965). Another study (Kuhlen and Arnold 1944) found that there was little to substantiate the hypothesis that Catholic adolescents wondered about fewer beliefs and thought they had fewer problems than non-Catholics. Thus we have the general picture of Christian adolescents being more or less interested and active in their faiths, and some not being religious at all in the conventional sense. Where the religious label applies, they are liable to follow the aims and ideas of their denominations with greater or lesser intensity. It is an oversimplification to distinguish between religious and irreligious adolescents; they are in a process of change. Effects on biologically relevant activities are bound, therefore, to be uncertain and generalizations cannot be made.

Religious restriction on adolescent association

Christian denominations, whether they express it openly or not, are concerned with the maintenance or increase of their numbers in general, and more specifically with avoiding the loss of potential as a result of their young persons marrying into other denominations with the consequent loss of their children to other faiths.

Even if a denomination does not actively involve itself in restricting association socially or by religious injunctions about the undesirability of such meetings, the preference many persons show for associating with others who share their views rather than with strangers, logically produces patterns of association based on similarity of religious beliefs. In fact it will be shown in Chapter 7 that even persons who do not actively practise their faith prefer to marry someone of the same faith, and that this holds even in populations which have a generally very low level of religious involvement.

Where there are choices of association in colleges which take in pupils from a number of denominations, it has been shown that students prefer to associate with others from the same denomination. Those who have no religious avocation at all prefer to associate with those in the same situations (Bonney 1949).

There is no doubt that some denominations do devote considerable direct and indirect effort to restricting association between their younger members and persons whom they consider to be 'unsuitable' marriage partners, though this is not so effective in the wider world of the multi-denominational city as it is in small, geographically restricted sects. Youth clubs, youth camps, youth services and activities of all types bring adolescents together and this propinquity is the social matrix in which potential marriage partners select each other, only in part on the basis of shared beliefs.

While there is normally some degree of pressure to prevent inter-denominational association and possible marriage, this pressure is particularly strong at the socially conceived 'limits' of legitimate association. Here pure prejudice may emanate from religious belief and practice. Studies in the USA have shown that those with no religion are more likely to have a low level of prejudice in racial matters than those professing a religion (Burnham 1969). In one study Catholic children were found to be anti-Semitic rather than generally race-prejudiced as a result of religious teaching about the Crucifixion (Gruesser 1950). In some periods the pejorative label 'Christ-killers' has been a common form of Christian street abuse for Jews. Among Catholics it has been shown that anti-Semitism in students has diminished since the 1965 Vatican Ecumenical Council (Ward 1973). This Council in its statement on non-Christian religions enjoined: 'Remember the bond that spiritually ties the people of the New Covenant to Abraham's stock' continuing, 'God holds the Jews most dear for the sake of their Fathers' and concluded 'this Sacred Synod wants to foster and recommend that mutual understanding and respect which is the fruit, above all, of biblical and theological studies as well as of fraternal dialogues'. In particular, it refuted the view that Jews in general were killers of Christ and stated that no support can be given to any form of persecution (Vatican II Council 1965).

Judaeo-Christian thinking on the occasion of sin

In the past a widely held view has been that 'keeping company' by couples intending to marry was potentially an occasion of sin. St Alphonsus 'would not permit a young man to go to the home of his betrothed more than once or twice . . for I have rarely found one who does not sin in such a visit, at least in word or thought' and 'I believe they ordinarily find it difficult to be outside the proximate occasion of sinning mortally' (Alphonsus 1905–12). Jewish Rabbinical thought expressed in the Torah has similarly held that any sexual relations outside marriage were unlawful and, that being so, any meetings in private between individuals of opposite sexes were to be strictly prohibited.

No modern theologian would attempt to justify such a ruling for engaged couples but these religions are certainly concerned over teenage associations when there is no prospect of early marriage or even any thought of marriage or 'going steady'. Among Catholic thinkers there are widespread feelings that personal sex attraction is both limiting and dangerous for persons who are ineligible for marriage, such as those who are legally too young, or who cannot conveniently marry because they have nowhere to live, or who are looking after elderly parents (Kelly et al. 1943: 25).

So adolescent intersexual contact is in the Judaeo-Christian tradition discouraged on the grounds that it might lead to a hasty and regrettable marriage, it exposes one to sexual temptation too early in life, and, for students, it may impose a strain on educational possibilities. As late as 1916 the Vatican forbade, even for pious purposes, dances which went on far into the night (Acta Apostolicis Sedis 1916). But this is an isolated, anachronistic and perhaps forgotten injunction. Many modern moralists appear to have greater confidence in the wholesomeness of the young, turning their attention to concern over the time and place of teenage associations, the availability of alcohol, the abuse of cars and the time that adolescents are expected to be home (Ford and Kelly 1963: 172).

The stigma of illegitimacy – a restraint on adolescent coitus

In the preceding chapter we looked at the effects of illegitimacy on birth rates and mortality. Here we look at prevailing attitudes to illegitimacy as they apply to the young parent. Where the stigma of illegitimacy is very great following the religious definition of all sexual relations outside marriage as immoral, as in Muslim Arab countries such as Egypt and Algeria, the illegitimacy rate is very low; where illegitimacy sanctions are slight, the rate is often quite high, as in Sweden (see Table 6.1).

Country	Year	Group	Illegitimacy rate (%)
Egypt	1935	—	3.8
Egypt	1957	—	1.0
Algeria	1950	Urban	2.2
Algeria		Non-urban	1.0
Sweden	1973	—	28.3

Table 6.1 Illegitimacy rates in three countries (From: Goode 1960 and Merton and Nisbet 1976)

The rules defining legitimacy and confining sexual relationships to marriage alone cannot be ascribed to prudishness. Such rules exist among Hindus who extol the virtues of sexual activity in all its many varied forms as a life-giving and joyous pastime that puts man into an almost divine condition. It is not sex that is tabooed but the breaking of category rules. Religious groups are in fact more concerned about illegitimate births than about mere sexual relations before marriage because the former make public the fact that the rules are weak and threatened. Catholicism provides mechanisms of absolution such as prayer, confession or sacrifice for the removal of the taints of minor sins. Absolution is available for those who feel that the sexual relations they have had before or outside their marriages are wrong. However, illegitimacy provides something of a problem. Various strategies exist to deal with the situation but in general adolescents are warned not to get into it.

The disapproval of premarital conception in Christianity may perhaps be shown by the fact that couples in which the girl is pregnant tend to choose civil weddings rather than religious ceremonies. A study in Detroit showed that half the brides in civil weddings were already pregnant, as against less than a sixth in religious weddings (Blood 1969: 145). There is no certainty that the former would not have chosen civil weddings even if they had not been pregnant, but the figures show that couples claiming religious affiliation to the Christian Church had a premarital conception rate lower than that for all couples (Blood 1969: 145).

What about attitudes to sexual activity? Adolescents involved in Christian institutions have been found to be generally less permissive in sexual matters than those not so involved. A study of US Methodist Youth leaders showed that 80 per cent held to a standard which did not allow premarital intercourse although at least a third approved of non-coital sexual activity (Glass 1972). Studies of sexual behaviour among older adolescents showed that sexual liberality decreased in proportion to increased frequency of church attendance and that in general non-believers reported more liberal sexual attitudes and behaviour than believers (Sutker 1970).

Apart from the social problems resulting from premarital sexual relations, it may also be that there are desirable health consequences from observing such restrictions. It has been shown that women who have had sexual intercourse during adolescence face a higher probability of eventual cervical cancer (Rotkin 1962). The incidence of venereal disease is also known to vary in proportion to the number of sex partners, and VD is at present widespread in the adolescent populations of the UK, USA and other countries where, in general, religious controls are not strong.

Male sexual relations in adolescence

Because of the social problems of pregnancy, the religious systems of most cultures have been more permissive about sexual intercourse for unmarried boys than for girls. In Western countries, frequency of sexual intercourse is, as expected, higher among males the less actively they are connected with religious groups. Studies in the USA show that among males under the age of 20 years only active Protestants and Catholics have rates of premarital coitus below average (Kinsey et al. 1949: 447–80). From this one may conclude that such moral sanctions as exist against premarital sexual intercourse are not particularly effective in controlling young men's sexual behaviour except when they are devout. In a sample of church-going and non-church-going Protestant men between 16 and 20 years without college education, the proportions reporting that they engaged in coitus were 70.4 per cent and 90.5 per cent respectively. With college education the frequency for the church-going group fell to 27.3 per cent and of the non-church-going to 45 per cent. So it can be seen that the educational factor is paramount, but that a practised religion does have some restraining influence on premarital coitus for males.

The effect of these religious and social restraints on sexual intercourse with socially acceptable girls is reflected by the high rates of visits to prostitutes by young single males which varies between 48.2 per cent for those without college education to 19.3 per cent for the college-educated between 16 and 20 years (Kinsey et al. 1949: Table 65). In terms of fertility, these figures suggest that severe restrictions do operate on the breeding potential of these teenagers as their coital activity is directed towards women who are least likely to conceive.

Female sexual relations in adolescence

Accordingly, in modern Western (as well as many other) societies, there are severe restrictions on the sexual relationships of unmarried girls, and religious rules to support them. This is certainly the case in Christian, Hindu and Muslim societies and was also the case in ancient Greece and

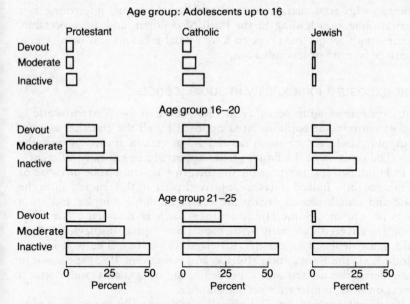

Fig. 6.1 Premarital coitus, by age, religion and degree of religious involvement. (From: Kinsey *et al.* 1953)

Rome. With the approach of adolescence, social and thereby potential sexual contacts between boys and girls are restricted if not totally prevented. In a modern Rajput community it was regarded as extremely scandalous for a young man and a girl to exchange glances publicly and they would be beaten if they were seen to do so (Carstairs 1961: 72).

Most data for Western societies show that premarital sexual intercourse is most frequent among girls least actively connected with religious groups and lowest among those who are most devout.

Western societies from their Christian background have very generally transmitted the viewpoint that premarital sexual intercourse is potentially dangerous and damaging. This general attitude is translated into a prevailing feeling among devout adolescents that sex is sinful. This feeling is reinforced by a private sense of guilt and by public disapproval. Additional physical dangers are pregnancy, abortion, venereal disease; social dangers include forced marriage and legal difficulties. Moral objections from within and without are probably the principal factors restricting premarital intercourse in girls. To some extent such rules can be self-defeating. If a girl assumes that sexual intercourse will not take place within a particular association, she is more likely to become pregnant if intercourse does occur, since she will not have taken contraceptive precautions in advance.

While Judaism (Deuteronomy 22: 13–21) and Islam (Koran, Sura 24.2) and almost all Christian denominations judge coitus before marriage to be morally wrong, there has developed a 'double standard' which disproportionately affects the girl. Many religions have expressed the no-sex rule in the form of a concern for the virginity of the girl at marriage while the boy may even be expected to have sexual experience at marriage. Virginity rules have had, and continue to have, widespread support and there is, in many cultures (USA, Italy, parts of Africa, even Samoa), a preference among some men for virgin brides.

One effect of this 'double standard', maintained in part by religions, has been the development of a social distinction between 'respectable women' who are marriageable and with whom sexual intercourse is a marital obligation leading to the birth of children, and 'unrespectable' women with whom men seek to have sexual relations and with whom marriage is more or less ruled out.

The exposure to sexuality in adolescence

The exposure to adult sexuality in adolescence in the Western world is almost entirely surreptitious. It is opposed by all the churches as pornographic, indecent or immoral and is, in certain forms, against the law. The position of the Eastern faiths appears to be radically different.

In Hinduism it is not possible for the growing child to be unaware of adult sexuality, indeed it has an approved place in the religion since the male and female sexual organs are central in some temples and are a focus of worship. Some Hindu temples, such as Khajuraho (see Plate XIV), are covered externally with copulating figures displaying a 'languid and calculated eroticism' (Rowland 1954: 164). The well-known Hindu text, the Kama Sutra (Burton and Arbuthnot 1963) spells out in great detail the desired and approved range of sexuality and instructs lovers on how to interact with one another.

Hinduism applauds marital sexuality and the child grows up within an ideology which is ostentatiously procreative and sensual to most Westerners, though for Hindus themselves, lacking Christian sex

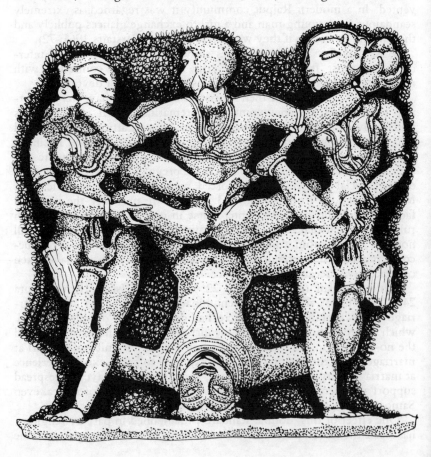

XIV. A sculpture from the Hindu temples at Khajuraho, India dated from tenth century AD.

taboos, it expresses in physical form the union of the soul with the divine. Hindu adolescents seeing the sexual imagery of temple paintings and sculptures as they grow to maturity think, perhaps, mainly of the physical and sensual aspects, but their religion makes them aware of complementary symbolic aspects. So we have in Hinduism an encouragement of marital sexuality that has never been overt in the Western world. Such a situation must contribute to encouraging adolescents to aspire to, or at least willingly agree to, an early date for their arranged marriages, if indeed they are not already betrothed before puberty.

Among Muslims, despite an external aloofness by women and the fierce condemnation of illegitimate sexuality, there is an equally open and divinely encouraged sexual activism for married couples. The Arab world has produced a number of erotic books, especially *The Perfumed Garden of Shaykh Nefzawi* (Burton 1963) which has for centuries had a wide currency in Islam. For present purposes, what is interesting in these books is not so much the ingenious variety of the sexual practices described, but the way in which they are included within the Islamic religious doctrine.

An Egyptian book about sex thus starts with the preamble: 'Praise to the Lord who adorned the virginal bosom with breasts and who made the thighs of women for the spear handles of men' (Jalal al-Din al Siyuti 1900) while *The Perfumed Garden* starts similarly with: 'Praise be given to God, who has placed man's greatest pleasure in the natural parts of woman and has destined the natural parts of man to afford the greatest enjoyment to woman'. This particular book is filled with numerous pious phrases and reflections such as: 'I, the servant of God, am thankful to him that no one can help falling in love with beautiful women; God, the magnificent, has said, "Women are your field. Go upon your field as you like"' and: 'I profited by this moment to admire the beauties of her vulva. The blessing of God the best creator, be upon it.'

There is nothing in this literature to suggest that it is not read by the young. Indeed it is intended for their erudition. Sir Richard Burton in his *Introduction to the 1001 Nights* says that he 'noticed among barbarians the system of... teaching lads first arrived at puberty the nice conduct ... of a branch of the knowledge tree which our modern education grossly neglects thereby entailing untold miseries upon individuals, families and generations' (Burton 1963).

Conclusions

We began this chapter with a general discussion of the relevance of the period of adolescence to the theme of this book. Individuals, at this stage of the life cycle, are able to reproduce, but the question arises: is adolescence the best time to do so, or would it be better to wait awhile? We then looked at the ways in which socio-religious rule structures led to a variety of solutions to this problem.

In small-scale societies we found that puberty ceremonies were widespread, sometimes with scarification rituals for social marking and other methods for toughening up or ensuring the bravery of young men. Instruction was included, conveying information on socially approved timing of sex, on marital duties and attitudes to sex, rather than on sex itself which was well understood.

Whereas emphasis was heavily laid on sex-in-marriage for some small-scale societies, in others adolescent sex was the approved norm. In the latter case, we found that widespread promiscuity did not inevitably lead to the expected high premarital birth rates.

Coming on to larger societies and the major world religions, we found that they all tended to disapprove of premarital sex to a greater or lesser extent. We interpreted this in the light of the known facts of religious endogamy, and also of status considerations which in the case of the caste system were linked to Hindu ideas of purity and pollution. In the case of Christian societies the situation was complex – some adolescents were unusually devout and were aloof from sexual activity which was seen as sinful; others were permissive and even irreligous and might even be promiscuous. Despite modern contraceptive techniques, we noted higher rates of illegitimacy and premarital conceptions among the less devout; but this phenomenon was far more influenced by educational level, both the frequency of coitus and rate of adolescent (premarital) pregnancy being lower in cases where education was more prolonged. We noted too a double standard for the two sexes. Boys were often far freer with regard to sex than girls before marriage, and prostitution was seen to play its part in making this possible.

Perhaps the most interesting contrast occurred within marriage itself, where Islam and Hinduism extolled the religious and virtuous nature of sexual activity whereas in Christianity it remained a shadowy area. Oriental sex manuals, until recently, were classed as 'pornographic' in the West, and even now are so regarded by many devout Christians. The idea of sex-in-itself, even within marriage, as sinful is peculiar, among world religions, to Christianity.

The range of religious attitudes to sex was the focus of this chapter because it is peculiarly during the teenage years that such attitudes are all-important to the reproductive process. Where the environment is variable, with good and bad years, times of glut and times of famine, as in parts of India and the Arab world, and in many areas occupied by small-scale societies, an early start to reproduction may be advantageous, because losses will be inevitable later on. But the social advantages of reproduction within marriage are not to be denied. We do in fact find a tendency for adolescent marriage to occur, and a wholehearted religious endorsement of sex within marriage in such societies, indicating a trend towards $r+$ selection. By contrast the more tightly controlled availability of resources and the smaller approved family size in the West seems to have been accompanied by more general religious taboos on teenage sex, a delaying of marriage until after the teenage years, and an emphasis on sex-for-reproduction rather than sex-for-itself in Christian sects and denominations. All these features are consistent with the idea of $r-$ selection. We turn, in the next chapter, to the time of marriage itself and the period of full reproductive activity.

Marriage 7

In this chapter we shall consider the institution of marriage with particular reference to how marriage is controlled by religious organizations or rules, and its significance with regard to human biology.

Every known society practises marriage in some form or other; every society makes some effort to bring the mating activities of its adult members under social control in order to establish rules for the orderly transmission from parents to offspring of material and non-material things such as land and membership of clans. The object is to bring order to bear on essential processes such as rights of land use, rights of access to other individuals, obligations to help with important tasks and so on. A marriage is not to be construed as an event involving just the two persons concerned and their families; it is an institution which has widespread ramifications and involves large numbers of people.

The institution of marriage affects reproduction by making it 'legitimate'. The offspring of a legitimate marriage are often given prior access to the resources of the kinship unit and are accorded the full benefits of membership of this social group, whereas offspring born outside marriage may not have these advantages and may go short of food, medical care, or affection thus reducing their chances of survival. It is thus with the survival of the offspring that the biological aspects of marriage are partly concerned. But they are also concerned with the reproductive success of the parents since it is often easier for them in the long run to rear offspring as married rather than unmarried partners. However, the complexity and permanence of marriage do seem to vary according to how mobile or settled family groups are, and where mobility is greater there is sometimes less emphasis on marriage, without necessarily any adverse effects on the offspring.

Christian pressure against concubinage and infant mortality

Before the sixteenth century in continental Europe, concubinage was, like marriage, a comparatively long-lasting union within which it was relatively easy to bring up children. From then on the Church campaigned continuously against it so that within a century it had virtually disappeared except for monarchs and the most powerful aristocrats who maintained it for political as well as other reasons (Flandrin 1979). In the sixteenth century 50 per cent of illegitimate births were the result of concubinage in the Nantes area of France but by 1787 this had fallen to 2.5 per cent. For children born out of wedlock the chances of survival became much lower than in the past. There was a steady increase in the

In Greek Orthodox churches in Crete thin metal plaques are placed around certain popular ikons testifying to the hope that the donor's prayers would be successful over the matter depicted. In this case a bachelor is praying for a wife.

number of children abandoned to public charity (Fig. 7.1). In France it became extremely rare for a girl to have more than one illegitimate child in the same parish. Such mothers were often driven out of their parishes. By the seventeenth and early eighteenth centuries the rate of illegitimate births decreased markedly in the rural areas and increased proportionally in the towns (Fig. 7.2).

Despite the redoubtable work of Christian innovators of charity such

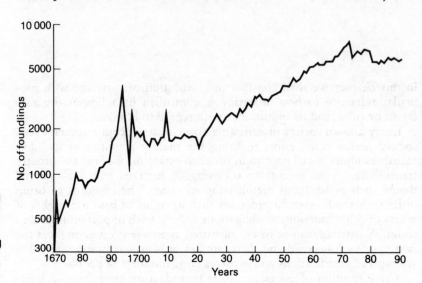

Fig. 7.1 Increase in the number of foundlings admitted to the Paris foundling hospital, 1670–1790. (From: Flandrin 1979)

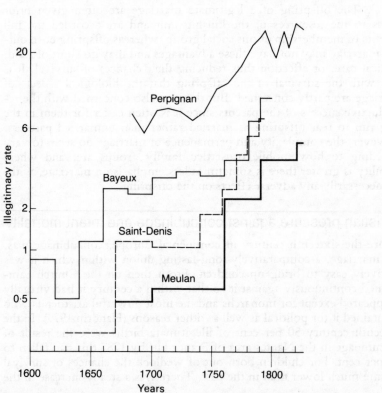

Fig. 7.2 Trends in the rate of illegitimacy of births in some French towns. (From: Flandrin 1979)

as St Vincent de Paul, the mortality among such foundlings as were taken into the care of Christian religious orders remained much higher than that of children brought up by their parents, including those brought up within concubinage in the sixteenth century. During the early eighteenth century 90 per cent of foundlings died in Rouen (Bardet n.d.) Among poor children 'assisted' by the town the death rate in the nursing stage was 38.1 per cent. For those nursed by their mothers it was 18.7 per cent. For Lyons the death rates for foundlings were between 62.5 per cent and 75 per cent around 1771–73 (Garden 1970). While the causal connection cannot be proved, it seems likely that the Church's pressure for social and religious recognition of monogamous marriage, the Christianization of conjugal life and the Church's refusal to recognize concubinage, resulted not only in the growth of illegitimacy but also in the raising of the death rate among the illegitimate young.

Marital stability

In hunting and gathering tribes, there is often little emphasis on marriage as a life-long arrangement. Among the Mbuti pygmies of Zaire (Turnbull 1966) and the Hadza of Tanzania (Woodburn 1968) betrothal and marriage are not tightly controlled, couples want a 'real' rather than an 'empty' marriage, and divorce is common.

In less nomadic societies in which the community is settled on its own land and its members do not have to move frequently in search of their livelihood, more concern is shown for the survival of social groupings which distinguish families from one another. Among the Sukuma of Tanzania the living, the dead and the yet-to-be born are one continuing family patri-clan which can only be interrupted by the infertility of its male members or their failure to contract legitimate marriages. There is considerable social and religious pressure on men to marry and propagate descendants legitimately, as without such children clan ancestors are prevented from surviving in the memories and religious practices of their descendants. Such ancestors may turn malevolent and harm their remaining descendants within the extended family as a whole. The man who does not marry out of selfishness or poverty and has children in a series of love affairs, is not carrying on his own patrilineage, as such children belong to their mothers' patrilineages (Tanner 1958).

A relationship between a Sukuma man and woman is legitimized into marriage by the passage of cattle from his family to her family. These cattle represent a congeries of rights and obligations between the husband's family that receives the bride and the wife's family that gives her. It is not a transaction between the couple involved, although the man will have chosen a particular girl and she will have accepted him beforehand. Sukuma marriages are not undertaken lightly and in fact the divorce rate is low (personal observation, R. Tanner).

From the biological point of view it is not so much the absolute stability of marriages that affects child rearing as the relative stability of any given marriage to the norms of the community. Depending how much emphasis there is on marriage and its stability, the effects of illegitimacy will be greater or smaller. A Sukuma lover, if he makes an unmarried woman pregnant, not only has to pay compensation but he gains no long-term advantages from his procreation (Cory 1953). He can, however, legitimize such a child before its birth by paying bride-wealth and marrying the woman. At a later stage he can pay cattle for each illegitimate child to the mother's family as compensation for their rearing. Finally, he can pay bride-wealth on behalf of an illegitimate son when the latter comes to marry. Only poverty would restrain a man from legitimizing his illegitimate children. Besides immediate there are long-term benefits of a spiritual kind, since a man can only become an ancestor if he has legitimate children. Most systems of ancestor recognition have within them positive inducements to marry and legitimize offspring even if this is delayed through poverty or irresponsibility until comparatively late in life. An ancestor cult can thus produce good care of and concern for children, and it is a sound reproductive strategy for individuals to work within it rather than outside it. This the Sukuma can do, however, even if they convert to Christianity or Islam.

Spirit possession and the survival of marriages

In unsettled societies where there is considerable migration to work and husbands are separated from their wives, or when the husband or wife lives somewhere like an urban slum, or in the mixed-sex labour lines of an agricultural estate or near a mine, separated from her or his family, the usual social methods of settling marital problems are lost and religion in the form of spirit possession may provide answers.

Some stable African societies have well established systems of spirit possession in which ancestors 'speak' through their descendants about the trouble particular individuals are bringing on themselves by their offences against the unity and survival of the lineage. For such men and women the reason for their troubles in life is ascribed to the disapproval of their possibly even unknown ancestors. It is probable that this type of possession is increasing as more people get involved in personal troubles caused by social changes for which there are no traditional institutional solutions. Certainly possession occurs much more frequently in communities in or near urban–industrial areas than in traditional areas (personal observation, R. Tanner).

Spirit possession is particularly common in areas of coastal Tanzania and Kenya (personal observation, R. Tanner) and in Somalia (Lewis 1971), where wives suffer from the difficulties of urban life and have to manage without the support of their own extended families. This situation seems to be heavily loaded against the wife, who is particularly vulnerable to poverty if her husband does not support her adequately. In such cases the spirits of the family or of the locality in which the woman is living are invoked. The wife becomes possessed and is thus incapable of performing her domestic obligations properly. The husband cannot negotiate directly with his wife as she is out of his world, and thus he has to organize her exorcism. During this exorcism the infesting spirit speaks through the wife giving its reasons for troubling her and the price it expects to be paid to her if she is to be relieved of its presence. Thus she becomes the centre of her husband's attention and he has to pay for her restoration to normality.

Possession occurs frequently in Sukuma communities near to Mwanza town in Tanzania (personal observation, R. Tanner). In Dar es Salaam the urban witchdoctor would lose clients by suggesting spirit exorcism since the local Zaramo would have to go to their country homes for the ceremony. As a result, outside Dar es Salaam exorcism is common but not within the city, despite the fact that an estimated 8,000 urban dwellers visit witchdoctors every day (Swantz 1970). The 1963 initiations to the Buchwezi Spirit Society in Usukuma, Tanzania, contained a majority of married, divorced and widowed women. Thus religion in the form of involvement in a spirit cult can be seen to respond in a variety of ways to the particular needs of women with marital problems, in the case of the married women for the survival of their marriages and in the case of divorced and widowed women as a response to the loss of their husbands. In such ways religious ideas and ceremonies can bolster the faltering institution of marriage in times of stress and change.

Hinduism and marriage

Marriage in Hindu life has unique features of biological importance since it is characterized by the obligation to marry within the caste or sub-caste. In addition bachelors have lower religious status than married men and cannot perform certain rituals. The married state, not just the marriage ceremony, is regarded as sacred rather than secular. The Hindu scriptures state that 'the husband receives his wife from the gods' (The Laws of Manu; Carstairs 1961) and among Brahmins, a wife is enjoined to treat her husband as a deity, and to eat on the dining leaf from which her husband has already eaten, which for others would be considered impure (Srinivas 1962). While polygyny is permitted when the first wife is infertile or has produced no sons, monogamy is held up as an ideal, typified by the mythical heroes Rama and Krishna.

The social requirements of Hindu marriage are so important that the experience of this most important of all family ceremonies cannot but have indirect biological consequences. It is the principal cause of debt among Indian peasants. It impoverishes them and makes life more of a struggle. Although the religious injunctions of Hinduism apply more strictly to the higher castes, it is, even among the peasantry, a ceremony of great complexity with a lengthy series of rituals and complicated expensive prestations.

Hindu marriage is indissoluble under the Laws of Manu, and there is a religious ban on the remarriage of high-caste widows. The latter is biologically significant owing to the celebration of pre-pubertal marriages long before cohabitation can begin, with the result that there can be virgin widows who may not officially remarry. The inducement to marry off daughters as early as possible is great; parents who have not succeeded in finding husbands for daughters past puberty are regarded as being guilty of a great sin (Srinivas 1962). The net effect of these attitudes and rules is to increase the birth rate, since reproduction begins at an early age, after the period of adolescent infertility (see Chapter 6).

In Hinduism there is preference for virgin brides and this leads (because marriage involves prepayments to the family of the bride) to the older and wealthier men getting younger virgin women as wives. The Laws of Manu state that 12 and 8 are suitable ages for brides, or even earlier if necessary. From the biological point of view, the husband's age may render him less fertile and active, but if older men are better able to care for their wives and children than younger ones, this arrangement could still be biologically advantageous. The lowest sub-castes are the most stringent in their marriage requirements and the youngest ages for brides have been found in the socially lowest endoga-mous units (Klass 1966).

Despite a general taboo, Hindu widows of lower castes have always remarried. These are not religiously sound marriages and a wife's hope is usually to predecease her husband and thus avoid widowhood which is itself considered attributable to sins committed, in a previous incar-nation. Second marriages have always occurred and thus the dictates of religion cannot be seen as having a direct restriction on fertility; the de-ciding factor is how the spouses and their families see themselves in relation to Hindu orthodoxy. Orthodoxy is maintained where there is considerable stability in social relationships, and families know each other well within a restricted area.

In any case first marriages are generally arranged by the parents even when some initial interest in a particular girl may have been expressed by a boy. The unmarried are seen as children who have little com-petence in the matter (Klass 1966). Attempts to determine the desires of either the boy or girl have been described as rare and at best circuitous and perfunctory. Thus for Hindus, marriage and first sexual experience are socially highly structured. A man's wife comes to him as a stranger and their relationship in its initial phases is one in which sexual experi-ence is combined with religious ideas and concepts of Hinduism learned in childhood.

In such delicate matters as obtaining socio-religious prestige from the marriage of a virgin daughter, a father is not likely to want to risk the uncertainties coming from marrying her into a little-known family. So there is not only the importance of marrying her within the local sub-caste (or higher) but within the range of families of whose habits one can be assured. There is also the fact that marrying into neighbouring families keeps the cultivable land in large parcels; more food is grown as less land is taken up with boundary hedges and 'bunds' (earth walls) be-tween rice fields and less time is spent getting to and from cultivable plots.

One is inclined to think that caste as a pervading institution must be in decline; human rights and democracy are guaranteed to citizens by Article 29 (2) of the Indian constitution, and all social disabilities were removed from the so-called 'Untouchables' by Articles 15, 17, 25, 46 and other sections. The Westernized members of the upper classes have theoretically shed caste restrictions to a large extent, but they are still members of caste-minded families and find it useful to use caste to procure economic and social advantages. There have, however, been changes. In public health matters the provision of piped water and sanitation has reduced the biological significance of the idea of 'im-purity'. The widespread use of public transport is incompatible with the idea of 'contamination' from an endless succession of fellow travellers. Certainly some educated and urbanized middle-class Indians are chang-ing and they marry more widely outside the previously sacrosanct en-dogamous units, but they are still only a small minority.

With these changes we can see a rise in the female age of marriage. There is not the same competitive element as where the families con-cerned are in long-term association. We can expect a decline in the amount and closeness of consanguineous marriages as families gradually become dispersed. But first marriages, except among a relatively small urbanized middle class, continue to be endogamous within the sub-caste. We can also see the creation of new sub-castes within which marriages will begin to take place, such as those of taxi drivers, and it may be that even 'anti-caste' communities will discover to their chagrin they have become sub-castes when it comes to the marriages of their daughters.

Buddhism and marriage – the resort to spirits

There are few references to marriage in Buddhist canonical texts, commentaries and contemporary studies, except in terms placing it as a second-best institution, irretrievably inferior to the monastic life according to the demands of the Eightfold Path.

Marriage for Buddhists in many areas is celebrated by the public witnessing of a ceremony accompanied by a feast with a propitiatory offering to the village spirits (Spiro 1967). It is the spirits which are particular to the area, together with those of the houses on both the mother's side and father's side, that are held responsible for the personal protection of those who propitiate them at marriage ceremonies and in childbirth. Buddhism thus has a protective edifice of personalized spirits within the general structure of the prohibitions and injunctions of its faith. We have discussed the possible effects of Buddhist ideas on conception in Chapter 3, pointing out that Burma has an unusually low birth rate for an Asian country. The support of the spirits is secondary to the main Buddhist culture in Burma, and a recent study (Nash and Nash 1963) has shown that older persons, divorced and widowed, being conscious of the inevitability of rebirth, tend not to remarry as 'there exists at the level of values a Buddhist rationale for extreme hesitation in marriage and remarriage'. In the six north Burma villages studied, 80.6 per cent of the widowed and divorced men and women did not remarry (Nash and Nash 1963).

A very interesting study of a particular type of marriage – polyandry – in Sri Lanka is that of Hiatt (1981). It is very relevant to our book because Hiatt is concerned with this marriage type in relation to sociobiological theory, and parental investment theory in particular. Hiatt considers the prevailing sociobiological argument that polyandry would be expected in families living in poor ecological circumstances, where polygyny occurs at the top, in relation to Sri Lanka. The evidence from Sri Lanka is that while this strategy does occur there, polyandry also occurs at higher socio-economic levels. In these cases, the most acceptable explanation is that in this patrilineal society it is a strategy adopted to keep family landholdings together, since it is mostly brothers who share a wife. Also, by limiting the number of offspring they produce, the land is not subject to extensive sub-division between the male heirs.

As to whether the process is related to genetic transmission, and if so how, Hiatt concurs with the view that there can be no direct connection, and that where men, even brothers, share a wife this will present a psychological problem of jealousy. Polyandry is unusual because of the basic human occurrence of sexual jealousy between males, but in the cases where it does occur this is because economic circumstances make it imperative that such jealousy should be carefully controlled.

Jewish attitudes to marriage and procreation

Judaism holds that marriage is for procreation and companionship and that this is based on Biblical injunctions (Genesis 1:28 and 2:18, 24). It is held that the Song of Songs, paralleling divine with carnal love, clearly had monogamous marriage in mind as do numerous other biblical passages in Psalms and Proverbs. Jewish scholars have in general felt that although the Bible mentions polygyny, it has no overall religious validity and its survival in Indian and other Asian communities rests on local social conventions. To summarize a complex topic, Judaism emphasizes procreation, restricts the number of spouses to one at a time, disapproves of divorce but does not forbid it and allows remarriage, and combines the obligation to marry with an affirmative attitude to sexual passion, though immodest conduct is not allowed even between married couples.

Rabbinic literature as expressed in the Talmud typifies the sinner as the unmarried man who 'spends all his days in sinful thoughts' and 'he who has no wife is not a proper man'. Celibacy thus has no place in Judaism since it is not advocated as one of the biblical acts of self-denial (Numbers 6: 2–8) nor imposed on the priesthood (Leviticus 21: 1–15). There are many cases of scholars not marrying but it is often held that the aspiring scholar should marry first and then study.

Sexual desire is not evil or shameful in itself, as it is linked to the idea that without it men would not marry or beget children and that absence of children would diminish man as the Image of God. For orthodox Jews following the scriptures, marriage is so important that in theory a man would be justified in selling a Torah scroll in order to get the money to marry. Again in theory, if he is not married by the age of 20 years God curses him; for a girl there is the danger that she will become unchaste if she is not found a husband. Marriage in Judaism is not a sacrament in the Christian sense since it is possible to dissolve it by divorce but it is more than a legal contract since the wife is consecrated to her husband and forbidden to others. Thus we see in Judaism the biologically relevant factors of early monogamous marriage and an acceptance of sexuality as something morally good: essentially a pro-reproductive ideology.

Early Christian sexual intercourse and marriage

The Gospels tell us nothing about the physical aspects of marriage and it is on St Paul that the Christian interpretations tend to rely. He states: 'It is good for a man not to touch a woman, but for fear of fornication let every man have his own wife and let every woman have her own husband. Let the husband render the debt to his wife [i.e. have sexual intercourse with her] and the wife also in like manner to the husband. . . . Defraud not one another, except, perhaps, by consent, for a time, that you may give yourself to prayers; and return together again, that Satan tempt you not for your incontinency' (I Corinthians 7: 1–6).

So it was not surprising that many early ecclesiastical writers took a very negative view of sexual activity both within and outside marriage. The ritualistic kissing in greeting by the early Christians was suspected by Athenagoras (1972: 32) of being a highly erotic act, so it was classed as immoral to kiss for a second time after having enjoyed the first. John of Damascus (1955: 4,97) even suggested that if Adam and Eve had obeyed God, human reproduction would have taken place in a less sinful manner. St Augustine (1844) was particularly severe, holding that sexual concupiscence was a vice and contamination and in no way to be considered as one of the benefits of marriage (*De Nuptiis et Concupiscentia* and *De Bono Conjugali*). In his arguments against Manichaeism he concluded that the only justification for sexual intercourse, which was evil, must be the procreation of children. Thus those who knew themselves to be sterile were not free from sin when they continued to have intercourse (*De Conjugiis Adulterinis* and *De Bono Conjugali*). The idea of sex-in-itself as sinful has been a consistent theme of Christian moralists up to the present century.

The great theologian St Thomas Aquinas (1964) held to much the same views, stating that 'there are two ways in which married people are free from all sin in intercourse, to wit, by reason of procreating and by reason of rendering the debt; otherwise there is always sin in it at least venial'.

While the view that sexual intercourse was sinful unless aimed at procreation faded with the centuries it did not disappear. In the early eighteenth century it was still held that sexual activity and pleasure were shameful but unfortunately necessary for human survival. Thus it would seem that sexuality in marriage must have been severely inhibited during this lengthy period of moral rulings. It made sexual intercourse during pregnancy sinful, likewise intercourse when a child was not wanted. And sex of all other kinds was sinful within as well as outside marriage. Biologically, it is reproduction and rearing that count. Thus despite the hostility to eroticism and libidinousness, Christianity is clearly and openly pro-reproductive. But it does not extol large family size, or stress the need for sons. Rather, it enjoins modesty and restraint.

Contemporary Christian approaches to marriage

While Catholic theologians have maintained for many centuries that the principal end of marriage is the procreation and rearing of children, it has now come to be accepted that the actual realization of these ends is not essential nor indeed that the absence of procreative acts invalidates an enduring marriage.

The contemporary view is perhaps that the fundamental rights in marriage 'embrace merely the acts by which the primary ends are achieved' and that 'the essence of marriage, the fundamental marriage right, includes a right not only to procreative and educative acts but also the acts of mutual help (life partnership), the remedy for concupiscence (sexual fulfilment) and conjugal love' (Ford and Kelly 1963).

Thus we see that there has been a turning away from the narrowly procreative idea of production of children as morally good in itself to the needs of married couples themselves. These new interpretations if we disregard any wider social or economic considerations are likely to have the effect of reducing fertility in modern contracepting marriages. The description of marital intercourse as 'the remedy for concupiscence' seems derogatory, or at least depreciatory of sexual activity as having any positive value in itself. It is now widely considered as the embodiment of natural affections. It has also come to be considered as having a value in itself apart from its natural biological consequences. This could reduce the fertility of Christians since it is in effect advocating sex for its own sake and not for the purpose of producing children, i.e. promoting non-reproductive sex.

Second, the stress on mutual help: 'cohabitation, community of board, use of material goods, earning a living and administering it, help of a more personal kind in the various circumstances of life, in psychic and bodily needs, in the use of natural faculties' (*Acta Apostolicis Sedis* 1944), as a part of the essential character of marriage, can be seen as contributing to the survival of such children as may be born. But it lays emphasis on quality of care, not quantity of offspring. As such, these features are the results of $r-$ selection.

Of conjugal love the moral theologians tend to avoid a specific definition but state it 'is that virtue which effects a union of husband and wife by which they wish to give each other the marital benefits' (McAuliffe 1954). This should provide a satisfactory environment and promote the survival of any children that may be born, on a basis of love of a rational rather than romantic order; the latter is 'too fleeting and uncontrollable to be the essence of permanent unions' (Ford and Kelly 1963). Thus in general we conclude that these religious attitudes emphasizing parental harmony must be conducive to the survival of such children as are born, of either sex, but are not in themselves procreative or conducive to the production of large numbers of children.

Establishing a community – the Muslim case

The move of the original Muslims from Mecca to Medina effectively isolated this small number of converts from their own clans. Their apostasy from their ancestral religion prevented any further marriages according to the currently accepted customs. The first Muslims were isolated socially, religiously and geographically. Muhammad at the battle of Badr was able to field only 300 fighting men of whom he lost 16 (Watt 1968). At the battle of Uhud the following year the Muslims lost 70 men out of 1,000 engaged. From the earlier battle there already existed the problem of the support of many widows and orphans. The battle of Uhud created an even greater number of bereaved, and it was impossible for these widows and orphans to return to their own families.

In a community used to feuding and fighting, as the pre-Muslim Arabs (who were a mixture of pagans, Jews and Christians) had always been, there would often have been a surplus of women because of men killed in these persistent skirmishes. Available land, wealth, resources and above all kinship obligations would, however, have ensured that such women and children were taken care of. Muhammad appears to have been worried by the problems of such a number of women without male support in a small religiously innovative community in an alien and often hostile environment, where the surviving men were in no position to marry further wives and care for their offspring because of the uncertainty of their own economic situation.

Thus it seems very probable that Muhammad needed actively to encourage a new and liberal kind of polygyny as way of coping with widows and orphans. As we saw in Chapter 5, he had always been greatly concerned with orphans because he himself had been one and had suffered from a difficult childhool (Watt 1968). He actually recognized that with some 10 per cent of his fecund women as widows, the community's rate of expansion and the chances of establishing a sizable population for his new Islamic community would be reduced, as the early Traditions show (*Mishkat al-Masabih* 1963). In the words of Muhammad: 'Marry women who are loving and very prolific for I shall outnumber the peoples by you' (*Mishkat al-Masabih* 2: 659). Thus we see that one of the principal features of Islamic marriage started with the biological issues of population size clearly in mind.

Muhammad was certainly strongly in favour of marriage and remarriage. The Koran has many references to marriage, and the Traditions give even greater support. Thus: 'when the servant of God marries, he perfects half of his religion' and 'those of you who can support a wife should marry, for it keeps you from looking at strange women and preserves you from immorality'. This idea is further supported by the long-standing practice of veiling Muslim women (Plate xv) which is seen at its most extreme in Afghanistan and Saudi Arabia.

The principal innovations regarding marriage were that it was declared by a secular contract and not a religious rite, thus making it possible for all newcomers to marry into or within the 'community' whatever their religion. This was also aimed at improving the position of women, who would thereby achieve a greater ability to rear children successfully. In the community of Islam, a marriage was valid by mutual consent before witnesses. The Koran laid down that a man might have up to four wives at a time (Koran, Sura 4.3) and that he must treat them with impartiality.

Muslim men may marry any woman except an idolatress (Koran, Sura 2.220). In particular they may marry Christians and Jews to whom the Scriptures have been revealed (Koran, Sura 5.7). But Muslim women are allowed to marry believers only (Koran, Suras 2.220 and 60.10). The prohibited degrees of kinship for marriage generally follow the Old Testament restrictions (Leviticus 18: 7–18 and Koran, Sura 4.27) but the

XV. Veils of Muslim women take many forms, from complete covering to a wisp of cloth round the mouth and throat. These women illustrate varieties of veiling in contemporary Afghanistan (behind, standing) and Morocco (in front, seated).

Koran also forbids marriage to the divorced or widowed wife of one's father (Koran, Sura 4.26), and to women who are sisters to each other (Koran, Sura 4.27). A regulation unique to Islam prohibits marriage between persons who have been nursed by the same foster mother or between a foster mother and her fostered child (Koran, Sura 4.27). This restriction is maintained in the modern Tunisian Code of Personal Status (*News from Tunisia* 1960 Jan., Bulletin 51: 3).

Slavery and concubines in early Islam

There were no barriers in Islam to having Muslim, Christian and Jewish slaves as concubines but having unbelieving women was forbidden. Any child begotten to a slave belonged to its father and was free. A man could not marry one of his own slaves except under certain conditions, for instance if he was too poor to afford a free woman and had no slave of his own for a concubine.

Since the original Muslims were mainly in contact with Christians and Jews these rules enabled their numbers to expand very rapidly. The automatic freeing of the children of concubine slaves must have led to a considerable increase in Muslim populations and it is clear from the variegated physical appearance of some existing Muslim populations, e.g. in Arabia, Zanzibar and along the coast of East Africa, that there has been a progressive mixing of the original Arab Muslims with neighbouring populations over time, coupled with the spread of the Muslim religion by non-reproductive means (persuasion, adoption, conversion etc.) to new peoples in new areas.

The age of marriage, incidence of divorce and place of virginity in Islam

No age limits for marriage have been fixed by Islam and quite young children may be betrothed and married on the authority of their parents, but a girl is not handed over to her husband until after she has started to menstruate. Since the Prophet, in the Traditions, spoke approvingly of marrying virgins (*Mishkat al-Masabih* 2: 659), although he himself only did so once in a dozen marriages, there is a religiously supported preference for virgins (Momeni 1972). The cost of their dowries is correspondingly higher and the cost of the extensive marriage celebrations can be very substantial. This being so, the husbands of virgin brides in Muslim countries tend to be older than their brides and moreover proportionately older than non-Muslim bridegrooms. In Libya the difference in age between Muslim and non-Muslim husbands is 9 years and in Iran 6.5 years (Dixon 1971). This age factor would not of itself reduce the birth rate unless older men were appreciably less fertile than younger ones and there is no evidence of this in the areas concerned; improved facilities for child rearing where the father is wealthy probably increase the survival rate of offspring. Table 7.1 shows the husband/wife age discrepancy in Shiraz, Iran in recent times.

A similar situation exists in Hinduism where the insistence on virgin and even pre-pubertal brides is even stronger than in Islam. Large differences in age between bride and groom cause no adverse comment. A study (Ross 1961) showing the average age difference between couples in a sample of urban Hindus indicates that this difference remains, but that there is in addition a general shift on the part of both sexes towards later marriage. This can be seen by comparing older married couples with younger ones (Table 7.2).

Years husband older than wife	Marriages (%)		
	1956	1966	1973
0–4	21.6	18.0	29.6
5–9	33.1	32.1	39.7
10–14	27.1	29.7	19.7
15–19	10.3	12.2	6.4
20+	7.9	8.0	4.6

Table 7.1 Husband/wife age differentials for couples marrying in Shiraz, Iran in 1956, 1966, and 1973 (From Momeni 1976)

Age at marriage (in years)	'Old marrieds'		'Young marrieds'	
	Husbands	Wives	Husbands	Wives
10–13	—	12	—	2
14–15	—	4	—	5
16–18	6	7	—	12
19–24	13	4	19	14
25+	9	—	15	—

Table 7.2 Age at marriage of urban Hindus (From Ross 1961)

The study in Iran (Momeni 1976) showed not only that brides tended to have older husbands but that the proportion of couples divorcing in 1973 with 15 or more years' age difference was about twice as great as the proportion divorcing with smaller age differences. An additional consequence of the taking up of young virgin brides by the older and richer men is thus higher divorce rates than when the couples are nearer each other in age and this may tend to be reflected in the reduced efficiency of bringing up children. However, if, as suggested, older men can do more in material terms to support their families this reduction may be more than compensated for, and if divorcees remarry with younger men, which would seem to be a concomitant of the system, the entire system may be very pro-reproductive.

Puritan marriage – the dominance of reason and moderation

In Islamic and Hindu societies we have found marriages to be arranged by families within a socio-religious conception of 'right' marriage, often with little regard to the couples' prior ideas and personal wishes. In the case of early Puritan Christianity there was a much stronger emphasis on the individual. This emphasis, however, was placed in a general context of very restrictive beliefs regarding sexual indulgence, and clear statements about the rights and wrongs of marriage. Let us take as an example seventeenth century Puritans in America. Here, a Puritan's initial decision to get married was usually made by a man or woman without reference to any particular other person. The problem, once this decision had been made, was matching with an equal in birth, religion and education. This being so it is not surprising to find that good Puritans controlled their affections even in their love letters; love for one's spouse required moderation because the highest love was to be reserved for God. Marriage was almost a statutory requirement in some places, at least to the extent that single persons were penalized. This occurred in both Massachusetts and Connecticut (*Massachusetts Records* 1636 and

Connecticut Records 1637) where single men and women had to live with
families whose general pattern of living had received the approval of
community leaders.

The Puritan New England sect was quite explicit on the way in which
marriages were to be conducted. Sexual union constituted the first
obligation of married partners to each other. The husband had a duty to
support his wife and this was enforced by law. The couple were forbidden by law to strike each other, a rule which was supported by the courts
on numerous occasions. Adultery in Massachusetts, Connecticut and
New Haven was a capital offence which appears to have been brought to
court on three occasions only (Morgan 1966); offenders were branded,
whipped, fined, made to wear the letter 'A' or symbolically executed by
having to stand on a gallows with a rope round their necks.

The duty of the wife was 'to keep at home, educating her children,
keeping and improving what is got by the industry of man'. The couple's
first duty was to give food, shelter and protection to their children and
indeed the courts enforced more care than the mere provision of food and
shelter. Thus we see in the Puritanically administered states of New England a very positive attitude to marriage with religiously motivated regulations to support it; the biological effects of this would be to promote
the care of children.

Puritan ideas were also unusual in recognizing that relatives by marriage had equal status with those related by birth, because Puritans took
literally the Biblical statement that man and wife were one flesh. This
definition extended the range of kinship obligations to all relatives
through marriage. While we do not know the extent to which such help
was provided, it must mean that the number of people who qualified for
support was increased, but this reciprocally meant that any given person
would be able to draw on a wide range of others for help. In effect it was
just widening the kinship network, or the effective one, by equating the
rights of affinal with lineal kin, a good example of group consciousness
and one which should enhance the chances of both individual and group
survival in difficult times.

Choice of spouse – the phenomenon of religious homogamy

Most religions have rules to prevent their adherents from leaving their
faith. The rules exist because it is felt, with some correctness, that to
marry outside the faith leads to an even greater possibility that the children of such marriages will do likewise. Tertullian (1884, *Ad Uxorem*
II:3) stated that out-marriages were like fornication and that they created
similar problems. Religious rules thus often favour homogeneity in the
marriages of their adherents, so that like marries like. The justification
for marriage within a faith is remarkably uniform in many religions. It
has been well stated by the seventeenth-century New England Puritan,
Cotton Mather, who wrote of the justification that 'it is lawful for all
sorts of people to marry who are able with judgement to give their consent. Yet it is the duty of Christians to marry in the Lord; and therefore, such as profess the true reformed religion should not marry with
infidels, papists and other idolators' (Mather 1853, 2: 202). And of the
consequences, Increase Mather wrote: 'Take heed how you dispose of
your children. It may make us to dread to think what's coming, in that

	Religious group		
	Protestant	Catholic	Jewish
% of US population	66	26	3
% expected homogamy if marriage were at random	53	16	2
% actual homogamy	91	78	93
Actual: Expected ratio	1.7:1	4.9:1	46.5:1

Table 7.3 United States: Homogamy by religious group (c. 1960) (From Blood 1969)

	Expected (on basis of random marriage) N	Actual N	Actual as % of expected
Anglican	191.0	56	28.8
Baptist	33.9	7	20.6
Congregational	31.8	9	28.3
Methodist	32.0	9	28.1
Presbyterian	7.9	6	—
Roman Catholic	64.9	21	32.4
Other, not stated etc.	16.7	9	—
Atheist, agnostic etc.	31.8	11	34.5

Table 7.4 Bishops Stortford, Herts., United Kingdom: Actual and expected number of spouses of different faith, 1966 (From Spencer 1968)

it is with us as it was with the Old World . . . the Sons of God are marrying with the Daughters of man' (Mather 1685: 128–9).

Even in the absence of positive injunctions, as in much of modern USA, selection of acceptable spouses often involves similarity of religion as one of the many constraints (see Table 7.3). In the United Kingdom today the proportion of religious intramarriages is high (Table 7.4) and in Ulster, Catholic–Protestant marriages are heavily proscribed, even physically dangerous, and can best be enabled and maintained by emigrating to mainland Britain.

There are plenty of data that mixed religion marriages are more prone to divorce and separation than intramarriage (Heiss 1961; Gordon 1964) and a large US study (Zimmerman and Cervantes 1960) has shown that the children of mixed religion marriages are more likely to be arrested as delinquents than those born within a single faith. If we accept that parental unity of ideas and practices in general is conducive to the survival of marriages, then inter-religious marriages, since they are 'accident-prone', have implications for the social and psychological well-being of the children.

The inbred marriages of Muslims

While most religions encourage the intramarriage of their followers, they also restrict the categories of kin who may be married either by absolute prohibitions (as for brothers and their sisters) or they allow certain close categories with special permission (as for cousins in Catholicism). Islam alone of major religions has developed a positive encouragement of cousin marriage as preferential for the first marriages of girls and this has existed very widely for many centuries (Patai 1955). In some cases this type of marriage extends to cross as well as parallel cousins (Tanner 1964) and in communities where there are few children this results in considerable inbreeding (Tanner 1958).

This type of marriage occurs in widely divergent Islamic societies. The reasons for it thus seem to be of a general kind rather than in response to local conditions. The Koran (Sura 4.128) enjoins that marriage should be between 'equals' and indeed refuses to permit the marriage of a female slave with her owner unless she has been manumitted first. Why the emphasis on equality and (relatively) close kinship? One compelling reason is the acknowledged consequence of the Islamic system of inheritance which can lead to the endless subdividing of land into smaller and smaller lots. Marrying a relative reduces this and also ensures that land will stay within the family.

Apart from these major economic concerns, there are also social and other economic advantages from such marriages. The expenses and the prestige are shared between one set of relatives and where there is prestige to be gained from discussing and publicizing a high bride-price it is highly advantageous if very little money actually has to change hands, and the family *as a whole* loses none of it. The likelihood of divorce is also reduced because the parents-in-law of one spouse are the uncles and aunts of the other and there is thus a ramifying kinship network which can provide support in difficult times. Tanner (1964) has shown how in Mombasa, Islamic cousin marriages (including cross and parallel cousins, unilateral and bilateral) were helpful in ensuring the success of as many children as possible. A child of parallel- or cross-cousin marriage has advantages over other children. He or she is less likely to suffer from family instability. Whether the child is male or female, support under Islamic law and inheritance are assured, and the custom is more likely to integrate him or her into the family than to be a source of contention. In Mombasa among the Afro-Arabs the proportions marrying cousins were as shown in Table 7.5. Among the Nubians (Hussein 1971) it was found that in the current generation 45.1 per cent had married their first cousins although in the parental generation the proportion was 35.3 per cent. While this degree of endogamy may be socially advantageous, there could be biological disadvantages if disadvantageous genes were present in the lineages concerned. It has been suggested that congenital malformations, stillbirths and prenatal deaths tend to be higher in consanguineous unions (Stern 1960, Stevenson *et al.* 1966), though there are contrary findings and the correlation is not certain. On this point the Nubian data referred to above showed that the average number of live-born children per first-cousin marriage was higher than for other types of marriage, but this may have been due to

Table 7.5 Frequency of marriage types in Mombasa, Kenya, over three generations (From Tanner 1964)

	Bilateral Cousin		Unilateral Cousin		Non-cousin	
	No.	*(%)*	*No.*	*(%)*	*No.*	*(%)*
Father's father's generation	66	37.7	59	33.5	51	28.8
Father's generation	130	31.4	179	38.4	157	30.2
Subject's generation	102	21.4	198	41.5	178	37.1

the fact that such marriages tended to last longer, because child mortality also was consistently higher. The data showed 35.4 per cent deaths of children in first-cousin marriages as against 27 per cent of children born to remoter kin and unrelated marriages.

Incest taboos

Incest taboos are universal, prohibiting with varying degrees of horror, distaste and penalties, marriage and sexual relations between mother and son, father and daughter and brother and sister. Such relationships are thought to damage the very essence of the family and the community of which it is part, and are even thought of as being against the laws of nature itself. Amongst the Zigua of Tanzania, sex between mother and son is seen as witchcraft, between father and daughter as bestiality, but between brother and sister as something quite likely to occur, which ruins the marital chances of the woman but is not totally reprehensible in itself. One of the sanctions used to support incest taboos is the threat of deformity for the children born to such relationships. This does not imply any knowledge of genetics, i.e. the danger of excessive homozygosity, and such threats are a common sanction for a wide variety of norms.

This does not of course mean that malformations, diseases etc. associated with incestuous relationships are not the result of increased homozygosity, but it is a fact that often they are not; Bittles (1981) has emphasized a number of other factors associated with incest that could lead to abnormalities, diseases and death of the offspring. Among them the main ones are as follows. First, incest is often associated with low maternal age, and this in turn can mean an unprepared and inexperienced mother. Second, conversely, there is often an advanced paternal age, with a consequent greater likelihood of mutations in the male's sperm. Third, incestuous relationships have a positive association with mental subnormality on the part of one or both parents, and this may be genetically transmitted. Fourth, incest tends in some societies to be associated with low parental socio-economic status. Finally, incest can lead to a good deal of psycho-social stress on the part of the mother, and she may attempt to procure an abortion, so the foetus may be subject to various insults during pregnancy which become apparent after birth.

The incest taboo is often extended to relatives outside the nuclear family but these extensions are not universally the same. Except for the primary incest taboos, there are many variations of the rules between societies and even within pluralistic societies. An absence of coincidence between biological distance and taboos makes it difficult to see them as having any universal genetic basis (Murdock 1949: 286–7). For instance in many societies the terms 'brother' and 'sister' are used between the most distant relatives of the same generation but the taboo still applies. Use of the terms and the taboos is probably more related to ensuring the perpetuation of ramifying social systems than to avoiding genetic malformations.

In some societies, when rather uncomfortably close marriages do occur they can be 'put right' by the carrying out of the appropriate socio-religious ceremonies. The Sukuma of Tanzania on such occasions sacrifice a goat which is split in two, each half eaten separately by the

XVI. Among the Sukuma of Tanzania there occurred a marriage which was in breach of the normal exogamy rules. To propitiate the ancestors, a goat was sacrificed and divided, each 'side' of the marriage eating the other side's part of the goat thus separating the spouses.

close relatives of the marriage partners (Plate XVI). Incest within the nuclear family is generally punished very severely indeed.

Although many may consider that religious rules concerning the categories of kin whom one may or may not marry are fairly standardized in the Western world, this is not so. There are some curious survivals in the USA. For instance, the laws of Rhode Island state that marriages between Jews permitted by their religion are valid, and so an uncle may marry his niece. The laws of Georgia hold that the prohibitions of consanguineous marriages are dependent on the Levitical code, and therefore do not explicitly prohibit a man from marrying his daughter or his niece, while prohibiting nephew–aunt marriages (Farrow and Juberg 1969).

Jewish intermarriage

For Jews, marriage with non-Jews is both prohibited and invalid as a religious marriage should it take place. This law is based on Biblical injunctions (Deuteronomy 7: 3–4) supported by Rabbinic declarations. In Israel this is more than a purely religious ruling, for it is illegal to contract a religiously mixed marriage (Rabbinical Courts Jurisdiction (Marriage and Divorce) Law no. 5713–1953), though there is no punishment if one is in fact contracted. This ruling is supported by other injunctions towards spouses, e.g. that they should have similar social backgrounds and age. Jewish men are unlikely to intermarry with non-Jewish women and Jewish women are even less likely than Jewish men to marry outside their faith. In Indiana, USA, only 33.2 per cent of the previously never-married, and 20 per cent of the previously widowed, married non-Jews (*Encyc. Judaica* 1971). The Jewish maintenance of intramarriage rather than intermarriage can be seen partly as the result of the endogamous tendencies of other religious groups and partly of the Jewish tendency to maintain a somewhat exclusive social and economic life, reducing potential contacts with marriageable outsiders. A US study has shown that the larger the Jewish community, the easier it is to organize communal activities and to maintain an organized intra-Jewish system. In smaller Jewish communities there is more intermarriage with outsiders (Rosenthal 1968).

Mixed marriages and the trend away from religious homogamy

We suggested earlier that to have parents of the same religion with the same religious practices is advantageous in certain respects. What biologically relevant data are there regarding the effects on children of marriages between parents of different religious practices? The conclusions of one lengthy study (Burchinal and Chancellor 1963) showed that couples in mixed-religion marriages had fewer children than those who married within their own faith. Their children were less likely to finish secondary school, and very generally the children rejected religion. The converse has also been shown, namely that the children of parents who attend the same church regularly stay at school longer (Morgan *et al.* 1962). The divorce rate of mixed-religion marriages seems in general to be higher than for those who marry within their own faith: for Catholics three to four times as high, for Protestants two to three times, and for Jews five to six times higher (Burchinal and Chancellor 1963). This may well affect the attitudes and hence the reproductive performance of offspring. The teenage arrest rate for the children of mixed-religion marriages tends to be high. But it is well to remember that a religious difference between the spouses may be associated with other differences, e.g. in socio-economic, ethnic or racial background, so that the difficulties in such marriages are unlikely to stem from religion alone (Monahan 1973).

Some religions are so strongly against the possibility of intermarriage that it would involve not only the loss of religious affiliation but the removal of those involved from their families as well. A Kenyan case, in which a woman who was a Muslim physiotherapist married a Hindu surgeon, resulted in the wife's father placing a newspaper advertisement to state that his daughter was no longer a member of his family (personal observation, R. Tanner). In such cases the range of issues goes far beyond formal religious rules and involves deeper issues of pollution concepts and family name survival, so that only the most persistent and strong-minded of couples are likely to even contemplate such a marriage. Another Kenyan case initially involved the forced separation of the engaged couple by sending the Muslim girl to Britain for higher education, and it was only her persistent refusal to consider marrying anyone else that eventually resulted in the marriage taking place to the Hindu man concerned.

Today religious intermarriages are in some areas becoming more frequent than in the past. Despite Judaism's absolute prohibition of intermarriage, US Jewish intermarriages in 1963 varied from 34.2 per cent in cities to 67 per cent in rural areas, where there was also the smallest pool of eligible mates (Rosenthal 1968). A 1961 study of Catholics (*Official Catholic Directory* 1962) reported their intermarriage rate to be 27 per cent while other studies have put this rate as high as 42 per cent (Gordon 1964). There is evidence that the proportion of interfaith marriages is increasing in both Canada (Heer 1962) and the USA (Bumpass 1970).

An even more important cause of the increasing inter-religious marriage rate in Western societies is the extent of mobility of the typical Western urbanite. Socio-religious association is often the sign of a stable community or at least a core of stability in mobile communities. Within modern cities, individuals tend to seek sectarian consolation because of the loneliness and instability of city living. A study (Chancellor and Burchinal 1962) has shown that inter-religious marriage rates tend to be higher for migrants into cities than long-term residents. Even when it occurs there is a consistent trend in mixed-religion marriages for one spouse to convert to the faith of the other, and wives convert more frequently than husbands. In the past some governments, as in Poland and Prussia, have decreed that the children of mixed-religion marriages had to follow the religion of the father. A US study (Salisbury 1962) showed conversions in the direction of the spouse with the higher social and professional status. Generally, intermarriage at the present rate is a recent phenomenon and has only been legal in Europe since the eighteenth century. There have been widespread legal prohibitions against Christian–Jewish marriages arising from the Emperor Constantine's law in AD 339. Some countries such as Poland, Lithuania and Yugoslavia prohibited religious intermarriage prior to the Second World War.

The Islamic polygynous marriage today

Islam requires the husband to act impartially between his wives. This was at one time felt to relate only to material benefits and sexual access. Now it is increasingly felt that this requirement of equality of treatment has an emotional quality to it as well. The frequency of polygynous marriages varies between 11 per cent of all marriages in some Palestinian villages (Putai 1958) to 1.9 per cent in Algeria (Seklawi 1960).

These marriages have often been hard to manage and today they are as full of quarrels and difficulties as when they were first observed (Lane 1954). Wives sometimes compete for the attention of their husband and to get additional advantages for their children over the children of their co-wives. Some of the pressures which have made the step-mother a figure of dislike to Western people are present in the polygynous marriage, where to the children the co-wives are like step-parents. Admittedly there is prestige from being one of the several wives of a prominent and wealthy husband, but the competitive element is still there. In one such marriage the husband had to give each of his two wives identical household goods, such as cookers, freezers, etc. (personal observation, V. Reynolds). The Islamic record in caring for the welfare of the wives rather than indulging the pre-eminence of the husband is not good, despite inevitable denials. Islam has always opposed any restriction on the principle of polygyny despite the considerable modernist pressure to abolish it as being derogatory to the status of women. Secular governments in Islamic countries have however done much to restrict it. Tunisia outlawed it in 1957. Syria insisted on prior judicial approval for a polygynous marriage in 1953 in order to protect the first wife financially.

Does polygyny have biological advantages or otherwise for the children? The number of a man's wives shows his prestige and there may be benefits to the children deriving from this. Polygynous households have some advantages over monogamous ones: where a wife is ill or absent another is available for cooking and caring for children. The children may not encounter the wide range from emotional deprivation to over-stimulation which is characteristic of societies with monogamous marriages. As the Islamic polygynous husband is usually richer and more socially prominent than the monogamist there are more money and goods in the household as well as people. Thus the children receive better facilities and should have better chances of survival than in monogamous marriages. While the sexual arrangements tend to operate on a shift system, the domestic arrangements have an advantageous continuity unknown in Western nuclear families.

The aim of many polygynous husbands in contracting more marriages is often prestige rather than increased sexual activity. This is shown in the reaction of some Sukuma tribesmen. On becoming Catholic and thus meeting the prohibition against taking extra wives, they become godparents to more children, and thus achieve high status. One man had over a hundred godchildren, providing them with the same kinds of help as he would have given full sons and daughters, while they in their turn gave him the same help as would have been due to him as a full father (personal observation, R. Tanner).

One of our main concerns in comparing the two major world types of marriage is their relative fertility. We need to examine fertility records of married women to see which type of union produces the largest number of children and rears them successfully to reproductive age. This is no simple problem. Some cultures and their religions decree that a woman who has produced a child which she is nursing should not have intercourse with her husband because a further pregnancy would damage the existing child's chances of survival. We have discussed the effects of this belief in reducing the chances of over-rapid conception in Chapter 3. This is mostly an excellent arrangement as far as the survival and rearing of children goes but in monogamy it leaves the husband without the opportunity for sexual access to his wife. This problem is solved in polygynous marriages if the husband has access to another (non-nursing) wife, which will sometimes, though not always, be the case.

There are other factors in polygynous marriages which have a bearing on fertility. In a monogamous marriage coital frequency is, if we exclude extra-marital arrangements, equal for each partner. In a polygynous marriage this is not so, as each wife has equal rights to the sexual attentions of her husband and the husband thus has to circulate, with an equal number of nights with each wife. Thus equality of coital frequency disappears and each wife has a half, a third or a quarter the coital frequency of her husband, depending on how many co-wives are sexually available (i.e. not nursing a young infant). The more the husband has to circulate, the lower will be the output of sperm as a result of repeated ejaculations. Also, in polygynous marriages, husbands are almost certainly older than monogamous husbands. Among the Temne of Sierra Leone (Dorjahn 1958) out of 121 men with more than one wife, 70 (58%) were over 43 years of age. Men who are past their optimum age for libido obtain, in polygynous marriages, younger women during their most fecund period. Age of the spouses thus works in two directions: if anything it reduces male fecundity but it increases that of the wife, who tends to be older at marriage in monogamous systems.

Another factor affecting fertility is the incidence of divorce. For the polygynous husband there is no great difficulty or inconvenience in divorcing a disliked wife. Also he probably has funds and prestige available to attract another. Whether polygynous marriages are more unstable than monogamous ones is too wide a question to answer in general. Christian polygynous marriages among Mormons in Utah have, or had, the reputation of being long lasting. By contrast, monogamous marriages in some parts of the USA such as California are particularly unstable at the present time. But the reasons for this are so many and varied that no general conclusions are justified.

In polygynous marriage, as stated above, the wife experiences less coitus than her husband, but does she have less than an average monogamously married woman? The answer is not known. There exists the possibility that in some polygynous households wives are not satisfied by their share of intercourse by rota and have extra-marital affairs, possibly leading to conception. There may also be a higher coital frequency in monogamous marriages than that of husband with wife owing to extra-marital affairs, and some of these may lead to conceptions.

The effects of monogamy and polygyny on sexual activity and fertility are thus complex. The polygynous wife probably has fewer children at risk owing to wider birth spacing than the non-contracepting monogamous wife, but religious attitudes can reduce sexual activity as we have already noted. The polygynous husband has more children to provide for than the monogamist but he may be more wealthy. In the large number of surveys of African tribes brought together by Dorjahn (1958) the monogamous wife had higher fertility than the polygynous wife in 18 cases, and lower in 5 cases (see Table 7.6).

Population	Size of group	Ratio	Monogamously married	Polygynously married	Source
Fertility equal or higher in polygynously married segment					
1. Ikela (Belgian Congo)*	672	Children/ wife	2.65	2.78	Baker (1950:44)
	487	Children/ fertile wife	3.54	3.95	
2. Kondale (Belgian Congo)	?	Live births/ wife	1.9	1.9	Schwetz (1923:336–7)
3. Wamuzimu (Belgian Congo)	940	Children/ wife	3.3	3.5	Salmon (1951:140)
4. Bamvele (French Cameroons)	344	Pregnancies/ wife	1.95	2.14	Wilbois (1934:64)
5. Wabena (Tanganyika)	472	Children/ wife	2.38	2.43	Culwick and Culwick (1938:379)
Fertility higher in monogamously married segment					
6. Akamba	52	Children/ wife	4.44	3.02	Lindblom (1920:87)
(Kenya)	52	Live births/ wife	7.00	3.91	
7. Katako-Kombe (Belgian Congo)	492	Children/ wife	2.6	2.2	Hemerijckx (1948:495–6)
	?	Children/ fertile wife	4.3	4.0	

Population	Size of group	Ratio	Monogamously married	Polygynously married	Source
Fertility higher in monogamously married segment					
8. Nkundo-Mongo (Belgian Congo)	770	Children/wife	0.99[†]	0.34[†]	Boelaert (1947:42)
	?	Children/fertile wife	2.72[†]	2.00[†]	
9. Bofiji-Ouest (Belgian Congo)	1,054	Children/wife	0.93	0.73	(ibid.:43) Study by Ruppol
10. Bashi (Belgian Congo)	328	Children/wife	5.8	3.6	Colle (1925:402, n. 1)
11. Kibali-Ituri (Belgian Congo)	?	Children/wife	0.95	0.57	Duren (1943:359, 379–80, 380)
	?	Children/fertile wife	1.97	1.41	
12. Kibali-Ituri	12,532	Children/wife	0.87	0.80	(ibid.)
13. Sara-Madjingaye (French Equatorial Africa)	289	Births/wife	2.8	2.3	Muraz (1928:143)
	289	Children/wife	2.0	1.5	
14. Betsenga (French Cameroons)	169	Children/wife	1.2	0.8	Wilbois (1935:64)
15. Bamvele	304	Live births/wife	1.47	1.08	(ibid.)
16. Wute	243	Pregnancies/wife	1.88	1.75	(ibid.:65)
	243	Live births/wife	1.49	1.26	
17. Efok	138	Births/wife	3.40	2.70	(ibid.)
	138	Children/wife	1.50	1.25	
18. Eton	?	Children/wife	1.44	1.35	Olivier and Aujoulat (1945:39)
	?	Children/wife	1.12	0.90	
19. Kotoko	?	Children/wife at least 35 years old	1.66	(1.2–0.7) (2.4–1.4)	Vincent (1951:458)
20. Ibo (Nigeria)	1,416	Live births/wife	3.4	2.9	Thomas (1913:18–19)
21. Mossi (French West Africa)	25,441	Children/wife	1.5	1.1	Ouédraogo (1951:52)
	21,652	Children/fertile wife	2.0	1.2	
22. Mossi	299	Children/wife	2.42	1.44	(ibid.)
23. Temne (Sierra Leone)	486	Children/wife	2.1[†]	1.7[†]	Thomas (1916:21)

Table 7.6 The fertility of women in monogamous and polygynous marriages, 23 studies in sub-Saharan Africa (From Dorjahn 1958)

* 'Monogamously married' includes women always monogamously married and also fertile monogamous marriages followed by sterile polygynous marriage. 'Polygynously married' includes women always polygynously married, and women polygynously married first, though subsequently monogamously married.

[†] Monogamously married women and the first wives of polygynously married men combined.

[†] Second and subsequent wives of polygynously married men combined.

	Crude birth-rates per thousand							Net reproduction rates		
	1960	1965	1970	1971	1972	1973	1974	1958/59	1969/70	1972/73
USSR	24.9	18.4	17.4	17.8	17.8	17.6	18.0	1.262	1.126	1.128
Latvia	16.7	13.8	14.5	14.7	14.5	13.9	14.2	0.879	0.911	0.937
Russia	23.2	15.7	14.6	15.1	15.3	15.1	15.6	1.186	0.934	0.936
Ukraine	20.5	15.3	15.2	15.4	15.5	14.9	15.1	1.042	0.960	0.965
Estonia	16.6	14.6	15.8	16.0	15.6	15.0	15.1	0.882	1.021	1.009
Byelorussia	24.4	17.9	16.2	16.4	16.1	15.7	15.8	1.253	1.092	1.074
Lithuania	22.5	18.1	17.6	17.6	17.0	16.0	15.8	1.183	1.109	1.079
Georgia	24.7	21.2	19.2	19.0	18.2	18.3	18.0	1.146	1.233	1.195
Moldavia	29.3	20.4	19.4	20.2	20.6	20.4	20.4	1.570	1.190	1.205
Armenia	40.1	28.6	22.1	22.6	22.5	22.1	21.9	1.990	1.488	1.388
Kazakhstan	37.2	26.9	23.4	23.8	23.5	23.2	24.1	1.947	1.559	1.526
Azerbaijan	42.6	36.6	29.2	27.7	25.6	25.4	25.0	2.132	2.085	1.827
Kirghizistan	36.9	31.4	30.5	31.6	30.5	30.6	30.5	1.909	2.231	2.175
Uzbekistan	39.8	34.7	33.6	34.5	33.2	33.7	34.2	2.142	2.598	2.562
Tajikistan	33.5	36.8	34.8	36.8	35.3	35.6	37.0	1.693	2.657	2.661
Turkmenistan	42.4	37.2	35.2	34.7	33.9	34.3	34.3	2.116	2.685	2.595

Table 7.7   Birth-rates and net reproduction rates of the population of USSR (From: Borisov 1976)

A considerable body of literature exists on the relative fertility of the population of the USSR. Such figures as are available show an appreciably higher rate of reproduction in the eastern (Muslim or ex-Muslim) countries than in the western (ex-Christian) ones. The data for a number of years are shown in Table 7.7.

Despite the extensive evidence on fertility rates, there appear to be no follow-up studies on the reproductive success or otherwise of the offspring of monogamous and polygamous marriages. If, as suggested above, conditions in polygynous households are marginally more advantageous than in monogamous ones, the extra fertility found in Dorjahn's survey would be compensated for. Fertility itself is not a very meaningful biological statistic, yet it tends to be the only one available for study – an indication of how far we are from understanding the long-term effects of marriage systems.

Conclusions

What conclusions can we draw about the biological effects of the institution of marriage, its structural rules and the ways it influences the behaviour of individuals? In many past studies, marriage systems have not been clearly distinguished by human biologists from mating systems but clearly the two are quite distinct, and not just with respect to the partners involved, but their children too. Thus it is necessary not only to draw a distinction between the pair of individuals who constitute a married couple and the pair or pairs who actually reproduce; it is also necessary to remember, as this chapter has shown, that marriage rules determine the legitimacy or otherwise of the young, and this can affect their chances of survival, depending on how easy or difficult any given religious group makes it for parents to succeed in the rearing process, when they are not married, or for the single parent (mother or father) to manage without a spouse. We noted that in some societies, generally those with a high degree of mobility, marriage tends to be unstable and there is little stigma to illegitimacy. In others, especially settled agricultural societies, marriage and legitimacy are focal issues and the problems raised by illegitimacy are greater. This tends to give legitimate children advantages over illegitimate ones, and thus marriage is, in biological as well as social terms, a good thing.

Where changing social circumstances have imposed new stresses, as in newly urbanized communities, old marriage patterns have often broken down and religion in the form of spirit possession has been adapted accordingly.

Not all religions are pro-marriage for all members. Hindus and Jews are actively exhorted to marry and to have children, the former in particular to have sons. In such cases the effect of such encouragement must be to increase the birth rate in the absence of efficient birth control, abortion or infanticide (see Chapters 3 and 4). Buddhists place far less emphasis on marriage, and indeed many do not marry. In the case of Christianity a curious situation prevails: the religion tends to be in favour of marriage as the pathway to parental stability and it is pro-reproductive within marriage, but it is anti-sex. Sex in itself is, or was until recently, seen as sinful unless in the service of reproduction within marriage; though today some churches approve openly of sex between married partners even if not for child production. Christianity as a whole, in common with Hinduism and Islam, does not approve of sex *per se* outside of marriage.

Islam provides an interesting case. Muhammad established a form of polygyny, at first to remarry widows whose husbands had been killed in battle. Together with new rules about the case of orphans, a new rule that slaves could marry, another that the children of slave concubines were free, and a rule enabling marriage with women of other religions (mainly Christians and Jews), Islam put itself on a strongly expansionist tack. This whole programme was, we know, based on a policy of politico-religious expansionism. It was designed in the first place by one charismatic individual, but later must have been added to by many others. It has all the characteristics of group thinking and group process, and if we want evidence of group selection at the cultural level, this is a good illustration, for the whole family programme of Islam (like the secular programmes found in other places and times, e.g. Stalin's family programme in the USSR) was aimed at, and achieved, both rapid population growth from within and increased numbers by proselytization of outsiders.

Evidence of group processes leading to economic advantages for members of religious groups was found in the way Puritans treated their affinal kin like lineal relatives, and the use of religious sanctions for cousin marriage, which keeps property within the extended family. Both economic and psychological benefits were seen to arise from religious homogamy, i.e. more or less clearly formalized rules enjoining marriage with a member of one's own religion or sect. Such benefits promote parental harmony, marital stability, and successful child-rearing.

The effects of monogamy and polygamy on fertility and the rearing process were seen to be complex. Modern Western Christian monogamy, with its emphasis on parent–parent love and care by both parents of a small number of young who are expected to survive (rather than production of many offspring of whom some will be expected to die) can be seen as the outcome of what we are calling $r-$ selection, i.e. cultural selection acting where food and other scarce resources are tight but reliable all the year round.

Where environmental resources are unstable for many, and few men are wealthy enough to support wives and children over the prolonged period of rearing, polygyny will be advantageous for survival and religions favouring it will be selected for and will gain momentum; hence Hinduism and Islam will be at an advantage, and the results of r+ selection may be observed in the form of religious exhortations to fathers to have large numbers of children.

Celibacy 8

Introduction

The issues raised by the practice of celibacy bring into sharp focus some of the points discussed in general terms in Chapter 1. Celibacy confronts very clearly the strictly biological question: How do religious practices affect individual and kin selection? There are other equally important questions: What does it mean to the individual to be celibate? What is the role of the celibate in the religious community and in society? Why does celibacy exist? Who are the celibates? What do they get out of it? Is celibacy an indication of man's ultimate freedom to choose and not to be bound by innate desires, normal conventions or the motives of the majority?

Again there are questions of adaptation and function: Can there be a credible phylogeny of the celibate state? Is celibacy something which developed in response to environmental conditions? Is celibacy subject to short-term fluctuations according to social conditions? Can we see celibacy as some sort of demographic adjustment? Is celibacy adaptively neutral, i.e. has it no especial bearing on the extent to which individuals or groups are adjusted to the world? Last, is celibacy actually disfunctional, that is can we see it as actively detrimental to the health, wellbeing, inclusive fitness, survival or general usefulness of the individual and/or his or her social group?

Celibacy and sexuality

First of all, what do we mean by celibacy? To many laymen undoubtedly, the term implies a negative – a turning away from marriage and sex, a voluntary, self-imposed decision by a religious devotee not

A procession of Cistercian monks, a celibate order of Roman Catholic men dedicated to a silent life of work and prayer within the boundaries of their monastery.

to engage in marriage and sexual activity. The early pre-Reformation Penitentials, manuals for the guidance and administration of the Church, give horrendous penalties for religious officials who deviate from celibacy. The Penitential of Finnian decrees, for a single act of fornication by a cleric, a year's penance on bread and water (Bieler 1963) and in the so-called Roman Penitential a lustful intention calls for half a year on bread and water (McNeill and Gamer 1938). Nor are the celibacy rules concerned only with heterosexuality. The penalties for homosexuality are even greater. The Penitential of St Columba states: 'If anyone has committed fornication as the Sodomites did, let him do penance for ten years, for the first three on bread and water' (Bieler 1963), while the Paris Penitential prescribes seven years for a layman (McNeill and Gamer 1938). The contemporary position is, however, different. While the sins may be the same as those listed in the works of past moral theologians, corresponding penalties are not given and the present training of priests in the hearing of confessions is towards repentance and reconciliation with a minimal penalty, such as the saying of a few prayers for even the most grievous sexual sin.

Celibacy and spirituality

But the sexual side is only one aspect of celibacy; it is also a spiritual state. In this respect, celibacy is particularly associated with a state of extreme spiritual involvement and comprehension, such that it enables the individual to transcend the everyday passions and concerns of ordinary life and achieve enlightenment. This applies also to the Buddhist celibates in the Mahayana northern school. Both Christianity and Buddhism stress the importance of sex and marriage for ordinary people, while denying them to those who seek the spiritual life. Thus if the flesh is denied, the spirit is felt by some Christian celibates to be freed. There is a greater possibility of service to the community, proximity to the Almighty or the desired spiritual state.

Neither Judaism nor Islam have ever had any wide interest in celibacy. In the sense of being a holy state, celibacy falls at the opposite end of the spectrum from the Hindu orgiastic cults of Chakra Puja or Vamachari in which sex and especially incest are seen as purifying. Hinduism tends to consider that unrestrained sexual intercourse in the right social context is good and in keeping with the general fertility of nature. The Chinese cult of Tao holds sexual union to be a close form of contact with the divinity, perhaps even the most divine state of being. Indeed it is not really possible in Tao thinking to divorce sex from the whole pattern of life; sex is everywhere represented by the symbolism of the yin (female) and the yang (male), the elements of the two sexes, which find their expression in the trees, the fields, the rock pools, the weather and all things natural and good (Rawson and Legeza 1979). In some Tao works (Chang 1977: 35–46) men (the yang element) must withhold their ejaculation as long as possible while they satisfy many women, but eventually they must ejaculate, as it is considered harmful to restrain oneself for too long. By contrast, Christian and Buddhist celibates hold that sex deflects from preoccupation with things divine, and celibacy may be defined, for the celibate, as a total dedication to God, or the Holy Trinity, and a giving of one's life to spiritual endeavour and helping others.

For the Christian, celibacy is defined as the canonical state of abstinence from sex and hence marriage, freely undertaken for the purpose
of dedicating one's life totally to God's service (*New Catholic Encyclopedia* 1967). For the Buddhist lamas, abstention from marriage and all
sexual relations is a necessary detachment from the world as part of the
process of conquering desire in order to achieve Nirvana. In all the
world religions celibacy is a specific condition separate from, though
overlapping with, the general condition of chastity. Celibacy for religious reasons must be considered a widespread contemporary and
historical phenomenon. Aztec celibacy included both sexes; all Aztec
priests were celibate (Thompson 1933); the seducers of girls associated
with temples, and priests who failed to remain celibate, were executed
(Bandelier 1880). Inca celibacy was religious and confined to women
(Rowe 1944).

The feeling that sexual congress must by its very nature prevent the
attainment of true religious states has been taken to extremes by certain
sects like the nineteenth-century Russian Skoptsy sect who castrated
themselves *en masse*. This has also happened in the case of isolated individuals with fervent religious convictions (Kushner 1967).

Celibacy and reproductive success
How does celibacy affect a person's reproductive success? The obvious
immediate response is that it diminishes it to zero. Then one begins to
qualify this. First, what about illicit liaisons and illegitimate offspring?
Quantitative data are hard to obtain but some historical material does
exist on the extent of celibate failure and public and institutional reactions to this. Celibacy for the Christian clergy was first written into
canon law by the Council of Elvira in AD 306. The Council of Carthage, AD 419, extended the condition to include sub-deacons. But the
celibate condition was a constant source of difficulty, particularly in
areas where the clergy could not be adequately supervised. In the
eleventh century some clerical fiefs were virtually hereditary with
parishes and bishoprics being passed from father to son and it was then
that Pope Gregory VII (1073–85) began the reaction to the lax observance of celibacy.

Lea's *History of Sacerdotal Celibacy* (1966) quotes a long series of celibate failures, mostly as isolated cases, spread over the Christian world
between the fifth and nineteenth centuries. Lecky in his *History of European Morals* (1877) refers to a similar range of cases, quoting the case of
the Bishop of Liège who was deposed in 1274 when 65 bastards were
cited against him. He does show, however, that Church Councils and
bishops have often been seriously concerned over the extent of these
failures and the possible reactions of the faithful to an obvious abuse of
priestly discipline. The Council of Aranda in 1473 bitterly denounced
the failures among celibates and so did a number of other Councils, before and after the Council of Trent which met in 1546. Pius IV in decrees dated November 1563 made the vow of chastity specific for
priests. The decrees were resisted passively in that priests continued to
have housekeepers, but at least they prevented the formation of a legitimate hereditary ecclesiastical class. The Council of Trent stated that the
married minister of religion is too preoccupied with his wife and family
to give practical charity to all men and that the priesthood, even in the
Old Testament required a form of sanctity that implied the curbing of

carnal desires. It has been suggested that in fact the main reason why the medieval Church was deeply in favour of celibacy for priests was that it wanted to safeguard its property from appropriation by clerics and then transmission by them to their legitimate or even illegitimate offspring. Fearing the loss of its lands and houses, especially in far-flung parts of Britain, it stigmatized priests who broke the rule of celibacy, and especially any offspring of such unions. It preferred its priests to be dependent on central authority and in addition to the economic reason for preferring celibacy, there was a political one, for the development of a landed priesthood would give the clergy greater independence and present a threat to its autocracy.

An Archbishop of Canterbury enacting the policy of Queen Mary I put into reverse the anti-Catholic activities of her predecessor Henry VIII. He estimated that out of 16,000 clergy in England, he had deprived 12,000 of office for having married (see Lea 1966 *passim*). As a result of the French Revolution, the 1791 Constitution provided that no profession could debar a person from marriage, so marriage for the clergy became a pledge of civic loyalty and continued celibacy became a silent political protest against republicanism. Considerable official pressure was put on celibates to marry even to the extent of executing some who refused (Duguit and Monnier 1898).

Latin America has always figured high in the folklore of the anti-celibate, of which Graham Greene's *The Power and the Glory* (1971) is a good fictional example. Lea (1966) again gives more exact figures (based though they must be on no more than hearsay) and quotes statistics that were produced to the Plenary Council of Latin America held in Rome in 1899, to show that out of 18,000 priests, 3,000 were living in regular wedlock, 4,000 in concubinage with their so-called 'housekeepers', and some 1,500 in relations carried on more or less openly with women of doubtful reputation.

The record of Burmese Buddhist monks, as far as the meagre historical evidence allows, shows a long record of their fidelity to their sexual vows. Very few contemporary lapses are recorded outside the major cities where there are often coteries of pseudo-monks who are referred to as 'humans in monks' costume'. This strict observance is not surprising when it is recognized that celibacy is laid down as the first of the first four rules, the breaking of which involves leaving the monastic order (*The Patimokkha* 1966). However there is evidence that the position is not so clear-cut in Thailand and Sri Lanka, either now or in the past, as it has been in Burma, and that lapses and liaisons have been tolerated to some extent.

In conclusion, with regard to the question about reproductive success, we need to acknowledge the existence of more or less sexual activity and even marriage on the part of some religious officials who have taken celibacy vows or are engaged in occupations that call for celibacy. Sexual activity by celibates may constitute a grave breach of moral law and warrant severe punishment; in other places and at other times it may merely be frowned upon, or treated with relative indifference. What seems to matter most to celibates themselves is the extent to which the celibate state, defined either with respect to sex or marriage or both, is seen as a precondition for spiritual enlightenment or service to the community. Religions which emphasize celibacy tend to stress the opposition between the natural and the spiritual; only by transcend-

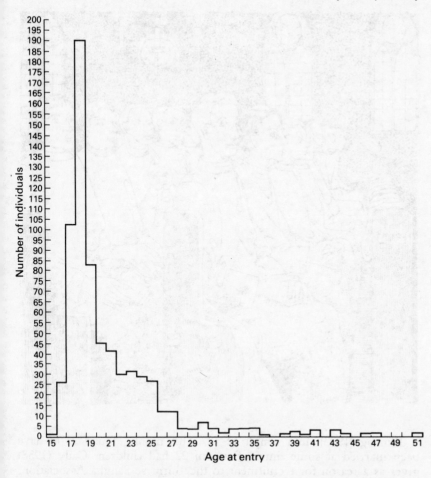

Fig. 8.1 Society of Jesus (English Province): age at entry taken from living members in 1978

ing the natural can man achieve the spiritual. In such conditions priests and lay celibates will tend to suffer a more severe curtailment of their reproductive activities than in more permissive circumstances. They may well, as in Burma where celibacy is widespread (5–10% of the adult male population), be totally debarred from parenthood.

But there is another aspect: depending on the age at which vows are taken, celibates might conceivably have reproduced beforehand, or if celibates tend to renounce their vows after a number of years, they might again reproduce successfully. What do we know about these matters?

We undertook an analysis of male entrants into the English Province of the Society of Jesus during the period 1900–69 (Fig. 8.1). By comparing the birth date with the date of entry, the data show that the majority of entrants committed themselves to celibacy between the ages of 15 and 20 (see Plate XVII). This applies to 516 of the total of 754 (i.e. 65.8%). The remainder joined the Society after the age of 20 years. This percentage was rather lower under the founder St Ignatius (1540–56) and his successor Laynez (1558–65) when 396 out of 748 members entered before 20 years of age (52.9%) (Ganss 1970). Thus in some of these older cases there may be men who have already married and reproduced.

XVII. Young men dedicating themselves to a life of celibacy in the Roman Catholic Church. They are seen here at the ordination ceremony.

Bunnag (1973), in a sample of 187 Thai monks, found 25 to have been married at some time, of whom 22 had children. Cady (1958) gives as a reason for recruitment to the Burmese Sangha Association, which provides social services, a disinclination to undertake the responsibilities of supporting a family. This was expressed as the necessary avoidance of parental responsibilities by anyone wishing to achieve Nirvana. There are certainly well-known examples of reproductive activity prior to religious conversion and the assumption of celibacy. St Augustine in his *Confessions* refers to his common-law wife and child, and St Elizabeth Setton (1774–1821), canonized in 1976, foundress of the American Sisters of Charity, had five children prior to being widowed and answering the call to a very specific and unusually powerful celibate religious commitment.

The recognition of the canonical requirement of celibacy frequently led to delaying ordination until after a family had been successfully completed. Theodore of Tarsus (*c.*602–90) was ordained at the age of 62 years so that he could become the Archbishop of Canterbury.

Father Michael Hollings, M.C. (1977) states the issue more obliquely: 'On the whole, perhaps more in the past than today, there was I think a general assumption that all priests were ignorant of what the textbooks used to call "carnal knowledge". This is not so, though it does not mean that clergy go around saying publicly "I am a virgin" or "I had intercourse before I became a priest and know all about it"'.

Continents/nations	1962/3	1964	1965	1966	1967	1968	Total	No. of priests 1966	Ratio of requests to no. of priests (%)
Middle–South America	29	75	118	133	148	158	661	21,854	3.02
France	10	67	115	117	128	116	553	41,076	1.35
USA and Canada	8	30	7	91	89	230	455	46,196	0.98
Germany, Austria Netherlands, Switzerland }	3	30	73	90	82	136	414	32,979	1.24
Spain	5	29	62	85	94	125	400	25,906	1.54
Italy	21	65	56	94	76	63	375	44,240	0.85
Slav countries	10	28	68	49	39	44	238	★	—
Portugal	—	11	20	26	28	21	106	4,773	2.22
Asia (incl. Philippines)	1	13	22	10	22	30	98	15,053	0.65
Great Britain	1	9	14	13	19	39	95	9,667	0.98
Africa	2	6	8	13	19	27	75	4,505	1.66
Belgium	1	6	11	—	17	23	58	10,350	0.56
Australia	—	1	4	5	10	13	33	2,382	1.38
Malta	—	1	1	2	—	1	5	558	—
New Zealand	—	—	—	2	—	—	2	513	—
Total	91	371	579	730	771	1,026	3,568	Ratio of dispensations	
Requests accepted	—	200	374	649	709	1,017	2,949	to no. of requests = 82%	

★ Approx. no. of priests: 25,000

Figures for renunciation of celibacy or chastity over the period 1962–68 have been collected by Denzler (1973–76). These show that this occurrence is not very common (Table 8.1). In general, then, during the commitment to celibacy in modern times, as in the previous century, it is uncommon for the vow to be broken. When this occurs it is a subject of general distaste, and even scandal. Renan (1883) testified strongly to the effective celibacy of the priests under whom he had studied for 13 years as a seminarian.

It would appear that the decision to be celibate is mostly made in the late teens, and that it effectively debars most of those who make it from reproduction. The trainee priest has a spiritual director with whom he works to control his spiritual and physical problems including that of his sexual desire, principally by prayer rather than, as in the past, by fasting and flagellation. If he fails, he cannot become a priest.

Canon law and the rules of the different religious orders insist on a good physical and mental condition in candidates for the religious life. The Constitution of the Society of Jesus details the impediments against entering the priesthood: to be mentally ill or to have a notable disposition toward such illness so that judgement becomes obscured and unsound. Conversely, the requirements for membership are: to have the health and strength to sustain the work of the Society as well as the good appearance and age for this work (Ganss 1970: 86, 89, 129 and 133). Most orders require a physical examination and pay particular attention to inherited illness as a disqualification from training. On the other hand several orders, such as the Sisters of Jesus Crucified, welcome those who are physically incapacitated claiming that poor physical health and handicap should not be an obstacle for someone wanting to live the religious life.

Table 8.1 Diocesan priests' requests for dispensation from celibacy rules in various countries (From: Denzler 1976)

Celibacy and inclusive fitness

In terms of Darwinian fitness, true celibacy would thus far appear to be largely disfunctional. But what of the celibate's *inclusive* fitness? Do celibates have larger numbers of reproductively active kin (especially brothers and sisters) than non-celibates? Do celibates 'farm' their siblings rather than reproduce themselves?

There is, in fact, some evidence that Catholic celibates do come, on average, from larger families (i.e. they do have more brothers and sisters) than non-celibates. The average US family providing 'vocations', according to Fichter (1966) who analysed a large number of US surveys, had 4 children in the early 1960s, as against a national average of 3.3.

In an Irish family from Limerick, details of which were reported to us (Hunt, personal communication), the breakdown of children's occupations and life styles was as follows: total number of children 13; 2 entered the Marie Reparatrice Sisters; 1 entered the Jesus and Mary Sisters; 1 entered the Jesuit Brothers; of these, 2 eventually left their religious orders and 2 died before the age of 10. The remaining 9 sons and daughters married.

How much bigger would a family need to be to more than compensate for the reproductive loss involved in celibacy? Assuming that a celibate loses 100 per cent of his personal reproductive value, he or she needs one extra sibling in reproductive activity to 'replace' him or her and anything over this is potential reproductive benefit. Thus if average family size in a community is three, then in a family where one child is celibate, compensation for this loss can be achieved by having four children, and if there are five or six children the help of the celibate sibling would make functional sense if we could say that it was as a result of his or her altruistic activities that the extra brothers and sisters were helped to survive and reproduce, and that without this help they would have died or failed to have children, or as many children. Is there any evidence for this?

Many prominent Christian Churches operate a wide range of supportive institutions not specifically directed at their own followers, but certainly providing places for those of them who are considered to be especially deserving. This would apply to Church hospital and school places in Africa. Even if a celibate failed to ask for a specific benefit for his or her relatives it would certainly tend to be the case that his or her siblings, nephews and nieces would get places in the Church schools of their parents' choice, and receive bursaries and general educational help. Siblings, particularly sisters, would receive places in Church-based hospitals, receiving personalized attention from the religious as well as the lay staff. Also jobs would tend to go to the relatives of those permanently dedicated to the faith (personal observation, R. Tanner).

This brings us to the next logical question: Does celibacy run in families? Or are celibates drawn from the community on a random, or at least non-family, basis? Fichter (1966) gives data on this point, stating that about two-thirds of candidates for celibate religious service had one or more close relatives (siblings, first cousins, uncles and aunts) following the religious life as seminarian, novice, priest, brother or sister. All of the surveys he studied showed consistently that about a quarter of priests and nuns had a brother or sister or both following a religious vocation; these proportions were much higher than for the average US family in the early 1960s. It thus looks rather as if celibacy does tend to run in families and is not a sporadic event in the community. This does not, of course, make it any 'more biological' than such hereditary events as attendance at a particular school in the general community, but it does invite further comparison with the situations in other species where some individuals forego reproduction.

Animal comparisons

The best known animal groups in which non-reproductive members are found are the social insects. The workers in the bees and wasps are wholly non-reproductive. In fact these individuals are not just non-reproductive, they are sterile. It has, for particular genetic reasons, come about in the social insects that genes can replicate themselves more effectively by confining reproduction to one 'egg-factory' individual, while the rest put all their energies into the tending of the factory and its products – their own genes. This whole process is specific to the special genetics of the Hymenoptera, which differs from the genetics of mammals, and as a result there is little to be learnt about celibacy in man from the social insects.

What about other animals where there are groups or individuals that do not reproduce? For instance, in some monkey species, such as hamadryas baboons, patas monkeys, and some langurs, there are so-called 'bachelor bands' – wholly non-reproductive, non-copulating groups of males out of the reproductive process. What are the advantages of this, and how are the genes underlying these patterns transmitted?

The fact is, we really do not know. We do not know the genetics of primate social behaviour in any detail at all. The bachelor males are not sterile; if one of them is able to take over a female or group of females from a reproductive male he does so, and is usually fertile. In hamadryas baboons, the bachelor males are effectively inhibited from engaging in reproduction. If one approaches a female who is attached to a male, the latter attacks, curiously not the intrusive male, but his own female, who returns to him. Conflict is engendered, the new pair is forced to abandon, and the intrusive male leaves.

It is clear, therefore, that the bachelors, though inhibited, have a motivation to mate, a motivation which in their case is swamped by fear of causing attacks. There may be a physiological/psychological switch mechanism in such species which is set at 'go' for a few males, 'stop' for the rest. The genes that the 'go' males transmit must programme for both conditions – a situation not hard to accept since many gene-based body processes are of this kind. Thus we must assume that the reproductive males transmit genes which can produce brains capable of the inhibition of sexual activity in one type of social environment, and its expression in another. The former environment could most simply be specified as 'sexually available females absent', the latter as 'sexually available females present'. Such two-way signals exist throughout the animal kingdom; rats respond to 'infant in nest' by care and attention, but to 'infant outside nest' by retrieval. Female birds like red grouse and female mammals like the African waterbuck respond to 'male on territory' in the breeding season by adopting mating postures, but to 'male off territory' in non-mating ways.

Can human celibacy be understood in similar terms? Whatever the processes underlying celibacy, it seems rather naïve to suppose that they could be transmitted in the form of 'go'/'stop' systems based on neural inhibition and facilitation of social responses. Are we really going to reduce the long, subtle and well-documented process of development of the idea of 'self' (Mead 1934) and the lessons of social psychology to this? (see Reynolds 1980). Do we assume that celibates 'want' to mate, but their wanting is curtailed by more powerful inhibitory processes? Are we to assume that the non-celibates who do reproduce pass on in their genes a programme to inhibit sex, or at any rate copulation, in particular circumstances? Is this not to reduce the spiritual element we have stressed earlier in this chapter to some sort of rationalization of a weak or cowardly disposition? Are celibates cowards?

There seems no reason to doubt that humans in general do inherit to a remarkable, perhaps unlimited degree the ability to inhibit inherited tendencies. Indeed this is a hallmark of the human condition in the thinking of writers such as Freud and Levi-Strauss, although we would want to see this as a primate characteristic found to greater or lesser degree in other species such as macaques and baboons. Chance and Mead (1953) have seen it as a central feature of primate and human social evolution.

Whether celibates 'want' to copulate and would engage in copulation if circumstances permitted it, is another matter. Human cultural inhibition is not like animal inhibition. We make ourselves, and in so doing we can make ourselves into people who are sexually uninterested and disinterested. What we 'want' sometimes has biological foundations and sometimes not, but in either event it reaches us through the customs, rules and social prohibitions of our particular society during the socialization process, and it is with reference to the expectations of those around us that we set up our own projects with their aims and standards of conduct. To elect for the celibate life may involve inhibition of libido but it involves a lot more besides – a conscious choice to follow a certain way of life, with its own opportunities for self expression, its own rewards. To inhibit mating, for man, may be a 'best', not a second best, as indeed is the case in Pauline Christianity or in some forms of Buddhism and other cults.

Likewise, regarding the arguments for kin selection (based on family size) and for reciprocal altruism (based on mutual benefits), all such processes in man would have to be seen in terms of cultural or sub-cultural meaning systems. Just because celibates have more siblings than non-celibates, and contribute to their survival and reproductive success, we cannot and should not conclude that this is evidence of phylogenetically evolved causes unless we can show it is *not* caused by the ordinary bases of human action, i.e. the self-construction process, and the process of making choices that are considered 'rational' and 'sensible' in any given culture or sub-group. Thus a big family may promote celibacy in one or more of its offspring as a sensible economic choice, or a child may come to this choice on his or her own. An only child, who stands to inherit a parental estate, may not think much of recourse to an institution of monks or nuns, whereas for a child with many competing siblings or in a system of primogeniture, this may be a very wise choice. This is not to say that the idea of celibacy is dependent on material matters; for some it is attractive in its own right. Whatever the

XVIII. Buddhist monks in Thailand receiving gifts of food in the early morning with downcast eyes and without speaking, from women devotees.

circumstances, and however close the biological parallels, it is certain that any explanation of celibacy needs to be based on a theory of human action, not a theory of animal behaviour (Reynolds 1980).

The Buddhist case of celibacy illustrates how culture presents its rules of inhibition. *The Patimokkha* (1966), the monastic rules which monks recite twice a month on Buddhist Sabbath days, contains many regulations aimed at minimizing the occasions for interaction with females. (See Plate XVIII.)

Monks are even forbidden to touch their mothers. For example, if the mother of a monk should fall into a ditch, her son may offer her a stick but not a hand and has to think of himself as pulling out a log of wood. Nor may monks sleep under the same roof as a female animal. The main object of the rule is to lead to the suppression and ultimately the extinction of bodily and especially sexual desire. This, combined with such comments from the Buddha that 'it were better for you, foolish man, that your male organ should enter the mouth of a terrible and poisonous snake, than that it should enter a woman' (*The Book of the Discipline* 1:36) must inhibit the sexual interests of any men who take their Buddhist faith seriously. Also the monk is sustained in his fidelity to celibacy by the fear of karmic retribution, punishment in hell and rebirth in a form delaying his final deliverance from desire, as well as by the fear of expulsion from the order and public disgrace.

Functional aspects of celibacy

But granted that cultural prescriptions and proscriptions rather than physical perceptions, lead to inhibition of the sexual life, what purpose does it all serve? What are the benefits? We know that the Christian celibate has eschewed marriage not in response to a basic Christian injunction to avoid sexual relationships, but to enable him to be of greater service to others. We can examine the families from which celibates come to see whether they receive any biological advantages from the religiously motivated celibacy of their siblings.

We have been unable to ascertain whether such celibacy has enabled other siblings to have more children than they would otherwise have done if there had been no celibate in the family. Prior to the Second Vatican Conference in 1963 religious orders and dioceses did not accept candidates for training without charge; candidates were expected to pay dowries or maintenance fees during their years of training and this in most cases would have come from their families initially. So a sibling going into religious life would not have immediately relieved his family of any financial strain; just the contrary, in fact.

There are, however, special cases. We have already cited the case of a poor Irish family with 13 children of whom 4 were taken into religious orders without cost to their family, as a result of which the remaining children were doubtless better able to marry, for in the case of the daughters the parents had to provide an expensive dowry. Perhaps of some importance is the support given by religious orders to the elderly parents of their members. This would have better enabled grandparents to care for their grandchildren in the past, but today the dispersal of the three generation family makes this less likely.

Contemporary religious celibates we have spoken to in the affluent West were unable to provide any examples of reproductively advantageous help to families, and none could think of siblings of celibates who received such help. We have similarly tried to find out whether such siblings might receive any preferential medical services particularly in a Catholic country. While we are inclined to think that this must occur or did in fact occur up to quite recently in places where such facilities are run by religious orders, we have been unable to get any hard data to support this contention.

In developing countries it is more likely than elsewhere that the families of religious celibates might have a biological advantage over other families. Catholic religious orders run many medical and educational institutions in tropical areas and priority would be given to their families. It has been reported to us that in the Diocese of Benin the sisters of priests and nuns would be given free fertility treatment at Roman Catholic hospitals should they ask for it. However, very few Congolese senior seminarians thought that they would be able to aid their families materially rather than spiritually; most thought that once they were ordained, their families would be able to help *them* materially (Noirhomme 1969). We can perhaps conclude at the most that where the celibate is highly thought of, his family will benefit medically from his unmarried state wherever the Roman Catholic Church runs enough separate medical institutions to make this feasible.

In some primates it can be argued that the advantages of non-reproductive all-male groups are that they provide a 'reproductive reserve'. In the case of hamadryas baboons, a semi-desert, arid environment means that the big groups that sleep together on the cliffs have to break up for foraging during the day. This they do every day, mostly into groups consisting of one male and a number of females and their young. The remaining males form all-male bands, where a mating inhibition operates. No species has been described in which the females form non-reproducing bands. This arid environment puts the obtaining of adequate nutrition at a premium; there is no time of year in which resources are super-abundant; the all-male groups are permanent not seasonal and a male may spend all his life as a 'bachelor'.

In the human case, we must consider whether r^- selection is the process underlying the religious insistence on celibacy and the idea that the spirituality of the holy life is incompatible with the life of reproduction and sexuality. We have already suggested that r^- selection is a basis for the idea that non-reproductive sex is sinful, even in marriage. We have also seen that Christianity, the dominant religion in the secure but resource-tight West, expresses r^- – selection, while Hinduism tends towards higher levels of sexual and reproductive activity, as does Islam. It therefore seems not unreasonable to think of Christian celibacy as an outcome of r^- – selection; it thrives where man can plan adequately for the long-term utilization of a secure but tight basis of scarce resources. Where resources and other aspects of the environment are hard or impossible to foresee and control, celibacy does not thrive, and r^+ + selection favours customs and institutions that maximize the reproductive, and further the sexual, activity of all members of the community, to provide the surplus necessary for the times of severe losses that, inevitably, lie somewhere ahead.

In Christian countries the number of celibates is never very great, but it has varied according to time and place. Flick (1930) states that 6 per cent of the adult women in fourteenth century Frankfurt were in religious houses. This may, in terms of proximate causation, be due to the disproportionate excess of women to men in the populations of late medieval European cities: Nuremberg had 1,207 per 1,000 men, Basel 1,246, and Rostock 1,295 (Heer 1962). Both Le Bas (1840–45) and Chabot (1827) give the number of religious celibates in pre-revolutionary France at over 400,000 which was approximately 2–5 per cent of the adult population.

Celibates in Buddhist societies are always men. The Burmese Ministry of Religious Affairs estimates that monks constituted 10 per cent of the male population in the late 1950s (Spiro 1971). Waddell (1967) referring to an 1894 opinion, estimated a fifth of the male population of Sikkim and Bhutan were monks and that the proportion for Tibet and Ladakh was a third, while contemporary estimates for Thailand and Sri Lankha suggest much lower figures not exceeding 2 per cent.

As important as the question of numbers however, is the question of whether these celibates can be considered as a reserve of 'breeding partners' waiting to take over where active reproductives die or fail. In the case of Christianity it seems certainly not to be the case that where, say, a father dies or a husband dies, a monk steps in and takes over the relevant reproductive activities, although a dispensation can be obtained in such situations when a sufficiently strong case has been made out. Nor do nuns see it as their duty to take over the uxorial functions of wives who die before their husbands. The celibate is already married – to God. His or her life has been dedicated to the Almighty and such vows are for life. In the case of Buddhist monks, Spiro asked a small sample of 20 Burmese ex-monks their reasons for leaving the monastery and only three cited family responsibilities, but these fell short of actual reproduction (Spiro 1971: 407).

Thus whereas the explanation for the evolution of non-reproduction in some animals is based on the fact that those genes that achieve most replication do so by programming for non-reproductive behavioural strategies that enhance kin fertility through certain kinds of relationships, this whole gene-based pattern of explanation is not applicable to the mechanisms involved in the human case. The condition of celibacy is not an outcome of differential selection at the genetic level, and consequent behaviour programming. Instead, we suggest that the idea of the godly, ascetic, humble, chaste life of the celibate is transmitted in and by those religions and cultures in which long-term planning is based on the assumption of a tight but secure resource base. Are there advantages of celibacy to large groups as well as individuals and families? We have already seen that sometimes celibates come from larger than average families. Are there also advantages, e.g. of food distribution or living conditions or health care, for the community in general?

Christian celibates in fact run a wide range of institutions which benefit the community in general and have done so from early medieval days. Indeed some orders are considered to have played an essential part in the development of medicine and the place of the Society of Jesus in education is well known. Celibates in religious orders run both general and specialized hospitals for the old, the insane, alcoholics, drug addicts and for child-bearing. They also run homes for unmarried mothers, orphans, cripples, the homeless and the disturbed, and provide food and care for homeless transients. But no generalizations are possible: both Islam and Hinduism run institutions for the help of the community but they are not run by celibates. Buddhist priests, perhaps the largest proportion of celibates in their societies in the world today, do very little social work and run few institutions. Buddhism is not greatly concerned with alleviating immediate physical suffering (although there is traditional Buddhist science of medicine and there are doctors). But some suffering is considered by Buddhists to be a necessary condition of human existence. For parentless children in Burma, however, there is the Social Service Sangha Association which in 1962 had 77 orphanages affiliated to Buddhist monasteries, catering for male orphans only. Nevertheless, it has been said that for the vast majority of Buddhist monks 'social service is viewed not only as irrelevant but an obstacle to their quest for salvation' (Spiro 1971).

One of the main social contributions made by celibates in countries such as those we have looked at, where a considerable fraction of the adult male population is celibate, seems thus to be a slowing of the birth rate and consequently a limiting of the rate of population growth. Can we substantiate this idea?

It is commonly stated in arguments against celibacy in developing countries, that celibates fail to contribute children to what are seen as 'the nation's needs'. Discussions in what used to be Tanganyika (now Tanzania) (personal observation, R. Tanner) prior to independence certainly focused on this aspect and made no reference to the usefulness of celibate priests for the needs of their parishioners. Much the same idea seems to have been current in the French Revolutionary government in its campaigns to make Christian celibates marry. They may have had grounds for taking this line, for both Chabot (1827) and Le Bas (1840–45) put the pre-revolutionary number of celibates at over 400,000 in a population of perhaps 10–20 million. The Russian demographer Dondog (1972) has related the number of lamas in Outer Mongolia to the low rate of population growth there. It thus seems that if celibacy is a population control device, some governments do not know this, or do not approve of it. This is scarely surprising, however, for few if any governments are ecologically-minded. Our own conclusion is that celibacy cannot be seen in isolation, but if treated as part of a complex of ideas it does fit into the demographic picture as a means of using existing resources, human and environmental, efficiently.

Conclusions

What conclusions can we draw from this examination of celibacy from a biological point of view? One finding would seem to be that a false interpretation of this phenomenon could be quite easily mounted from a genetic starting point. We have what can be considered in socio-biological terms an 'altruistic behaviour pattern' involving 100 per cent loss of personal reproductive fitness. This loss is sometimes compensated for by the fact that celibates have larger-than-normal numbers of kin, and their own activities help those kin to achieve a higher level of reproductive success than in families without celibates. Also, we do have some evidence that celibacy runs in families.

However, despite its biological attractions, we must reject this interpretative scheme. The focus on reproductive sex, genes, altruism and inclusive fitness is a distortion induced by excessively narrow biological thinking. In fact, celibacy is but one aspect of a much wider call to service, service to the community and to God. Such a call occurs during the process of self-construction of the developing person, in his or her contact with the religious elements of the community and culture. We suggest that the benefits of such service have persisted in the way so many aspects of the division of labour have persisted in human societies – by the conscious selection, among available alternatives, of activities useful to individuals, families, and groups. Conscious traditional transmission by religious groups would favour such a process over the centuries if the groups that obtained better social service from specially designated religious people, dedicated to give their life's efforts to helping others, did better in the obtaining and distribution of scarce resources than those without such specialist orders.

At the individual level, self-esteem and a satisfying life style lead some people into celibacy. The group itself provides the institutions and training necessary. In functional terms this is done to provide various kinds of charity towards group members who are in some kind of difficulty. But functionalism only takes us a little way. In wider terms it seems very commonly the case that celibacy is a concomitant of high levels of spirituality. This clearly expresses a widespread dualism in man's thinking, as if it were not possible in certain cultures to be both sensual and godly. This, however, is not universal, for we have noted religions in which the very opposite is the case.

So, whatever 'functions' celibacy may have, they are not universally applicable. In some cultures, such as those embracing Hinduism, Islam, and Judaism, celibacy has little if any religious backing for all but a very few sects, and the practice of celibacy goes against common ideas of what is 'good'. We thus end up with the curious polarity: that in some cultures celibacy is next to godliness while in others it denies the holiness of sex.

This polarity is of the greatest interest, following, as it does, the one we came across in Chapter 7 in which sex *per se* within marriage was considered good and spiritually desirable in some cultures, but sinful in others (unless consciously for purposes of reproduction). The chief line of division in Chapter 7 was between Christianity, especially Roman Catholicism, and other cultures and religions, especially Islam and Hinduism. With regard to the present chapter we can see the division is between Buddhism and Christianity (again Roman Catholicism) and Hinduism and Islam together with Judaism. We noted also the presence of celibacy in the ancient civilizations of the Aztecs and Incas.

Always when it occurs, it concerns priests, who may be of one or both sexes. The crucial relationship seems to be the connection between sexual activity on the one hand, and spirituality on the other. This relationship can be positive or negative. Where it is positive, i.e. where sex is spiritually good, we suggest that cultural selection has tended to be of the $r+$ variety; where it is negative, i.e. where sex is thought to impede full spiritual growth, we suggest that a more $r-$ type of cultural selection has been at work.

Divorce and widowhood 9

In Chapter 7 we dealt with religion and marriage: how different religions organize marriage; the ratio of males to females in marriage; the reproduction rate of married couples; the advantages there may be for children born within marriage; how marriage is important for the integration of the family into society (with benefits to food supply from help of kinsmen, and so on). These aspects of marriage have biological implications in that they affect the health and welfare of the adults who are doing the reproduction and of the children produced; thus these issues are central to a proper consideration of the reproductive success of individuals within a human community, and hence to the process of human evolution itself.

In this chapter we want to look at the opposite side of the marriage coin – marital breakdown in one form or another, either because of death or accident to a spouse or loss of other kinds, and such ways and means as may exist to change the situation so that reproduction in its proper social context can continue.

From a biological point of view it is clearly debatable whether marital 'breakdown' may not be advantageous in certain circumstances. For example, if a marriage is infertile and one of the partners is responsible, then the remarriage of the fertile partner would be biologically advantageous for that individual (or his/her genes) as soon as he or she had children.

Another point which could be made in favour of having mechanisms of marital dissolution is that the children might benefit from the termination of a difficult marriage and therefore be more inclined to grow up as healthy individuals to reproduce in their turn. For instance if one of the marriage partners was permanently sick and unable to bring food into the household or cope with the children's needs, it would be good biological policy for a way to exist by which the affected person might be replaced.

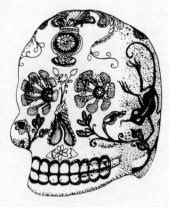

Sugar coffins, marzipan graves and skulls are made to be eaten on All Souls' Day (November 2) in Mexico. In this way the family remembers its loved ones now deceased.

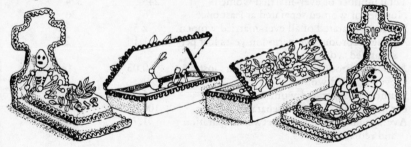

In wider terms, the terms of real life situations, for marriages in which this actually occurs the problem posed will be one of the depth and quality of the relationship between the married couple, so it may be preferred to keep the sick partner within the marriage. In this case marriage acts against the interests of the children from a biological point of view if (and only if) their reproductive success is impaired by their parents' difficulties. It is often, however, the case that the children of divorced marriages do get some degree of preferential treatment, either in the form of goods and services from near kinsmen or in the form of financial assistance from public or private institutions.

Clearly also this problem has many psychological aspects. Modern Western society promotes the ideal of a marriage as being 'happy' and the belief that family-reared children are better adjusted and happier thereby. This ideology does not exist in all parts of the world. We are concerned with psychological aspects if they cause direct physical breakdown of the marriage in biological terms, as in many cases they certainly do.

The possible effects of divorce

Let us start with a consideration of divorce, that is the termination of a marriage by either partner. This may in fact be impossible in some religions or very difficult, as in Roman Catholicism and the first marriages of high caste Hindus. Or it may be a relatively simple matter as in some African societies where a wife has only to break a cooking pot and put it outside the door of the hut for her husband, on returning home, to discover that he has been divorced.

What are the biological effects of divorce? For a start there is clearly the termination of the reproductive partnership. If the divorce comes before children are produced, the reproductive success of these two spouses will remain at zero if they do not remarry. Very often, however, divorced individuals do remarry and so their reproduction is just delayed. A study made of Bengali Muslims (Nag 1962) calculated the reproductive period lost through separation (see Table 9.1). In a sample of 819 wives the average period lost was between 1.1 years for higher class women and 2.5 years for lower class women. The average interval in years between separation and remarriage was between 1.7 and 2.4

Table 9.1 Loss of reproductive period to women due to separation, in two Muslim groups (From: Nag 1962)

	Sheikh Muslims	Non-Sheikh Muslims
Total number of ever-married women	245	574
Number of women separated at least once	6	36
Per cent separated of all ever-married women	2.5	6.3
Average reproductive period in years lost per separated woman	1.1	2.5
Average reproductive period in years lost per ever-married woman	0.03	0.17
Number of separated women remarried	6	34
Per cent remarried of all separated women	100.0	94.4
Average interval in years between separation and remarriage	1.7	2.4

	Sheikh Muslims	Non-Sheikh Muslims	Hindus
Total number of ever-married women	245	574	237
Number of women widowed at least once	37	93	31
Per cent widowed of all ever-married women	15.1	16.2	13.1
Average reproductive period in years lost per widowed woman	6.8	7.4	9.6
Average reproductive period in years lost per ever-married woman	1.0	1.2	1.3
Number of widowed women remarried	2	28	0
Per cent remarried of all widowed women	5.4	30.1	0.0
Average interval in years between death of husband and remarriage	10.0	3.6	

Table 9.2 Loss of reproductive period of women due to widowhood, in two Muslim and one Hindu groups (From: Nag 1962)

years. Virtually all these women married again as most separations occurred very early in their first marriages. Among widows there were numbers who failed to remarry as their ages were higher, and the average reproductive period lost by them was between 6.8 and 7.4 years. In a Hindu group the comparable figure was 9.6 years (see Table 9.2). Comparative data relating to remarriage of widows in a Christian society can be found in Marris (1959, Ch. 5).

There is thus a difference by religion, with a greater loss for Hindu widows than Muslim ones, a point to which we shall return.

The infertile marriage and religion

In tribal systems which are deeply concerned with the survival of the clan, the family or the individual as a descendant, the infertile wife is the most miserable of women. Among the Sukuma a barren wife crisscrosses the tribal region seeking the reason for her condition in an endless series of consultations with traditional spirit investigators who might be able to tell her how to get her ancestors to withdraw their malevolence so that she can conceive. The Sukuma marriage ceremony only initiates a marriage; it becomes a continuing and developing institution if children are born. The marriage then becomes part of the social and religious fabric of the community instead of remaining marginal (Tanner 1957 and 1958). Among these people infertility of the wife is cause for divorce irrespective of the length of the marriage (Cory 1953). To a lesser extent this is also true of incapacity of the husband to beget children. This situation is paralleled in many African tribal societies.

Where cultures and their religions are heavily procreative in tone, as in Islam or especially Hinduism where the husband has a direct religious need for a son to prevent him suffering in the next world, the position of the infertile wife is extremely uncertain and full of anxiety.

In Hinduism, even if she is fertile but has produced only daughters her status is still low; she has failed in her main role as the producer of male children. The pressure is even greater on the wives of prominent men. The status to which she aspires in both these religions is to be known as the mother of a son, a more important role than being known as the wife of a certain man.

Infertility has often been adequate grounds for divorce in Islam as well as among the lower castes in Hinduism. In Judaism it has similarly been a suitable ground for divorce provided that it is proven. According to Jebamoth vi:6 'If one married a woman and waited with her 10 years without her bearing a child, he is not permitted to remain exempt from the duty of procreation. When he divorced her she may remarry and the second husband waits with her 10 years' (The Talmud). In Christianity the infertility of either the man or the woman is no grounds for divorce, nor even for an annulment, since any assessment of infertility must come after consummation and it is the act of consummation that seals the marriage in the eyes of the Church and of God. It may well be that in medieval and modern Christian agricultural communities this fact resulted in the high rate of premarital conceptions of many brides, as farmers and others would not risk being stuck with an infertile wife whom they could not divorce. We should note, however, that the relation between divorce and reproductive failure is just as the r^- / r^+ principle would lead one to expect, with, interestingly, Judaism on the r^+ side.

Many tribal societies, and indeed most societies (including sectors of the most urbanized Western ones) pay considerable attention to invoking the help of the Divine in making marriages fertile. The Lugbara of Uganda (Middleton 1971) have fertility shrines to which offerings are made if any wives or daughters of the lineage are barren, and in fact the Lugbara ancestor cult and similar cults in other African societies are concerned among other things with maintaining fertility. Prayers, sacrifices and visits to the local witch-doctor or medicine man are made by individuals seeking fertility.

Hinduism and Buddhism have always had special shrines in their temples for 'problem solution' purposes (Bhardwaj 1973) and some shrines are particularly devoted to curing barren women. Dubois (1972) and El Saadawi (1980) have suggested that Hindu and Muslim women subject themselves to sexual intercourse by the priest of the temple or the mullah in the hope of becoming pregnant. Alternatively the women may offer to grant sexual intercourse to a certain number of pilgrims to the shrine as a thanks offering to the titular deity for his aid in becoming pregnant. All these methods are in fact religious solutions to the problem deeply felt by infertile wives, which they perceive as a danger to their marriages. But even where the danger of divorce is less real, wives and their husbands continue to want children. Visitors today to Greek Orthodox churches will see beside the more popular icons the plentiful little silver panels which testify to answered prayers, and numbers of these show they are expressing gratitude for babies born in answer to their prayers (see Plate xix). Some religions allow for the replacement of an infertile wife and Hinduism provides such a woman with religiously sanctioned support. Christianity however forbids the abandonment of an infertile wife, thus inevitably involving a reduction in fertility for affected spouses.

XIX. Another plaque of the kind shown at the beginning of Chapter 7. This one expresses thanks that prayers for a child have been answered.

Annulment of unconsummated marriages

The procedure of annulment has been favoured by the Judaeo-Christian religions because in their eyes the unconsummated marriage has never properly existed in the first place. In the same vein St Paul refers to marital intercourse as the debt which the spouses owe to each other because of the marital contract. Roman Catholic theologians such as Davis (1946) have held that unconsummated Christian marriages can be annulled on account of the impotence of the husband, or the physical incapacity of either party to complete the marriage act. Some have gone beyond this to allow annulment for incurable incompatibility of temperament, as in the case of arranged marriages in France and Italy in the nineteenth century, when the bride cannot stand the sight of her new husband, or when she lives in dread of family discord after having been talked into a marriage by her family when she wanted another man, or even when her husband wanted another woman; also on the grounds that one party has obtained a civil divorce in order to marry religiously; also in situations in which the spouse is forced into marriage in order to keep a man or woman out of further sexual trouble or 'incontinency' as it may be called. Finally there is annulment on the grounds of contagious disease, where one spouse suddenly realizes that the other has venereal disease or leprosy, or for reasons of behaviour, namely that one partner requires the other to perform an act of sexual perversion.

Islam provides (Russell and Suhrawardy n.d.) for the annulment of marriage if either party is sexually incapable of carrying out intercourse which both husband and wife have the right to receive from each other. Islam has additional grounds for annulment where the marriage contract has not been fulfilled if the bride was described as a virgin when she was not, or if promises to pay the dowry before consummation were not kept (Westermarck 1914).

Judaism makes similar allowances for annulment on the grounds of defects or disabilities in the wife or husband preventing 'cohabitation'. This term is somewhat wider in its possible interpretation than the mere absence of the ability to have sexual intercourse and goes beyond questions of dangerous and contagious diseases (*Encyc.Judaica* 6:128).

All the above rules make 'good' biological sense in that they terminate partnerships that would be reproductive failures, and limit the spread of disease. The emphasis on sexual and psychological compatibility, found in Christianity especially, can be related to the process of $r-$ selection, if we assume it is an important feature of long-term parental care of offspring rather than mere reproductive success, as seems very probable.

Remarriage after divorce in Hinduism

Divorce is not permitted in high caste Hinduism but it occurs in lower castes. So any assertion of higher caste status requires the relinquishment of the opportunity to divorce (Kane 1950). Since traditional Hindu marriage was sacred and therefore indissoluble this restrained the breakdown of marriages except by desertion; now a series of new laws has made the civil dissolution of a religious marriage possible under somewhat onerous grounds (Hindu Marriage Act 1955). While the number of divorces has risen, Hindu marriage remains very stable. Studies of contemporary Hinduism often do not contain any description or details of divorce. The relation between ease of divorce and caste is as would be predicted on the assumption that resources are more stable in higher than lower castes, which must be the case.

If divorce occurs under this new legislation it is tantamount to a reduction in caste status and this itself prevents or certainly reduces the possibility of the divorced or divorcing person remarrying except lower down the socio-religious scale. In addition there is the Hindu insistence on the sanctity of first marriages which goes far beyond most concepts of a sacramental marriage: the husband is held in high religious esteem; divorce involves something approaching apostasy. Again this restrains divorce from the woman's side.

Furthermore in Hinduism we see not only religious sentiment against divorce but a proscription against remarriage. Just as the remarriage of widows is scandalous, that of female divorcees is even more so. The rejected or rejecting wife is expected to devote herself to sexual abstinence and the care of such children as she may have. We should recall, however, that these rules are characteristic of the higher castes only, and thus constitute less of an anomaly in what we have designated a 'pro-reproductive' religion than would otherwise be the case.

Islamic divorce and remarriage

Muhammad, according to the Traditions, did not approve of divorce calling it the thing most hated by God (*Mishkat al-Masabih*). Nevertheless the Koran gives the husband complete freedom to divorce his wife by simply saying 'I divorce you' three times (Koran, Sura 2.229). Should the husband wish to remarry the same woman, she has first to be married to another man, and then re-divorced (Koran, Sura 2.230) with three menstrual periods delay between each divorce and marriage.

The Koran contains many details of the procedure for divorce but little on the grounds for it. Since no justification for divorcing a wife is demanded by the Koran, the husband can do so without any reason other than his own caprice (Russell and Suhrawardy n.d. and Aghaba-

bian 1951). The only restraint on divorce by the husband is that he is required to pay the unpaid part of any marriage agreement with his wife's
family, but alternatively the wife could encourage her husband to divorce her by agreeing to forfeit any part of the money that was still
owed.

So there are restraints on Muslim divorce apart from the expenses of
paying the bride-price for a new wife. While it may have been possible
for the richer man to divorce frequently, there are restraints from the
fact that many Islamic marriages are alliances between two families.
The poor subsistence farmer must always be circumspect in the use of
his powers to divorce. Islamic countries generally have put secular legal
restraints on the husband's religious right to divorce. From 1950 in
Egypt husbands have to give their reasons in court before a divorce can
become effective, and both Algeria and Tunisia have ruled that divorces
can only be decided in the courts. So the religious aspects of divorce,
except where there is collusion between the parties, seem to be of dimi-
nishing contemporary importance, especially in the larger, modernizing
North African states, which is just as we would expect if $r-$ selection is
beginning to replace $r+$ selection in these areas.

In dealing with the biological aspects of Muslim divorce we must
first be concerned with its effects on the fertility of women. Quite a
number of divorced women remarry their original husbands; about 11
per cent in Egypt in 1948. Presumably in such cases the only interrup-
tion in the wife's fecundity would be the minimum period of three
months' separation to allow her to remarry (see above).

As Islam lauds the married state and most Islamic countries provide
few if any roles for the unmarried or divorced woman who does not
wish to remarry, it is certain that if they can they will remarry quickly
after the obligatory delay. This is again not the case with divorced
women in Western countries. The younger divorced woman in the
West may or may not decide to remarry, but there is normally a longer
time gap: 50 per cent of divorcees in the USA are still unmarried two
years after their divorces (Goode 1965). So what we have in Islam in
biological terms is a relatively small reduction in fertility consequent on
divorce. Remarriage is often arranged by families, particularly when the
divorce is of a childless woman in the first few years of her marriage
(Jordan, *Statistical Yearbook* 1960). In any system depending on arranged
marriages few women are left 'on the shelf' as this is considered to be
bad for the prestige of their families, quite apart from other considerations. As regards fertility we have already shown in Chapter 5 that
Muslim natality is consistently high. Thus ease of divorce together with
a short post-divorce period and a relatively frequent remarriage rate, all
characteristic of Islam, can be seen as products of $r+$ selection.

Islam and fornication
The killing of adulterous persons rather than mere divorce is often considered to be a specific characteristic of Islam so we shall examine the
issue, since the biological effects of such a procedure are clearly profound. Muhammad's views on this subject appear to have changed during the course of his public life and the Koran reveals these changes
when it is examined according to the probable time sequence of its
verses and chapters. The avoidance of fornication, i.e. sexual intercourse between persons who are not either married or in concubinage,

is the mark of the believer (Koran 17.34 and 25.68). Proof of adultery requires four witnesses (Koran 4. 19–20) and if it is proved, the adulteress is to be confined in her house until she dies. But the text allows for repentance. Muhammad took a different line after the suspicions of others about his own wife Aisha, stating that fornicators should be beaten with a hundred strokes (Koran 24.2) and he doubled the penalty for his own wives should they be involved (Koran 33.30).

There is nothing in the Koran which authorizes the killing of an adulterous woman as such and yet this appears to have happened frequently (Antoun 1968; Canaan 1931; Gibb and Kramers 1953). Much seems to rest on the 'verse of stoning', not usually considered to be an original part of the Koran (Gibb and Kramers 1953) which states: 'If a man and a woman who have reached years of discretion, commit adultery, stone them in every case as Allah's punishment'. This is one of a number of verses which the Caliph Omar thought were laid down in the Koran until he was convinced to the contrary by lack of evidence (Watt 1970a).

It seems unlikely that there was ever such a harsh ruling, and if there was we should note its inclusion of men. Possibly we have here a ruling used to cover a small residue of cases which involved complicated issues of honour which could not be resolved by the usual processes. The killings of adulterous women are not Islamic religiously imposed solutions in the Muhammadan sense, but arose from subsequent falsifications and distortions.

Christianity: divorce and remarriage

Almost all Christian denominations prohibit divorce for their adherents or allow remarriage only for what is regarded as the 'innocent' partner. They actively discourage their members from breaking their marriage vows since these are based on the Gospel statement 'what therefore God hath joined together, let not man put asunder' (Matthew 19:6).

Although in earlier centuries various Councils and Divines wavered over the issues involved, it was from the sixteenth century Council of Trent that separation rather than divorce was allowed on the grounds of adultery, apostasy, cruelty and heresy, but in all such cases the tie of matrimony was not broken so remarriage was forbidden.

In all this, Christianity has taken a different line from Judaism which has always allowed divorce by the husband, though with certain restrictions (Westermarck 1921). For instance, barrenness of the wife had to be proved, and if there was premarital intercourse with the bride this disallowed subsequent divorce (Deuteronomy 22:29). Divorce was also disallowed in cases of the wife's insanity, or her youthfulness making it impossible for her to understand the implications of what would happen to her, and in addition a false accusation that she was not a virgin on her marriage disallowed her husband from subsequently divorcing her (Deuteronomy 22:19). But there was no restriction on the wife's remarriage after divorce (Deuteronomy 24:2).

The Christian hard line against accepting marital failure reinforced the structure of marriage. Before Christianity became a popular religion attracting enormous numbers of converts, the early Christians may well have encountered the same problems that faced Muhammad at an early date in his creation of the new Muslim community. It was logistically necessary to hold Christian marriages together so that the new communities could continue to exist and build up into further generations of Christian families. In later times Christian cultures have evidently maintained or reinforced the idea of marriage as a life-long, indissoluble institution.

Christian Sukuma women in Tanzania prefer to be married to Christians rather than traditionalists because of the added security which the Christian concept of marriage gives to their unions (personal observation, R. Tanner). By its stress on permanence in the eyes of God, Christianity reduces the strain of possible failure and contributes substantially to the persistence of the social and biological unit of society within which children are reared. Marriage is held in high esteem, and the security it brings is favoured over and above the satisfaction of sexual desire and reproductive success.

In most religions, adjustment to marital problems has been required in the main from wives. This is less so in Christianity where wives have a much higher standing than in Islam or Hinduism. Christian wives are further felt to gain a special ethical dignity from their forbearance, perhaps even suffering, in difficult marriages; this concept of 'unselfish love' encourages marriage survival.

What effects does Christianity have on keeping marriages going and restraining divorce? The Catholic Church with its total prohibition on divorce has the lowest actual divorce rate among Christian denominations (see Table 9.3). In comparison with the non-religious, religious people generally have lower marital breakdown rates if only because the former find it easier to accept the idea of divorce (Burchinal and Chancellor 1963). Inter-religious marriages fall in between these two rates. These rates are in the expected direction and indeed it would be surprising if the practising members of Churches prohibiting divorce were not affected by their rulings. Religiosity holds spouses together; its absence in a sample of marriages surveyed by Landis (1960) raised the divorce rate fourfold. This survey also found that where there was a divorce,

	(%)
Maryland (Bell 1938)	
Both parties Catholic	6.4
Both parties Protestant	6.8
Mixed	15.2
No religion	16.7
Spokane, Washington (Weeks 1943)	
Both parties Catholic	3.8
Both parties Protestant	10.0
Mixed	17.4
No religion	23.9
Michigan (Landis 1949)	
Both parties Catholic	4.4
Both parties Protestant	6.0
Mixed	14.1
No religion	17.9

Table 9.3 Divorce rates by religions (From: Landis, 1949)

Table 9.4 Catholic and
Protestant rates of
remarriage by time since
divorce, Metropolitan Detroit
1948 (From: Goode 1965)

	Catholics (%)	Protestants (%)
Divorced 8 months	13	17
Divorced 14 months	35	41
Divorced 26 months	49	59

more Catholics than Protestants considered themselves to have been
seriously emotionally upset, even to have displayed symptoms of physical ill health.

There is little information on differential rates of remarriage in different religions except that the percentage of Protestants remarrying
seems always somewhat higher than among Catholics (see Table 9.4).
Goode (1965) discloses that nearly half of divorced Catholics refused to
be interviewed for his study which suggests that they were well aware
that they were violating their Church's doctrine. It also appears that in a
religious marriage, it is the spouse who rarely attends services who
makes the first suggestion about divorce (Goode 1965).

The widowed and remarriage: the levirate

Let us now consider the phenomenon of widowhood. Where a man
dies leaving a widow with or without children and the woman is still
fertile but has no mate, many societies have developed social mechanisms to enable her to continue married life. One such is the 'levirate'. In
the levirate the woman is remarried to her dead husband's brother.
From a socio-biological point of view this is a splendid arrangement as
it has the required genetic properties: the new husband is investing his
energies in the rearing of children who bear his brother's (i.e. 50% of
his own) genes. In the terms of social anthropology the levirate is carefully constructed to keep the existing children and any future ones within the clan of the dead husband. This type of remarriage is widespread
in human societies, and has an ancient history.

There is an ancient Semitic tradition given in the Bible, (Genesis
38:8; see also Deuteronomy 25:5–6; Matthew 22:24; Mark 12:19; Luke
20:28) encouraging the brother 'to marry her [the widow of a brother]
and raise up seed to thy brother' so it is not surprising that in Judaism a
brother had the obligation to marry such a widow, especially if his
brother had died without offspring (*Encyc. Judaica* 1971), and had to release her formally before she could remarry anyone else. Indeed this
rule has recently caused trouble in Israel where the deceased husband's
brothers may be living abroad. Legal provision has had to be made for
Israeli women to be able to apply to the Rabbinical Courts to get a formal release in cases where the brother was not traceable or refused to
give it.

The Nuer of the Sudan practice 'ghost marriage', a form of levirate
(Evans-Pritchard 1956) in which the widow is neither inherited nor remarried but continues to be married to her dead husband while cohabit-
ing with his brother until she dies. Any children she bears to the
brother carry her dead husband's name. The Nuer also have a further
kinship fiction to ensure the survival of the name of a dead bachelor
who has no male heir and of course leaves no widow to bear him male

heirs through a brother. In such cases the lineage can marry a woman *to his name* in a properly legitimate marriage and whatever sons she may bear from whatever lover will carry the dead man's name even though he will not even have known the woman while he was alive; so he will survive as a social entity. Here we see most clearly the distinction between social and genetic inheritance.

The levirate is certainly common in some Arab communities where about half of all widows marry their husband's brothers (Rosenfeld 1958). There are many biological advantages in such arrangements. As the widow is inherited by her husband's brother, she will not have far to go to her new husband's house, and will stay together with her own children. If she refuses to be inherited, not only may she not have a home nearby on remarriage but her children will be lost to her and kept by her dead husband's clan. From the new husband's point of view, any property she inherits under Muslim law is available to him (Gaudefroy-Demombynes 1954), and he also gets a new wife without having to pay more than a minimal marriage settlement for her.

In Musoma, Tanzania, despite the prohibition in 1929 of the levirate by local government regulations and the Christian Church, it was still well in evidence 30 years later. Widows still found it to their advantage to enter the households of their late husband's brothers even as subordinate wives, and even if it meant breaking with their church (personal observation, R. Tanner). In Hinduism where we have seen that upper-caste widow remarriage is generally discouraged, the levirate is encouraged and has occurred widely among lower castes (Karve 1953). Only in the form of the Nuer 'ghost marriage' discussed above are the children of the widow reared in a truly fatherless family. Especially where the wife is still young enough to bear children, we can see the levirate as a pro-reproductive institution.

Remarriage of widows in Hinduism

In Hinduism the concept of indissoluble marriage is most effective in the higher castes and they are better able to prevent the remarriage of widows. The overall fertility of such castes is lower than would be the case if remarriage of widows occurred (Davis 1951). Lower castes, by contrast, allow their younger widows to re-enter marriage and continue to benefit from their fecundity.

The best known aspect of this interdiction on the remarriage of upper caste widows was the custom of 'suttee', for widows to immolate themselves on the funeral pyres of their husbands (Altekar 1956). (See Plate xx). It is difficult to know how many widows killed themselves in this way though there exists a figure of 706 for the Bengal Residency in 1817 (Dubois 1972). The British attempted to stop the custom by the 1829 Act for the Prevention of Sati (Suttee) but it had little effect as there was no provision in that law for the remarriage of widows. To live on as a widow was regarded as morally wrong and it continued to be an intolerable existence: a widow's head was shaved, she wore white, she ate one meal a day only and was avoided on all social occasions as an inauspicious omen (see Plate xxi).

These customs may well have been generally followed for centuries (Dubois 1972) and have exerted considerable pressure on widows. Alte-

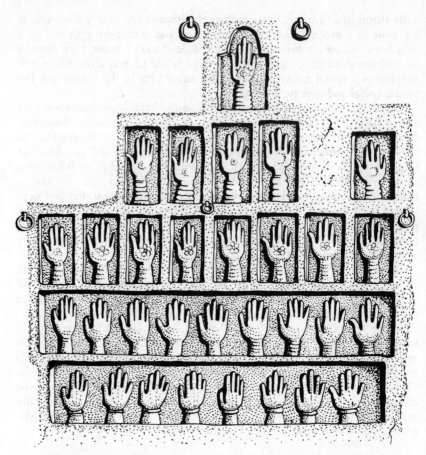

XX. The suttee gateway to a Rajasthan palace has carved impressions of hands in commemoration of widows who had burnt themselves to death on the funeral pyres of their husbands. Such women placed red ochre palm prints on the wall as they passed through on their last journey. These were later carved in relief so that the memorial should not be lost.

kar (1956) gives a figure of 2–10 per cent of widows in priestly and noble families burning themselves to death in the areas where it was most common. One of his own sisters killed herself on the funeral pyre of her dead husband, a retired senior army officer, in 1946, and there have been still later cases. Such self-immolating widows are still widely venerated as supreme examples of the wifely devotion expected of the best Hindus (Mayer 1965). In one especially venerated case on record, the widow who burned herself was still a young virgin (Carstairs 1961:74).

We have already discussed in Chapter 7 the large age difference between Hindu husbands and wives and the fact that brides tend to be as young as the law and local opinion allows. Age for age, male mortality is in any case usually higher than that for females. Thus there will always be substantial numbers of widows in Hindu communities. While it is doubtful whether there are still any noticeable numbers of pre-pubertal brides (a group which in the past led to the existence of virgin widows), there is still the problem of large numbers of youngish widows. In 1901, 18 out of every 1,000 girls aged 10–15 years were widowed and the figure was 92 in the age group 20–30 years (Census of India 1901). Goode states that in the last 50 years over half of those over 40 years of age had been already widowed. The inevitable result is that a large number of fecund women are made infertile. However

XXI. A group of Hindu widows living communally and devoting themselves to prayer. Their costumes are decorated with the word 'Rama', the seventh manifestation of the god Vishnu.

attractive the widow may be, it takes considerable courage and conviction for a Hindu man to marry a widow. There is a counter-pressure from her kinsmen favouring remarriage of widows in non-agricultural castes because of the obligation on them to maintain her. A second counter-pressure favouring widow remarriage is the possibility that she will have illicit sexual liaisons, leading to disapproval and harassment by male relatives and a social stigma on her and others too (Kapadia 1957).

As mentioned above, some studies (Dandekar 1961) have shown that the ban on widow remarriage is less strong in the lower castes, except where they are attempting to establish higher caste status. Remarriage is also more frequent generally than it has been in the past since families cannot afford to have unproductive women in the home. But there are further complications which can prevent the remarriage of widows because of its perceived inferior status and the general lowering of the religious status of all those involved in the arrangements. The relatives of the first husband will not wish to meet the relatives of the second husband of the divorced wife or widow, so the second marriage has to take place in a different village from the first one, but usually villages form communities and some relatives are present in all the local villages. If the two sets of relatives cannot be disentangled, then a remarriage may not be arrangeable (Mayer 1965). In any case the new husband will be socially restricted as well as debasing his future family's ancestral purity and his reputation.

Quantitative data on the effects of widowhood on women's fertility are given by Nag (1962) for low- and high-class Muslims and for Hindus (see Table 9.2). As can be seen from these figures, of 31 widows (drawn from a sample of 237 women) none remarried. Thus we see in Hinduism formidable forces keeping widows out of further marriages which might increase their fertility. This pattern keeps down reproduction rates as compared with systems that facilitate remarriage.

If we want to designate Hindu restrictions on the remarriage of widows in terms of r selection we meet with a problem. On the one hand, the custom is anti-natalist and to that extent fits $r-$ thinking. On the other hand it, and more especially the extreme action of suttee, would have decreased the care available to any existing offspring, unless there was special provision for their upbringing. It seems likely that the children of Hindu widows in upper castes (i.e. those involved in suttee or non-remarriage) would in fact have received adequate care because the wealth and resources of the joint family would be sufficient to meet their needs. T. Raychaudhuri (personal communication) writes that 'children were seldom the responsibility of parents only. It is extremely unlikely that women committed suttee or were made to do so when there was no such provision' (i.e. through the joint family). Their father's death would represent an economic blow, but less of a blow than in lower castes. If therefore we find, as we do, that lower caste widows did tend to remarry and not to commit suttee, we can perhaps reasonably suggest that these phenomena were products of $r -$ selection operating in the upper castes.

Christianity and the widow

St Paul opposed (1 Corinthians 7:8–9) the remarriage of widows except on the grounds that it would be better for them to marry than to burn, and elsewhere suggested (1 Timothy 5:13–14) that they had better remarry as otherwise 'they learn to be idle, wandering about from house to house; and not only idle, but tattlers also and busybodies, speaking things which they ought not. I will therefore that the younger women marry, bear children, guide the house, give none occasion to the adversary to speak reproachfully.'

Since first marriages were anyway regarded by St Paul as a poor alternative to virginity, it is not surprising that second marriages were even more vehemently opposed. Athenagoras in the second century called them a form of adultery (*Legatio pro Christianis* 33) and St Jerome wrote (*Epistola* LIV) even more strongly that young widows in remarrying were prostituting themselves 'for a paltry and passing gain to pollute that precious chastity which might endure forever'.

In modern Western societies we do not find clear-cut mechanisms for replacing the deceased partner of a marriage. It is left to the surviving individual to find a new partner and this can be difficult for a widow with a large number of children, or even a few.

Even though in contemporary Christianity younger widows can and do remarry, it is sometimes covertly felt that older women who have been widowed ought not to experience a new outburst of sexual feelings, or indeed expect to remarry, but to accept widowhood. These quasi-religious sentiments do nothing to provide the widow with economic support, and there are strong economic, as well as social and psychological grounds for her remarriage, both for her own and her children's welfare. Christianity is not helpful to widows. They are not encouraged by the Church to remarry, least of all to remarry quickly and there are no Christian organizations which cater particularly for the widowed, though this is the normal experience, late in life, of almost all married women. For such older people, their isolation and often loneliness is not a biological loss of fertility, since they are already post-menopausal. They can still perform grandparental functions. However there is evidence of increased mortality in that group. The mortality of bereaved women is substantially higher than that for the non-bereaved of the same age and sex (Rees and Lutkins 1967 and Parkes et al. 1969). This heightened mortality has also been found for the younger widowed between 20 and 34 years of age in a USA study (Kraus and Lilienfeld 1959), where it does, clearly, have reproductive consequences. These features are anti-natalist. Provision for dependent children left fatherless is nowadays a matter of state concern and has always in Christian countries been a community concern. Unlike the levirate, which stimulates further reproduction by widows, Christian teaching tends to reduce it and can be regarded as a product of r^c–selection.

Conclusions

Our concern in this chapter has been with the biological effects of divorce and widowhood, that is with their effects on the reproductive success of the parents involved, and also on such children as they may have produced or will produce in the future.

We saw that in Bengali Muslims there was a loss of reproductive time through these events, amounting to some two years for divorce (separation) and seven years for widowhood. Such figures are useful in that they indicate some idea of the scale of the setback; in this case the time lost is to some extent compensated for by the expectation of re-marriage and resumption of reproductive activity.

In both Islam and Hinduism we found evidence that reproductive failure was grounds for divorce, as also in Judaism. This was not so in Christianity, where annulment of a marriage was possible in cases of sexual inadequacy but not reproductive inability. We interpreted these attitudes in terms of r^c+ and r^c- orientations respectively.

The Hindu case of suttee and Hindu disapproval of the remarriage of widows would have provided a setback to the principle of r^c+ selection in cultures where resources are unstable and life is hazardous but for the noteworthy fact that these are associated with the upper end of the social scale, and we concluded that they did not therefore constitute an anomaly, but represented elements of r^c- selection in a culture which is in general a product of r^c+ selection.

In modernizing, as opposed to traditionalist, Islamic cultures we found evidence that divorces were harder to obtain owing to the intrusion of new secular legal safeguards; we saw this in terms of a movement from $r+$ to $r-$ selection.

The Christian attitude to divorce is hostile, and in the case of widowhood there is no ready method for remarriage. These features we saw as associated with the idea of lifelong monogamy, confirmed in the eyes of God and indissoluble – all anti-reproductive, as opposed to the levirate which is a specially designed custom to promote continued reproduction, as well as bringing economic security, to widows. As anticipated, the levirate does not occur in the religions of cultures resulting from $r-$ selection.

Middle and old age 10

Introduction

During the preceding chapters we have been concerned with children or with people of reproductive age. In the case of children, anything that religious rules bring about that tends to foster their survival until they reach reproductive age is adaptive biologically as they are going to be the reproducing generation in their turn. In the case of adolescents and adults, religious concern with sex, marriage, divorce and remarriage tends to affect reproduction in various ways. We saw that rules about reproduction serve to increase or restrict fertility and through this to affect the chances of bringing children up successfully to child-rearing age.

In this chapter for the first time we shall be dealing with women who are post-reproductive, and men who are past their prime but not necessarily post-reproductive. If religions were mainly concerned with ensuring reproductive success, we would not immediately expect them to devote too much attention to post-reproductive old people. However, religions are, to a greater or lesser extent, concerned with them. Are there any biological reasons for this? One's first thought might well be that if religions do spend a lot of time and effort on older people then biologically this effort is wasted, but this conclusion is premature.

First of all let us consider women who are post-menopausal. By definition these women cannot give birth any more. Can belonging to religious groups give them children? One way this could happen would be if such women were given children by religious agencies. They might not be able to suckle young infants, but they might be able to look after them in other ways. And with older children there seems no

In this scene at a Shinto shrine in modern Japan a group of old men and women are seen praying.

reason why older women should not rear them, or help their mothers rear them, perfectly adequately. Let us look first, then, at adoption processes, and second at grandparental roles, in the religious context.

Adoption through particular denominations

As we have already described, certain religions, particularly the Judaeo-Christian and Islamic, have long been interested in the survival of children who have lost their parents or who have been abandoned. Christianity has gone further than most in institutionalizing this practice to the extent that it has become the professional as well as religious preoccupation of certain groups of persons. Of the persons in religious groups who look after such children, some are parents themselves, others are unmarried but fecund, some are adult and celibate, others are older and post-reproductive. Through their concern they can, nevertheless, provide the setting for the prospective fertility of many children who might otherwise, in many parts of the world, have gone short of food and succumbed to disease. Older, senior men and women can play important roles in such contexts, by organizing and running adoption agencies.

The special role of grandparents

Does religion affect whether post-menopausal women and their husbands have some biologically significant role to play as grandparents? There appear to be few, if any, Christian religious rules which instruct them how to look after grandchildren. Children do not get instruction in Sunday school about how to behave towards their grandparents; good behaviour is anticipated by Christianity rather than subject to special rules. In other religions the position may be different.

Dead grandmothers jealous of their surviving children have been reported among the Veddas (Seligman and Seligman 1911: 140) where they have to be placated as spirits if they are to continue to be helpful. There is a cult in Sri Lanka of the 'Seven Grandmothers' to, whom offerings are made, particularly when children are sick (Gombrich 1971); some unrelated 'grandmothers' in the public ceremony concerned get quantities of free food and are the centre of attention.

Grandparents are often responsible for the continuing of religious feeling in a family. They have more spare time for their grandchildren than other relatives, often more than the children's own parents. Without special authority the interrelationship between them and their grandchildren is almost universally a pleasant one (Radcliffe-Brown and Forde 1950: 30; Radcliffe-Brown 1952: 68). Grandparents can thus encourage the religious beliefs and practices of their grandchildren even if parents neglect the matter. They can also be a brake on religious disaffiliation, and help promote the transmission of religious ideas down the generations, as well as sharing in the rearing process in countless other ways.

Elderly men marrying young women

Male dominance in society, which as we have seen is underlined by some religions, combined with stress on the importance of virginity at marriage and therefore on early marriage, as in Hinduism, leads in

Age of mother:	Age of father										Total
	Under 20	20–24	25–29	30–34	35–39	40–44	45–49	50–54	55 and over	Not stated	
Under 20	40.0	35.1	31.8	33.3	37.6	37.9	43.9		42.8	70.3	38.4
20–24	40.0	31.3	27.5	26.6	30.6	31.5	34.6	37.0	42.5	76.9	30.4
25–29		35.3	28.4	28.2	29.6	32.3	35.2	38.5	36.4	92.5	29.9
30–34		45.8	36.3	32.4	34.3	36.4	38.5	42.7	46.1	105.8	35.1
35–39		61.0	51.0	43.3	42.7	46.1	47.9	50.9	51.5	117.9	45.9
40 and over			59.3	55.5	55.0	57.3	60.9	63.3	64.5	138.3	60.2
Not stated	85.4	72.7	72.2	64.9	88.6	88.5	106.4	116.4	84.2	133.6	125.6
Total	40.2	33.1	28.8	30.0	35.7	43.2	48.8	52.3	52.3	91.3	35.7

Table 10.1 Stillbirth rates per 1,000 total births, by age of parents, US Birth Registration Area 1931–35 (From: Yerushalmy 1939)

some cases to husbands being much older than their wives. This occurs in tribal societies too, for instance among the Aranda (Arunta) and many other Aborigine tribes in Australia (Meggitt 1965). Second or third wives, often young and attractive girls, are taken by older and more successful men. The same age differential also occurs in Muslim marriages in traditional societies (Levy 1969: 106–8; Butler 1978). We have already shown that marital age differentials in Muslim Iran are greater than in Christian marriages there (Momeni 1976), and these differentials are likely to be even greater where richer men are concerned. Such men dominate the marriage market and marry wives much younger than themselves (Butler 1978).

As regards the biological significance of such arrangements, we should remember that polygyny most frequently consists of the gradual accumulation of wives. There will therefore tend to be less of an age difference between husband and first wife than for second and third wives, and the last wife to be married may be 30–40 years younger than her husband. Will this affect fertility? It has been shown in a general US survey (Yerushalmy 1939) that there is an increase in the general stillbirth rate associated with paternal age (see Table 10.1). A later study (Ressegui 1976) in Wisconsin found no indication in general of excessive stillbirths among fathers except in one age-grouping of fathers of 35 years or older and mothers aged 20–24. In general, differences were attributed to social rather than biological phenomena. A further study of over 1.5 million pregnancies in New York state (Selvin and Garfinkel 1976) found that foetal death rates increased as male parental age increased: for the paternal age group 25–29 years the foetal death rate per thousand pregnancies was 10.1; for the 40–44 years group the rate was 22.2; and for fathers over 55 years, 32.2. In this connection we can note that the transmission of mutations to succeeding generations is not necessarily increased with older fathers as the mutant genes tend to be eliminated during gametogenesis i.e. before conception (Bishop 1970; Sonneborn 1960). Another American survey showed that stillbirths were significantly associated with increased maternal and paternal age (Woolf 1965) and a further Canadian survey found high risk-rates of stillbirth and handicaps in babies born to women much younger than their husbands (Newcombe and Tavendale 1965). A specifically Islamic study (Awan and Mobashar 1975) confirms this for a sample of Pakistani women; in cases where the husbands were more than 15 years older than their wives, the total foetal loss rate was 331.19 per thousand pregnancies, whereas the rate when wives were the same age as their husbands or when the husband was older by 1–4 years, was 179.34. There does therefore seem to be some evidence of increased reproductive failure where fathers are old. However, there are compensating factors. Where wealth accumulates slowly and such wealth is advantageous to children in the form of land and produce, clearly the more wealth the family has, the more viable the children will be, and so it will be a good thing for children to have older fathers. Thus a 60-year-old man marrying a 20-year-old woman can be a biologically favourable arrangement, and lead to the successful rearing to reproductive age of very many offspring.

Birth control and the fertility of the older woman

There is some evidence that menopausal age has occurred progressively later in life during the twentieth century in affluent countries. In Britain it now averages 50–55 years, 4 years later than it was a century ago (Frommer 1964), and in Basle it occurs 3 years later now than it was 50 years ago (Hauser *et al.* 1961).

This may not be an important reproductive issue in contraceptive-using cultures, but it may well be significant in religious groups which taboo the practice of contraception such as the Amish and the Hutterites. In such cases, this extension of fecundity would be expected, other things being equal, to be reflected in the birth rate, and indeed it is. Cross and McKusick (1970) have shown that in Hutterite and Holmes County Amish women, net reproductive rates are considerably greater than in California and New York (Table 10.2). The figures also show that the excess fertility of these religious sub-groups occurs in the period when the mother is over 25 years of age; prior to this the rates for California and New York are higher than the Amish–Hutterite

Age of mother	Number of years lived in age interval by a birth cohort of 100,000 Females*	Calculated number of births			
		Amish	Hutterites†	California†	New York†
15–19	484,208	3,632	5,810	49,777	27,358
20–24	482,693	104,986	111,454	129,024	108,944
25–29	480,803	176,310	184,003	90,920	93,901
30–34	478,259	90,104	187,047	49,452	54,330
35–39	474,665	83,636	163,570	22,926	25,822
40–44	469,409	32,061	97,778	6,102	6,149
45–49	461,537	5,354	19,431	323	277
Total		496,083	769,093	348,524	316,781
Net reproduction rates		2,454	3,830	1,701	1,546
Sex ratio		1.022	1.008	1.049	1.049

Table 10.2 New reproduction rates of Amish and Hutterites compared to those of California and New York residents in 1960 (From: Cross and McKusick 1970)

* US Department of Health, Education, and Welfare, 1960, Sec. 5, life tables.
† Eaton and Mayer, 1953.
† Thompson and Lewis, 1965.

ones. As a result of this excess of reproduction later in life, the Amish net reproduction rate is one and a half that of the New Yorkers and Californians, while the Hutterite rate is twice that of the latter two groups.

It is, however, certain that this extension of the years of fertility involves extra risk both for the older mothers themselves and for such children as are born, mainly owing to the higher rates of mongolism. The proportion of Down's syndrome (mongol) children is three times higher for mothers over 40 years compared to those under 30 years, both for children born (Murphy 1947: 22) and for aborted foetuses (MacMahon *et al*. 1954). Older mothers have almost five times the risk of death in child-birth in comparison with the rate for all age groups combined (Francis 1970).

Thus we can see that religious attitudes involve these communities not only in the possibility of losing mothers who are looking after existing families, leaving orphans, but also that these communities will have the burden of looking after a larger number of defective children than would otherwise have been the case. In biological terms, these disadvantages need to be weighed against the single advantage of increased fertility.

We are thus left with a complex biological conundrum. For both older men and older pre-menopausal women there is a greater risk of producing a defective child, and in older women the mother runs in addition an above average risk of death at childbirth. Nevertheless, the chances of the above outcomes are never as great as those of producing a perfectly normal child. However, where the outcome is unfortunate, those children already in existence may be disadvantaged. Religions, as we have seen, may in some cases sanction older fatherhood or older motherhood. Where they do so they impinge on this biological situation. Where, alternatively, they tend to emphasize youth as the time for reproduction they avoid the consequences of older parenthood.

The idea of preferential older parenthood is not common in modern Christian countries, where children are preferred in the 20–30 age range. In these $r-$ cultures the remaining parental years focus on intensive, almost 'hothouse' rearing of the few children produced earlier, and the later, grandparental years are also dedicated to helping to rear rather than to reproduce. By contrast in some Islamic, Hindu and tribal cultures the older years can be the main reproductive ones for men, while women continue reproduction up to the menopause. As we saw in the last chapter, religious ideas play their part in all this through the rules and ideas pertaining to divorce and widowhood. The lessons learnt there need not be repeated here.

Religions maintaining the old

A purpose served by many religions is ministering to the sick and to the aged, who often become sick as they get old. What is the biological significance of this? It would seem, biologically, to be a cost with little benefit to the community. Here are people who are not reproductive, perhaps not looking after grandchildren, taking food and other resources from younger folk in ways sanctioned by religious rules. In this light it looks as if religion is disfunctional in the biological sense. (see Plate XXII).

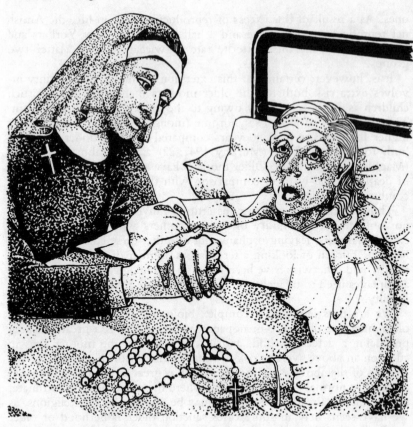

XXII   A Christian nun in an
institution run by a religious
order is here seen comforting
an old bed-ridden woman.

Judaism certainly pays particular attention to the old. The Torah
says: 'Who is sure of heaven? He that honours the aged.' Reverence and
tender consideration for old age have an important place in Jewish life:
'The old must be helped; their infirmities must be borne with patiently;
their society is to be sought out.' The aged who unite in their lives both
piety and learning are made the object of singular veneration (Joseph
1917). Buddhism makes no such provision for care of the aged, nor indeed for any form of social work. Christianity has been responsible for
widespread institutional care of the aged through religious orders which
regard this work as their particular vocation. Islam, with its insistence
on charity as one of its five basic tenets, makes provision for some sort
of general support for those who have no families. Islamic Egypt has
large numbers of welfare societies, but the expenditure of these bodies
for the care of the aged and beggars in 1960 was only 0.069 per cent of
their total expenditure of nearly 4 million Egyptian pounds, and only
914 persons are said to have benefited (Berger 1970). It seems there that
although these voluntary associations are expressed in a Muslim idiom,
the movement they reflect is also a new development under the stimulus of socio-political events.
    It is difficult to distinguish between the natural concern of a family
for the care of its own aged members and the moral requirements of religion. Religious care for the old is often a response to a need in urban
situations when families were, or are, no longer fulfilling their normal
obligations. Christianity may have responded more institutionally to

this problem than most religions because the nuclear family with its neglect of non–nuclear obligations largely arose within the geographical boundaries of urban medieval Christendom. Today Mother Teresa's response to the abandoned old and dying in Calcutta has received grateful attention and financial support from the Indian authorities because it is meeting this same need, unmet by other religions and secular institutions. Christian religious orders in particular seem to have the organizational form and underlying motivation to develop this type of charitable work.

The biological question remains: Given the human effort, time, food and other resources which go to the care of older people and to looking after infirm people, is this care of any positive biological significance? We could argue in a number of ways that it is. For instance, there is biological significance in the way that religion, by its attitude to old people, puts forward or expresses the general value it holds about all human life. If the religion lays stress on the value of *all* human life, human experience, and the significance of the individual, and attempts to promote the health and happiness of all individuals, then it must logically do so for old individuals as well as younger ones. The value which it places on human life and which we see in the care of the old, which takes up such a large part of the expenditure and time of Christian organizations such as the Salvation Army, is also part of the general value system that helps the survival of younger people.

This is not, however, to suggest that religious concern for older folk exists wholly to maintain some kind of consistency about the value of life as a whole. Force of logic is not the driving force behind the Christian care for the aged. It would be more accurate to say they are expressions of a sympathetic concern for the old and helpless in particular, enjoined by the teachings of Christ, who emphasized the virtues of self-sacrifice as well as of suffering, and upheld the positive value of meekness, mildness, powerlessness and the quality of being a 'victim'. It is the same sentiment that leads to care of unwanted pets, and opposes cruelty to animals and vivisection as a whole even when it is of medical importance. It does not put function first. Religions can be very concerned to channel human efforts into ends that produce relatively few if any results of biological value, and care of the old and infirm is a case in point. We can see in all this a background of r – selection, but clearly to overemphasize that is to distort one of the main Christian virtues out of all recognition.

However, we do in some sense seem to have reached, here, the opposite extreme from the attitude of some nomadic tribal societies of abandoning old people who are unable to keep pace, or the 'benign neglect' of them found in many of the poorer subsistence economies of the present day world. In such areas all 'soft' feelings, for young and old alike, are mitigated by the constant reality or possibility of actual starvation. We cannot ignore the level of control over food resources in the causation and persistence of religious rules about care of the aged. Even Christ exhorted his disciples to concentrate on the living (the young) and 'leave the dead to bury their own dead' (Luke 9:60). Only with the increasing prosperity of Christendom has the intensity of 'age concern' increased to present levels, and with it, incidentally, an increasingly aged overall population structure, as death rates have fallen owing to improved medical facilities and care. In the Christian West, the old are probably now reaching a better health situation than ever. The one remaining obstacle is that they have become isolated from their families, have thus lost the benefits of family involvement and tend to feel lonely and depressed. This obstacle must surely be resolved in the next century as it is so pressing. At the same time in other parts of the world poverty may increase steadily, with rising populations, and r+ thinking will probably not give rise to any general improvement as far as the old are concerned. Their existence will remain as precarious as ever, and perhaps even more so, and their relative numbers in the vast populations of the Third World will not increase as they have in the West.

Old age and religious involvement

While it is often assumed that religious involvement increases with the approach of death, this is not always so (Moberg 1965). Among Christians in the West there appears to be a peak of church attendance around the time of retirement and a steady decline thereafter related to increasing infirmity, the absence of transport and inability to continue driving, and the dislike of being dependent on others for transportation to services (Barr 1970). Religious attitudes and feelings as such increase among those who already have an acknowledged religion (Barrow 1958); these feelings can become more intense even though their institutionally oriented practices diminish (Hinton 1963). This increasing divergence between faith and church attendance among the old can be balanced to a limited extent if religious services are brought to old folk in their private homes or in the institutions in which they live, by peripatetic priests or, more often, by religious services on radio and television.

Men appear to lose interest in Christianity in old age much more frequently than women. There is no rush to religious belief and practice among the terminally ill. The approach of death does not produce a large number of conversions or a return to earlier beliefs. Christianity has no last-minute influence on the dying, who are influenced 'more in their reactions by the religious practice of their whole lives and by the general socio-religious environment from which they come (Wingrove and Alston 1971).

Other religions tend to have a more active approach to the involvement of the old in religious practices. Elderly Buddhists observe rituals more frequently than do those of other ages, particularly at the village level where monastery ceremonies occur near to their homes. The higher attendance of older women there has been accounted for by their desire to be reborn as men (Spiro 1971: 218). Hinduism has the preferred state of 'sannyasi' for the elderly; to achieve this they must detach themselves from their work and family responsibilities and become wandering ascetics (Dubois 1972: 522–7; Carstairs 1961: 96–7).

Religions and techniques for the prolongation of life

Prayer for the prolongation of life and the avoidance of suffering is ubiquitous and it is only recently with the growth of concern for, and scientific research into, psychosomatic disease that interest has been

shown in the possibility that prayer is an effective agent for the reduction of pain and the lengthening of life.

Faith healing at shrines has an almost worldwide occurrence as well
as a very ancient history. Today perhaps Lourdes is the best known. It
has been estimated that up to 3 million sick persons have visited this
shrine since 1858. Of these, between 6,000 and 10,000 are said to have
been cured; 62 cases have been claimed by the Lourdes Medical Bureau
to be 'miracles'. A figure of 1,500 miracles at medieval English shrines
in the twelfth and thirteenth centuries has been reported (Finucane
1973).

Galton made a quantitative study of the 'success' of prayer, positing
that because the British monarchs had more regular prayers said for
their welfare than anyone else in Britain, they should have lived longer
than the average citizen; he found that their life expectancy was in fact
lower than the average (Galton 1883: 277–94). Perhaps it is quality
rather than quantity that counts!

Some purposive praying for specific patients paired with unprayed-
for controls has been attempted under clinical observation. A small
British study of chronically ill patients initially showed that those
prayed-for did better than the controls, but subsequent pairs showed
that the controls did better. The authors thought this might be
accounted for by the prayer group's waning interest in the patients
(Joyce and Welldon 1965). A small American study in which the sick
and the prayer group did not know each other and the latter were kept
up to scratch by reminders, showed a marked delay in the deaths of the
sample in comparison to the control group (Collipp 1969).

Ancestor cults and old age

Certain religions, in China and Africa for instance, use the 'social fact'
of an after-life, in which retribution on the living by angry ancestors
can occur, as the sanction for their moral belief system during life. In
that sense the after-life is, or can be, the basis of the rules promoting the
biologically significant actions that occur during life, and understanding
this helps us to understand the esteem in which older people are held in
certain societies. They are close to ancestral status.

In the tribal religions of pre-literate societies which stress lineality,
we often find the phenomenon of ancestor propitiation. The deceased
members of a family have an influence on their descendants and ceremonies are carried out to maintain beneficial contact with them and to
placate their anger when it has affected the family's well-being. Thus it
comes about that grandparents are seen as prospective ancestors and as
such it is considered unwise to anger them because of what they might
do in revenge after their deaths.

Do such beliefs lead to a waste of family resources on the old? It is
arguable that they do not, because acceptance of the interest of the
ancestors in the good behaviour and cohesion of their descendants can
promote reproduction and survival among the young (Tanner 1958).
Couples are under pressure to marry and have legitimate children to
satisfy the departed by continuing their lineage, and to ensure their own
survival as ancestors. Children are to be properly cared for, so that the
lineage will persist. The natural affection of parents is thus supported by

religious beliefs and there is a healthy, if somewhat selfish, interest in a trouble-free present and a satisfactory future after death. A belief in the ancestors' continued involvement in family affairs helps maintain family solidarity and gives individuals a proper motivation to reproduce. Ancestor cults are thus clearly pro-reproductive and should be favoured where r+ selection is in the ascendant.

Reduced fear of death through religion

Religions, through rituals, provide an orderly progress through life and into death. Believers know the stages involved, and are given some self-assurance by ritual occasions; they become habituated to death by taking part in funerals or ancestor worship during their active lives. Such events tend to be played down in Western societies, and it is known that close relatives of the deceased in countries like Britain and the USA have an increased risk of themselves dying after the death of a close relative (Kraus and Lilienfeld 1959; Parkes and Brown 1972; Young et al. 1963). An 'orderly' death in which the deceased dies at home in the midst of his or her family has also been shown to have a less fatal effect on the bereaved close relatives, siblings as well as spouses, in a study in Wales (see Table 10.3). The risk of close relatives dying during the first year of bereavement is almost doubled when the death causing bereavement occurs in a hospital rather than at home, and it rises to five times when the death happens at a site other than a caring institution or at home (Rees and Lutkins 1967). For the aged and infirm, therefore, other people's deaths need careful socio-psychological management, and religions are very often deeply concerned with this.

Table 10.3 Percentages of deaths at the sites listed when the death was followed by the death of a close relative (From: Rees and Lutkins 1967)

| | *Years of bereavement* | | | | | |
	1	2	3	4	5	6
Died at home	7.1	5.0	1.2	2.5	0.6	0.6
Died in hospital	12.6	3.7	3.8	4.0	2.0	1.0
Died in chronic sick unit	17.5	8.1	6.7	—	—	—
Died in old people's home	—	—	20.0	—	—	—
Died at other sites	37.5	—	20.0	—	—	—

The religious concept of a 'good death' is one in which the person dies in a properly sanctified state, for example as Roman Catholics sometimes put it 'fortified by the rites of the Holy Church'. The dying person is the centre of rituals to put his own mind at rest and to concentrate it on the promise of the next world, while at the same time it is beneficial for the agitated survivors to be able to recite special prayers.

Burmese Buddhists believe that an individual's position in his next incarnation can be influenced by his state of mind immediately prior to death and to achieve this Buddhist devotions are recited at the deathbed by his friends, relatives and, as often as possible, monks (Spiro 1971: 248). While these Buddhist and Christian ideas involve the dying in essentially restful rituals, Hinduism, at least for high caste Brahmins, involves the removal of the dying man from his house and bed to be ceremonially purified outside on the ground by a priest and the nearest relative (Dubois 1972: 482–3).

In most cultures there is a proper way to die; usually surrounded by one's relatives and involved in the socio-religious ceremonies of one's faith. This idea sustains not only the aged but all the living. It is being increasingly recognized that death ceremonies are an essential part of the process of mourning, without which the surviving close kin have no accepted and successful way of working out their sorrow and their re-integration into society and a return to a useful social life.

A part of the last rites in the Sukuma involves a farewell to the dying person in which all the relatives present touch the feet of the moribund individual. In contemporary Western society touching by any except the most intimate relatives may have fallen into disuse because of fears of infection, or general distaste for being too closely associated with dying and death, and also the fact that those who are expected to die as part of a diagnosed disease or senility usually die away from their families in institutions for the aged or in hospital. Such separation is unim-aginable in most smaller-scale societies. For instance, in the Lodagaa (Goody 1962: 49–50) it is preferred that an individual should die sitting up in the arms of a close kinswoman.

We can thus see two contradictory kinds of biological effects on the survivors arising out of death-bed rituals. On the one hand there is the life-enhancing aspect of reassurance that all is as God or the spirits in-tend, which is actually pro-reproductive in the case of religions with ancestor cults. On the other hand such gatherings round a death-bed must in some cases be a potential focus of infection.

Suicide and religion

Suicide is predominantly found, in our own kind of society, among the old (see Table 10.4), and among men (see Fig. 10.1). Because of the association of suicide with old age, we shall look at it here as well as in the next chapter. According to Dublin:

With advancing years habits become set, reactions run in established grooves, and forced changes become more difficult and disturbing. Impairments are accumulated, particularly of chronic and painful diseases. Many older people suffer from psychoses of one type or another, especially from depressions, and from feelings of loneliness and futility as relations with family and friends and

Age	Rate
Below 1 year	0
1–14	0.1
15–24	5.2
25–34	9.9
35–44	13.7
45–54	19.8
55–64	23.7
65–74	24.5
75–84	25.8
85 and over	23.3

Table 10.4 Suicide rates in the USA by age, 1959 (Source: US Department of Health, Education and Welfare *Monthly Vital Statistics Report Annual Summary for 1959* Part II)

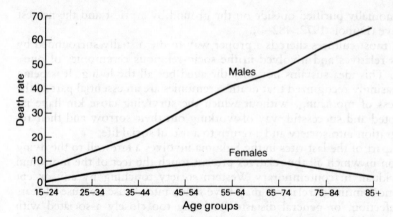

Fig. 10.1 Sex and age variations in suicide, death-rates per 100,000 among white persons, United States 1959 (From: Dublin 1963)

productive work drop off. Economic insecurity is often a serious problem, as is also inability or unwillingness to tolerate hardships. Young people, when difficulties arise, can more readily work off their pent-up emotions without resorting to self-destruction. They have more and safer methods of relieving emotional tensions. (Dublin 1963: 22)

Considerable attention has been paid to suicide in relation to religious belief and practice, and there have been several detailed studies of it (Durkheim 1932; Dublin 1963). Western religions have always taken a strong stand against it, even in old age. Early Christians mostly considered that God had sovereign power over life and man therefore should not interfere in any way with his own life; it was not his to terminate and the self-killer was guilty of mortal sin and buried outside consecrated ground. This idea is still widespread: 'The suicide prevents the divine purpose from being realised and interrupts his service to God. Man like all else must subserve the glory of God' (Davis 1946: 142–3). Suicide is certainly infrequent where the guidance and authority of religion are accepted without question and where the Church forms the background of communal life and its duties are rigidly prescribed.

We have already discussed (in Chapter 9) the, now vanished, custom of Hindu widows destroying themselves on their husbands' funeral pyres, concluding that they were probably confined very largely to the upper castes. Even allowing for the widows to have been younger than their husbands, they would have been in the main at the end of their reproductive life, though still very capable of looking after grandchildren. Hindu women still, however, commit suicide more frequently than men (Shah 1959) and it is probable that the self-destruction by women is just one aspect of a certain concept of womanhood due to a number of specifically Hindu factors (Meer 1976); firstly there is the inferior status of women, shown clearly in their lower survival rates at birth and in early childhood; secondly, the fact that a very early marriage is often arranged for them by their fathers, without, or with very restricted choice of bridegroom; and thirdly, there is the subordination and oppression of the daughter-in-law by her husband's mother and father. We can contrast the traditional 'socially embedded' kind of suicide of high caste widows with the more general suicide of women nowadays, out of feelings of inferiority and not being wanted, which more closely resembles the Western type except that women, not men, are mostly involved.

Altruistic suicide and the survival of the reproductively active

Finally, we should consider the situation in hunting and gathering societies in which such suicides as do occur tend to be for altruistic purposes (Durkheim 1932) where the loss of an older life will allow others to survive. When an individual's needs and his continued living begin to be a liability to the group he or she may turn to suicide. Among the Eskimos it used to be the case that old people would kill themselves (Nansen 1893; 151) and other cases are well known and documented in which old folk who no longer could manage the nomadic existence were expected, and able, more or less passively to accept abandonment (see Carr-Saunders 1922).

Conclusions

In this chapter we have been looking at some of the religious attitudes and beliefs we have been able to discern in relation to the period of life after the youthful reproductive years are over; in women the start of the period is marked by the menopause. As we saw, not all cultures and religions regard older men as post-reproductive. Indeed there are vast regions of the Hindu and Muslim worlds and some smaller-scale societies in Africa, Australia and elsewhere in which older, often quite old, men are regarded as ideal husbands, mainly because their wealth is essential for adequate security for the wife and children.

In the West this attitude is also found, but is infrequent and tends to flourish only among the very wealthy; even there it is not institutionalized. In the main, marriage and child-rearing are done by people in their twenties, thirties and forties in our society, rather than by fathers in their fifties and sixties married to younger mothers in their teens and twenties.

Nevertheless we found good evidence of a strong religious concern for older, largely post-reproductive, people in the Judaeo-Christian tradition, and there are at present many Christian institutions (old folks' homes, charities, etc.) especially devoted to channelling money, goods such as food and clothing, and housing towards older people in distress or need.

Are such efforts biologically wasteful? We saw a clear function for grandparents: sharing care of their grandchildren with their parents, and transmitting religious teachings and moral values to them. Indeed, a socio-biological argument has been advanced in terms of genetic kin selection for such post-reproductive grandparental care in non-human species. We can interpret the difference between religions and cultures that emphasize the reproductive functions of older men and those that emphasize their usefulness as grandparents as the outcome of $r+$ and $r-$ selection respectively.

In addition, there is the fact that much religious care is directed to old people who either have no children or are without a family circle. That indeed is often why they need care. In such cases an argument in terms of biological utility has to be of a very general kind: the care of such people promotes the altruistic morality supporting other, biologically relevant, care. Doubtless true, but such arguments appear rather vapid; the fact that care of the aged is encouraged by Judaic or Christian belief does not need such support and our understanding gains little from it. We noted, in fact, that in the modern, Christian West, old people were rather subject to neglect and consequent loneliness, as if altruism gave out at a certain point. This could perhaps be interpreted as a result of the fact that in such cases (which quite possibly run into hundreds of thousands, or even millions nowadays) neither the emphasis which $r-$ selection places on grandparenthood nor the emphasis which $r+$ places on procreation are relevant. Rewards for gerontological care are few and in general only next-worldly, and not many people seem adequately motivated to give the extensive time and care such old folk need. Dare we suggest that $r-$ selection favours neglect of the very old in favour of those in a more active state? It seems a cruel idea, and could be a false one. A related problem, that of euthanasia, will be examined in the next chapter, which in some respects overlaps with this one.

In other cultures the old may, we saw, have considerable status and respect, especially if they are seen as close to an increasingly powerful and active participation in life after their death. Ancestor worship is widespread in Africa, and even in the West there are many sects who maintain relations with the departed, but it is not a Judaic, nor a Christian idea.

We concluded that ancestor cults had a pro-reproductive function, in that they kept up pressure on the living to produce a healthy, active lineage. They would thus result from $r+$ selection, as would the consequent positive attitude to old folk arising from them.

In more strictly biological terms, we saw that a number of characteristics of the old are directly relevant to survival, either of the old themselves or of their survivors. Sperm-based fertility is reduced and mutation frequency increased in older .men; ovarian chromosomal anomalies increase with age; and so the incidence of defective children is increased in older mothers especially for the chromosomal abnormality trisomy 21, or Down's syndrome. Perhaps because of this neither $r-$ nor $r+$ selection appears to have favoured older motherhood.

Religious ceremonies and customs can also, we saw, bring people into close physical contact with the old and sick, even dying persons; we concluded that in many places this must lead to the spread of infection, especially in the poorer parts of the world where modern health services are lacking, where infectious diseases are most common, and where, paradoxically the old and sick are most closely associated with the rest of the community.

Finally we looked at suicide, noting its greater frequency among older men than women in Western society, whereas the reverse was true in India and China, at least in pre-modern times and among the wealthy. Christianity taboos it, whereas other religions such as Hinduism approve it in certain circumstances. Biologically it removes post-reproductive people from the community so that their resources can go to younger and actively reproducing elements. In the case of upper caste widows, perhaps we could say that they are already dead, because they are also regarded as irretrievably married to their dead husbands. In the case of Westerners we have noted that the Judaeo-Christian religion appears to have neglected the old; the old suicide is often a neglected person, and older men are, as we saw, less bound up with church-going than older women.

11 Death

In this chapter we come on to the inevitable next stage of the life-cycle, death itself. This involves the actual process of dying, a time after this for funeral and mourning ceremonies, dealing with the bereaved, and a subsequent period when the dead person is, or may be, psychologically or socially active among his or her descendants and others in the community.

Religions are very concerned with this crucial point in the life-cycle; very concerned with ministering to the dying person, preparing him or her for the world to come, a general involvement in his physical needs and psychological feelings at this time, and likewise helping those people who are especially close to the dying person. In many religions the actual dead person whose body requires disposing of, is left largely, or entirely, in the hands of religious organizations which have special ways of dealing with the situation.

Dying and death are key areas of focus for the religions of the Western world. One reason for this could well be that religions have lost much of their day-to-day significance for the living in modern Western society; there is a general lack of preoccupation with religion as an everyday consideration among the living. This, as we saw in the last chapter, extends into old age. Nevertheless it seems that at the time of death itself, even in modern Western societies, the services of local religious bodies are called in. The social services may to some extent be active until death, in care of the aged, but they are not adequate for the scale of the problem provided by death itself. Nor, it seems, does the wish to 'face the facts' of a loved one's death necessarily succeed for the bereaved. We are not only concerned here with what religions do about dead people; we are also concerned with whether these activities help the survivors and make them better able to cope, to recover, and

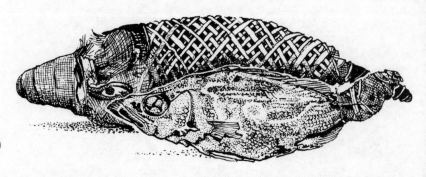

In ancient Egyptian tombs, food was provided in preserved form for the departed. These examples are a preserved crocodile (behind) and a fish (front).

to resume reproductively active lives. Despite its efforts, Christianity is not always able to cope, as we shall see; Hindu, Muslim and tribal religions probably do better, and we shall suggest a reason for this.

Mourning procedures and funerals

What are the effects of death on the survivors? We can distinguish social and psychological effects. Socially, the death of a person who occupies an important place in the social structure of the group leaves a gap in the structure. Most deaths occur to the aged who in our society (though not in many others) are mostly marginal. Less often, a person dies in the middle of his or her life-cycle at the peak of his or her prime and social significance. The death of a child is, again, socially a marginal event.

Psychologically, things are different. In the case of a child's death there is the important question of bereavement of the surviving members of the family which in our society tends to be severe. There is not a big social structure deficit here, but a major emotional upset, and this can, if not given adequate expression, cause loss of parental libido and non-replacement of the child, to put the matter in its briefest, most biological, and crudest form. When a man dies in his prime, bereavement is again severe, and the wife and children have to be cared for and their reproductive futures assured. We have already discussed this problem in relation to remarriage (see Chapter 9). The psychological impact can still be sharp, though it must normally have been anticipated. The rituals surrounding death are as much for the living as for the dead person and indeed biologically they are strictly for the living. Bereaved people feel a sense of grief; they do not necessarily comprehend a death and they may not know what to do about the situation. Therefore religions need to have rules for the expression of grief, for the explanation of death and for the management of situations which arise when people do not comprehend. The grief itself is given legitimate expression and religions have places and times when this should be done. They sometimes have rules about who in particular should grieve, and how long they should grieve. The funeral is not only the method by which the body is disposed of and the final termination of that particular person's active life, but also a message to the mourners.

The psychological effects have to be brought under control or damage to the physiological systems of the bereaved persons results, rendering them prone to infectious and even non-infectious diseases. Prolonged grief is also disruptive to the social life of the individual and his or her community.

Death has a wide range of psychic and psychosomatic effects on the bereaved (Table 11.1). These tables compare data for recent widows in two cities, Boston and Sidney, with a set of matched widows no longer suffering from grief reactions. Grief can upset the stomach (Landauer 1925) and is related to rheumatism, skin irritations, headaches and asthma (Marris 1959). A number of psychologists have referred to grief as a disease (Spiegel 1977: 53–6).

The importance of the rituals of death is that they are socio-religious requirements which have to be carried out by the bereaved within the social context of friends, relatives and neighbours who are less bereaved. The bereaved are not left alone to generate and multiply the

Death

Symptom or complaint	Total widows (%) n = 375	Total controls (%) n = 199
Neurological		
Migraine	4.8	3.0
Headache	17.6	9.0
Dizziness	9.1	4.5
Fainting spells	1.3	0
Blurred vision	13.7	7.5
Dermatological		
Skin rashes	6.1	2.5
Excessive sweating	9.3	5.0
Gastro-intestinal		
Indigestion	9.9	4.5
Difficulty in swallowing	4.8	1.5
Peptic ulceration	2.1	2.0
Colitis	0.5	0
Vomiting	2.7	0
Excessive appetite	5.4	0.5
Anorexia	13.1	1.0
Weight gain	8.5	9.0
Weight loss	13.6	2.0
Genito-urinary		
Menorrhagia	4.3	0.5
Cardio-vascular		
Palpitations	12.5	4.0
Chest pain	10.1	4.5
Respiratory		
Dyspnoea	12.0	4.5
Asthma	2.4	1.5
General		
Frequent infections	2.1	0
General aching	8.4	4.0
Neoplastic growth	0.8	0
Diabetes mellitus	0.8	0.5

Table 11.1 Psychosomatic grief reactions of widows in Boston and Sidney (From: Maddison and Viola 1968)

psychosomatic symptoms of their grief, but are required to be active and in many cultures there is a special role for bereaved persons over quite a long period, such as the 40 day mourning period for Muslims, by which time their recovery from bereavement is well advanced.

Not only are there the visible physical effects which are shown in Table 11.1, but hormonal effects on the reproductive libido of the grieving individuals which are of biological concern. Islam forbids the remarriage of widows for four months after the death of the husband; also it was, and still is, the convention among many Christian cultures for remarriage to be discouraged for up to a year after bereavement. The reason for such rules is no doubt partly that they prescribe and thereby guide the way back to normal functioning, social and physiological, and it is significant that the period is shorter in the Islamic rules, so often associated with pro-natalist ideas resulting from *r*+ selection, than in the Christian ones.

Most societies have prescribed mourning behaviour which varies on a common theme: that the bereaved are in some ways abnormal and that this abnormality diminishes with time. The Buddhist Lepchas of Sikkim prohibit any married person in any way connected with the dead person from sleeping with his or her spouse for three days after a death. On the death of a spouse, parent or sibling, the survivors are debarred for a year from marrying. For affinal and classificatory relations this prohibition lasts for 49 days (Gorer 1938: 361).

There is little doubt that contemporary Western society has increasingly simplified mourning rituals, even removed them from the family context; families move too often and the nuclear family is too small to provide either the environment or the personnel for big family rituals. The bereaved are very often alone after the funeral and it is tempting to see in this social isolation a direct connection with the physical symptoms shown in Table 11.1.

The involvement of the bereaved in special activities from the moment of death is very obvious in some societies, particularly where extended families exist. In Islamic societies the women of the bereaved family maintain formalized wailing from the time of death up to the burial, beating themselves, scratching their faces and tearing their clothes (Gaudefroy-Demombynes 1954: 171) and even in some cases hiring professional wailing women (Lane 1954: 517).

Religious ideas as a cause of death

Religions approach the problems of 'death management' where death arises from any cause whatever. There are also, however, instances where religions themselves cause death. They can bring death to individuals or to whole groups, and to old and young alike.

A case in point is snake-handling, using poisonous snakes that have not been 'milked' or had their fangs or poison-sacs removed. Religious ceremonies using such snakes occurred among the Hopi Indians of the south-western USA (Parsons 1939: 652–75). Young men had to go out before the snake ceremony, find, and collect certain poisonous snakes alive, a dangerous business indeed. Then, at the time of the ceremony, the snakes were handled in a great variety of ways. The religious functionaries involved were men, often in their prime; they are reported to have avoided snake bites to a great extent, but we have no accurate data on the extent of bites and fatalities.

The members of some small Christian denominations such as the Holiness Churches of the southern USA, even today have their entranced members test their faiths by handling poisonous snakes, following the Gospel of St Mark (16:18). They also apply torch flames to their bodies and drink strychnine (Schwarz 1960). In this study it is stated that although there has been widespread handling of poisonous snakes, very few people have been bitten; despite refusal of treatment about 30 Holiness members are known to have died from snake-bite since 1910 (Alther 1975). G. W. Hensley, the founder in 1909 of snake handling in Tennessee died of snake-bite. The practice of snake handling continues despite its legal prohibition in Tennessee, Kentucky and Virginia (Wilson 1970) (see Plate XXIII).

A further, well documented, but rather different way in which religion can cause death is through psychological suggestion. The subject, sometimes called 'Voodoo' death, has been well reviewed by no less an

XXIII. Poisonous snake handling by the Rev. Doyle Morrisy, a member of a fundamentalist Christian sect in the southern USA.

authority than Walter Cannon (1942: 189) who concluded that 'it may be explained as due to shocking emotional stress – to obvious or repressed terror'. He finds valid evidence of it in South America, Africa, Australia, New Zealand, the Pacific Islands and Haiti. In many of the cases he cited, the death concerned followed upon the discovery by an individual that he or she had broken, sometimes inadvertently, a sacred taboo, e.g. by eating a forbidden food. Death could occur either soon after or long after the breach. Cannon was concerned to assess the possibility that death was in fact an outcome of wholly physical, non-psychological processes of poisoning or self-starvation. This was difficult. The latter was indeed often involved but it was an outcome of the initial psychological shock. 'The question arises', he wrote, 'whether an ominous and persistent state of fear can end the life of a man.' (1942: 186). His interpretation of the underlying physiology indicated that it could. He described how the sympathetic nervous system and the hormonal adrenal medullary system between them could, if their action was prolonged, bring about a fall in blood pressure due to a reduction in the volume of circulating blood, which, together with reduction of food and water, could cause death as a result of 'shock' in the surgical sense. One of the authors (V. Reynolds) observed a case of near-death from 'witchcraft' in Uganda in 1962; the patient recovered, however, when he moved from his home community to another village. This individual was a well-educated African who spoke fluent English. Other studies relevant to this phenomenon, besides that of Cannon, are those of Barber (1961), Johnson (1964), Lester (1972) and Lex (1974).

The use of corpses in magical and religious rituals

The traditional Western picture of the witch and wizard using human ingredients in magic potions, boiled and stirred while chanting powerful spells, is well illustrated in Shakespeare's *Macbeth*: 'Nose of Turk and Tartar's lips, finger of birth-strangled babe, liver of blaspheming Jew'. There is indeed evidence that human ingredients are used in contemporary rituals in parts of Africa (Cory 1951: 35–6; Goody 1970: 219). Some well-known cases of this use are from Lesotho where at least 60 ritual murders occurred in a 10-year period (Ashton 1952) in which the victims were mutilated while still alive to supply the blood and flesh ingredients of magic medicines needed for the support of political power. Among the ancient Aztecs too, hearts were routinely taken from living victims for ritual purposes. Likewise in the old West African Kingdom of Benin. In such cases, religions cause considerable loss of life.

The consequences of disease arising from the consumption of human tissues for ritual purposes is known from the New Guinea disease known as *kuru* studied among the Foré people (Gajdusek 1973). This is a severe degenerative disease of the central nervous system affecting much of the population of certain areas, resulting in death within nine months of the appearance of the first symptoms. Foré women practised ritual cannibalism of their dead kinsmen, particularly eating the brain tissues which were squeezed into a pulp with the bare hands and eaten. With the decline of the practice after 1957 there has been a steady decline in the incidence of *kuru*.

This New Guinea case is interesting in so far as it involves eating dead relatives, thus it tends to keep this particular disease within the extended family and as a result was at first thought to be a genetic disease. In certain American Indian tribes, however, such as the Hurons and Iroquois, captives were regularly eaten either cooked or raw; indeed the latter ate the Jesuit priest de Brébeuf raw in recognition of his bravery under torture (Kenton 1925).

Cannibalism of old people was reported during the nineteenth century, in which the old were killed and eaten by their relatives. Early literature contains many references to this practice, as for instance among the Battak of Sumatra (Leyden 1811: 202) and the Birhors of Central India (Dalton 1872: 220). While the explanation has been put forward that this occurred as an act of filial piety to retain within the family the powers of the old, it has been observed that 'like so many other funeral customs which are supposed to comfort the dead (this) may be the survival of a practice which was originally designed to promote the selfish interests of the living' (Westermarck 1912, i:390).

It has often been assumed that cannibalism is related to the religious beliefs of the eaters but this need not always be so. In a detailed study of Azande cannibalism, Evans-Pritchard (1965) concluded that the motive was simply a taste for human meat, sometimes accentuated by extreme hunger. But the author pointed out that this whole subject was full of hearsay, quoting the Azande's conviction that British doctors were cannibals who performed surgical operations to obtain meat. A variant of this view was often encountered by one of the authors (R. Tanner) in Tanzania, where it was widely believed that the parts of the body removed in hospital operations were used in the preparation of magical medicines. The other author (V. Reynolds) heard the view expressed in Uganda in 1962 that whites, in general, were cannibals from time to time.

Though cannibalism excites our interest (because of our own taboo on, not to say horror of, eating human flesh) the practices subsumed under this term are many and the causes various. For this reason it seems unwise to try and generalize on the subject (for a brief review, see Clark 1975).

The preparation of the body for disposal

An idea expressed in many religions is that the dead should not be left alone. This may in some societies have been or still be to prevent the use of the body for witchcraft. In other cases it ensures that the dead are always 'properly' disposed of. Judaism has burial societies and medieval Christianity had religious orders specifically dedicated to the disposal of dead people who had no relatives. Few religions, if any, have ever considered it proper that the dead should be disposed of without due preparation. When the dead are left unattended or disposed of in mass graves, it is usually because religious concern for the individual person has broken down under some kind of stress or disaster such as war, epidemic or earthquake. Religions do not as a rule make provision for this and their normal death rituals are not appropriate for mass disposal.

We know that some death customs such as cradling the corpse, found in Java (Geertz 1960: 69) and other places (see Plate XXIV) are quite extraordinarily dangerous to health. The Bontoc Igorot, a mountain people living in North Luzon, Philippines, have their dead placed on a chair under the house for several days and

> . . . as a rule decomposition sets in well before the third day. Often the corpse swells greatly; the liquid escapes through the nose and the mouth. Insects also swarm around the corpse and a couple of women chase them almost continually with a kind of fan which they make for this purpose. Although the odour is at times unbearable, the people remain on the house-ground and eat their meals with no less appetite. One can imagine how it must have been when the corpse was kept on the death chair as long as ten days. (Lambrecht 1938: 342; see also Jenks 1905)

In many parts of the world, the dead body is prepared for burial by being washed and dressed by special personnel. In Islam, body washers are entitled to keep the clothes of the deceased (Lane 1954: 518). In Buddhism this job is done typically by relatives and always by men (Spiro 1971: 249).

Among Buddhist societies we encounter some unhygienic religious

XXIV. Among the Kukukuku people in New Guinea a dead grandfather who has been smoke dried over the fire in the living hut for two months is surrounded by his family.

practices concerning the dead. David-Neel (1977: 33–4) wàs an eye-witness of the custom of drinking tea out of a cauldron that had just held a corpse, during a funeral ceremony in Tibet. In Nepal, Faul (1979) observed an unhygienic religious practice, which she described as follows:

The two parts of Pashupatinath Stupa [a Buddhist shrine] lie on either side of the Bagmati River [in Kathmandu, Nepal], connected by a bridge. Huge numbers of people come there to worship every morning. And, when there is no hope of recovery, it is there that the dying are taken to the dying house. When their time is near, they are carried to the edge of the river, so that they may die with their feet in the holy water (p. 51).

Such practices seem likely, if only occasionally, to spread infection. There are, of course, in hygiene-conscious societies, special washing practices after touching a dying person or a dead body. But not everywhere.

XXV. This scene from contemporary USA shows relatives of a deceased man paying their last respects at a funeral parlor.

In many cases relatives and neighbours come to some form of lying-in, to say farewell or pay final respects to the deceased, and there is often a steady stream of visitors (see Plate XXV). Even if death has been due to infection, relatives may be required or may want to kiss, touch and otherwise handle the bodies of their loved ones. This heavy involvement of relatives will tend to spread any infection present along kinship lines, a process that hardly makes good sense in terms of positive kin selection. The West has seen a massive reduction of frequency of death from infectious diseases, so that the dead are more likely to be perfectly 'safe' to those nearby. Yet many Westerners no longer seem able to touch dead bodies of any except their most beloved without extreme reluctance. The effort made by the Jewish and Christian religions to help those involved see death as a necessary and not particularly dreadful part of life seems often to fail in modern Western society where psychosomatic illness often follows a death (see above and previous chapter). Almost the first thing we do with a dead person is to cover him or her with a sheet, as if the sight of a corpse was not appropriate, was frightening or even disgusting. Not so in societies in what we call the underdeveloped or 'third' world, where general instability and high mortality makes death, if not an everyday, at least a familiar event. We can therefore distinguish between 'open' funeral customs and 'closed' ones, meaning by those terms the extent to which feelings are openly expressed and given ritual expression or kept in check. In the former case the living and the dead mingle together in harmony; in the latter they remain at an hygienic distance from each other.

The disposal of dead bodies

Dead bodies have to be disposed of and religions often provide the rules and personnel for this, even when the dead and their survivors are not specifically religious. From a biological point of view this process is important, since the corpse, even if not unhygienic at first, is bound to become so sooner or later.

Religions advocate particular ways of corpse disposal, the Hindus by burning and the Christians traditionally by burial, though nowadays very much by cremation too. These are adequately hygienic methods of disposal. However, in the Hindu case, there is not always enough wood to burn the body completely and as a result the Ganges receives large numbers of half-burned bodies (see Plate XXVI). With burial, in some non-Western societies, the soil may be too hard in the dry season, or the tools too inadequate, to allow for burial to be at a sufficient depth to eliminate all possibility of infection. Nomadic people often do not have the tools to dig graves. The Masai of East Africa expose their dead, and do not kill hyaenas as an accompaniment of this practice. The Parsees expose their dead in specially constructed 'towers of silence', built well away from habitation.

XXVI. At Benares, India, bodies are dipped in the River Ganges prior to cremation. After cremation the remains are disposed of in the river.

Until the growth of cities, Christian dead were traditionally buried in graveyards surrounding village churches, usually situated in the middle of housing. Each house had its own well or access to a communal well nearby. One of the authors (R. Tanner) lives in an old house with its own well directly downhill from a graveyard, which is less than 50 yards away. The through-put of water in a constantly used well could be expected to have had adverse health effects in the Middle Ages and later, especially for the transmission of cholera.

Even where we might wish to explain the burial of the dead near the living in religious terms, as for instance in a society with an ancestor cult stressing the need for communication between the dead and the living, there may also be more prosaic factors. The Sukuma of Tanzania bury their dead in their cattle pens, and their own explanation for this is only partly a religious one; they also state that the soil is softer there. They do not like the burial grounds provided by modern mission churches because the graves are not guarded and they are concerned that the newly buried body will be dug up by witches and wizards, or by hyaenas.

Religious attitudes to autopsies

Every religion, as we have seen, has an idea of what is the 'correct' attitude to the body of a deceased person. Judaism holds that respect for the dead prevents the mutilation of a body for dissection or post-mortem examination. There have been divided rabbinical opinions as to whether dissection is permissible for the purposes of advancing learning and research. The anatomy needs of Israeli hospitals have at times been disproportionately met by the use of non-Jewish bodies. Thus the refusal of permission for autopsies in New York Jewish hospitals has not affected the 36 per cent minimum quota of autopsies required for hospital accreditation owing to the availability of the bodies of non-Jewish people dying in those hospitals (Jakobovits 1961). In these New York Jewish hospitals the rate of refusal for permission for an autopsy was 62 per cent among Jews and 38 per cent among non-Jews. There have been occasional cases (Curran 1977) in which relatives have sought to prevent an autopsy on religious grounds when it has been legally required in cases of unusual sudden death. In 1942 Chief Rabbi Kook forbade autopsies of Jewish bodies but his successor, Rabbi Herzog, allowed autopsies designed to save future lives and in cases where it would be humane to establish the presence of hereditary disease. In 1965 there were orthodox objections to this broad range of permissions so the use of autopsies was limited to saving future lives when there was an immediate possibility of doing so, e.g. in cases when there were several patients in the same hospital suffering from an undiagnosed disease and one of them has died. This ruling in fact resulted in a greater proportion of autopsies among non-Jewish corpses to reach the 36 per cent quota.

In 1965, in Israel, there were 'allegations of widespread abuse of the safeguards contained in the Law of Anatomy and Pathology' (*Encyc. Judaica* 10:1,182) and the then Chief Rabbi Y. Nissim of the Sephardi and Head of the Rabbis of Israel, and Chief Rabbi Y. Unterman of the Ashkenazi, supported the orthodox agitation for strictly limited permission for autopsies, i.e. autopsies only allowed in cases where they would assist in saving the lives of other patients. The contrast between the Christian and Jewish attitudes is striking here. Of the two, of course, Christianity is the newer faith; in the modern world its management of death is, as we have seen, deficient. It is hygiene-conscious rather than putting feelings first, and it has thus been able to absorb the ideas of autopsy by specially trained personnel, and reap the benefits of the information so obtained for the improvement of care of the living. This trend continues at the present time and can be seen as the outcome of r–selection.

Organ transplants from the dead

Dead people can help the living, increasingly in modern times, as their bodies can be used for replacement parts for other living people. This can happen during life or at the death of one person, giving a sick person a new lease of life. If a dead person acts as the donor of a kidney to a younger person, then in a very real sense he or she is responsible for the latter's reproductive success. This is a very recent event so that one cannot expect religions to have developed a great deal of thought and practice concerning it. However it does seem that religions have reacted differently to this use of dead bodies for transplants.

The Jewish view is ambivalent; many rabbinic authorities permit organ transplants if the absolute and positive death of the donor has already been satisfactorily established. However, failed transplants have also been condemned as 'double murder' (Rosner 1971, 15:1,337–40). This follows through the rulings against the mutilation of the dead that govern autopsies (see above); not only is the dead person wrongly mutilated, but so also is the recipient, especially when the transplant fails.

The Roman Catholic view is that organ transplants present little moral difficulty provided that consent has been obtained from the donor or the legal custodian of the corpse, but the grant of a part is not a duty or an obligatory act of charity. Pius XII stated that financial circumstances and social status should not be related to availability of body parts and that it is best to refuse financial compensation for them (Paquin 1967, 10:754–6). In general the Christian world has adapted easily to these modern developments.

The economics of death and mourning

While there is a movement in the Christian Church, particularly in the United States, for the simplification of funeral ceremonies and a reduction in their cost, most religions have developed extremely complex funeral rituals which use up a good deal of scarce resources. Does this use of scarce resources lead to biological disadvantages for those involved? The enormous expenditure on the cult of the aristocratic dead in dynastic Egypt involved the extensive use of the labour of families at the lower social levels, especially when it came to the burial of the Pharaohs themselves. The construction of pyramids rather than canals would seem to be economic nonsense in a subsistence economy.

What, indeed, are the forces at work in the rise and fall of ancient civilizations? This is a question that has puzzled historians of all times who have noted the rise, flowering and decline of civilizations. Many, such as Toynbee, Spengler, Gibbon, Hegel, and Marx have seen this as the historian's central problem. We shall return to this issue in chapter 15, but provisionally let us hint that, in our terms, the answer will be found in the extent to which the resources of an environment can be successfully managed. Whenever and wherever this comes about, the stage is set for a move from r^c+ to r^c- selection, and all sorts of customs and ideas, including religious ones, begin slowly to swing from the central pivot of survival and reproductivity to that of population control and care of the living. The process of r^c- selection is first seen among the wealthy aristocracy; it permeates down to the lower classes; eventually, if the ecological system is adequate it takes in the whole society. But usually something in the environment goes radically wrong and the carefully constructed edifice falls apart as unpredictable and unstable conditions return. Thus civilizations do not, in this view, have to contain the seeds of their own destruction (though they may do). They often simply lack the foresight to predict, or the power to withstand, environmental change. The pyramids were built to last for ever, and so they may. But their significance was that the civilization producing them was going to last for ever. The same is true elsewhere: among the ancient Indus Valley peoples, the Mayas and Aztecs, in China, Greece and Rome. Our preoccupation with biology and adaptation has led us deep into issues of central concern to the study of history along a new path. For us, to return to our current concern, pyramids do make sense as the outcome of a move towards control of resources along the Nile, and with it the rise of the religion of ancient Egypt through r^c- selection.

Human sacrifice and ecological survival

While human sacrifice for religious reasons has been widely recorded in a number of societies, it was perhaps in pre-Columbian Mexico that it became most frequent with the mass sacrifice of war captives in the century immediately prior to the Spanish conquest.

The Nahua civilization of Mexico, in which religion centred around human sacrifice, raided outside its boundaries to obtain victims (Cook 1946). Human blood was pleasing to the gods, and the more blood the greater the benefits which they would confer on their worshippers. Records show that an average of 700 war captives were sacrificed per year and that the total sacrifice of captives between AD 1442 and AD 1507 averaged 9,400 per year, or 12,000 when children and slaves are included. A skull count carried out on the orders of Cortés (Tapia 1866) totalled 136,000 excluding two *towers* made of skulls which were not counted. This occurred at a time when the population density in central Mexico was reaching the maximum that could be supported at the current level of subsistence agriculture, according to Cook (1946).

Cook estimated that there might well have been a mean annual sacrifice rate of 15,000 and that this in a total population of about two million was a major factor in controlling population and balancing it with the maximum available economic resources. In the eyes of the Mexicans themselves it was seen as ensuring the benevolence of the gods by human sacrifice.

If we can assume that war captives were men in their reproductive prime, then the reproductive loss in the long run must have been very considerable. Thus we have here an extreme example of religion resulting directly in the reduction of population levels by bringing about a massive loss of reproductive capacity.

However, groups would not be benefiting themselves by reducing the populations and reproductive rates of their neighbours, at least not in the short run. To entertain the notion of population control seriously we have to assume that in the longer term all populations became subject to reduction as a result of defeats in warfare and so each group 'benefited' in turn. This hypothesis is rather fanciful and smacks of a rather naïve form of ecological determinism; nevertheless there may be something in it and more research is needed on the subject. Useful research on the functions of war has recently been done (Vayda 1969; Chagnon and Hames 1979). If it were to be construed as an evolved pattern, it would need to be seen as some kind of group selection process in which, through a form of intergroup altruism, groups helped other groups by decimating them while remaining overpopulated themselves; in due course they could expect to reap the ecological benefits when they themselves were decimated by their neighbours. Such processes, not impossible perhaps, nevertheless demand considerable leaps of imagination!

We can extend these ideas in relation to our own as follows. If, as a result of r+ selected cultural processes together with improving levels of ecological stability, population levels increase and the resource base is threatened, a resort to violence, internal and/or external, may result but the losses involved will lead to social disintegration, as does appear to have happened in Mexico and many other places. The only long-term solution by which cultures can achieve a successful adaptation to improving conditions is to adopt restrictions on reproduction rates and other processes that we have described in this book as processes of r− selection. Groups must help themselves, not wait to be helped, and since groups and their cultures are composed of individuals it is finally the choices made by the individuals of different groups that will determine patterns of survival. The crashes of civilizations resulting from ever greater levels of religiously sanctioned violence are predictable, for these blind responses are inadequately geared to a problem of resource management, which can only be solved by the construction of alternative rules for action that bring about peaceful population reduction.

Suicide, self-destruction, and martyrdom

Suicide among the aged was discussed in Chapter 10. Here we shall consider other kinds of suicide to see how religious affiliation affects the probability that a person will or will not take his or her own life in particular circumstances.

Suicide has in the past been an important characteristic of the Japanese, particularly towards the end of the Second World War in connection with the religions of Shintoism and Buddhism. Many Japanese believed that they had the religious obligation to die for their Emperor as a divine figure and did so in so-called *banzai* charges by groups of soldiers; very large numbers of Japanese committed suicide at the end of the war on Saipan and Iwojima when an estimated 22,000 civilians died, mostly by suicide (Toland 1971). *Kamikazi* or 'Divine Wind' suicide was practised by pilots in their bomb-carrying aircraft. The cause was not only the shame of personal survival but the shame that survival would bring to their families.

The names of 4,615 *kamikaze* pilots who lost their lives in the Pacific war are inscribed in the Kannon temple in Tokyo (Morris 1975: 459). These young men in early adulthood were steeped in the Japanese idea of honourable death as expressed in their traditional samurai philosophy and by their religion. These acts of suicide were the result of carefully pondered and prepared acts considered to be the only reasonable course of action for honourable men in the circumstances of personal and national extremity. The state religion of Shinto promised that those giving their lives in the service of the Emperor would return as divine spirits to be worshipped in the Yasukuni Shrine. But many of these pilots were Buddhists, not Shinto. They came from a university background and many do not appear to have paid much attention to any of the popular forms of religion which would assure their believers of happiness in some future existence; some indeed were openly sceptical (Inoguchi and Nakajima 1960: 80). It would not be correct to see Buddhism as a main motivational force in their suicides since this faith is essentially pacific. It could not be seen as endorsing the destruction of human beings by men riding bombs at them. Such a death would not be seen as enhancing the killer's position in the next life as a stage nearer the extinction of self. We can conclude that these suicides were principally part of the Japanese military tradition and that they were only supported in part by Buddhist and Shinto ideology (Okumiya 1980).

There have been other examples of large-scale suicides on the part of religious groups. The 960-strong Jewish community at besieged Masada in AD 73 killed themselves on the last night of the siege; only two women and five children hid and did not kill themselves (Yadin 1970). In York in AD 1190, 150 Jewish men and women killed themselves to avoid further persecution.

However, Judaism distinguishes clearly between *suicide* and *self-destruction* (*Encyc. Judaica* 10:978–9). The latter is the appropriate term here. Self-destruction should be undertaken willingly and is called *Kiddush ha-shem*, or sanctification of the (divine) name. It is the proper course of action if the person finds himself faced with an unavoidable threat to his or her religious principles. This is so clearly a part of the Jewish faith that medieval Jewish prayer books included a benediction to be recited before a Jew killed himself and his children, and special memorial lists were compiled to preserve the memory of those who had sacrificed themselves in this way.

Self-destruction by religious sects occurs also in Christianity, as in the case of Jonestown, Guyana (see Plate III). The motivation here was complex, but certainly a strong component was the fear that the US authorities were about to break up the sect, remove its leaders and try to reintegrate the rest into the world from which, for various reasons, they had fled. Their unity was expressed in a fervent religious idiom, it was in that idiom that their vow of self-destruction was phrased, and that is why it had such a powerful hold.

In other Christian cases a strong element of altruism can be detected underlying actions that brought about death, often on quite a large scale. Again, such cases can be considered to a great extent suicidal. For example, the story of the plague at Eyam in Derbyshire, 1665–66, illustrates this. When the disease began to appear there the Rector, together with his Non-conformist predecessor, urged his parishioners to stay put, pointing out the danger of scattering the seeds of infection among neighbouring villages so far unaffected. So this village cut itself off from outside contacts and 260 people died in 14 months, including the wife of the Rector, out of a total population of about 350 people (Daniel 1966). This seems to have prevented the plague from spreading as virulently elsewhere. We can only guess at the strength of character of the Rector which enabled this community to behave as it did, and we can only guess whether more people would have survived if they had dispersed, but the principal motive in this fatal self-abnegation was religious.

There are many other cases of Christian altruistic actions leading to death. Right from the earliest years of Christianity, Christians seem to have courted death in their care and treatment of the sick particularly during plagues. Eusebius (1890: 307) writes about the AD 263 plague at Alexandria:

Most of our brethren were unsparing in their exceeding love and brotherly kindness. They held fast to each other and visited the sick fearlessly and ministered to them continually, serving them in Christ. And they died with them most joyfully, taking the affliction of others and drawing the sickness from their neighbours to themselves and willingly receiving their pains. And many who cared for the sick and gave strength to others died themselves, having transferred to themselves their death.

How are we to interpret religiously inspired self-destruction by large numbers of healthy adults at times of crisis? In our terms, the explanation needs to be based on environmental circumstances which are suddenly very seriously worsened: situations of crisis or catastrophe. Individuals see themselves, their families, their beliefs and their communities threatened. What should they do? A turn to any new customs or ways of life is too ponderous and slow, the threat is too imminent. And so, where a prescription for self-destruction already exists, it is followed through. Such prescriptions are, if anything, the result of r– selection. They are not to be expected in pro-natalist cultures that are determinedly fighting a day-to-day battle with survival in unstable conditions. On the contrary, they are a r– selected last-ditch measure for foreseeable crisis situations, reflecting by their intensity the need, in normal times, to take the greatest pains to avoid such situations by the greatest adherence to the normal rules of life. They are saying, 'Stick to the rules, they are precious and vital; but if you cannot, destroy yourself!' Such ideas can clearly have complete control over the human will to live; they are not, by this or any other token, as 'adaptive' (or even 'sensible' to use a less value-laden word) as rules that might bring about a rational solution to the crisis and a return to some new, future, stability.

Martyrdom

There is little accurate information on early Christian deaths other than the listed martyrs of whom there are somewhat less than 5,000. Some researchers have considered the number of martyrs small (Dodwell 1684) and others large (Hertling 1944) suggesting there were 100,000 executed martyrs from the persecution by Nero who was emperor AD

54–68, to the end of Diocletian's period as emperor in AD 305. Except for the persecution by Nero there may not have been any wholesale killing which could have greatly affected the birthrate. Some accurate figures come from Palestine where, from the spring of AD 303 until Galenius' edict in AD 311, there were 44 killings, but for other totals there is no corroboration; it does seem for the length of the period involved (Grégoire 1951) the totals must have been modest.

Ecclesiastical records are filled with references to martyrdom such as the 80 clerics who petitioned the emperor Valens (AD 364–78) about the treatment of Christians. He, pretending to send them into exile, arranged for their boat to be set on fire so that they might even be deprived of burial (Socrates 1891: 104).

Later, the Inquisition is widely considered to have burnt to death large numbers of those opposed to Roman Catholicism in the early Middle Ages. Some commentators have denied this, however, stating that it marked an improvement in the treatment of criminals and its procedures considerably diminished the number of those condemned to death (Vacandard 1908). Records have survived for Toulouse from 1307 to 1323 (Maycock 1927). During this period the Inquisition pronounced 930 sentences. Of these, only 42 were given over to the secular authorities and burnt; 307 were imprisoned, but of these only 9 were strictly confined; the remainder being allowed to live with their spouses under more or less communal living conditions. The secular authorities were far more active, on occasion burning Albigensian heretics in large numbers, 200 at Monsegur in 1244, and 80 at Berlaiges in 1248.

Religious massacres

More serious damage is likely to have been caused by sieges occasioned by religious wars in which whole communities died. Thus in the siege of the Saracen fortress of Damietta (lower Egypt) in 1219, only 3,000 Muslims survived out of an estimated 80,000 inhabitants because of starvation and disease when besieged by Christian crusaders (Oliver 1894). As we come forward in history, larger numbers have been killed for their faith or because of their religion with the invention of ever more efficient weapons and means of destruction, though this impression may be due in some measure to better historical records. The St Bartholomew's Night massacre of French Protestants in 1572 probably totalled some 10,000 men, women and children (Erlanger 1962). In this case, figures for Paris come from the payments paid to gravediggers who disposed of bodies floating down the Seine (Weiss 1888).

Russian pogroms of Jews involved large numbers, for example 300 killed in Odessa in 1905, 80 in Bialystoil in 1906 and during the period 1917–21, mainly by the White Ukrainian Army, possibly as many as 60,000 killed in 887 major and 349 minor pogroms (*Encyc. Judaica* 1971, 13:694–701).

It is only with the Jewish holocaust during the Second World War that we have more detailed figures. These are admitted to be incomplete (*Encyc. Judaica* 1971, 8:889) as no records are available of the actual numbers liquidated by Nazi Germany. Certainly something like six million Jews died, involving in some cases the virtual obliteration of whole communities. The complexity of such events in social and political terms, their ideological implications and origins are vast and libraries have already been written about them. For our purposes, the biological effects seem to require little comment: the twentieth century destruction of Jews marks such an enormous loss of viable human potential that it dwarfs all other such events. Judaism clearly puts its members at risk to life and limb every now and again. This risk the group and its members know all about and are prepared to accept, since every Jew has the personal option to convert to another religion which will be safer, if not for him or her, then surely for his or her descendants. Such a strategy would thus be sensible in terms of kin selection. There can be no doubt that if Hitler's policies and ambitions had succeeded, all overt traces of Jews and Judaism would have been erased, at any rate for a considerable length of time.

In the case of religious wars we need to be exceptionally careful before making any generalizations. Wars phrased in a religious idiom are often more accurately understood in terms of the political ambitions of leaders who use the added zest of religious conviction to increase the fighting power of their armies. In such cases the wars may indeed be related to shortages of resources, or to internal stresses (Russell and Russell 1968, have written extensively on this in relation to biological processes) and the religious aspects are secondary. Besides the violence of wars about resource shortages, there are wars of conquest in which propagation of religious ideas and militaristic methods of conversion are significant causal factors from the outset.

We have developed the idea that the particular beliefs and customs of religions are related to the stability of the resource base and the extent of control over it. Where religions are based on instability and poor control they are unlikely to be expansionist in the very active way demanded by military regimes. There is insufficient spare energy and an altogether unfavourable socio-economic basis for this. In such cases, $r+$ selection is in operation and will not produce large and efficient armies. The preoccupations of people, religious and otherwise, will circle around the immediate problems of subsistence and survival. Only when conditions have led to the emergence of $r-$ selected cultural patterns can we expect religious ideas to become violent or aggressive, as opposed to resigned and fatalistic. War can then be made rather than avoided or endured; but it need not be. Nothing Jesus said was militaristic though many bloody wars have been pursued in the name of Christianity (see Plate XXVII). In other cases and at other time things are different. The Baghavad-Gita, perhaps the best known of Hindu religious works contains a long discussion of this very point, namely whether it is appropriate to go to war for the sake of the faith, or not. The young Prince, Arjuna, is not inclined to do so; but his charioteer Krishna (an incarnation of the god Vishnu) emphasizes that it is vital for him to do so. Such dilemmas could be related to a transitory phase of a culture, or sub-culture, from $r+$ to $r-$ selected religious ideology. Such theoretical possibilities call for further investigation than is possible here.

Conclusions

The subject of death in relation to religion has turned out to be inordinately complex and difficult to comprehend, but very interesting. At first one thinks of religion as the agency that 'smoothes the troubled

XXVII. During the recent Christian/Muslim fighting in the Lebanon, a Maronite priest is seen shooting from a church wall. Another young Maronite has a picture of the Virgin Mary on the butt of his rifle.

brow' of the dying person, and of those who are left behind. Indeed it does, and at the level of individual psychology this may be its most important function. But what we discovered in our broader survey was that religion and death are intertwined in far more extensive ways than this.

For instance, on occasions the pursuit of religious ideas and practices can lead to the sickness or death of the individuals and groups concerned, whether it be the occasional victim of snake-handling ceremonies, or of brain-eating, of drinking water contaminated by the dead, or handling a corpse. In such cases, the outcomes are a result of a lack of adequate comprehension of the infective agents involved, or a lack of care, or both. In the case of snake-handling, faith is being tested and forms of religion emphasizing a high degree of care in normal circumstances may be buttressing this with such 'miracles' to strengthen their hold on the community; if so, we should see them arising through r– selection. But other cases of snake handling could have quite different causes, as in the activities of oriental 'snake charmers' who are quite frankly performing for money (and use de-fanged snakes in any case).

Funeral customs are a central consideration and we distinguished 'open' from 'closed' in terms of the degree to which they encouraged or discouraged the expression of feelings by the mourners. In more r– selected cultures, where death is less frequent in the experience of individuals, we found the 'closed' approach, which could, together with other aspects we described, be a result of the awkward threat of death to the prevalent ideas of control and permanence. The result of such closure was a failure to meet the psychological needs of survivors. By contrast, in cultures resulting from $r+$ selection religions had such 'open' expressions of grief as mourners paid to wail, customs involving cradling the dead person's body, and placing of the dead nearby or even under the living house.

We looked at attitudes to autopsies and transplants and found a greater readiness to accept these rather modern practices in Christianity than in Judaism. We argued that a positive attitude to them would result from $r-$ rather than $r+$ selection.

With regard to the monuments to the dead, often huge and demanding vast energy resources to build, that various religions have from time to time produced, we concluded that these were only possible in sub-cultures associated with aristocracies intent on demonstrating their permanence and their wealth. It would seem appropriate here to quote the sonorous lines of Shelley's 'Ozymandias':

I met a traveller from an antique land
Who said: Two vast and trunkless legs of stone
Stand in the desert . . . Near them, on the sand,
Half sunk, a shattered visage lies, whose frown,
And wrinkled lip, and sneer of cold command,
Tell that its sculptor well those passions read
Which yet survive, stamped on these lifeless things,
The hand that mocked them, and the heart that fed:
And on the pedestal these words appear:
'My name is Ozymandias, king of kings:
Look on my works, ye Mighty, and despair!'
Nothing beside remains. Round the decay
Of that colossal wreck, boundless and bare
The lone and level sands stretch far away.

Religion and death were further associated in a number of dreadful ways, involving human sacrifice, self-destruction, and wars of conquest, often causing deaths on a massive scale with consequently devastating results on the reproductive powers of the groups concerned. Where religion demanded extensive human sacrifice, and this could be linked to overpopulation as in the Mexican example we looked at, we indicated that it was an inappropriate long-term solution to a situation where a culture was apparently moving from $r+$ to $r-$ selection. Self-destruction by religious groups was, we found, associated with situations of internal social crisis in which this particular form of suicide could be seen as a device maintaining the vital importance of the ideas of the group prepared to destroy itself in their defence, and most likely associated with $r-$ selection. Wars of religious conquest, finally, we linked to $r-$ selection or to a transitory period from $r+$ to $r-$ selection where the war and its inevitable death-toll was seen as the prerequisite for peace and prosperity.

Part Three

Religion and
disease

12 Concepts of disease

In Part 2, we were mostly concerned with ways in which religion affected the survival and reproductive success of individuals in the normal course of their lives. The topic of sickness cropped up from time to time, for instance in cases where religious practices could be seen to have unhygienic consequences, or where they could be seen to spread infection, thus lowering the Darwinian fitness of the individuals concerned. Again, sickness was a central topic during the last phases of the life-cycle, though at this time its implications for an individual's own reproductive success were minimal.

There is more to religion and disease than the ways in which religious practices affect the spread of various diseases. Diseases, however they arise, have to be dealt with. They can and do cause widespread havoc, whether we think of the spectacular epidemics of plague in bygone times, or the less spectacular but nevertheless very far-reaching effects (on productivity, for instance) of the 'flu epidemics of the present day. What attitudes can we discern among religions to the occurrence of diseases that can strike at any moment, and to which we all from time to time succumb?

Fatalism

It would seem that if a religion imparts fatalistic ideas, these will lessen the efforts individuals make to overcome any diseases they have. Other individuals may feel that they need not make any effort to cure them either and this will reduce the reproductive rate of affected individuals, and may completely eliminate certain people from the reproductive process. At the population level this would, if not compensated for, keep the death rate high and the birth rate low, reducing the growth

The grotto at Lourdes in the early twentieth century showing crutches and other appliances hung up by those who have been cured there.

rate or replacement rate and hence the size of the population. From the genetic, individual and population standpoints, this might be no bad thing, especially in countries lacking a sustained food surplus or permanently adequate food supplies. Thus a reasonable suggestion would be that fatalistic ideas leading to passivity in the face of disease would be associated with poorer countries that cannot sustain their long-term food supply or other essential scarce resources. This kind of hypothesis makes good sense in arguments that religions are adaptive. It would be maladaptive for religions to make great efforts to save life in countries where life was a burden on the community and there was not enough food to go round. It would be advantageous to have a religion which said it was God's will to have people fall sick and die and that nothing should be done to save them. The same could be said for ideas emphasizing a joyful acceptance of death, and of beliefs in a glorious after-life for those dying young. These features, then, would be expected to result from $r+$ rather than $r-$ selection.

Such crude ideas must overlook many of the complexities of the actual world. Wherever we turn our attention, we find a vast range of illnesses and of attitudes to them. Also, we can designate certain zones as having adequate long-term food supplies and others as being prone to severe shortages and surpluses but there are variations in such zones depending on altitude, proximity to water, and social factors such as caste, which partly determine how much food people get in time of need. These are facts we must take into account, and they will complicate any answers we can attempt to produce. So will entirely other matters, such as level of technological sophistication in relation to food supply, level of food imports, use of spare land (if any exists) and improved use of existing land. Further, there is the extent to which other religious ideas, e.g. about science, agriculture, fishing, hunting or nature, enable or restrict the development of processes of thought that are directly concerned with disease management and cure. We cannot hope for much by putting our question too boldly and naively; we need to look at the situations that exist in all their complexity. Only then can we draw sensible conclusions and avoid the fallacy of a naïve ecological determinism.

Religion and disease within the Western setting

In the United States, particularly in the mid-nineteenth century, there was widespread intense pietism, a stress on religious feeling which acted as a stimulus to social reform (Niebuhr 1937) and to public health reform in the case of New York City. Two figures dominated this trend in public health attitudes, Dr J. H. Griscom, a Quaker, City Inspector and principal health officer, and R. M. Hartley, a Presbyterian merchant who helped found the New York Association for Improving the Condition of the Poor in 1842 (Rosenberg and Rosenberg, 1968).

Griscom, the son of a Quaker educator and philantropist, held that hygiene and physiology had a spiritual as well as material content, holding that:

Indulgence in a vicious or immoral course of life is sure to prove destructive to health. Our Creator afflicts us with diseases that we may know how frail and dependent we are. But he has also given us a knowledge of the laws which

*regulate our growth, and our lives, so that by attending to them and living
purely and uprightly, we may avoid those diseases in a great degree. (Griscom
1847: 132–33.)*

He drew habitually on arguments from design, taking the view that
New York's mortality rates could not be a normal part of God's world
because they were so high (Griscom 1857) and stressing the unnatural
quality of city life. The neglect to remedy these evils was culpable and
an affront to God. He wrote: 'Cleanliness is said to be next to godliness
and if after admitting this, we reflect that cleanliness cannot exist without ventilation, we must then look upon the latter as not only a moral
but religious duty.' (Griscom 1850: 137.)

He produced a detailed and critical report on the city's sanitary condition (Griscom 1843) and it has been contended that 'this study already
contains in essence the principles and objectives that were to character-
ize the American sanitary reform movement for the next thirty years'
(Rosen 1958: 238). He carried out his campaign for the state's involvement in improving the health of the city over two decades at legislative
hearings, public meetings and through journals, consistently displaying the pietistic origin of his concern for public health. As a result an
increasing number of doctors became interested in public health
problems.

Hartley in the long run was more influential than Griscom as the
principal organizer and long-time director of his Association, and is
considered to have been the shaper of America's first social welfare
agency, leading its involvement in tenement and public health reform.
His social activism was founded on the evangelical enthusiasm of his
youth and despite his success in business in New York City, his spiritual commitment continued throughout his life; for example, an entry
in his diary for 1856 stated: 'At evening attended a sanitary lecture at the
Cooper Institute. Today my mind has been pervaded with a deep
seriousness and a desire to dwell on spiritual things' (Hartley 1882: 288.)

His Association in 1852 opened the first public wash-house in New
York City and, after a long campaign over their findings of remarkably
high infant mortality, the production and sale of milk came under legal
control in 1862. He fought with others for the establishment of an effective professionally staffed City Board of Health in 1866.

Thus both these vigorous reformers were basically motivated by a
religious commitment to saving and helping the unfortunate, with an
assumption that there was a close relationship between environment,
health and morals.

Traditional and modern medical ideas

Modern medicine is to some extent an outgrowth of Christian religious
concern for human suffering, but its demonstable effectiveness for human survival in terms of reduction of death rates is not much more than
a century old. Prior to this, and still today in many parts of the world
even among those directly affected by modern Western medicine, local
traditional religion and indigenous medicines have continued in use in
the treatment of human misfortune. Traditional healers have attempted
to solve health problems in many ways, e.g. by herbalism (see Plate
XXVIII), exorcism or the confession of sin, and have mostly dealt with

XXVIII. A contemporary scene at the market place in Zomba, Malawi. On sale are a variety of herbs, pangolin scales, snake skins, tortoise shells, imported cowrie shells and various liquid medicines.

the whole person and his or her problems as a single unit, rather than with the affliction alone as if it were to all intents and purposes separate from the person suffering from it.

It is now becoming recognized in the West that traditional 'medicine men', whether diviners, diviner-herbalists or shrine priests, can have an important place in any 'Third World' public health system (Ademuwa-gun 1969). This view can be justified on the grounds that such practitioners have developed valid and successful skills in dispensing curative, preventative substances and in rehabilitative care; they often use an astute approach to human health; they belong to the same culture as their patients, sharing common beliefs, values and symbols of communication with them and they have skills in interpersonal relations including counselling with sympathy, identification and concern. Yet despite these advantages there has been little overall utilization of their services by Western doctors in the Tropics.

In this relationship between traditional and Western medicine, it is important to remember that good doctors cure, rather than that cures make good doctors. Overall there is little doubt that considerable confidence exists in Western drugs, but much less confidence in Western-style processing of illness particularly as regards what is seen as the aloofness of medical personnel. Peasants and the urban poor mainly have dealings with nurses and medical assistants who often, owing to the shortage of doctors, prescribe rather than refer cases on which they may not be competent to reach a diagnosis (Alland 1964). The choice can often be between the local traditional healer and a small Western-style bush dispensary with few medicaments often in short supply, and

Concepts of disease

it is the former who in practice provides the health service for most of the population most of the time (Imperato 1977).

There is little recognizable ritual associated with Western medical treatment and the medical examinations are usually both detached and cursory. Western medicine places the accent on the clinical and biological evidence and this point of access closes off contact with the socio-religious forms of diagnosis used by traditional practitioners (Bibeau 1979). The Western system considers itself to be all-embracingly effective so that it is far from ready to accept 'untrained' traditionalists, who can nonetheless be surprisingly effective (Lambo 1971).

While Western medicinal outposts often have a mission-station basis, they do thus seem very secular to non-Western tribal groups. Sometimes the doctor in a hospital with religious backing may be in a better position to bridge the gap. The patient can at least assume that there is a religious dimension to the treatment because there are religious symbols in association with the doctor and his staff; religious dress may be worn; a crucifix may be seen or religious slogans on the wall; or the hospital may be situated in the grounds of a church.

Traditional healers are, in some areas, relatively more common in the towns than in the more rural areas. Mwanza town in Tanzania had about 10 times more diviner-herbalists in the mid-1950s than more rural areas (personal observation, R. Tanner). That the numbers of medicine men is huge everywhere seems certain (Harrison 1974 and see Table 12.1).

Table 12.1 Estimated number of traditional medicine men in selected Nigerian cities, 1973 (From: Harrison 1974)

City and state	Population estimate	Number of medicine men
Lagos, Lagos	665,246	15,168
Ibadan, Western	627,379	14,304
Benin, Mid-western	100,694	2,296
Enugu, East Central	138,457	3,117
Kano, Kano	299,432	6,736

In addition Christian and other syncretic religious organizations have proliferated so that the modern man can get religiously related 'health treatment' in a clearly religious environment which does not have the status shortcomings of traditional treatments. A long queue of people waited to go through the laying on of hands for their health and other problems after a Legio Maria Mass in Nairobi in 1969 (personal observation, R. Tanner), and both indigenous and foreign clergy are under constant pressure to use their religious powers if not to cure, at least to stave off misfortune.

The extent of co-operation varies from place to place, but overall appears to be low. Some Malaysian medicine men have attended government-sponsored elementary medicine and hygiene courses (Bolton 1968) and in India there has been some co-operation over family planning (Neumann and Bhatia 1973). What appears to be happening in Zaïre, and may well be the case elsewhere, is that traditional healers as locally powerful men are receiving de facto recognition from the political authorities and that in general they continue to practise both because it is impossible to stop them and because these new states find it hard to provide the expensive alternative of even a minimal modern public health system (Janzen 1974).

The co-existence and combination of largely incompatible medical systems raises an interesting possible interpretation in terms of r^c+ and r^c- selection. Whereas in r^c- selected Western Christian ideas emphasis is on active practical and physiologically effective methods of cure, traditional methods quite often, still to this day, stress elements of social discord and witchcraft and suggest a variety of kinds of cure, from use of herbal medicines to the recital of spells, performance of rituals and handling of objects with curative powers. We have seen that such methods are not entirely ineffective, but they are less effective for severe illnesses such as typhoid, malaria or cholera. Where they persist, in cultures subject to uncontrolled epidemics, we can consider them as products of r^c+ selection. In such cases we can agree that adoption of more successful Western medical practices will achieve higher rates of cure but unless this is matched by a greater extent of control of food supply and provision of stable food resources for the population, r^c- selected medicine will be disfunctional because the more appropriate culture in such ecological circumstances will in fact be the r^c+ one. Hence, whatever the other circumstances, there will clearly be a return to r^c+ selected medicine if r^c- medicine tends to lead to long-term disaster, such as must result if the death rate declines and leads to overpopulation in relation to food supply.

It is interesting to compare the healing practices of a Coptic (Christian) priest (Giel et al 1968) and a Muslim sheikh (Workneh and Giel 1975) in Ethiopia. The people coming to both these religious practitioners of medicine were suffering from physical and mental illnesses and, as well, they were seeking solutions to social misfortunes. In both the situations referred to above, the cures were gradual and consisted of a combination of medical treatment and services offered by the two priests, supported by the confidence in them of the patients by virtue of their religious faiths.

Both priests had rigid methods which they applied to all persons who came seeking their help. The Coptic priest induced trance states by his dominating personality and his standardized and suggestive method of questioning. The Muslim sheikh was equally dogmatic in his therapy, stating that suffering could only be cured by faith in Allah, and supporting this by hitting sufferers with his hand on the afflicted part of the body. According to Workneh and Giel (1975), these divers religious therapies appear to 'work'. This raises the general question of what it is that 'cures' disease and how far Western science, with its emphasis on pharmacological cures for so many symptoms, has, in departing from traditional methods, lost as well as gained.

Perhaps in important ways magico-religious practices give their participants the conviction and the courage to carry on with their lives instead of giving way to despair (see Plate XXIX). It is here that we can consider one of the most important aspects of religion and its relationship to medicine: the question of the 'miracles' which are recorded as having occurred at Roman Catholic shrines such as Our Lady of Lourdes. The shrines at which such miracles are alleged to have occurred are quite numerous including, besides Lourdes, St Joseph's Oratory (Montreal), Our Lady of Guadalupe (Mexico), and Our Lady of Fatima (Portugal).

The number of miracles at Lourdes accepted by medical authorities is extremely small in relation to the number of pilgrims. The chance of

XXIX. A Sukuma
witch-doctor exorcising an
ancestral spirit from a sick
woman so that she can
propitiate this ancestor who
will then withdraw the illness.

being cured for a desperately ill person has been put at 300 to 1 against
(Garner 1974). If we accept that figure as correct, miracles would not
have much direct biological significance. But there are other aspects that
may be more important. As Garner writes: 'And so the sick leave
Lourdes, still with their bodily ailments, all but a few. But they are
cured – cured of despair, of sadness, of their inability to accept mortality. What is the definition of health? Optimum adaptation to one's
environment. In this sense, nearly every pilgrim, bodily sick or not, who
goes to Lourdes receives a benison of health.' (1974: 1264.)

Not all writers, however, have seen Christianity as a health-giving
faith. Darlington (1969) for example described the pre- and post-
Christianization of Rome as follows:

*Christian ideas on cleanliness must be counted a step back from those of civilized
people either pagan or Jewish. When Jerome came to Rome as an Illyrian
immigrant he found a city with 900 public baths. But he felt that these resorts of
profane pleasure would be better converted to sacred baptisteries. The man who
had bathed in Christ, in his opinion, needed no second bath.*

And he added the footnote:

*Other factors helping in the decline of washing were perhaps the decay of the
Roman aqueducts and the Christian idea that nudity and mixed bathing led to
sexual promiscuity (whence the transference of the word bagnio in Italian to
mean brothel).*

He continued:

The Christian rejection of washing and tolerance of filth was to continue down to our own day. It was to devastate Christian cities with plague, generation after generation. Milder epidemics began in Rome with Marcus Aurelius but became more serious with Justinian in Constantinople. They continued, one disease replacing another, up to the last century in Europe. The damage was selectively disadvantageous to Christians in relation to Jews in the same cities; and also in relation to non-Christian cities, notably, as we shall see later, in Islam.

The consequences have been far-reaching. Until recently rules of hygiene have always depended on religion for their enforcement in multiracial and stratified societies. The right rules have therefore been indispensable for any religion that was to expand into warm countries with dense populations. Christendom had thus been permanently deflected away from southern countries by its neglect of cleanliness, its opposition to nudity and washing. (Darlington 1969: 299– 300).

This is an interesting idea, though one which, as a reading of this book will show, we do not in fact find necessary, adequate or indeed well-documented in the relative absence of Christianity in 'southern countries'. We must, surely, accept that Christianity in the Roman Catholic form *is* the predominant religion in much of South America. In those hot countries to which Darlington no doubt refers, such as India, China, North and tropical Africa, Indonesia, etc. we have suggested other more compelling reasons for the predominance of other religions over Christianity.

In a very thoughtful and carefully-worded study, Vaux (1976) analysed the possible, and in some cases, actual, interrelations between the Judaeo-Christian commitment and health. He wrote:

Religion may contribute to physical and mental health. Certainly in the deep meanings of well-being, good religion brings health. Salvation tends one's being toward health. But in a more profound sense, sound religion may render one weak rather than strong, dependent rather than independent, critical rather than adjusted, non-conformist rather than well-rounded, ecstatic rather than integrated, pain-bearing rather than tranquilized. In fact, at the radical heart of the Christian tradition, where prototypic man is crucified man, we find the notion that normative man, man at his best, is suffering man, broken man, pathetic man, dying man. In one sense the hale and hearty, robust man of our perennial Promethean mythmaking is the inversion of what our religion sees as ideal man. This man is pathetic, sympathetic and empathetic, dying into life. In normative personhood masculinity is graced by inclination toward the feminine. The Greek hero is not model humanity in this tradition. (Vaux 1976: 525.)

He continued:

There is a related conjecture worth exploring. Could it be that the traits of tenderness and compassion, though avant-garde in mankind's spiritual development, are actually dysfunctional from the evolutionary point of view of fitness and survival? Perhaps the spiritually sensitive person is also vulnerable to heartbreak and cardiovascular crisis. The studies that attempt to correlate personal disposition and propensity to myocardial infarction find the vulnerable personality to be introspective, emotionally and volitionally intense, given to bursts of passion, serious and meditative, dutiful and conscientious, all of which in one sense are ingredients of the religious life. Though the idea is often overstated, there may be certain affinities between sickliness and saintliness. (p. 526)

He then went on to examine the health-giving properties of some religious rules, especially among more Puritannical sects, such as the Seventh Day Adventists 'who enjoy dramatically better health indices than the general populace' (p. 527), together with the view they often express that sickness provides a welcome opportunity for amending and purifying one's way of life. Christianity favours moderation in working, resting, eating and drinking, and hence promotes health. Yet, he continued:

Although purity may mean simplicity, singleness of purpose, frugality and integrity, the purity impulse may also degenerate into sickness. In the Lady Macbeth syndrome, the woman washes her hands all night and all day. Dirt and germ phobia are factors in many illnesses. Many mental disorders originate in the obsessive need to isolate oneself from the millions of microbes, poisons, and contaminants closing in on the vulnerable body. Paranoia is fear of contaminants disproportionate to their reality. As the elder Zossima tells the novice Alyosha Karamazov, however, true purity is loving the creatures, loving the earth. Being earthly, like the humus, means to have humility and humor. Real purity of life could be seen as willingness to get your hands dirty, sweat with the brow, take life's anguish with relish, standing with the other, living with abandon. Hothouse caution which isolates one from soil and toil, from life's challenge, achieves neither purity nor health. (p. 528)

Vaux continued his survey with a consideration of the various ways in which religiosity can affect a person's will to go on living, by generating purpose in life, and how this in turn can affect survival, e.g. by affecting how a patient progresses post-operatively, or survives anaesthesia. He contrasted the idea of the survival, after death, of the soul (as in Plato's account of the death of Socrates in the *Phaedo*) with the Christian idea of the resurrection of the body. Socrates faced death confidently, Jesus approached it with trembling and distress (Mark 14:36, 15:34, Luke 22:44). The question put by Vaux was:

Does a Socrates-like confidence in immortality lead one to easily accept death, even to the extent of inflicting it on oneself? Does a Hebraic dread of death lead one to preserve life, cling to every modicum of vitality, undergird every effort of biomedical science to forestall, perhaps even defeat, this last enemy? (p. 591)

And he felt that:

Intrinsic to beliefs about life after death are commitments to present health concerns. Depending upon whether immortality or resurrection controls the belief, we find varying positions regarding:
(a) resistance to natural fate (epidemics, infectious disease, malnutrition, degeneration and ageing, death) through preventive medicine and public health programmes;
(b) extending the life span through biomedical research and clinical therapeutics;
(c) 'willingness to die'. Positions are found ranging from rage and resistance at

one end of the spectrum through reluctant or peaceful acceptance, to pathological
yearning for death at the other end of the spectrum. (p. 531–2)

We have quoted from the paper by Vaux at length because it is so
germane to our own theme. It was in fact the outcome of a symposium
on religion and health. Vaux's conclusion is chiefly that more research
is needed on the complex interplay of *beliefs* about disease and health
and *actual* disease and health. He certainly does not prejudge the issue or
take a naïve 'functionalist' standpoint.

It would perhaps be wrong, in view of his caution, to suppose there
is an easy answer to his question, but our ideas do prompt us to give
some sort of explanation. We contrast, throughout the book, those religions and cultures in which man feels himself to be a victim of environmental difficulties and disasters, with those in which he has achieved a
good measure of control. It is mostly in the former that resignation
occurs, in the latter that life is held dear and death dreaded. We shall interpret these attitudes as reflections of the general trend towards selection for $r^c +$ strategies in the former, $r^c -$ in the latter.

Medical care in medieval Islam and Hinduism

While the origins of Islamic medicine and hospital care came from
Byzantine models (Runciman 1933), its record is distinct since its care of
the sick was not carried out by religious orders. The first institutional
care of the blind, disabled and lepers was a hospice built in Damascus in
AD 706 by the Caliph Al-Walid as a philanthropic gesture. By the end of
the century two hospitals had been founded in Baghdad under the aus-
pices of the Caliph Al-Rashid; from then on hospitals became a feature
of all the main cities of the Islamic world (Hamarneh 1962).

One of the basic requirements of Islam is the giving of alms which
was considered as religiously important as prayer, fasting and the pilgrimage to Mecca. It is not surprising therefore that Islamic rulers welcomed the opportunity to build and equip new hospitals to fulfil their
religious obligations as well as to testify to the wealth and grandeur of
their regimes. Further, the services of these hospitals and their doctors
were in the first instance supported by philanthropy and then by public
funds, and were provided free to all regardless of age, sex and social
standing.

We do not know what the demographic effects of these hospitals
may have been on the populations they served but we do know that the
larger hospitals were also medical schools. These schools were responsible for raising both the standards and quality of the medical profession
within the Islamic empire, particularly as they employed Christian and
other non-Muslim physicians and so were not closed off from new ideas
by religious restrictions.

We also know that the patients in these hospitals were systematically
cared for. Islamic medical treatment was based essentially on Greek origins and consisted of therapy by exercises, baths and diet based on the
humoral theory introduced by Hippocrates and elaborated by Galen. If
these treatments had no effect a comprehensive *materia medica* was used
which was widely available (Al-Kindi 1966; Elgood 1951). Finally manipulations, bone-setting, cauterizing, venesection and minor eye surgery

were used. However the development of major surgery was hindered by religious and traditional opposition to human dissection. The Adudi hospital in Baghdad built in AD 981 had 24 physicians who called daily on the patients, and at the Al-Nuri hospital in Damascus physicians were required to keep regular records of diet and medication after their daily rounds.

In the Al-Fustat hospital in Cairo built in AD 872 there were separate wards according to sex and with regard to the kind of illness or surgery involved. Separate baths for men and women were installed and each patient was required to wear special clothes provided by the hospital authorities while their clothes and valuables were kept in a safe place until their discharge. The Al-Dimnah hospital in Tunisia built in AD 830 had specially employed Sudanese women as ward attendants and nurses. Maternity does not however seem to have been the occasion of organized concern.

Medieval Hinduism also had religious institutions which carried out substantial medical work but regrettably information about them is limited to a few surviving inscriptions on temple walls (Reddy 1941). Details are known about a small hospital with 15 beds attached to the Vishnu temple at Madhurantakam endowed by the Chola king, Rajikesari Veerarajendra (AD 1063–69). Another temple at Sriranganadha had a dispensary for pilgrims in the thirteenth century, and during that period dispensaries and hospitals existed at the educational and religious centres of Kanchi, Draksharama and Pithapuri.

The monasteries of southern India are known to have provided medicines and relief for the treatment of the sick and the Kodia monastery in an inscription dated AD 1162 was described as a place for the treatment of diseases of the destitute and the sick generally, and for the distribution of food to the poor, lame, blind and deaf. Perhaps we have in these medieval inscriptions is evidence not so much that these Hindu charitable institutions cured the sick, but that they kept alive many who would otherwise have died of neglect.

Hindu medicine today

The Hindu Laws of Manu see physical ills as being the result of evil acts committed in a previous incarnation and state 'thus in consequence of a remnant of the guilt of former crimes, are born idiots, dumb, blind, deaf and deformed men, who are all despised by the virtuous'. The adulterator of grain results in redundant limbs, the stealer of the words of the Veda in dumbness, the stealer of clothes in leprosy, and the stealer of a lamp in blindness. These sufferers for the sins of a previous generation are also not allowed to sacrifice (Laws of Manu 1969, iii:151–5) and indeed by their very presence they penalize the giver of a sacrificial feast (Laws of Manu 1969, iii:161 and 177). Those who have genetic deformities or the stated diseases are effectively prevented from marrying by very strong social and religious sanctions.

Besides the serious, and mostly genetic or constitutional diseases referred to above, that are believed to arise from events during a prior incarnation, the Hindu view of health and sickness is that there should be harmony and balance between the elements controlling the proper functioning of the body (Opler 1963). Any disharmony creates non-inherited disease and is caused in the main by faulty diet and by immoderation or inappropriate behaviour in physical, social or economic matters, sexual excess, loose conduct with women, harshness in business dealings, intra-familial quarrels over land, and the activities of ghosts.

This concept of balance comes from the religious conviction that there is a cosmic order for the universe by which even the gods are governed (Kane 1946), a moral and physical order enforced by truth, righteous duty and observance of religious rites in which the activities of sacrifice are connected with prevention and cure. Within this system of order under the great gods Brahma, Vishnu and Shiva, there are local-ized cults, with goddesses often related to specific diseases such as smallpox, chickenpox, cholera and boils (Dube 1956).

It may come as a surprise to some that there have been continuous modern efforts in India to retain the ancient Hindu Ayurvedic system of medicine, and that these efforts have been supported by modern govern-ments who have appointed a commission to increase the usefulness of the indigenous systems of medicine (Government of India 1948). Quite apart from the question of the degree to which a modern govern-ment is involved in promoting what must be accepted to be unscientific methods of medical practice, there is the extent to which these practices are actually used among both peasants and townspeople. This govern-ment commission assessed the use as involving more than 80 per cent of the population.

A study of medical care in a rural Indian community in the Punjab (Singh et al. 1962) for a series of fatal illnesses, compared the proportion who had gone to Westernized physicians or auxiliary health workers with those who had gone to local spiritual healers, and the practitioners of indigenous medicine (Table 12.2). The youngest age groups had the lowest levels of any kind of medical care, and spiritual healers and the practitioners of indigenous medicine dominated their terminal care. We cannot know how the course of any of the fatal illnesses might have been affected if the people concerned had seen another kind of healer than the one they did.

Table 12.2 Medical care in 615 fatal illnesses of Punjab villagers; by age, 1957–59 (From: Singh et al. 1962)

Age	Patients receiving medical care from local and nearby sources, by kinds of medical service					No medical care	No medical care other than by staff member	Unknown	Number of fatal illnesses
	Physician	Practitioner of indigenous medicine	Auxiliary health worker	Spiritual healer	Total patients treated				
0–27 days	8	7	16	28	44	48	3	8	103
28 days–11 mos	17	45	42	39	86	18	6	6	116
12–23 mos	13	30	30	27	59	7	17	1	84
24–35 mos	8	9	13	10	19	2	2	—	23
36–47 mos	3	2	4	—	6	1	2	—	9
48–59 mos	2	1	1	1	3	—	1	—	4
5–14 years	2	5	7	5	12	4	1	1	18
15–44 years	26	17	29	16	48	6	4	—	58
45–64 years	29	32	32	11	57	14	3	—	74
65 + years	19	29	35	9	67	38	20	1	126
Total all ages	127	177	209	146	401	138	59	17	615

	Infectious diseases (B1–17, B23, B30–32, B36, B43)★	Non-infectious diseases (B18–22, B24–20, B33–35, B37–42, B44–46)★	Injuries (B47–50)★	Total
Number of fatal illnesses	283	307	25	615
Patients receiving medical care from local and nearby sources:	226	167	8	401
Physician	63	64	—	
Practitioner of indigenous medicine	108	67	2	
Auxiliary Health Worker	111	91	7	
Spiritual Healer	98	46	2	
No medical care	33	90	15	138
No medical care other than by staff member	23	34	2	59
Unknown	1	16	—	17

Table 12.3 Medical care of 615 fatal illnesses in eleven villages of the Punjab, India, by class of disease, 1957–59 (From: Singh *et al.* 1962)

★ Numbers refer to the abbreviated list *Manual of the International Statistical Classification of Injuries and Deaths*, World Health Organization 1955.

This study also showed that fewer females (49.1%) than males (60.5%) had some sort of medical care during their fatal illnesses and generally were seen by attendants of a lower level of professional competence. As can also be seen (Table 12.3) spiritual healers and practitioners of indigenous medicine were consulted more frequently in cases of infectious than non-infectious diseases.

A further study of the morbidity of children below five years (Malhotra and Prasad 1966) in Delhi showed that many of the cases studied had been treated by practitioners of indigenous medicine. Even when the families concerned were members of a contributory health scheme many still visited homeopaths and practitioners of indigenous medicine (Seal 1964).

A study of the personal health expenses in the North Arcot district of southern India showed (Table 12.4) the high proportion of families spending money on native and allopathic medicines, prayers and offerings. The expenditure on health care of all types for the lowest income groups was 7 per cent of their incomes as compared with 2.5 per cent for the highest income groups (Rao *et al.* 1973).

From these various points we can see that in Hinduism especially, attitudes to disease take an r^s+ rather than r^s- pattern. The idea that constitutional diseases are predetermined, and the facts that the younger people, and women, get less adequate treatment (by Western standards) than do the older ones, especially men, are more in line with r^s+ than r^s- selection. And the heavy reliance on indigenous medicines for infectious diseases can again be seen as the outcome of r^s+ selection, though no doubt in all these cases the intervening variable is the cost of treatment. We should, however, note that attitudes (which cost nothing) often favour indigenous over modern Westernized medicines and medical personnel, and (as stated) government schemes continue to

Income	Percentage stocking		
per capita (rupees)	Native medicines	Allopathic medicines	Food supplements and tonics
0–199	28.1	31.6	3.5
200–399	23.8	40.6	6.6
400–599	38.1	46.0	11.1
600 and above	30.0	64.0	25.0
Total	28.8	45.5	10.8

Table 12.4 Proportion of families spending money on stocking native and other medicines, North Arcot district, southern India (From: Rao *et al.* 1973)

promote indigenous methods. These are the mechanisms by which treatments are discovered and chosen by the sick, and can be seen as the kind of elements that disappear under r^- selection but are characteristic of cultures where r^+ selection is in operation.

Judaism and medicine

It has been written:

The medical principles of the early Hebrews, as enshrined in the Pentateuch, represent a notable advance upon contemporary theories of disease in that they repudiated magic completely, and sought to consider disease either from an empirical standpoint or else in terms of the personal spiritual relationship between the sufferer and his God. The principles of personal and social hygiene contained in the medical sections of Leviticus are unique in antiquity as rational assessments of pathology. (Harrison 1974.)

Here, by way of example, is a short but typical section of Leviticus, Chapter 13:

And when a man or woman hath a plague [i.e. sickness] upon the head or the beard, then the priest shall look on the plague: and, behold, if the appearance thereof be deeper than the skin, and there be in it yellow thin hair, then the priest shall pronounce him unclean: it is a scall, it is leprosy of the head or of the beard.

And if the priest look on the plague of the scall, and, behold, the appearance thereof be not deeper than the skin, and there be no black hair in it, then the priest shall shut up him that hath the plague of the scall for seven days:

And in the seventh day the priest shall look on the scall: and, if the scall be not spread in the skin, and the appearance thereof be not deeper than the skin; then the priest shall pronounce him clean: and he shall wash his clothes and be clean. (Leviticus 13:29–34.)

Most of the ideas given in the Old Testament were concerned to segregate those thought to have leprosy and to proclaim their uncleanliness. The Jews regarded leprosy as brought about by the sins of shedding blood, taking oaths in vain, incest, arrogance, robbery, envy and benefiting from sacred objects (*Encyc. Judaica* 1971).

If we compare the Hindu and the Judaic views of sin and disease, an interesting contrast emerges. In the Hindu case, the sin was committed in an earlier incarnation, and thus the afflicted person is not a victim of his own wrongdoings; in the Jewish case, however, he is. Second, and more importantly for our book, is the fact that whereas a lot of the medical treatments in Hinduism, even in modern times, are what we in the West would consider somewhat magico-religious, in the case of even ancient Judaism a rather more practical and prosaic medical text was available and treatment consequently more effective. Nor was there a discernible cost factor involved in the Judaic case, since from the outset it was the priest (rabbi) who was consulted, and his services were available to rich and poor alike. In any case there was no equivalent of the caste system in ancient Jewish society, nor any less concern for women and children than for men: all life was sacred and to be saved. Thus we can see the differences in religious attitudes to disease between these two cultures in terms of $r+$ (Hindu) and $r-$ (Judaic) selection: the former more fatalistic and less effectual, the latter less fatalistic and more effective, in both curing and restricting spread. As we shall see in the next section, things are not always so neat and tidy.

Epidemic and personal disease as the result of sinful actions

The Black Death was widely regarded as a Holy punishment for the sins of the world.

The Europeans were possessed by a conviction of their guilt. They were not so sure of what, exactly they were guilty, but the range of choice was wide. Lechery, avarice, the decadence of the church, the irreverence of the knightly classes, the greed of kings, the drunkenness of peasants; each vice was condemned according to the prejudices of the preacher, and presented as the last straw which had broken the back of God's patience. . . . The European, in the face of the Black Death, was in general overwhelmed by a sense of inevitable doom. (Ziegler 1970: 36 and 39.)

Ziegler makes the important point that 'the Black Death descended on a people who were drilled by their theological and their scientific training into a reaction of apathy and fatalistic resignation. Nothing could have provided more promising material on which a plague might feed.'

There was no consistent secular search for the cause of the disease and the cure was left to the clergy, who in some areas, notably Germany, advised extreme penitence, giving rise to the Flagellant movement. The rationale behind the movement was that since the pestilence was God's wrath the only cure lay in demonstrating penitence, and this could best be demonstrated by public acts of self-punishment. Flagellants on the march moved in a long crocodile from 200 to 1,000 strong. Arriving at their destination, they formed a circle round the market place and into this circle came sick people from the area. Self-scourging then took place, until the flagellants were in a state of near hysteria, using whips with nails in them to tear at their flesh and occasionally actually killing themselves. One of the promises Brethren had to make on joining the movement was not to change their clothes – they wore long skirts down to their ankles. It is hard to think of a more efficient method of spreading the plague than the practices of these people, which were specifically designed to eliminate it.

Some modern African sects such as the Christian Aladura of Nigeria hold that disease, besides being a natural phenomenon and caused by evil agencies, 'is a punishment for sins sent by God or His ministers and can only be cured by the moral repentance of the sufferer; to use medicine, even as a palliative would deceive us as to our sin and would so be wicked' (Peel 1968: 129). The break of the Aladura with the Apostolic Church in 1939–40 made this formulation even more explicit, and there was an exposition of their doctrine that sickness was the result of sin or unbelief of some kind. Peel concludes: 'It is a mark of the secure hold of this institution on its members that they have so far acted to maintain the Church's institutional goal . . . that sin is the origin of sickness, both being traced to the Fall' (Peel 1968: 134–5).

Further, the Aladura believe that drugs and other human remedies weaken faith in Christ, that faith must not be 'assassinated' by the bad example of leaders, and that denial of divine protection would send their people back to idolatry since 'it is our common experience that fetish priests and witch doctors have both good and bad medicines' (Peel 1968: 132). During a smallpox outbreak in Ibadan, Nigeria in early 1965, the head of the Aladura Church said sanctified water was the best protection possible.

The 1938 constitution of the Aladura Church stated:

It is forbidden to go to doctors or to use medicine of any kind . . . be it native or any (other) . . . We trust in heavenly healing in this Church. . . . The power of herbs has been ended, the power of medicine reduced to vanity, the power of incantation exterminated. The Lord laid down the spiritual water for everyone, and Christ is the rock of the water!   (Turner 1967, 2:142.)

Christian Scientists state that illness is a state of mind and that the true believer should concentrate on prayer and refuse medical treatment. Mary Baker Eddy, the foundress of the Christian Science Church taught that 'materialist' healing was unnecessary for true believers as only the action of the divine mind on the human mind could cure diseases. Being ill is being in error, and the recommended therapy is prayer.

Here are some quotations from her book *Science and Health* (1906):

Christian Science reveals incontrovertibly that mind is all-in-all, that the only realities are the divine Mind and idea. (p. 109)

Christian Science explains all cause and effect as mental, not physical. (p. 114)

Christian Science eschews what is called natural science, in so far as this is built on the false hypotheses that matter is its own lawgiver, that law is founded on material conditions. (p. 127)

We must abandon pharmaceutics, and take up ontology – 'the science of real being'. (p. 129)

Treatises on anatomy, physiology, and health, sustained by what is termed material law, are the promoters of sickness and disease. (p. 179)

Small wonder, then, that orthodox medicine considers Christian Scientists to be problem patients! (Hoffman 1956). They are likely to seek medical help later than the average patient and to feel guilty about doing so. The actress Doris Day and her husband sang hymns when she was suffering from a tumour which nearly proved fatal (Hotchner 1976: 196). A study of Christian Scientists in the state of Washington (Wilson 1956) showed that deaths from malignancy were nearly double the national average and it was estimated there that at least 6 per cent of all Christian Scientist deaths were preventable in the sense that their condition would have been amenable to surgery. This sample tended to die at ages slightly below the national average and the cases of malignancy averaged 34.75 years at death, while the average age of all cases considered to have been preventable was 26.8 years. Christian Scientists are thus at a biological disadvantage; they may die from a preventable cause and at an age when they are still quite clearly capable of reproduction.

What are we to conclude from the above examples – the Flagellants during the Black Death, the Aladura of Nigeria, the Christian Scientists and others who put themselves at risk? First, we should not overlook the differences between them. The Flagellants were actively trying to escape sickness and death. They were operating in a perceptual environment that was at odds with the operational environment. Their actions strove towards improved survivorship but in fact probably reduced it. Their strategy was thus, as seen by them, an effort at long-term cure in quite exceptional circumstances.

The Aladura, by contrast, combine the idea of sin as the origin of disease with a refusal to use such cures as secular Western medicine has to offer. Such ideas and actions are in line with r^c+ selection. Last, the Christian Scientists' belief that sickness is God-willed and must not be interfered with by man seems evidently to be an r^c+ strategy. We can perhaps interpret the cases of r^c+ responses as characteristic of small groups in uncontrollable disease or in hostile *social* environments. They react by a kind of social introversion. Both kinds of reaction mark, in different ways, an increase in health risk.

Blood transfusions

In Catholic ethics blood transfusions have always been approved and the donors have been praised for their charity (Pius XII 1960) and are not necessarily at fault if they accept payment. Whether a doctor can give a blood transfusion without the approval of the patient or of those persons morally and legally responsible for him is another matter over which there have been both legal and moral debates. However, some Catholic moralists (Häring 1972: 39) have held that a fully conscious adult patient has the right to refuse a blood transfusion.

These discussions usually centre on the Jehovah's Witnesses. This fundamentalist Christian sect expresses repugnance to transfusions on the Biblical grounds that man may eat anything 'but flesh with the life thereof which is the blood thereof' (Genesis 9:3–4 and Leviticus 17:10–14), and its members regard transfused blood as being 'eaten' in the sense that an infusion of blood supplies the body with nourishment.

United States hospitals have applied to the courts on many occasions to overrule a patient's objection to a blood transfusion (Georgetown

Coll. 331.Fed.2d.1000.Misc 2180.1964) and to override the wishes of
the parents of a sick child (Illinois S.Ct.104.NE2.769.1952). There are
no cases in which doctors have been sued by those believers who have
received blood transfusions against their religious beliefs (Schechter
1968), but recovered patients have appealed against court rulings
empowering doctors to give transfusions (Moore 1964). In Britain there
have been court applications with reference to adult refusals (*Lancet*
1960, **2**:976) as well as acceptance of the fact that such patients have the
right to die for their beliefs if they are fully aware of the implications of
a refusal to accept such transfusions. A further United States case
(Brooks Estate.205.NE.2nd 435.1965) held that where a patient had
clearly expressed her wishes, absolving the doctors from any civil liability, and no minor children were involved, then the state had no right
to interfere.

Considerable ingenuity has been shown by surgeons in devising
techniques for heart surgery using the patient's own blood so that they
can operate on them without moral problems or extraordinary clinical
danger. There have been cases in which surgeons have refused to operate (Minuck and Lambie 1961) once they have discovered that the
patient would not accept blood transfusions, and other cases in which
they have transfused against the wishes of their patients and even
against their own understanding of the legal position. This has to be
considered an important medical issue as the numbers of Witnesses is
increasing and, while this sect provides no membership figures, those
potentially liable to surgery cannot now be less than two million. There
is no doubt that a number of Jehovah's Witnesses have died prematurely
because of their beliefs.

Euthanasia

Euthanasia has several related meanings (see Firth 1981). These include
action or inaction based on the direct intention to shorten the agony
caused by fatal disease which could last months or years, through the
planned withdrawal or omission of life-prolonging treatment. Most
doctors admit that this possibility is a result of a new situation caused
by the unusual progress of medicine. A United States study (Williams
1969) showed that almost all Protestant doctors sampled were in favour
of negative euthanasia, 80 per cent indicating that they actually practised
it; but fewer Catholic doctors agreed. The points at issue are various.
One view is that, if life is to be prolonged, there has to be some faint
hope that a reasonably happy and significant existence may return to the
sick person in an anticipated period of time (Rhoads 1968). The decision
to prolong life must be primarily a medical one rather than an economic
one, though the effect of further futile treatment on a family's finances
has often to be considered. In cases of poverty the doctor in a state-
supported hospital system can make decisions divorced from this economic aspect while such is not the case in places where medical care is
private. A moral theologian may, however, hold that doctors should
not strive officiously to keep alive someone who is dying whatever the
financial aspects of the situation, or he may argue (with Hippocrates)
that doctors should always strive to cure and hence prolong life. Con-
fusion reigns! In principle, however, $r-$ selection would not favour
negative euthanasia, whereas $r+$ selection would do so.

Positive euthanasia – encouraging death for the 'useless'
Killing the 'useless' has certainly had a long history, starting with Plato (*Republic*, 3V.460c) who stated that those who were not physically healthy in the ideal state would be allowed to die. Thomas More (Utopia, 1965: 187) suggested that the incurably ill patient should 'either dispatch himself out of that painful life, as out of a prison or a rack of torment, or else suffer himself to be rid of it by others'.

The re-emergence of the concept of eugenic efficiency and the modern idea of euthanasia were created by Francis Bacon (1905: 106 and 487) who laid down the procedures to be followed. These principles have been outlawed by all modern states; only Nazi Germany has practised euthanasia on the incurably ill and mentally subnormal calling its programme *Todesgnade*, the 'boon of death', which is roughly equivalent in meaning to the Greek *euthanasia*. It is interesting to note that the state of Ohio in the United States passed a law referring euthanasia on demand to a committee of four (Flood 1956). This law was extended later to apply to malformed and idiot children before it was struck out by the United States government as being unconstitutional.

In the orthodox Jewish view there can be no shortening of life as all life has an equal and infinite value, and relief from suffering cannot be purchased at the cost of life itself (Jakobovits 1971, 6:978–9). The great Jewish philosopher Maimonides has stated that death by euthanasia should be legally codified as murder 'whether (the victim) is healthy or about to die from natural causes' (Maimonides 1949, Yad, Roze'ah, 2:7).

Has the policy of making euthanasia illegal been the result of Judaeo-Christian influence or other principles? One is inclined to think that legal prudence may have had the dominant hand in restraining the possibility of making euthanasia legal. Even when the aim of any such law may be conceived of as being in the best interests of the incurable or subnormal patient, the opportunities for misuse of any such law are many.

However behind this legal prudence is the fact that Judaeo-Christian tradition, starting with the Biblical injunction 'Thou shalt not kill the just and the innocent' (Exodus 23:7), has consistently condemned euthanasia and opposed it where it has actually occurred. Pope Pius XI issued a ruling (*Casti Connubii* 1931) which stated: 'If the state authorities not only fail to protect these little ones, but by their laws and decrees suffer them to be killed or even deliver them into the hands of doctors and others for that purpose, let them remember that God is the Judge and Avenger of the innocent blood that cries from earth to heaven.' Such pronouncements have provided the religious backing for legal prudence.

In biological terms the effects of an anti-euthanasia attitude are hard to assess. Euthanasia ('mercy killing') on a grand scale could eliminate all but the fertile young and reproductively active elements in a community, because, as with eugenics, there are no clear limits where the killing should stop. What life in such a society would be like is, fortunately, not known but it would probably be riddled with fear and the consequences on health and fitness could be disastrous.

Properly managed and controlled, euthanasia is not, however, biologically disadvantageous to individuals or groups. An older person may feel his or her dignity is enhanced and the lives of his or her children are made easier by seeking euthanasia, and in such cases there seems no clear biological reason to oppose it. The problem is, however, that of misuse, for instance in cases where a person requests euthanasia and then changes his or her mind, often at the very last moment, as fear of death intervenes, or for other reasons. Biological advantage may point in one direction, but biology is morally neutral (Reynolds 1980: 165; Singer 1981). Religion is founded in the province of morality and as such as is concerned with, and capable of, making value judgements and ethical pronouncements. Without these, human life as we know it would cease to exist, the concept of 'good' becoming synonymous with 'selectively advantageous' or 'conducive to inclusive fitness' or even 'conducive to group survival'. Such interpretations, while they sound reasonable in biological terms, could rapidly result in preposterous distortions of social health policies in today's efficient, rational bureaucracies, and so the relatively small biological 'load' imposed on the healthy (which is discussed at various points in this book) is probably best left outside the institutional realm altogether and in the hands of individuals reaching their own decisions on a personal basis, subject always to public scrutiny by the society as a whole.

The problem of positive euthanasia is in fact a severe moral dilemma in modern Western Christian states only, because only they have developed sufficiently advanced medical techniques to alter radically the time of death by alleviating really serious (and normally fatal) illness. The general ideological trend of such cultures, as this book shows, is $r-$ selected, emphasizing care of the sick and suffering with a view to their cure and rehabilitation. It is the certain knowledge that care will not produce these effects but will simply prolong life or delay death that typifies the modern situation. Opposition to euthanasia, positive or negative, probably reflects a wish to be consistent with care-of-all-life thinking but it need not, for instance where a pro-euthanasia policy is linked to a positive attitude to organ transplants, which are doubtless more effective in cases where the donor is younger than where he or she is older. Probably we should conclude that the current dilemmas exist between a number of cultural strategies and ideologies all of which are compatible with $r-$ rather than $r+$ selection.

Conclusions

Our survey of a number of concepts of disease has met with a limited amount of success in terms of our ultimate aim, which is to relate the ideas and actions of members of religious groups to their reproductive success and inclusive fitness. In general we found ourselves confronted from time to time with strong elements of fatalism, beliefs that sickness was God's will, and a consequently low level of response to the vagaries of the disease environment. Where disease ecology gives evidence of poor human control such beliefs are in evidence, and we can see the action of $r+$ selection, favouring pro-reproductive action and acceptance of death.

By contrast, we saw how, with the advance of modern techniques and medical know-how, Christian cultures which had for a long time stressed the value of all life and the virtues of alleviating the sufferings of others began, in recent times, to integrate ideas of piety with those of hygiene and public health reform in countries such as Britain and the USA. Here the attack on disease clearly arises from prior attitudes associated with $r-$ selection.

We looked at modern and traditional patterns of medical practice and the often complex relation between them, noting that emergence of the former did not necessarily accompany or even imply disappearance of the latter. Based on $r-$ and $r+$ selection respectively, we felt we could expect to see a persistence of traditional medical techniques in parts of the Third World where man has not yet achieved much ecological stability.

We were interested in Vaux' ideas of the difference between the robust energetic ideal man of Greek antiquity and the meek and even pathetic ideal of Hebraic man. The former was unafraid of death, meeting challenges head on, courting danger and, no doubt, dying young; the latter lived carefully, hoarding resources, and avoiding danger into a ripe old age of wisdom and respectability. This contrast is one we can rephrase in our own terms: the former is ideally suited to poorly controlled ecological circumstances, hence a product of $r+$ selection; the latter to the more tight-knit and carefully contrived life style where human ecology is based on effective management, and its vagaries are no longer a significant danger to survival.

Our survey of Hindu attitudes to disease showed that along with the idea that constitutional disease was the outcome of sins in previous incarnations, other kinds of disease were more often treated as the result of disharmony by immoderate actions, upsetting the body's balance. Such upsets called for recourse to the relevant gods for cures. But there was often a choice between such traditional methods and recourse to a modern Western-trained physician. In such cases we noted that older people, no doubt because wealthier, had more access to physicians; and men more such access than women. We also saw that fatal infectious diseases seemed to have been treated more frequently by traditional methods than by modern Western ones. No doubt in a poor country such as India there are vastly insufficient numbers of Western-trained doctors to go round, but there was evidence of preference for local medicine men, and of governmental support for them. All efforts at cure can be said to fall between some notional 'pure' $r+$ strategy in which no realistic effort is made and a 'pure' $r-$ strategy in which every conceivable realistic effort is made, and to the extent that different ideologies co-exist with different outcomes and even expectations of success, we can see Hindu attitudes to sickness on this continuum. We contrasted the Hindu situation with that of the ancient Judaic faith detailed in Leviticus, which gave out clear and realistic ideas of hygiene to one and all, and charged priests with their enactment; here is a much clearer case of $r-$ selection.

We looked at some curious cases where religious sects, all of them Christian and all fundamentalist, were guided by the notion of sickness being the outcome of sin. During the Great Plague this idea took massive hold; today it persists in some sectors of the Christian community. Throughout the mass of the Christian world sickness and suffering arouse pity, and the typical response is to seek to alleviate and cure: this was the characteristic response of Jesus as is well known. To relate sickness to sin is uncharacteristic of $r-$ care-based cultures, and we discussed the significance of such beliefs as moves towards $r+$ strategies.

Lastly, we considered the ambivalent attitudes to transfusions, transplants and euthanasia current in modern societies. It is perhaps hardest of all to see one's own culture as it now is, but the future will probably show that these are among the key areas in which the evolution of moral ideas is now taking place in the affluent West. If the ideology of the West is increasingly subject to $r-$ selection, beliefs and practices that are inappropriate in conditions of long-term ecological stability should eventually give way to more appropriate ones, but time alone will tell which ideas have the greatest persistence in shaping the future in the various cultural and ecological worlds we inhabit today.

13 Infectious diseases

Introduction

In the preceding chapter we laid emphasis on how religiously supported attitudes to sickness itself, or to medical treatment, or to other factors associated with disease, were likely to affect the chances of people contracting, or resisting adequate treatment for, those diseases. In this chapter and the next, we pursue the topic of religion and disease in a somewhat different way (although the distinction is not cut and dried). We want here to compare religious groups with regard to actual reported disease frequency data. Thus we are less concerned with predisposing attitudes that clearly seem to put religious groups at risk, or to reduce their risk, as with whether or not they actually do contract certain diseases with different frequency from their neighbours of other religious (or non-religious) persuasions. We begin with infectious diseases, and move on to non-infectious ones in the following chapter.

Perhaps before starting we should remind ourselves what we see as the relation between disease and our avowed centre of interest: reproductive fitness. Clearly we are here looking at medical rather than reproductive fitness. It is thus an oblique approach. Depending very much on age, (which is the guideline in the layout of the major part of this book), medical fitness will have effects on reproductive success; the younger a person is, especially during childhood and the so-called 'prime of life', the more serious to his or her reproductive potential is any kind of disease. A minor sickness may predispose for a major one; a major one can either be fatal or affect the reproductive system itself, leading to sterility or reduced reproductive efficiency. Lastly, what do we mean by 'infectious' diseases? By and large all diseases which are transmitted from one individual to another by 'agents' can be lumped together as infectious

A procession of medieval flagellants in the fourteenth century at the time of the Great Plague.

diseases. The opposing group are often called 'constitutional' diseases and arise from a variety of processes but not from contact with other individuals in the community.

Infectious disease can be spread in a number of ways. It can for instance be spread by physical contact between individuals, or by droplet infection from one individual to another through exhaled breath being inhaled by another person. It can also spread by the transmission from one individual to another of a virus, not breathed in but entering in other ways (e.g. through the conjunctiva as in the case of measles) or it can spread through the action of 'vectors'. A vector is an insect or other animal which carries a disease agent from one human host to the next. So we have a multitude of ways in which infectious diseases can be transmitted, and all of these may be considered with respect to the ways in which religions may wittingly or unwittingly reduce or foster them.

Infectious diseases need certain conditions in which to thrive. Most are not happy with very small populations. By and large, whether viruses or larger organisms are involved, they need big populations in order to survive, because in small populations one of two things is likely to happen. Either they wipe out the host population and hence themselves, or they produce immunity in the population and having done this the population survives while the disease agents die.

So infectious diseases tend to do best where they occur in large communities, especially where there is a shifting population, and in situations where individuals are moving around rather rapidly into new areas, where there are new people arriving and the disease agents can find new hosts. Therefore religious occasions which in any way bring people together are likely to promote conditions for infectious diseases to thrive, whereas aspects of religion which tend to cut people off from each other or close group frontiers are likely to be antagonistic to the entry from outside of infectious diseases.

This distinction can give us an important lever into the matter of r^c+ and r^c- selection. As we have constantly found throughout our work, r^c+ strategies are 'high risk' strategies geared to life in unpredictable ecological circumstances, while r^c- selection produces 'low risk' strategies. Thus large-scale religious festivals and pilgrimages in areas where infectious diseases were common would not be favoured by r^c- selection but could be favoured under r^c+ selection, if, for instance, they promoted ideas of religious unity or in other ways bolstered faith. In the relative absence of such diseases, as in the modern West, big get-togethers are less likely to promote infections, and so there will be no r^c+/r^c- contrast. However, we can speculate that in any cultural evolution from r^c+ to r^c- conditions such comings together and dispersals would tend to diminish and disappear, while the reverse would be likely if cultural evolution were going from r^c- in the direction of r^c+ selection.

We have already mentioned above the possibility of immunity occurring after infection but there is also another method by which immunity can be achieved and this is at the genetic level. With regard to malaria a number of genes have evolved conferring immunity. In such cases we can see that there might be a connection with religion if it kept together people who were genetically immune or had anything to do with the spread of genes responsible for genetic immunity, for example by restricting marriage to other people who happened to be genetically immune. If for example there were any correlation between an 'immunity' gene against malaria and a particular endogamous religious group, then the fact that this group kept up its level of 'immunity' genes by endogamy would maintain its resistance to malaria. Whereas if an anti-disease gene was not present in the members of a religious group and the group was proselytizing, constantly trying to gain new members in other parts of the world, then this could, especially if there was a lot of intermarriage, introduce into populations with some natural immunity, newcomers who had no genetic resistance and thus reduce the frequency of immune genes in the population, effectively leading to the spread of malaria.

Besides genetic immunity and immunity occurring after infection, there is artificial immunity created by inoculations and vaccinations. Certain religious sects, as we saw in the previous chapter, are hostile to medical intervention, including vaccination and inoculation; others, by contrast, are in favour of or actively promote such interventionist techniques. We interpreted such attitudes in terms of r^c+ and r^c- selection respectively.

Plague

The movements of the Flagellants were discussed briefly in the previous chapter but are worth a more detailed investigation. They toured towns in the Middle Ages trying to atone for the wrath of God manifested by the Black Death before appreciative and understanding crowds. Here is a good example of religious activity helping to spread infectious disease. Plague took on two forms: initially it was bubonic, transmitted by rat fleas, but later it became pneumonic, spread by droplet infection. Pneumonic plague spread rapidly where lots of people were gathered together in one place and so the penitents spread the disease widely as they went about atoning for it. How did this come about?

Plague had reached Europe from the East in 1348. It was considered to have been sent by God as retribution for the wickedness of the present generation. Langland (1935) wrote that these pestilences were for 'pure sin'. It has been estimated that about a third of the European population died (Ziegler 1969).

While 'infection' of some kind was recognized as the manner of spread of the plague, with some civil authorities trying to prevent its spread by keeping travellers away or quarantining them, its widespread and virulent attacks and high mortality against which nothing appeared to be effective, made it almost inevitable that there would be general support for both religious explanations and reactions.

St Bridget of Sweden, visiting Rome in 1349, stated that the proper method of tackling the epidemic was to avoid extravagant clothes, give free alms to the needy and celebrate special Masses in honour of the Trinity.

Pope Clement VI ordered a jubilee year in 1350 granting special indulgences to all who made the journey to Rome; it has been estimated that very large numbers came from all over Europe and returned home, thus spreading the infection into areas not previously touched.

The Flagellant movement (Leff 1967) in Europe, by which associations of men and women donned sackcloth and scourged themselves in public as they moved from town to town, was a reaction to the plague

XXX. At a Hindu temple in Bikanir, India, rats are being fed specially by the local Maharajah, Dr Karni Singh. Some 500 years ago the temple's goddess Karni Ma directed that the rats should be worshipped and there are now more than 100,000 rats in the temple.

that caused crowds to gather, thus spreading infection. Their numbers were often large (Cohn 1962); a single monastery in the Low Countries provided accommodation for 2,500 flagellants in six months and 5,300 visited Tournai in two and a half months. Whatever the good they may have done in awakening people's consciences, they spread the plague to young and old alike.

It is difficult to see what the Christian institutions of the time could in fact have done to slow down the spread of the disease and aid the sick, given the existing state of medical knowledge, but we can see that Christian reactions in many cases must have furthered the disease by encouraging large gatherings and the movement of penitential groups across whole countries.

Outside Christianity there are many other examples of religious actions that can increase the opportunities for spread of plague. One such is the practice of keeping live rats in certain Hindu temples (see Plate xxx).

Leprosy

We have already noted that ancient Jewish law forced suspected lepers to live apart from the settlements of healthy people. The contribution of medieval Christianity to leprosy control was the institutionalization of this separation. From the old Judaic precepts the idea of contagion gradually became the motive power in the development of an entire system of preventive measures, at first largely limited to lepers and persons suspected of leprosy (Sudhoff 1926). The recognition of the contagious nature of leprosy led to the gradual development of compulsory regulations to prevent the spread of the disease. Leprosy by the sixth century was sufficiently common in southern France and the Mediterranean littoral

XXXI. A Christian nun bandaging the hand of a victim of leprosy in present day East Africa.

for the Council of Lyons in AD 583 to promulgate an edict putting rigid limitations on the free movement of lepers. Other regulations prohibited them from going barefoot on public roads or touching articles for sale, provided that they made their presence known by blowing horns or shaking rattles. Their attendance at church was segregated.

Thus the Christian Church became a prominent factor in the establishment of the segregation of lepers, in the creation of leper colonies and a distinct factor in the gradual elimination of the disease (see Plate XXXI). The influence of the Church made leper colonies less oppressive than the term suggests (Walsh 1928). Lepers were not absolutely confined to them, and these colonies received a large measure of public support from prominent men since it was believed that the prayers of lepers on behalf of others were of particular value. The development of leper colonies can be readily accepted as a case of r- selection.

Contact with religious objects and infection

Some religions involve their faithful in touching and kissing certain objects (see Plate XXXII), or drinking and eating from certain utensils. Muslims as part of their pilgrimage to Mecca kiss the stone in the *kaaba*; Catholics kiss the feet of a wooden Christ during Good Friday services. In the latter case an altar server with a cloth wipes the wood between kisses. Muslims wash the exposed parts of their bodies prior to praying in the mosque and the cisterns containing the water for washing outside mosques has been found in the Yemen to harbour snails infested with schistosomiasis (Oliver and Ansari 1967). Similarly *Bacterium coli* has been found in the bowls containing blessed water at the entrances to Catholic churches in Perugia into which churchgoers dip their fingers to cross themselves before going into the church (Losito 1946).

In such practices it can be assumed that harmful micro-organisms are

XXXII. Kissing a crucifix outside a contemporary Russian Orthodox monastery at Pskouo-Petcherski, USSR.

deposited on the objects of devotion by some of the devotees, and that these micro-organisms are transferred to subsequent touchers. The sharing of a communion cup from which some Christian denominations drink wine has come under experimental study, using stimulated conditions, for the possibility of transfer of infections (Gregory *et al.* 1967). In this study, the wiping of the edge of the cup between drinkers was found to be remarkably ineffective in lowering the bacterial count, but another study (Hobbs *et al.* 1967) found that it reduced the bacterial count by about 90 per cent (see Table 13.1).

In the study by Hobbs *et al.* the bacteria recovered from a test cup after a simulated communion service included species of *Bacillus, Micrococcus, Neisseria, Staphylococcus* and *Streptococcus*. The communion wine killed certain micro-organisms within two to three minutes, but *Microbacterium avium* was undiminished after an hour and *Staphylococcus pyogenes* was

Experiment No.	1	2	3	4	5	6
1 Drinking from same place	485	2,700	1,700	7,820	9,200	1,670
2 Drinking from different places	910	3,020	3,320	7,840	4,290	5,200
3 Drinking from same place and wiping	215	125	320	790	1,730	2,300
4 Drinking from different places and wiping	765	305	465	920	9,440	80

Table 13.1 Effect of wiping and rotating the chalice on numbers of organisms recovered from the drinking surface (From: Hobbs *et al.* 1967)

completely protected by the saliva droplets in which it was suspended.

The study by Gregory *et al.* concluded that both the common communion cup and its contents could serve effectively as vehicles for the rapid transmission of infectious microorganisms, suggesting that the practice might be dangerous if an infected person were to participate in the communion ritual. In the past, for instance, tuberculosis might have been transmitted in this way. But the study by Hobbs *et al.* concluded that TB would not be a significant hazard except possibly in the case of an excessively salivating individual taking precedence in the communion queue! Medical opinions are thus divided. But for present purposes, in terms of the connection between high-risk actions and $r+$ selection, we can suggest that in areas where infectious diseases are common, persistence of practices increasing risk of infection may be perpetuated by $r+$ selection.

Use of left and right hands

Religious rules on which hand is to be used for excretory and/or sexual activities are widespread in Hinduism and Islam. In general the left hand is used for these purposes while the right is appropriate for eating and culinary actions. Thus, Islamic teaching has it that 'one must neither eat nor drink with the left hand for these are Satan's manners' (Ibn Taymiya 1950:); and that 'one holds the genitals with the left hand' (Ibn Rusd 1355 AH: 52). Again 'many of the Arabs will not allow the left hand to touch food in any case except when the right hand is maimed' (Lane 1954: 150). Regarding the Almighty himself: 'Allah has nothing left-handed about him since both his hands are right hands' (Tabari 1879: 56).

Hindu beliefs follow the same general rules. The sacred Laws of Manu state: 'He who desires to be pure must clean the organ by one application of earth, the anus by applying earth three times, the left hand alone by applying it ten times' (v: 136). This seems a clear indication of the idea that the left hand is actually dirtier and in more need of cleaning than the penis or the anus. As regards sex instruction, the Hindu husband learns: 'He should then with his wife get on the bed with his face toward the east or the north. Then, looking at his wife, let him embrace her with his left arm, and, placing his right hand over her head . . . next, let him place his (left) hand on her vagina' (Avalon 1963).

Finally, exclusion of the left hand for cooking and eating is prevalent in many African peoples, for instance in rural Tanzania (personal observation, V. Reynolds and R. Tanner) and in West Africa (Leonard 1906). All such practices are the result of $r-$ selection. What is perhaps most remarkable is the apparent absence of any such emphasis, or even mention, in Christianity or Judaism. It is as if these religions, so $r-$ oriented in general, had 'missed out' on a practice by which they could have immensely benefited themselves over the years. Of course, the *general* idea of hygiene has been promoted by these religions, but they might, nonetheless have been expected to embrace the idea of handedness just discussed. To the extent that, more in the past than now, infectious diseases, especially smallpox, could easily be transmitted by humans unhygienically contaminating their food with infected excreta, the absence of rules must be seen as an atypical case where these religions have, by default as it were, adopted an $r+$ strategy, or at any rate left one area of action untouched by $r-$ thinking.

Water, prayer, and religious pilgrimages

Whereas washing is normally thought of as a cleansing activity, and may in many cases be so, such is not always the case and much may depend on the precise circumstances at the time. A good example is that provided by Islam. The Koran commands: 'O you who believe! when you rise up to prayer, wash your faces and your hands as far as the elbows, and wipe your heads, and wash your feet to the ankles' (5:7), echoing the command referred to in the Old Testament (Exodus 40:32), which the Lord gave to Moses, to wash before coming near to the altar. Thus, today, the followers of Islam, before each prayer session (and there are up to five every day, though actual participation varies for each person according to circumstances) wash in the prescribed way if the situation permits. This practice can promote hygiene. For instance in the Grey Street mosque in Durban and many others, washing takes place in an anteroom beside the main prayer room, and there is a continuous supply of piped running water so that any disease agents from infected devotees are rapidly dispersed into the drains (personal observation, V. Reynolds). By contrast, in mosques in rural areas of the Yemen and Bangladesh, the water for washing comes from water storage tanks, and all those who wash before prayer run the risk of picking up up infections from Guinea worms (Underwood *et al.* 1980), schistosomiasis (Farooq and Mallah 1966) or any other disease agents present in the water (Plate xxxiii). Muslim prayer-washing can thus be associated with either $r-$ selection or $r+$ selection depending on the nature of the water supply and the disease environment.

Washing is often associated with religious pilgrimages. Many Roman Catholics (and not a few others) journey to Lourdes, in France, mostly during the warm weather from April to October. There they visit the grotto where Bernadette saw her vision of the Virgin; many of them are

XXXIII. A typical scene outside a mosque where water for pre-prayer washing of the hands, face and feet comes from a standing rainwater tank.

sick and go to Lourdes in search of miracle cures. Besides the grotto, there is the nearby holy spring which has been channelled into baths in which those seeking cures dip themselves, or are dipped.

The scene at the baths is described by Marnham (1980). Those who have come to immerse themselves first join one of the large queues. They then change clothes in a cubicle and walk down some steps into a stone tub. Those on stretchers are carried down by teams of *brancardiers*. At the far end of the tub is a small Madonna and prayer cards in 19 languages. The prayers are recited, and then the supplicant leans back, to be lowered into the water by the *brancardiers*. 'Early in the day (the water) is clean and freezing. Later, as the pilgrims pass through it, it becomes warmer. It is changed once, at midday' (p. 93).

There are altogether 13 tubs which at peak times handle an average of 85 pilgrims an hour. For instance, on 14th August 1978, 1800 men and 4750 women were bathed. Pollution of the water has been investigated on several occasions. A devout theory holds that microbes die in Lourdes water; words to this effect appeared in a recent *Guide to the Grotto*. This claim was based on tests carried out in the 1930's, which found Lourdes water to be polluted with colon bacillus, staphylococcus, streptococcus, pyocynaeus and other microbes, but showed that experimental animals were unaffected by these bacilli when derived from Lourdes water. Undoubtedly pollution is present in Lourdes water. But evidently this fact is not a consideration for those whose faith renders this water utterly pure.

The association between Christian, Muslim and Hindu pilgrimages and water has spread diseases among devotees, of which cholera has been the best documented. Cholera spreads when water contaminated by infected excreta is ingested. Christian pilgrimages to Jerusalem antedate Muslim pilgrimages to Mecca but by the early Middle Ages both were equally popular. The Crusades to the Holy Land involved large numbers of Europeans in long-lasting expeditions away from their homes. Crusaders generally sought the joys of sex with local women and sometimes married them; both they and the pilgrims brought back *Treponematosis* (syphilis), misdiagnosed at first as leprosy, which was alleged to have spread like wildfire in the fourteenth and fifteenth centuries (Hudson 1963). This disease was also spread by female pilgrims who were reported to have maintained themselves by prostitution, giving cause for religious concern (Boniface 1973: 140).

Table 13.2 Deaths from infectious diseases in Zalingei district, Sudan, attributed to West African pilgrims on the way to Mecca. (From: El Tayeb 1976)

Year	Disease	No. of deaths
1927	Relapsing fever	10,000
1929	Smallpox	359
1940	Yellow fever	1,627
1944/45	Relapsing fever	754
1949	Smallpox	Epidemic
1950/51	Cerebrospinal meningitis	9,741
1951/52	Smallpox	Epidemic
1952/53	Smallpox	578
	Relapsing fever	Epidemic
1958/59	Smallpox	90
1960/61	Cerebrospinal meningitis	892

Attracting a gathering of:	Number of fairs
Less than 5,000 people	3
5,000 to 10,000	143
10,000 to 25,000	142
25,000 to 50,000	41
50,000 to 100,000	58
100,000 and over	12

Table 13.3 Religious fairs held annually in the United Provinces, India (From: Banerjeà 1951)

Pilgrimages to Mecca in the 1800s involved about 30,000 persons per year, involving journeys at least as long as those undertaken by the Christians but with the added feature of sexual intercourse with African slaves. Pilgrimages to Mecca were occasionally accompanied by cholera epidemics (Pollitzer and Swaroop 1959). The first well documented occurrence, in 1831, has been estimated to have killed half of the pilgrims in Mecca. Pilgrims still today drink water from the spring of Zam-Zam and take home bottles of this holy water to be drunk by their nearest and dearest (Omar 1958).

In 1863 pilgrims brought cholera from India to Mecca, and one-third of the 90,000 pilgrims are thought to have died; the disease was subsequently relayed by returning pilgrims to Mesopotamia, Syria, Palestine and Egypt. The last serious epidemic involved pilgrims from Odessa in 1907 and killed more than 25,000; a recent minor outbreak occurred in 1974 among some Nigerian pilgrims, killing about 300.

The size of the problem is clearly immense. During 1973 there were said to be 1,290,364 pilgrims at Mecca excluding local Saudi Arabians. Overall standards of health care have generally improved at Mecca, but the problem of pilgrim infection is not just related to the end-point of the pilgrimage. It has been shown that the Sudanese have been consistently infected with a wide variety of diseases by West Africans passing through the Sudan on their way to Mecca (El Tayeb 1976) (see Table 13.2).

The connection between cholera and numerous Hindu places of pilgrimage was first noticed in the nineteenth century when mortality was seen to escalate after pilgrims had been to celebrate astronomically calculated religious festivals (Sen 1903; Anderson 1904). Apart from the major religious fairs each province has large numbers of minor fairs attracting many thousands every year (Table 13.3). The major festivals on the upper Ganges and elsewhere attract pilgrims from all over India (Bhardwaj 1973).

Every twelfth year there are large gatherings of Hindu pilgrims at Hardwar and Allahabad on the Ganges between February and early April in which millions gather for a few days. Every one of these gatherings since 1879 until quite recently has been followed by a cholera outbreak (Table 13.4). Pilgrimages outside the Ganges valley have also been associated with cholera as with the Madras epidemic in 1875–77 in which known deaths amounted to 357,430.

It is indeed hard to think of a more effective way of spreading a water-borne disease than the religious practices of these Hindu pilgrims (Plate xxxiv). 'Water is not only being drunk as part of the religious ceremony by all the pilgrims, but it is also taken back with them in bottles and drunk by their relatives very soon after their return home.'

Year	Fair	Mortality
1879	Hardwar	35,892
1882	Allahabad	89,372
1885	Hardwar	63,457
1888	Allahabad	18,704
1891	Hardwar	169,013
1894	Allahabad	178,079
1897	Hardwar	44,208
1900	Allahabad	84,960
1903	Hardwar	47,159
1906	Allahabad	149,549
1909	Hardwar	21,823
1912	Allahabad	18,894
1915	Hardwar	90,508
1918	Allahabad	119,746
1921	Hardwar	149,667
1924	Allahabad	67,000
1927	Hardwar	28,285
1930	Allahabad	61,334
1933	Hardwar	1,915
1936	Allahabad	6,793
1938	Hardwar	70,622
1942	Allahabad	7,662
1948	Allahabad	52,604

Table 13.4 Cholera mortality related to Kumbha and Ardha-Kumbha religious fairs in the United Provinces, India (From: Banerjea 1951)

(Rogers 1926.) On one pilgrimage 'two sufferers in the last stages of cholera were taken out of the pool and died immediately afterwards' (Rogers 1926).

While a particular Hindu pilgrim may perhaps visit only a single centre and do so only once in a lifetime, there are large numbers of persons who make a living out of the pilgrimages as beggars or priests, moving from one centre to another. They are almost perpetually on the move (Swaroop and Raman 1951). It has also been noted that most pilgrims have scant material resources and are isolated from the home society with its rules of health; they huddle together with their fellow pilgrims under ideal conditions for the spread of many different types of infections (Banerjea 1951).

How are we to interpret these great religious pilgrimages in terms of $r+$ and $r-$ selection? Most particularly in the Islamic and Hindu cases there seems to be a strong element of compulsion to go. In Islam, the requirement is stated in the Koran, and it is a once-in-a-lifetime command. Hindus, by contrast, make more frequent pilgrimages to the Ganges, and in the case of local 'fairs' may go annually. The early Christians, like the Muslims, made their journey to Jerusalem once only.

Cultures living in areas of relatively poor disease control and of relatively low ecological stability thus appear to be those that practise pilgrimages which, as we have seen, put people to the risk of further infections. Such cultures and their religious rules are, as this book shows, pro-reproductive and in many biological respects risk-taking rather than anti-natalist and risk-reducing. The advantages of these pilgrimages must indeed be great for them to have persisted and we must assume that the risk-takers have mostly survived and so the ideas have continued.

XXXIV. Hindu pilgrims engaging in ritual washing in the river Ganges at Benares, India.

Perhaps indeed disease immunity has acted during pilgrimages to eliminate the unfit and non-resistant and encourage the development of immunity in pilgrims thus enhancing their Darwinian fitness on return to the normal life at home. If prestige is positvely correlated with both having made the pilgrimage and ease of obtaining a wife or further wives, this could well be the case. And so we can see ways in which cultural selection of the r^c+ type could prevail and grow in such circumstances. The decline of pilgrimages in modern Christendom is perhaps a correlate of the increasing extent of a need to remain within the home area, as competition for its resources became more and more pressing with the increase in environmental control – conditions, in other words, favouring r^c- rather than r^c+ selection. Once conditions have been 'made safe' however, in terms of hygiene, property ownership, tenure of job etc., pilgrimages could be resumed.

Missionaries as sources of infection

While we have already discussed the movements of large numbers of pilgrims to a limited number of religious sites, it must not be forgotten that small numbers of people dedicated to particular religions have always gone beyond their usual places of residence in search of religious truth or in order to bring religious truth to those who have not yet heard it.

Such religious migrants have a long history. The early Buddhist missionaries travelled afar to spread their faith from its heartland in the Ganges valley to the farthest parts of Asia. Under Ashoka's patronage the Third Buddhist Council in 225 BC initiated a well-documented missionary movement (Thapar 1961) sending named monks to Kashmir, Sind, Mysore, Ceylon and Bengal.

The Buddhist faith with its doctrines of detachment from all earthly involvement has enabled monks to wander in a way which was only later paralleled by the wandering friars of medieval Christianity. A great period of Buddhist interchange began after the middle of the fourth century AD with Indian monks visiting China (Wieger 1929) and Chinese monks coming to India (Bagchi 1950).

While we do not know what infections these early travellers may have carried, we can assume that their travels had some medical significance as we do have parallel evidence from contemporary records of Christian missionaries carrying diseases from and back to their countries of origin. Missionaries on furlough to the United States (Table 13.5) have been shown to have high levels of intestinal protozoa and helminths (McQuay 1967) as well as icteric (Frame 1968) and viral hepatitis which in US missionaries was found to have a rate of 1,301 per 100,000 as against 24.2 for the US domestic population (Kendrick 1974).

Not only have missionaries reduced their own fitness by travel, they have also affected the health and survival of those they have sought to convert. Among the South American Indians this phenomenon in its modern form can be seen in Brazil. Isolated mission stations now have airstrips from which the missionaries themselves come and go, and by means of which visitors drop in on short trips from the USA, thus complicating health problems dramatically. A Yanomamö village of 179 people suffered 40 per cent mortality in 1974, resulting some years later in the village containing no children below the age of 10 years, as a result of infectious diseases brought in by missionaries and other air-borne visitors. Chagnon (1977) writes: 'The only thing that had changed...was the initiation of contact with the foreigners downstream whom they had been visiting regularly to obtain machetes. Rerebawä, in reflecting on what was happening, commented introspectively: "When I was a boy we did not have epidemics like this. It did not begin until foreigners started coming here."' The Wai-Wai of Guyana have also suffered from the diseases brought in by missionaries (Guppy 1958).

Infection from the practice of cannibalism

If individuals eat a fellow human being who is suffering from certain

Table 13.5 Parasites found in United States missionaries on leave (From: McQuay 1967)

	No. examined	% with helminths	No. examined	% with protozoa
Below 19 years	1982	27.0	1752	39.1
Over 19 years	2889	16.2	2563	39.0

transmissible diseases at the time of death, there is the likelihood of their being infected, depending on how the human food is prepared. In New Guinea a disease known as *kuru* has been found to be associated with cannibalism. We include it here because of its religious associations. *Kuru* is a severe degenerative virus disease of the central nervous system affecting women and children, and, more rarely, adult men, known to medical science only since 1957. It results in death within three to nine months after the appearance of the first symptoms. Among the Foré-speaking people where the disease occurred until the recent decline of cannibalism, human flesh was eaten because people liked its taste, but they did not kill in order to eat the flesh of their victims (Glasse 1967). They consumed the bodies of those who had died from injury in warfare, from accident, or from certain diseases, including *kuru*. When a relative died, rites of mourning were carried out before the body was dismembered, cooked and eaten.

While the flesh of leprosy and dysentery victims was not eaten, the flesh of *kuru* victims was especially preferred. The disease was regarded as caused by witchcraft. Most women were cannibals, observing few restrictions on eating anyone except close relatives, whereas among men it was less common as they believed that cannibalism robbed them of their vitality and protection from arrows in tribal warfare. Overall, men seldom ate the bodies of women because women, both living and dead, were believed to be physically dangerous to men and were avoided in many circumstances. Women prepared the corpses for eating, working bare-handed, squeezing raw brain tissue into pulp with their hands and ultimately eating the cooked flesh bare-handed.

For a time *kuru* was thought to be a genetic disease because of its pattern of family recurrence (see Chapter 11). The gene was thought to be female sex-linked and rarely penetrant in adult males but it was clear that this could not be the only explanation as the high frequency of *kuru* (it was the major source of death among the Foré) could not have been maintained in the face of such a high rate of gene loss (see Fig. 13.1). In fact, *kuru* mimicked a genetic disease. It was found to be caused by an infectious, heat-resistant virus passing from person to person through peripheral routes such as open sores, the respiratory tract, and by eating. The virus moreover was present in its highest concentration in the brains of the victims – a concentration of over one million infectious doses per gram (Gajdusek 1973).

What could be the advantages of selectively retaining a lethal eating habit? Why have not the non-cannibals long since won out? Why in fact do the Foré not have a strict taboo on eating human flesh? If cultural practices in any sense evolve 'blindly' as a result of the differential survival and reproductive outcomes of the choices of individuals and groups, why have not the individuals and groups banning or at least not engaging in cannibalism come to outnumber those practising it and hence led to the practice disappearing? Let us look at it another way: What would happen to a group banning cannibalism? It would reproduce faster, no doubt, particularly because it would sustain a higher number of reproductively active women. The one curious feature, which we could regard as the 'giveaway' of Foré cannibalism is the excess of women cannibals over men. Thus *kuru* selectively reduces the reproductively active female population. This feature resembles the female infanticide found in some societies; it is an anti-natalist, popu-

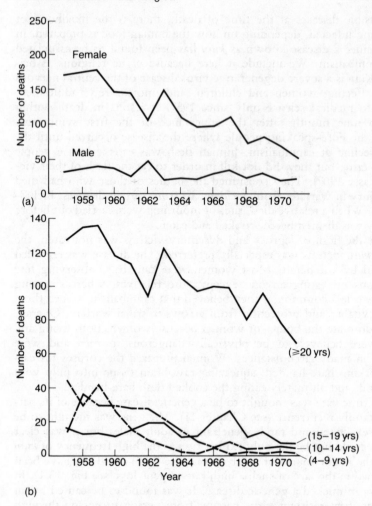

Fig. 13.1 Number of deaths caused by *kuru* (a) Sex distribution (b) Age distribution (From: Gajdusek 1973)

lation reducing social practice. This being so, we can expect to find it in circumstances in which environmental productivity is regular and adequate, and ecological stability is great. These conditions do apply to highland New Guinea. Cannibalism by women, and the resulting high female death rate, can be interpreted as the result of r- selection.

Circumcision

We have already considered this practice in Chapter 5. Here we consider it again because of its possible implications for the spread of infectious disease. For it has often been assumed that there is a close connection between the religious ritual of male circumcision and the absence of cervical carcinoma in women and penile carcinoma in men. It has been widely noticed and excellently documented that Jewish women have low rates of cervical carcinoma relative to non-Jews in the USA (Weiner *et al.* 1951; Kennaway 1948; Versluys 1949; Wynder *et al.* 1954). The latter authors in particular have also made a detailed 'blind' study with adequate controls and shown that circumcision of husbands is associated

	Bombay		Madras	
	Total female admissions	% cancer cervix	Total female admissions	% cancer cervix
Hindus	3,828	45	280	53
Christians	575	29	60	29
Muslims	818	16	67	18
Parsis	396	13	—	—

Table 13.6   Cervical cancer as percentage of total female cancer admissions at Tata Memorial Hospital, Bombay, 1941–50 and Premier Radiological Institute & Cancer Hospital, Madras, 1950–52 (From: Wynder *et al.* 1954)

with a five-fold lower incidence of cervical carcinoma in the wives of non-Jews in the USA.

A correlation between male circumcision and low rates of cervical cancer has also been noticed in Fiji (Handley 1936) where the rate for Indian women is eight times that of the Fijian women. Similarly in Malaysia, populations of circumcised Muslim Malays have a much lower rate of cervical cancer than those of uncircumcised Indians (Marsden 1958). In Macedonia (Kmet *et al.* 1963) the rate of cervical cancer and premalignant conditions for Muslims was found to be 2.7 per 1,000 women, whereas for uncircumcised non-Muslims it was 11.0 per 1,000 women.

The evidence in India is stated to be not quite so clear in comparing (circumcised) Muslims with (uncircumcised) Hindus (Nath and Grewal 1935 and 1937; Rewell 1957; Khanolkar 1948) but other data (Wynder *et al.* 1954) show clear differences (see Table 13.6).

However, data from Kenya and Uganda (Dodge *et al.* 1963) found little connection between cervical carcinoma and circumcision and in Ethiopia where all males are circumcised in early infancy, cervical cancer is reported to be common (Hauber 1960).

Little difference in cervical cancer rates has been found between Lebanese Christians and Muslims (Abou-Daoud 1967). However a survey for cervical cancer was done among the uncircumcised Amish (Cross *et al.* 1968) which showed that the risk of cervical cancer was several times *less* in the Amish than among the non-Amish. Further studies have found cases of cancer where the husbands had been circumcised (Aitken-Swan and Baird 1965; Graham *et al.* 1962).

Several studies have suggested that circumcision itself is not a clear category since the uncircumcised may have short foreskins, a natural occurrence in about a fifth of all men (Wynder *et al.* 1960). Also, data obtained from wives about whether their husbands were circumcised or not was unreliable in over a third of the cases observed, and for about 7 per cent of the men questioned and examined. This rate of inaccuracy would not occur in orthodox Jewish, Muslim and certain African tribes where all males are circumcised as a matter of course.

Avoidance of intercourse during menstruation and for some time thereafter is a major feature of Mosaic law, but this is not considered to be a contributory factor in the low rate of cervical cancer in Jewish women (Heins *et al.* 1958) since few Jews now observe the full avoidance requirements (see also Weiner *et al.* 1951). It has been noted that Indian Parsees also have a low frequency of cervical carcinoma and observe sexual abstinence for a similarly long period over menstruation (Kennaway 1948). However a study in Israel (Hochman *et al.* 1955) showed identical rates of 1.1 cases of cervical cancer per 100,000 women for Ashkenazi Jews who observe little avoidance beyond the actual days of menstruation and Mizraki Jews who mostly observe this avoidance with an additional seven days in accordance with the laws of Nidah.

Some writers (Lynch *et al.* 1963) have stressed the importance of penile hygiene and the influence of religion in determining this. Islamic instructional manuals such as the Maliki text *Mukhtas-aru* and Al-Ghazali's *The Beginning of Obedience* (Watt 1970b) contain detailed instructions on personal cleanliness in relation to urine, semen and faeces as religious obligations. It has been suggested that it is because of this that Muslim women in Macedonia have generally lower rates of reproductive organ infections than other non-Muslim women (Damjanovski *et al.* 1963).

Low risk groups for cervical cancer include Irish and Italian immigrant women into USA (Haenszel 1961), Catholic and Protestant women in Maryland, USA who regularly attend religious services (Naguib *et al.* 1966) and Amish women (Cross *et al.* 1968), and its virtual absence in virgins in USA is well documented (Martin 1967; Kottmeir 1953; Gagnon 1950 and Towne 1955).

Despite the confused state of the data, it is not unreasonable to put the question: If circumcision does reduce the risk of penile or cervical carcinoma, what effects would this have on reproductive success? The answer is that such success should be increased (all other things being equal) in families or groups practising circumcision. Circumcision would thus be a pro-reproductive practice and should be favoured in situations in which $r+$ selection was operative. We know that it is a characteristic of long-standing in Judaism and Islam. In the case of Judaism it represents part of Abraham's Covenant with God, the covenant in which God called him to leave Ur and to found a new nation; also in the Covenant was the promise from God that his 'seed' would inherit the land. A charter for $r+$ selection indeed! In the case of Islam, circumcision appears to have been simply continued without question from a prior Arabic tradition. The practice is not mentioned at all in the Koran and was adopted without question by Muhammad; it is regarded as an essential of the faith (Levy 1969: 251–2).

Conclusions

Following our efforts in the preceding chapter to indicate how religious attitudes and beliefs could be expected to, and do in fact, have a variety of biological effects, we have turned in this chapter to the evidence that religious activities and practices do have noticeable effects on people's health, and in particular we have looked at infectious diseases.

First we saw how plague, especially at the time of the so-called Black Death, was attributed to man's sinfulness by Christians, and this led to the Flagellants' practice of marching from place to place, inevitably increasing the opportunities for plague to strike down the marchers as well as those visited. In the case of leprosy, where the method of transmission is simpler and for a number of reasons disease control is more easily achieved, Christianity, by setting up well organized leprosaria, built on the existing Judaic practice of isolating lepers and helped to prevent the spread of the disease, thus in our terms reducing the chances of individual Christians being infected and constituting a case of $r-$ selection.

In the case of a number of religious practices, we discovered evidence of the spread of infectious diseases (inevitably, in matters as sensitive as this, disputed). Simulation studies of communal drinking from a single cup at the Christian service of Holy Communion showed some evidence of the spread of infectious agents. Islamic pre-prayer washing could be hygienic or could spread disease depending on whether the water was running and well drained, or semi-static. Bathing by Catholics at Lourdes seemed a particularly risky business from the health point of view since almost all the bathers are sick, though not many, in fact, as a result of communicable diseases. Use of the left hand for toilet and sexual purposes, and a taboo on its use for cooking and eating, were noted in Islam, Hinduism, and some African peoples. These various activities, either increased or decreased the risk of infectious spread, and could accordingly be seen as the outcomes of $r+$ and $r-$ selection respectively.

Then there were the really gigantic pilgrimages – to Mecca in the case of Islam and to Hindu fairs or festivals in parts of India, especially impressive along the River Ganges. The wholesale upsets of population involved, though highly organized, were shown to spread at least one fatal disease, cholera, not only among individual pilgrims themselves but also among those living along routes to and from the holy places. As with the other phenomena we looked at in this chapter, benefits must outweigh costs for their continuance, but in view of their undoubted risk-increasing nature, such pilgrimages would be associated with the operation of $r+$ selection.

Missionaries are another well-documented source of infection. Ironically, it is those they most want to 'save' whom they may infect and kill, and as we showed they themselves very often fall victim to infection.

The case of *kuru* was included here because it indicated in perhaps the most bizarre way of all how the practice of cannibalism, not by any means entirely religious but nevertheless with religious overtones, could spread a particularly unpleasant and deadly kind of disease, even if only among one small population. Owing to its association with women rather than men we saw it as anti-natalist and as such an example of 'blind' $r-$ selection.

Lastly, we looked at the situation with regard to circumcision and the spread of penile and uterine cancers. We can see, first, that it is severely complicated by our lack of understanding of the transmission process, if indeed there is one. The fact that many of the findings have been disputed is not unusual in a study involving as many variables as this one. But it does seem that there is more evidence pointing towards a positive correlation between circumcision of males and lowered frequency of both penile cancer and uterine cancer. If indeed this kind of cancer is infectious and can be transmitted by the reproductive organs it is of great significance for biology. Any disease of the reproductive organs rendering them less active or less fertile must serve to depress reproductive activity and reduce Darwinian fitness of the individuals concerned. If data show differential incidence of these cancers in groups of different religious persuasions and actions we must focus closely on these. This is not the place to enter into a close discussion of causal mechanisms, but whether through control of personal hygiene, the micro-environment in which any viral cancer agents might exist, time and frequency of intercourse, or number of sexual partners, circumcision may, it seems, be biologically advantageous, pro-reproductive, and as such constitute a case of r+ selection. In the Judaic case we saw that this interpretation fitted particularly well with the Biblical version of the circumstances accompanying the origin of the custom.

Non-infectious diseases 14

Introduction

Non-infectious diseases are here defined as all diseases not caused by transmission from person to person in the ways described in Chapter 13. They include genetically based and environmentally caused diseases. The former were looked at in Chapter 2; here we shall consider the latter. Just as serious or fatal infectious diseases are mainly found, at the present time, in the underdeveloped countries, so the non-infectious diseases come to the fore in societies like our own, where hygiene, care and medical advances have reduced risks from infectious diseases drastically, with a consequent rise from the non-infectious ones, especially cancers and diseases of the heart. This chapter will thus, inevitably, draw heavily on data from our own kind of society, in which r–selection has been occurring for a number of centuries now with unabated intensity (except during a few crises caused by epidemics and wars). Non-infectious diseases may be early-acting and cause death or incapacity during foetal development or childhood, or occur later in life during or after the reproductive stage. For instance, most cancers cause disease or death after reproduction is completed, but some can affect the young.

A very early prenatal or neo-natal disease which causes death is, from a biological point of view, less of a catastrophe than one in later childhood because a child is better lost early than late, otherwise a lot of parental time and effort will have been wasted. If a child dies just before or during adolescence, before he or she has had time to reproduce, 10 or more years of hard work and energy used in bringing up the individual that dies will have been 'wasted' in the biological sense.

Once a person has succeeded in reaching reproductive age and has in fact reproduced two or three times, his or her death is not so important

KEY OF THE HOLY SPIRIT against infantile convulsions

Amulet

In Italy children of Roman Catholics have silver keys hung round their necks to protect them from convulsions.

a loss provided the offspring are cared for adequately. Therefore constitutional diseases of late onset are not biologically harmful, in fact they can even be viewed as advantageous, since they leave resources to offspring; however, we should not overlook the biological significance of grandparents in helping with the care of their children's children.

If we look at non-infectious diseases through religious spectacles, a number of questions arise, for instance: What do religions do for or with individuals who are suffering from such diseases? When a severe disease can be spotted early in life, such as a child with a severe or progressive deformity, it does seem that in Christian societies there are rules, sanctioned by religious ideas, that lead to them being taken care of and given love and affection by their parents or sometimes by religious agencies. In the case of genetic diseases, affected individuals may not be allowed to marry, or religions may impose certain restrictions on them over marriage. These provide ways of preventing the transmission of deleterious genes into the next generation. Such pro-care and anti-natalist measures would fall into r – selection programmes.

There are some diseases of development which are to some extent caused by religious rules. Kwashiorkor is a widespread disease in parts of Africa, resulting almost entirely from the absence of sufficient protein in the diet of the child. This absence of protein is, in parts of East Africa, the result of religious taboos on the consumption of meat, chicken and eggs by children and also by their mothers who pass on the deficit via their breast-feeding of those children. This debilitating co dition may be fatal *per se* or the precondition for other diseases. The Baganda, for instance, do not allow their women to eat meat of any kind, so they have to subsist largely on cooked bananas (*matoke*). This is given as a staple diet to children andoften leads to kwashiorkor (Welbourn 1955; personal observation V. Reynolds and R. Tanner).

Some diseases occur when the environment has been so artificially reorganized by man that he has released a whole train of harmful events; religion can affect the probability of their occurrence. The most prevalent modern diseases of affluent societies are the various heart diseases. Of these the commonest is coronary artery disease, caused by the deposition of fat which becomes calcified on the arteries near the heart, eventually leading to coronary infarction. There are a number of dietary theories of its cause which variously implicate sugar, salt and animal fats. Other theories additionally implicate coffee consumption, smoking, and a sedentary way of life (Jenner *et al.* 1980; Reynolds *et al.* 1981). Other theories point to the pace of life in modern society and are based on evidence that our physiology is adversely affected by the psychological stress of modern life (see Cox 1978 and Reynolds 1980 for summaries of these findings).

A study by Friedman and Rosenman (1959) showed higher rates of coronary artery disease in 'Type A' people, who were characterized by forceful driving personality, competitiveness and adherence to deadlines, than in 'Type B' people, who lacked these traits. Religious beliefs, if taken seriously, should make people less desperately competitive, or at least not more so. Christian church-goers have indeed been found to show less heart disease than non-church-goers (Comstock and Partridge 1972). From the point of view of diet, Christianity, which regards gluttony as sinful, tends to reduce the intake of fats and sugars; likewise Islam, which has prayers involving physical exercise five times a day, must be conducive to fitness. Buddhism, which emphasizes the value of a contemplative life, disapproves of cut-throat competition, teaches meditation, and suggests a slow pace of life and a friendly, co-operative attitude to the business of making a living, appears to enable its followers to avoid the stress syndrome referred to above.

Some forms of cancer are known to be environmentally induced. Such for example is lung cancer which is definitely connected with inhaling tobacco smoke into the lungs; the smoking habit also increases the incidence of heart disease. Again, religious groups that taboo or object to smoking have low incidences of lung cancer.

However, both heart diseases and cancer of the lung tend to occur late in life when the reproductive stage is largely over. Thus the great modern killer diseases are less serious from a biological point of view than those affecting individuals before or during the reproductive period. So the interplay of religion and disease here is, paradoxically, of less vital concern to human biology than in the case of those diseases which affect individuals of all ages indiscriminately, or the young in particular.

Diet

We suggested above that religious rules affecting diet should be effective in promoting health if they prevented overconsumption of certain foods.

Some religions divide the year into periods of deprivation and/or periods of plenty and revelry. Thus in the Muslim holy month of Ramadhan, days of austerity alternate with revelry and feasting at night. The devout Muslim fasts for 30 days during daylight hours and suffers more from lack of water than food in areas where the holy month occurs in the hottest part of the year; he can eat what he likes during the night. There are widespread exemptions for the old or sick, for travellers, pregnant women and nursing mothers. Such periods of controlled fasting may be conducive to physical fitness.

The fasting rules of the Ethiopian Orthodox (Christian) Church, however, seem to go beyond this and can become a health hazard. They prohibit eating before midday and the eating of any food of animal origin except fish at any time during the 110–150 annual days of fasting. One result of this extensive fasting is *injera gastritis*, a stomach complaint caused by the required diet of baked flour pancakes. More lasting effects are especially visible in the six months to three years age-group of children who receive about 25 per cent less than adequate total protein during fasting and especially suffer from the virtual elimination of milk and animal protein sources. This change for the worse in the already inadequate diet of the poor, particularly their children, has been described as 'ominous' (Knutsson and Selinus 1970). Neglect of children is associated with *r*+ selection.

In other societies such as the Orang Asli of West Malaysia (Bolton 1972) we again find religious food taboos with a restriction on the intake of animal protein; this chiefly affects the protein intake of women of child-bearing age and children. This is combined with the fact that men eat first and whenever there is a general shortage of food in this community it is the women and children who must go hungry. When a large animal is killed, the flesh is taboo to younger women and children so that only men and women *past* child-bearing age benefit from this short-term protein boost. The rationale for these animal taboos is curious and complex. All animals are believed to have spirits and those of the stronger animals are more powerful. Disease is caused by a spirit attacking the body. The weaker members of society (women and children) are more easily attacked so they must only eat the small animals with weaker spirits. Here, then, we have a case where religious beliefs and the associated food taboos act in line with expectations under r-selection: reduction of reproductive activity (in this case by reducing capacity) occurs in the bad times not as a direct result of food shortage but as a result of the cultural rules.

In Zen Buddhism, Western-style, diet is sometimes related to the practice of Zen macrobiotics (Ohsawa 1956) in which the best diet for creating a spiritual awakening or rebirth is a largely cereal–vegetarian one combined with the avoidance of many fluids. This diet is believed to help in achieving a general state of well-being. It is even regarded as a prevention and cure for cancer, mental disease and heart trouble, and medical consultation is not advocated (Ohsawa 1965). An American promoter of the regime states: 'We shall demonstrate the macrobiotic preparation of delicious aesthetic meals that cure all illnesses (present and future) giving at the same time longevity and youthfulness to everybody, at no expense and with no special training' (Ohsawa, quoted by Sherlock and Rothschild 1967). In the opinion of the US Council of

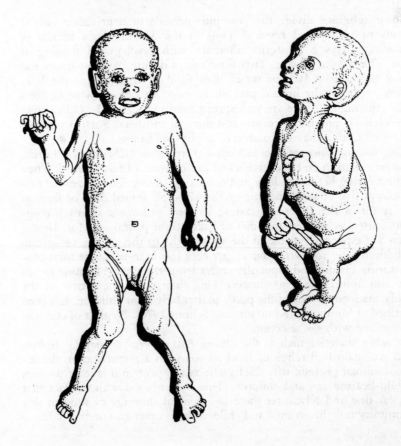

XXXV. Severe nutritional disorders in children fed on macrobiotics diets. (Roberts *et al.* 1979)

Foods and Nutrition individuals who, for long periods, rigidly follow Zen macrobiotic diets are in considerable danger of serious nutritional deficiencies, including scurvy (Sherlock and Rothschild 1967), anaemia, hypoproteinaemia, hypocalcaemia, and emaciation due to starvation; malnutrition in which infants were found to be taking only 40 per cent of the nationally recommended dietary intake (Robson *et al.* 1979) is on record (Plate xxxv). How do such movements, and their consequences, arise and continue? Child neglect of this kind would in general be selected against in affluent societies. So how can we explain it? The idea that certain parents are just acting in a misguided way seems quite inadequate; we are left without an explanation.

Church attendance and health

Medical surveys have occasionally tried to relate health to frequency of attendance at religious services. A study in Washington County, Maryland (Naguib *et al.* 1966a and 1966b) compared women attending church less than twice a year with those who went at least once weekly. The former had trichomonads in 17.8 per cent of the sample compared with 12.4 per cent in the latter. Cytological changes suspicious or positive for cervical cancer occurred in 1.88 per cent of the former compared with 0.64 per cent of the latter. Such results correlate with earlier conclusions showing a negative correlation between extent of extramarital coitus and frequency of church attendance (Kinsey *et al.* 1953).

	Usual frequency of church attendance		
	Once or more per week	Less than once weekly	Relative risk for less frequent attenders
1963 Census population	24,245	30,603	
Arteriosclerotic heart disease★			
Deaths	38	89	
5 year rate per 1,000	8.52	18.12	2.1:1
Pulmonary emphysema			
Deaths	18	52	
3 year rate per 1,000	0.74	1.70	2.3:1
Cirrhosis of the liver			
Deaths	5	25	
3 year rate per 1,000	0.21	0.82	3.9:1
Suicide			
Deaths	11	29	
6 year rate per 1,000	0.45	0.95	2.1:1
Cancer of the rectum			
Deaths	13	17	
5 year rate per 1,000	0.54	0.56	1:1
Cancer of the colon			
Deaths	27	28	
5 year rate per 1,000	1.11	0.91	0.8:1

★ Among white females only, aged 45–64 in 1963. Other figures are for both sexes.

Table 14.1 Deaths and death rates from selected causes by usual frequency of church attendance among persons 16½ years or older, Washington County, Maryland, USA (From: Comstock *et al.* 1972)

Non-infectious diseases

	Age group		
	25–45	45–65	25–65
England and Wales			
General male population 1863–71	1.15	2.52	1.84
Clergy in general 1860–61	0.52	1.72	1.04
Church of England clergy 1860–61	0.48	1.72	1.02
Protestant ministers 1860–61	0.54	1.58	1.01
Roman Catholic priests 1860–61	0.97	2.69	1.57
Prussia			
General male population 1776–84	0.97	2.59	1.68
Protestant ministers 1801–33	0.58	2.00	1.18

Table 14.2 Annual mortality rates (%) for clergymen in England and Wales and Prussia in the nineteenth century, by age groups (From: Stussi 1873–75, quoted by King and Bailar 1969)

A further survey in the same area of the USA (Comstock *et al.* 1970) found that those who went to church once a month or more had a rate of 84 in 100,000 for newly reported active tuberculosis, while in those who attended twice a year or less the rate was 138.

These conclusions were followed up in a further study (Comstock and Partridge 1972) which showed (Table 14.1) a relatively higher risk among infrequent church attenders than among regular churchgoers for certain diseases.

Can anything be concluded from this broad range of associations? It seems likely that the seriously ill would progressively fail to attend services rather than keep up their previous regularities, but in one study (Comstock and Partridge 1972) there were no such diminutions. It must however be the case that some bedridden patients who can no longer attend church services are visited at home or in hospital by the clergy. Comstock, who has specialized in this type of study, concludes that whatever the mechanism of association, it could still prove useful in identifying groups at increased risk of suffering from a number of important diseases. Any diminution of health risks consequent on religiosity in modern society can be seen in relation to r– selection.

The health of the clergy

If the rules and practices of a religion have any effects on the health of its followers, then those who adhere most strongly should show these

Standardized mortality ratios (All males in given year = 100)★ *age 20–65*				
Occupied and retired males	Clergymen	Lawyers	Physicians	Teachers
1921–23 101	60	107	102	71
1930–32 100	69	95	106	68
1949–53 100	81	88	89	66

Table 14.3 Mortality figures for males, age 20–65 in selected professions, England and Wales, 1860–1953 (From: King and Bailar 1969)

★ The standardized mortality ratio (SMR) for a given population is the ratio of the observed death rate to the rate in a standard population, adjusted to the age distribution of the study group. SMR is equal to 100 when the study population has the same age-specific mortality rate as the standard population.

Cause of death (nos. refer to International Classification of Diseases, Injuries, and Deaths, rev. 6)	England and Wales			United States White
	Church of England	Roman Catholic	Other	
All causes	81	107	78	83
Tuberculosis, all forms (001–019)	43	—	38	39
Malignant neoplasms, all sites (140–204)	60	90	80	86
Vascular lesions of nervous system (330–334)	119	208	126	106
Coronary disease, angina (420)	153	193	130	108
Hypertension (440–447)	105	180	82	73
Accidents (E800–E962)	67	—	67	63
Suicide (E963; E970–E979)	46	—	—	37

— Mortality figure not shown here because number of deaths entering into computation is fewer than 5.

Table 14.4   Mortality figures (SMR) for clergymen aged 20–64 in England and Wales, 1949–53, and the United States, 1950 (From: King and Bailar 1969)

most clearly. The expectation of life for the Christian clergy appears to have been longer in the nineteenth century than that for the general population of males of the same age distribution (Table 14.2). Many factors undoubtedly contribute to these findings, quite apart from the beneficent effects of income, diet, regular employment and good housing. For instance, longevity might also be influenced by selective recruitment of healthy individuals to the clergy in the first place; aspirants to the Roman Catholic priesthood often receive both physical and mental health examinations. In fact, however, Roman Catholic priests in the study referred to did not show a greater longevity than the general population in the 45–65 years age-group.

The general difference in mortality rates seen above referred to the nineteenth century. More recently there has been in England and Wales a general decline in the mortality of all occupied and retired males so that now the standardized mortality ratio of clergymen is at the level for lawyers and doctors and is higher than that for teachers (Table 14.3).

The data show a very low mortality among clergymen from infectious diseases such as tuberculosis and syphilis, but a mortality excess from cardiovascular diseases with particularly high rates of cardiovascular disease mortality for Roman Catholic priests (Table 14.4).

The average life expectancy of Roman Catholic missionaries was found to be 14 years less than the average lifetime based on the mortality rates in their home countries, with variations between temperate Asian and tropical and sub-tropical African countries (Boldrini and Ugge 1926).

A study designed to discover the effects of Christian monastic life on health (Groen et al. 1962) compared the nutrition of Benedictine monks in Holland who lived on a mixed 'Western' diet and Trappist monks in Belgium who lived on a frugal vegetarian diet (Table 14.5).

More obesity occurred among the Trappists, against expectations. However it has been noted (Groen 1964) that the Trappist diet between countries is not uniform, in line with the differences between the manual working brethren and the largely sedentary, contemplative fathers. Another study (Mirone 1954) concluded that the prolonged consumption of a diet low in animal protein had no apparent deleterious effects on the health of a Trappist community.

Data	Trappist monks			Benedictine monks		
	Fathers	Brethren	Both	Fathers	Brethren	Both
Number	96	84	180	102	66	168
Average age (years)	48	53	50	47	37	42
Average height (m)	1.69	1.66	1.68	1.71	1.70	1.70
Average weight (kg)	79	72	76	69	65	67
Obesity★ (no. of cases)	40	23	63	23	7	30
Average blood pressure						
Systolic (mm Hg)	147	147	147	136	136	136
Diastolic	83	80	82	85	83	84
Number with diastolic hypertension ≥ 100	9	4	13	7	3	10
Number with myocardial infarction	1	—	—	—	—	—
Number with angina pectoris	2	1	3	3	1	4

★ An individual was classified as obese when his weight was equal to more than 110 per cent of the normal for his age and height.

Table 14.5 Trappist and Benedictine Fathers and Brethren (From: Groen *et al.* 1962)

A further study showed that a markedly reduced mortality from coronary heart disease in a sample of monks was associated with a higher than average mortality from cancer (Keys 1961).

In conclusion it can be seen that there is no easy answer to the question: Do clergy have especially good health? There are differences between denominations, of disease patterns as well as life expectancy. In general we have seen that clergy do tend to have good life expectancy, but that mortality from heart diseases is high, especially among Catholic priests.

The health of nuns

Kunin and McCormack (1968) found that both systolic and diastolic blood pressure were lower for nuns than for controls in both a white and a black group (Table 14.6).

It has been observed for some time that there is an increased relative frequency of breast cancer in nuns, while marriage appears to increase the frequency of cervical cancer. A study of death rates in Verona from 1769 to 1839 (Rigoni-Stern 1844) found a ratio between cancer of the breast and uterus in the proportion of 1:4 for married women as com-

Table 14.6 Mean systolic and diastolic blood pressures, adjusted for age, in nuns and working women (controls), both white and black (From: Kunin and McCormack 1968)

Group	Blood pressure (mm Hg)	
	Systolic	Diastolic
Whites		
Controls	124.9	76.0
Nuns	121.2	71.2
Blacks		
Controls	129.6	79.0
Nuns	122.4	71.7

pared to a 3:1 ratio for single women other than Sisters, and a ratio of 9:1 for Sisters.

However a later study in the Netherlands during 1931–35 (Versluys 1949) found that death rates from all types of cancer among nuns and 'religieuses' did not differ significantly from those among other unmarried women. Another study (Gagnon 1950) found only three cases of cancer of the cervix in Canadian nuns out of a total of 140,000 pathological reports of malignant tumours of the uterus. Similar negative results are recorded from Germany (Schömig 1953) and Chicago (Towne 1955).

Low rates of cervical cancer were discussed in Chapter 13 in relation to male circumcision, and it may be that the data from nuns supports the idea of genital infection from the male, but the agent (if there is one) is not known. Perhaps of equal interest is the high incidence of breast cancer in nuns. To what can this be attributed? Gjorgov (1980) concludes with what must, to many, be the startling hypothesis that a substance occurring in human semen, when deposited in the vaginal canal, offers protection against breast cancer. The argument is too complex to enter into here, but postulates that certain biologically active substances in seminal plasma are essential to the maintenance of a healthy hormonal balance in the female. Gjorgov's study was based on a comparison of women whose contraceptive practices prevented contact between semen and the vagina, with those whose did not. The former methods, called 'barrier' contraception, were associated with a 4.5–5.2 times higher risk of breast cancer than 'non-barrier' methods.

As with studies of male clergy and monks (above), studies of the health of nuns run into difficulties of interpretation. In general, however, their health is good and in line with expectations under r^c – selection.

Disease and some smaller Christian denominations

There is little doubt that alcohol and tobacco contribute substantially to the aetiology of certain non-communicable diseases that affect the liver and respiratory tract. It is for this reason that we are interested in the disease profiles of the Seventh Day Adventists and the members of the Church of Jesus Christ of Latter Day Saints (Mormons) which prohibit the use of alcohol and tobacco. A study of Mormon men and women

Table 14.7 Percentage of raised and converted Seventh Day Adventists obeying dietary rules compared with practices of non-members (all over 30 years of age) (From: Wynder et al. 1959)

	Males			Females		
	Raised SDA	Converted SDA	Non-SDA	Raised SDA	Converted SDA	Non-SDA
N	210	253	417	228	266	404
Percentage of:						
Non-smokers	93	62	35	98	81	74
Non-drinkers	93	55	28	98	88	70
Non-meat eaters	56		2	52		1
Non-fish eaters	64		16	68		17
Non-coffee drinkers	82		17	82		14
Non-tea drinkers	90		38	89		34
Non-milk drinkers	17		15	19		21

(Lyon *et al.* 1976) showed very significantly low rates of lung cancer in comparison with both non-Mormons and the general population of the USA.

A study of Californian Seventh Day Adventists (Wynder *et al.* 1959) who prohibit tobacco, alcohol and a number of other dietary items, has shown that only a proportion of the membership obeys these prohibitions (Table 14.7).

This study showed that 93 per cent of born Seventh Day Adventist men had never consumed alcohol and that of the men who did drink only 1 per cent of born members and 9 per cent of the converts had taken one or more drinks per day for 20 years or more. The proportions for women were 1 per cent and 1 per cent respectively. Similarly none of the born and 13 per cent of the converted members had smoked 16 or more cigarettes per day for 20 years or more with the proportions for women being 0 per cent and 2 per cent respectively.

The distribution of cancer between the Seventh Day Adventists and the controls (Table 14.8) showed that for men the observed percentages were lower than the expected values and the differences were statistically significant and particularly striking for cancers of the bladder, lung, mouth, oesophagus and larynx. For women there were only statistically significant differences for cancer of the cervix. Subsequent studies (Lemon *et al.* 1964; Lemon and Walden 1966) of Californian Seventh Day Adventists have confirmed that their cancer mortality is considerably below that of the general population.

Although a large share of this reduction in cancers is clearly due to the very high rates of cancer mortality known to be related to smoking, there are numerous other differences. Other properties of the Seventh Day Adventists themselves and/or their life style may be involved besides their dietary habits, smoking, etc. A study (Phillips 1975) of the background and life style of Seventh Day Adventists states that they are by no means a representative sample of the general population; the proportion of college-educated persons is twice that of the general population. However, adjustment for education did not wholly eliminate the mortality differences, and it was suggested that an important variable may be their total dietary pattern. Their typical lacto-ovo-vegetarian diet has about 25 per cent less fat and 50 per cent more fibre than the average non-vegetarian diet and the unsaturated to saturated fat ratio is about double the average (Hardinge *et al.* 1958, 1962). Studies have revealed significant differences in their faecal microbial flora (Finegold *et al.* 1977). Lack of coffee consumption could account for a good proportion of their reduced bladder cancer risk (Cole 1971 and 1973) and perhaps have other beneficial effects on health (see Reynolds *et al.* 1981). Thus we can conclude that the Seventh Day Adventist pattern of food abstinence is significantly related to a reduction in certain diseases, avoiding certain conditions, and in the case of coronary heart disease delaying its appearance.

In respect of the vegetarian diet hypothesis, Armstrong *et al.* (1977) found that the blood pressure of Seventh Day Adventists, both systolic and diastolic, is significantly lower than that of non-members, and there is a gradient towards increasing blood pressure with increasing egg intake, and a higher diastolic blood pressure in those drinking tea and coffee. Their special diet may also cause a delay in the onset of the menarche (Frisch 1974; Kralj-Cercek 1956) as well as influencing hormone

Type and site of cancer	Non-Seventh Day Adventists	Seventh Day Adventists	Expected values Seventh Day Adventists
Males			
Lung	158	2	14.76
Mouth, larynx, oesophagus	176	2	16.54
Bladder	259	16	25.47
Breast	2	1	2.82
Lung (adenocarcinoma)	21	0	1.97
Central nervous system	46	2	4.51
Pancreas	52	4	5.26
Misc. 1[†]	351	19	34.69
Leukemia	90	7	9.12
Lymphoma	83	8	8.55
Stomach	162	10	16.17
Misc. 2[†]	82	2	7.80
Colon and rectum	314	25	31.68
Prostate	329	31	33.75
Totals	2,125	129	
Females			
Lung*	30	3	2.91
Bladder	122	8	12.22
Cervix	309	12	30.17
Mouth, larynx, oesophagus	68	1	6.39
Lung (adenocarcinoma)	7	3	0.94
Central nervous system	48	3	4.79
Pancreas	53	5	5.36
Leukemia	83	3	8.08
Lymphoma	101	9	10.34
Stomach	110	6	10.90
Misc. 1[†]	536	51	54.33
Uterus	179	22	18.61
Misc. 2[†]	162	21	16.73
Colon and rectum	415	40	42.39
Breast	614	61	62.89
Totals	2,837	248	

Table 14.8 Distribution of hospital cancer cases among Seventh Day Adventists (From:Wynder et. al., 1959)

* Includes anaplastic.
[†] Miscellaneous 1 refers to primary cancers not included in the sites listed.
[†] Miscellaneous 2 refers to all metastatic cancers whose primary origin was not determined.

status at other periods of life (de Waard 1975; Dickinson et al. 1974; Lipsett 1975; MacMahon et al. 1973).

Seventh Day Adventists have been compared with Mormons with regard to the incidence of certain kinds of cancer. Californian and Utah Mormons with no vegetarianism have an overall incidence of colonic and rectal cancer below that reported for Californian Seventh Day Adventists claiming a 50 per cent compliance with their vegetarian diet (Phillips et al. 1973; Enstrom 1974). Indeed Utah Mormons in 1972 were reported to eat 59 kg of beef per year as compared to 52 kg for the United States as a whole. This finding sheds doubt on the idea that a vegetarian diet is an antidote to colonic and rectal cancer. Similar conclusions were reached from a study (Jarvis 1977) of Mormon mortality

XXXVI. Members of the
African Israeli Church Ninevah
in central Kenya jogging to
church. This independent
Christian Church is widely
reputed to retain a strict
standard of sexual morality.

rates in Canada. A difference with particular significance for fertility is
the low rate of cancer of the cervix in Californian Seventh Day Adventists (Wynder *et al.* 1959), where it is a third of the expected US rate and
just under half that of the Utah Mormons (Lyon *et al.* 1976). We know
that both early and promiscuous sexual activity are far less common in
these religious populations (Christensen and Meissner 1953; Christensen
and Cannon 1964; Christensen and Gregg 1970) than in the general
population. The same is true of certain sects in other parts of the world
(Plate XXXVI).

Comparison with Jews
Mortality from cancer of the buccal cavity and pharynx which are
thought to be related to smoking are markedly low in Jewish males
(Greenwald *et al.* 1975; Seidman 1966, and 1970). Jewish men smoke
fewer cigarettes than either Catholics or Protestants (Hammond and
Garfinkel 1961). Mortality from cancer of the lung and bronchus has
apparently shifted over time from an excess over the national average
in foreign-born Jewish men to a significant deficit (Seidman 1966; Wynder and Mantel 1966) for which a pattern of declining cigarette smoking
may be an explanation. New York Jews may also have a below-average
proportion of men occupationally exposed to inhalants such as gas, dust
and fumes. A study of Montreal Jews (Horowitz and Enterline 1970)
confirmed this low lung cancer pattern for men but showed a relatively
high lung cancer rate among Jewish women which could not be entirely
explained on the basis of cigarette smoking habits. In other US studies
(Askovitz 1961; King 1965) both Protestants and Roman Catholics had

higher diagnosed rates than Jews for cancers of the lung, buccal cavity and pharynx.

Conclusions

In tribal societies and peoples living close to subsistence levels, religious taboos on eating high protein foods directed at women and children can perhaps be explained as devices resulting from r^c- selection; such 'group cultural selection' is theoretically feasible because of the nature of the human rule-transmission process. It marks a position along the 'scale' towards the r^c- end, being a population control anti-natalist device. Status considerations rather than energy needs may provide proximate explanations for the giving of high-value foods to men and people of high caste. In affluent societies under r^c- selection, religious food restrictions may on the contrary be beneficial to health since they reduce intake of excess or harmful foods, leaving a basic moderate diet which is adequate to produce good health. Such societies, which have passed the 'demographic transition' are faced with quite different problems of food consumption, and have in any case adjusted their birth rates by methods that eliminate the need for, and indeed do not permit, population 'pruning'.

The Christian idea that 'gluttony' is sinful leads to a sensible and healthy intake of nutritious foods under r^c- selection where no periods of starvation occur. Fasting periods are probably good for health where a return to plentiful food is assured and can be planned for. Where excessive fasting occurs, causing health hazards, as among Ethiopian Orthodox Christians and proponents of Zen macrobiotics, we are faced with a problem.

Religious practitioners have been much studied and there is in consequence a mass of data bearing on their health status in relation to their religious practices. Christian clergymen have, in general, good longevity; nuns have a tendency to develop breast cancer but very rarely develop cancer of the cervix. Lung cancer rates are, as expected, low in Seventh Day Adventists and Mormons, who have religious rules that forbid smoking.

In this third part of the book we have looked at the effects of belonging to religious groups on concepts of disease, and the incidence of infectious and non-infectious diseases. This completes our study. After a survey of some relevant genetic facts, we looked at the human life-cycle, with an analysis of the day-to-day decision-making of ordinary people. We argued that it was on the basis of those decisions, made in the light of ongoing cultural prescriptions and taboos, together with an assessment of the benefits, costs and risks of following or deviating from them, that some rules came to be perpetuated and others got changed or fell into abeyance. As a result, cultures could develop and change, and eventually whole civilizations could arise and collapse. Our ideas of r^c+ and r^c- cultural selection were in mind as we looked at the data, but it has always been our intention to let the data speak for themselves; indeed that was how we came by the ideas in the first place.

There remains one final task: to survey the whole subject and spell out such conclusions as have emerged. This is the purpose of the final part of the book.

Part Four

Conclusions

15 Theoretical considerations

For some time, now, anthropologists and others interested in human evolution have accepted that, on the physical side, man's body, brain and behaviour have evolved by similar methods to those of other animal species, by the action of natural selection on the variations produced by sexual reproduction. We include 'behaviour' above because it can be distinguished from 'action' (Reynolds 1980) to which the above would not apply. The word 'action' describes what people do, taking into account the instructions they receive from their cultures – ideas of appropriateness, right and wrong, etc. – as well as those received from the organic side. The arguments arising in the debate about where the cultures come from, and how they, and the elements of which they are composed ('memes', to use Dawkins' (1976) term, or 'culturgens' as Lumsden and Wilson (1981) have called them) are transmitted, continue unabated and it is to that debate that the present book has addressed itself, and to the effort to find a theory that will be general enough to embrace both biological (species) evolution and the evolution (if such there be) of the cultures of the single species, man.

That such a general theory is possible (though we are still searching for it) has been recognized from time to time. In our Introduction we mentioned the theory of Social Darwinism with its central notion of 'survival of the fittest' propounded by Herbert Spencer, and the more 'physiological' theory of the 'Cell State'. The former theory suggests that societies evolved like species by mutual competition between varieties under natural selection; it ignored the process of diffusion and failed to take account of the mechanisms of cultural transmission. The 'Cell State' is little more than a pretty analogy between the complex

Throughout Hindu India cows, because of their religious significance, roam freely in both town and countryside and are not prevented from eating human food exposed for sale in shops.

bodies of higher organisms and the complex structures of modern societies with their high levels of division of labour. It offers no real understanding of cultural evolution at all. A swing away from biological (internally organized) theories brought to the fore two new kinds of theory: the theory that cultures were not to be biologically understood at all, but either psychologically or sociologically (or of course a mixture of both). The names of Gregory Bateson (1936), Margaret Mead (1971), Ruth Benedict (1935) Boas (1966) and Kroeber (1952) are associated with this new paradigm, which owes nothing to Darwinism.

Secondly, there was renewed interest in theories of environmental determinism. Such theories have a long and distinguished history, going back to the fifth-century BC Greek writer Heraclitus, who wrote in his *Influences of Atmosphere, Water and Situation*, 'The countries which have the greatest and the most frequent seasonal variations of climate... also have the wildest landscape... and if the variation is great, the differentiation of (human) bodily type is increased proportionately... and their possessors have headstrong, self-willed characters and temperaments, with a tendency towards ferocity instead of tameness' (quoted by Toynbee 1935, **1**: 251–2 from his own translation).

Toynbee, reviewing a number of theories of environmental determinism finds them unacceptable for what he calls the genesis of civilizations because the same kinds of environments have produced great flowerings of culture in some places and at certain times, while in other places and times no such results have occurred (Toynbee 1935, **1**: 249 *ff*). Even if we widen our concept of the environment to include the human as well as the physical environment, and take into account both time and space, he finds the resulting theory wanting. For Toynbee, civilizations (we can say 'complex cultures') have a major internal component driving them forward, at least as long as they continue to grow and progress. The mechanism that spurs them involves environmental components, which are seen as 'challenges' to which there is a 'response'.

But for Toynbee the most important element shaping the evolution of a culture was its inner, more elusive and spiritual force, unique to itself, different in each of the civilizations whose development (and later decline) he describes. Each culture had its *geist* and Toynbee was indeed very interested in the question of religions, and in how religious ideas have provided the distinctive elements enabling challenges to be overcome and in determining how they have been, and still are overcome.

The eminent historian soon left the concerns of biology far behind in his quest for understanding. But modern biology retains, in its anthropological wing, a strong interest in the effort to find a theory that can link up the characteristics of human cultures with human evolution in the organic sense (differential reproductive success of individuals, etc.). For (and this needs spelling out) in so far as culture is *not* transmitted genetically, we need go no further than the individual and his or her impact on social thinking to explain the basis of cultural transmission, and one of a number of ways of achieving this impact is by reproductive success enabling lineal transmission of ideas from parents to their children.

For this reason thinkers about cultural evolution should consider biology. In other respects they can do without it. The theory of biological evolution has nothing to tell us about the process of 'diffusion'. Ideas and practices can and do spread widely and swiftly as and when they are taken to neighbouring groups by conquest, or taken up by neighbours because they are felt to be more satisfying or appropriate to prevailing conditions. Diffusion theories were popular earlier this century. The idea has left a lasting impact but still tells us nothing concrete about cultural evolution or selection mechanisms. There is no doubt that diffusion is a vital element in cultural change. Diffusion of technological innovations is perhaps the best example, whether of stone tools, pottery types, use of bronze, copper and iron, adoption of wheeled transport, the plough, the printing press or the electronic calculator. Joseph Needham gives a fine selection of items which originated in China and diffused westwards:

China produced a profusion of developments which reached Europe and other regions at times varying between the +1st and the +18th centuries: (a) the square-pallet chain-pump; (b) the edge-runner mill and the application of water-power to it; (c) metallurgical blowing-engines operated by water-power; (d) the rotary fan and winnowing machine; (e) the piston-bellows; (f) the horizontal-warp loom (possibly also Indian), and the drawloom; (g) silk reeling, twisting and doubling machinery; (h) the wheelbarrow; (i) the sailing-carriage; (j) the wagon-mill; (k) the two efficient harnesses for draught-animals, i.e. the breast-strap or postilion harness, and the collar harness; (l) the cross-bow; (m) the kite; (n) the helicopter top and the zoetrope; (o) the technique of deep drilling; (p) the mastery of cast iron; (q) the 'Cardan' suspension; (r) the segmental arch bridge; (s) the iron-chain suspension-bridge; (t) canal lock-gates; (u) numerous inventions in nautical construction, including water-tight compartments, aerodynamically efficient sails, the fore-and-aft rig, and (v) the stern-post rudder; (w) gunpowder and some of its associated techniques; (x) the magnetic compass, used first for geomancy and then, also by the Chinese, for navigation; (y) paper, printing, and movable-type printing; and (z) porcelain. I come to a stop, having exhausted the alphabet, but many more instances, even important ones, could be given. (Needham 1975, 1: 240–41)

But diffusion of religions has no such certainty about it. Why has not one religion long since swept the globe?

To return to Toynbee, is religion, or some kind of spiritual quality, the 'prime mover' of any given culture? There seem to have been two kinds of negative answer so far. The first is based on a materialist, sometimes called simply 'holist', philosophy that there is only one world, the world of matter. Arising from the physical world of non-living matter, there evolved life, and life gave rise to man, who devised religion. Religion and culture can, by reduction, be broken down to physical matter (in theory at least – it isn't a practical proposition!). In this view, a religion or spiritual quality could not be a 'prime mover' of anything as it is at the very end of a chain of causes and effects. It can no doubt be a 'mover' of sorts, affecting people's actions in all sorts of ways but it remains the outcome of events in the physical world and has no independent 'essence'. The idea that it has would be regarded as metaphysical, a return to pre-scientific thinking. Writers such as Wilson (1975) espouse this view.

The second kind of rejection is one we can associate with the sociology of Durkheim (1961) which holds that any religion is a mirror of society, its relationships and structure. Any given society, in order to validate its social world, first invents, then reifies, and finally uses its religion to provide sanctions for the rules of order and the political, economic, kinship and other systems of which it is made up. Materialism is not a preoccupation of such thinkers, who would not regard that as an important issue. Being concerned with the world of human thought and action, they would, however, want to reject any theory that proposed that a religion itself could give rise to or give form to a society; that would be putting the cart before the horse.

Sociology has undergone many changes and refinements during the twentieth century and religion has remained one of its chief concerns, as in the work of Luckmann (1967). But in turning its back on biology and the physical sciences it has been unable, through a studied lack of interest, to integrate them into any kind of general theory of life processes. For, as we have seen, religion, even if it does validate social processes and thus has an integrative function, also contributes in many diverse ways to people's health, survival, and reproductive fitness. It provides the conventional phraseology for decision-making with regard to biological processes (and thus biological outcomes). It provides the options and suggests which course to take, i.e. whether and when to engage in sexual activity, whether to rear or abandon a child, etc. It acts as an adviser on human parental investment.

It has in fact been the materialists who have reopened the question of the significance of religion. Evolutionary anthropology is a materialist science, as is evolutionary biology and both have provided relevant material to the debate in recent times, and continue to do so. We can distinguish a number of positions in the debate which we shall now briefly elaborate, after which we shall see how our own ideas relate to these and finally test them against a summary of the data contained in the present book, from which, albeit in a dim and hazy form, they did in fact first arise.

Let us begin with the approach of what has been called 'ecological anthropology'. A convenient central figure here is Marvin Harris, whose work on the Hindu sacred cow complex (Harris 1966) is an excellent example of the method. Attacking a very large number of proponents of the idea that the prohibition observed by Hindus on killing and eating cattle is disadvantageous, disfunctional, maladaptive and positively harmful to the health and welfare of people in India, and that it results from an outdated and, in modern times, harmful religious ideology, Harris argues cogently that this is not necessarily so.

He disputes the idea on two fronts. First, it is wrong to take an etic (outsider's) stance and pass judgement, when an emic (insider's) understanding yields insights that can alter our assessment greatly. Second, he disputes that the ideology should be taken as a 'prime mover' when in fact more mundane, practical considerations are far more likely to be the ultimate determinants of action, and the ideas of sanctity serve to perpetuate these. In particular he lays stress on:

such positive functioned features of the Hindu cattle complex as traction power and milk, dung, beef and hide production in relationship to the costs of ecologically viable alternatives. In general, the exploitation of cattle resources proceeds in such a way as not to impair the survival and economic well-being of the human population. The relationship between the human and bovine

population is symbiotic rather than competitive; more traction animals than are presently available are needed for carrying out essential agricultural tasks.
Under existing techno-environmental conditions, a relatively high ratio of cattle to humans is ecologically unavoidable. This does not mean, that with altered techno-environmental conditions, new and more efficient food energy systems cannot be evolved   (Harris 1966: 59).

Harris's views, later worked into a more general functional theory of culture with its basis in materialism, have ever since been subject to acclaim from some quarters and criticism from others. The criticisms have variously come from other ecological anthropologists or from social anthropologists wanting to emphasize the autonomy of cultural features, such as religious rules and ideas, from a materialistic basis or explanation.

Taking the latter first, there is quite wide opposition to the idea that the forms of religious life have a functional relation to the mundane business of getting a living. In many respects this is true. Many of the world's great mythologies, whether of old classical Greece and Rome, or of the Norsemen – the old Scandinavian and Teutonic tribes – or of the ancient and modern Hindus, Buddhists, Jews, Muslims and Christians, are not to be explicated in a functional way. Religions are many-faceted and the fine grain of sacred beliefs is rich in symbolic significance, colourful in its story line, poetic in form, memorable often for its contradictions and portrayal of the underlying ideas of human nature, good and evil of the peoples and their times. None of this discounts the possibility that there are strongly functional messages in some religious imperatives and taboos, however; but even then, as Hallpike (1973) has pointed out, we still need to know *who* benefits from such rules, and how they do so.

The second kind of criticism emphasizes an evolutionary perspective as well as an ecological one, and it is in this direction we want to move now. The point at issue is that the functional view as laid out above in relation to the sacred cow does not clarify how religious rules would come to change as a result of changed ecological circumstances. It does not deny change, but leaves the mechanism implicit, as a sort of gradual process which somehow occurs. Clearly, religions do change – one has only to think of the debates and changes in modern Christianity with regard to abortion, birth control, sexuality and so on. Around us we see the debates in progress, and always shall. But a theory that holds that religious ideology 'knows best' must put itself into difficulties in the face of change, for if people are best advised to 'stick to the rules' rather than try new ones and throw off the old, how does religion, and indeed culture as a whole, evolve?

Harris does, in fact, accept change and evolution as a result of 'altered techno-environmental conditions' as our quotation (above) shows. But we are not given a clear idea of how it takes place. It seems logical that change must be slower where religious taboos are more deeply entrenched, but how can we judge how entrenched religious rules are? Rappaport (1968) in his discussion of the functions of pig rituals (Chapter 1: 3–4) emphasizes the systemic nature of religious rituals, and argues that any system providing the appropriate solutions for life in the local environment will be viable. Thus the actual rules are not rigid, but there must be a set of rules. This idea is helpful in that it can account for what seem to be arbitrary features of religious rituals and associated beliefs. We need, however, to go beyond the 'systems' level of analysis to discover how individuals can and do respond to religious rules, and how these rules affect individuals' fitness; without such an understanding we may have an ecological analysis of religion but we shall never have a biological one.

What is needed, therefore, over and above the demonstration of ecological functionality, is a mechanism for continuous assessment, trial and error, and eventual change. Such a mechanism would, almost inevitably, be at the individual level, but it is by no means obvious how it would work or what processes would be involved in determining outcomes, and much current thinking focuses on these problems.

A consistent critic of Harris has been Diener (1980) who, with a number of colleagues, has emphasized the fact referred to above, that ecology without evolution is only half the story. At first this group focused on what they saw as a neglect of the evolutionary dimension; later (Diener 1980) the argument has come to emphasize quantum jumps in cultural evolution based on an analogy with quantum jumps in biological evolution (Gould and Eldredge 1977) and opposed to gradualist theories of change.

The arguments in this debate have been complex, hazy and heated as a perusal of Diener (1980) will show. Rather than enter the fray, which is not our main concern, let us return to the question of the nature of the supposed selection mechanisms by which culture passes from generation to generation, for here we shall find progress easier and less convoluted. A productive idea in regard to cultural selection is that of the anthropologist Durham (1976) and the psychologist Campbell (1975) who, meaning much the same process, refer to 'selective retention'. Selective retention implies that culture, far from being monolithic and homogeneous, consists of a variety of choices, and according to the choices made by people down the generations it remains either more or less static, or undergoes directional change. Two questions this gives rise to are: What is the criterion of a successful choice, i.e. What is it that determines whether choice (a) or choice (b), once made, goes on down the generations or fizzles out? Secondly, at what level are these choices made: individual, group, or wider, e.g. state? As we shall see, these questions are closely related to each other.

Both Durham and Campbell have been concerned with the relationship between human cultural evolution and Darwinian, organic evolution. It is today more or less universally accepted that Darwinian selection occurs principally at the individual level. As Williams (1966) and Dawkins (1976) have stressed, only those genes that can 'win out' in one generation can be transmitted to the next, and they are transmitted according to the relative success of their carriers in the reproductive 'rat-race'. Is the same true of aspects of culture? This question raises the basic issue of the relation between natural and cultural selection. Are they quite different and separate processes, or similar by analogy, or truly interactive? All shades of answer occur in the current literature. For Dawkins (1976) they were considered as rather separate. Dawkins coined the term 'memes' for the learned ideas transmitted by cultures, and differentiated sharply between their transmission mechanism from generation to generation, and the genetic one. Memes had the advantage that, being able to spread very much faster than genes, they enabled individuals to adapt faster; hence the whole evolutionary process in man was somewhat removed from the animal one. The idea of 'memes' was useful in that it laid emphasis on the unique properties of man's cultures and their unique method of evolution, but it was based on a rather close analogy with 'genes' and tended to deflect attention away from interactionist theories that saw cultural ideas and practices interacting with genes in some way or other.

This brings us back to the idea of 'selective retention'. In this view, the criterion of success for aspects of culture is not directly measured in terms of how far they succeed in perpetuating themselves, for that degree of success is itself a part of the wider process of natural selection. Thus cultural items are successful if they enhance the inclusive reproductive fitness of their bearers. The result is a 'co-evolution' of the cultural and physical aspects of human life (Durham 1978).

Some such idea as that of co-evolution is becoming quite widespread, particularly among evolutionarily minded anthropologists. They fall into roughly two camps. On the one hand we have a 'hard-nosed' group who wish to retain a genetic perspective, and on the other a 'softer' group who feel this is unnecessary or do not discuss it. The former group holds to a view that makes certain demands, which have been very well expressed by Alexander (1979: 77) as follows: 'One might suggest that there are *genetic instructions* which somehow result in our engaging in arbitrariness in symbolic behaviour in whatever *environments* it is genetically *reproductive to* do so' (his italics). Durham (1978) and more recently Lumsden and Wilson (1981) have gone to some trouble to produce a brain-based model that would do at least some of these things. In this model the process of natural selection, acting on individuals via their success or otherwise to reproduce themselves, has led to the emergence of brain structures that create biases in human behavioural tendencies. Such biases produce 'ease of learning' of adaptive actions (i.e. actions that have in the past been active) but can be overridden by ontogenetic processes if the culture is changing or the individual is for any reason unable or unwilling to follow them. A not dissimilar brain-based, genetic theory was produced by Hamilton (1975) to explain the in-group-amity, out-group-enmity found in the relationships between human groups. Hamilton had the idea of a 'template' in the brains of individuals, by reference to which human relationships would be organized; Lumsden and Wilson (1981) do not posit a brain template but a series of neural pathways along which learning occurs easily; Durham suggests three kinds of 'biases': adaptive learning; feelings of satisfaction, and canalized learning (1978: 23).

Clearly this 'hard-nosed' group is struggling to find a down-to-earth mechanism whereby the outcome of following the cultural rules that happen to prevail at any one time in any one place can be reflected, via the genetic process, in the next generation. This inclusion of the genetic process in the system can link up with natural selection theory and integrate human action into animal behaviour and general biological theory.

Nevertheless we need not accept such a theory, for it makes an unnecessary demand, namely that the transmission of culture should have any genetic basis at all. This brings us to the 'soft' view referred to above, and with it the end of our survey. We noted that the soft view de-emphasizes genes, tending to emphasize reproductive success as such. In brief, following, changing, choosing between or rejecting cultural rules will lead to people having more or less children and thus their ideas of what to do and how to do it will be perpetuated, by parent–child interaction and other processes, in proportion to their reproductive success. The anthropologists Chagnon and Irons (1979) have emphasized reproductive success in this general way, as also has Durham in his 1979 chapter, together with a number of other anthropologists, notably Hiatt (1981), by showing that cultures are based on individuals' strategies for maximizing their reproductive success. Irons, for instance, writes as follows: 'Human beings "track" their environments and behave in ways which, given the specific environment in which they find themselves, maximise inclusive fitness; what is observed as culture and social structure is the outcome of this process' (Irons 1979: 258). His statement arises from his field studies of the Turkmen, and he qualifies it with respect to post-industrial populations practising birth-control by contraception, but wishes nevertheless to maintain it as a general idea. Dickemann's (1979) argument concerning the occurrence of monogamy and polygamy in the Indian caste system, relating this to the prevailing levels of relevant resources and the amounts of parental energy needed to utilize these to maximize inclusive fitness, is of the same general type. Hiatt's (1981) paper on polyandry in Sri Lanka is a further good example. Following Trivers (1972) he concludes that parental investment must be working on non-genetic lines in man, and he accepts that such human strategies as exist are based on cognitive choices dictated by economic contingencies. He does also, however, consider that natural selection plays its part in determining the background against which such choices occur. He argues that the universal human emotions of 'sexual desire, sexual jealousy, parental love (and) kinship amity, guided by intelligence and self-control' underlie the connection between human reproductive strategies and natural selection.

Such arguments hold that the extent of genetic control of human cultural activity is either entirely absent or minimal. Even if, as in Hiatt's analysis, there is an underlying stratum of universality at the level of 'emotions', the cultural responses to these are 'free' in the sense that they can go along with, or oppose, the underlying tendencies. Hiatt's non-genetic parental investment implies that individuals learn or are explicitly taught during their lives the appropriate ways of behaving in their particular culture, taking account of their social position, gender, and possible future happenings based on a knowledge of the past. There is no need for gene-based 'node-link structures' channelling action towards certain goals rather than others (Lumsden and Wilson 1981). All we need to posit is a process whereby children are differentially produced by members of the community, and processes exist whereby they discover the cultural know-how to reproduce successfully in their turn, and to transmit the know-how down the generations. Providing a culture provides some rewards at least for reproduction itself, the process will go on. Where such rewards are strong, for example where old people are looked after by their children and no one else, the process will certainly go on apace, and the more so if life's uncertainties make it likely that a goodly proportion of children produced will die before their parents. If, in a society, there were few rewards for having children, the process would slow down; if there were rewards for having few children, or the safety of those born was largely guaranteed, it would lead to low levels of reproductive activity, and if a culture actually removed all rewards or even punished reproduction, it would be expected to stop. To use the terms of Trivers (1972) and Hiatt (1981), culture provides the rules for parental investment.

The world is full of cultures with different rules; some of these are encoded in religions and have religious backing; among them are many that affect the extent of child-rearing regarded as appropriate. Such rules and emphases might be entirely arbitrary ('culture by whimsey' as Blurton-Jones (1976) has memorably called it). In fact, however, we have not found this to be the case. In company with others who have emphasized the ecological circumstances of cultural forms, we have found evidence of rules within cultures that would tend to enhance the survival and reproductive success of individuals in the prevailing, and in light of the past, environmental conditions. Some of these rules are encoded in religious systems, which (contrary to first expectations) seem to be very much concerned with *this* life and its practical goings-on.

Cultural and natural selection: the theory 16

The biology of religion looks at religions in terms of their contributions to individual (and, though to a lesser extent, group) survival and reproductive fitness. As we have seen, it cannot do this without paying very close attention to ecology: the study of the environments in which people and their religions have to operate. Starting with rather naïve biological questions such as 'Who have more children as a rule, Christians, or Muslims?' we come up with the answer 'Muslims'; but this does not tell us a great deal, even though it is a fact of the greatest interest. Our next question is the difficult one: 'Why?'. The answer relates to the whole debate around which this book revolves, for as with many 'why?' questions, there are many real reasons: the need for support in old age; the number of children other local people recommend; government allowances; costs of rearing versus benefits from the economic support children can give; income and expense when they get married; hopes for grandchildren; wishes to demonstrate fertility; a desire to continue 'the line'; a love of children – perhaps expressed as the view that a home without the sound of children's voices is a sad and unhappy place . . .

Yet the fact is, as we have found, that Christians in many countries content themselves with two or three children, while Muslims in other countries prefer to stop at four or five, and as Davis (1967) showed, this is not for want of the means of birth control, or the advice on how to use it, or exhortations from authoritative quarters to have fewer children; in his valuable and pioneering work he showed that people only began using birth control seriously after they had reached their 'target' number of children. The same process can happen within one country and one religion: Chamie's study (1981) shows that 'Druze' Mus-

A modern wealthy African polygamist with his family.

lims in Lebanon want and have less children than 'Sunni' Muslims in the same country.

Returning to the concerns of biology and ecology, we can see just how far they are removed from the ideas in people's minds. They are at a very high level of abstraction. Yet, by reduction and reduction, they come down to the ideas in people's minds and their consequent choices. People feel free to choose and *are* free to choose. Nobody has to have any children at all; or we could all have as many as we possibly could. But we tend to settle for a certain number, so we come back to the question 'why?' Looking at the answers given above, we can see that there were what Harris (1966) has called 'emic' answers people themselves are inclined to give to account for their actions after the event. What we are looking for are 'etic' answers, that is answers behind the proximate answers people give; answers given, in this case, by students of biology and ecology. Such students interpret what people say in other terms; they in fact seek, not reasons for people's actions, but the causes of those reasons.

The quest for such causes is legitimate enough for students of a science, but whether or not such causes as are posited are in any sense 'valid' depends on 'validation'. Validation is not just a matter of falsification and verification. These two processes, valuable as they are, boil down to questions of 'reliability', namely how often the same or different students come up with the same or different causes for the reasons or actions concerned. Validation, by contrast, demands that quite different approaches based on different methods come up with the same answers, and is thus a more powerful method of 'proving' that actual causes are being found.

It is early days yet to suggest that validation is occuring in the biology and ecology of cultural variation. Insufficient time has passed; too few relevant studies exist. Nevertheless, we can say that from other sources we have confirmed some existing statements in the literature. Thus Dickemann (1979) has suggested that polygyny in upper caste Indian households is a twin result of: (a) the use of wealth by men to enhance their reproductive success; and (b) the upward social mobility of women in the system. The overall effect of the process is seen as adaptive. We too have found that in the Indian caste system polygyny occurs in the upper social strata especially, and have related this to the effects of wealth and a desire to enhance reproductive success. We did not, as it happens, concern ourselves with the total pattern of social mobility. But we have additionally shown that polygyny among wealthy men is a feature of other places and times. It is a feature of some Muslim societies in West Africa, East Africa, and the Middle East, and of some tribal ones such as the Aborigines of Central Australia described by Meggitt (1965). Hiatt (1981) refers to further examples.

Such widespread arrangements begin to have a 'validated' look about them, but in fact the number of variables involved is still far too great for comfort. That this is no simple cause-and-effect relationship is evident from the fact that in the Judaeo-Christian religions wealth does not lead to polygyny. However 'adaptive' the scheme may be, it meets a complete block when a religion, or a culture of which the religion is a significant part, taboos the institution or practice in question. The most a tycoon in the modern West can do is to take one wife after another; he may end up with a dozen wives and several dozen children all doing nicely but he will have been a 'serial monogamist', never a polygynist. The reason he cannot, despite all his worldly goods, be a citizen of a Christian state *and* a polygynist is that the law forbids it. But why, the bio-ecologist asks, forbid something half the world finds so satisfactory?

This brings us close to the heart of the matter. The biological ecologist cannot in his role as student rest content either with emic explanations (e.g. 'It says so in the Bible') or other etic ones (e.g. 'Monogamy goes with certain types of civilization'). He cannot even be satisfied with demonstrations that monogamy goes with higher levels of income or education. It is his duty to enquire whether there might be certain advantages for survival or reproductive fitness in certain circumstances for a given practice to be forbidden, when in other circumstances it would be preferred. He deals with a number of equations: equations of benefits relative to costs, and of risk-taking to risk-minimization, at different times and in different circumstances.

It is at this point that he meets, travelling in parallel, the sociobiologist and the animal ecologist, and discovers a number of shared concerns. These have already been touched on in Chapter 1, and are subject to considerable attention by Reynolds (1980). The conclusion there, and one expressed also by Durham (1978), was that although the prospects looked good for a general theory of culture that would link in with existing theories in biology and ecology, no such theory exists. Our study has raised the possibility that one idea, already present in the animal literature, could be a useful foundation stone for such a theory. This is the idea of r selection, to which we referred in Chapter 1. Rephrased as r^c selection, to take account of the particular and highly distinctive characteristics of human cultures, we could then propose a common socio-ecological principle applicable to both animals and man, which could utilize the symbol $r^{(c)}$.

This suggestion relates a reproductive variable to an environmental one. In the present book we have been very largely concerned with the former, but not with the latter which has been largely implicit. This situation needs to be rectified, but it would take another book to do that. In the meantime, we shall look at some ecological measures in the next chapter and shall use them in the final one. The environmental feature that concerns us, however, is what we have called 'unpredictability'. This can be designated U. As applied to the environment it becomes Ue. And as applied to the culturally perceived environment it becomes Ue^c.

How does Ue^c relate to r^c? We suggest that as one increases so does the other. Where the former is low the latter is low too, and *vice versa*. We suggest that *some kind* of a positive correlation exists between Ue^c and r^c. Where environments are perceived as secure, reproductivity is restricted in various ways; where environments are insecure, reproductivity is given positive inducements to ensure high levels.

Control of reproduction on the above lines is (in part at least) achieved by strategies encoded in religious rules. The word 'strategies' here refers primarily to culturally selected ideas and rules concerned with the regulation of reproduction and parental investment in offspring. But it also perhaps is not wholly inapplicable to the naturally selected behaviour patterns by which reproduction and parental investment are controlled in animals (see ch. 1). If such a parallel exists it is of the greatest interest. The matter requires much further study. But initially we can note that *r* selection in animals is associated with *seasonality* of environment, which includes great variations in food supply. This is comparable in some respects with what we are calling environmental 'unpredictability'. Whereas what has been called *K* selection is associated with stable environments and steady food supply. This is comparable to more 'predictable' conditions. For purposes of this book, however, the animal parallel must be left aside.

Our present purpose is to suggest a theory of cultural evolution which operates by an interactive process involving both cultural selection (by human choices) and natural selection (by reproductive success). Our theory is that the more unpredictable the total environment is perceived to be, the more people will want to create and support ideas favouring high levels of reproduction. They will accept the loss of some of their children as inevitable. Conversely, the less unpredictable the environment is perceived to be, the more people will develop ideas favouring low levels of reproduction. Our study of religion provides a useful set of data against which we can test this theory, and we shall do so in the final chapter. But first we must pay a little more attention to what we mean by 'perceived environmental unpredictability'.

The cultural environment 17

By the 'cultural environment' we mean to imply the physical environment in which people live, as interpreted or viewed or perceived by those people. Every human group has a set of rules determining what parts of the environment are suitable for the various processes of human life and what parts are to be avoided. As we have seen throughout this book, religions are very involved in the transmission of these 'do and don't' rules. To this extent religions are very concerned with interpreting the physical environment, and thus with establishing the cultural environment.

We can begin this chapter by envisaging a situation in which a group of newcomers, devising a new religion, enter an already occupied zone. What kind of religious rules will such a group need to have any chance of establishing themselves? If, and only if, their ideology contains a strong pro-natalist element, will their colonization succeed in building up numbers, unless they proceed by the somewhat more hazardous and perhaps politically dangerous, policy of conversion. In fact, we know that Jehovah told Moses 'to be fruitful and multiply' (Genesis 1:22), that Allah told Muhammad to allow each man four wives (Koran 4:3) and to spare the lives of daughters (Koran 6:138 and 81:8) and care for orphans (Koran 4:5–7), and that St Paul (who preferred celibacy and conversion tactics) nonetheless conceded that it is better 'to marry than to burn' (1 Corinthians 7:9). In India there are old erotic temples and men are strongly exhorted to have sons. Buddhists in Thailand have phallic shrines for women in quest of children (Plate v). Religions, in short, have rules to perpetuate themselves in the biological sense, some more characteristic in their early days, others still clearly in operation.

However, as time goes by, our colonizing human population will fill its environment and new food types will need to be developed, or more of the existing types imported, or fertilizers will need to be used if the population is to continue to thrive. These processes however, will tend to be expensive and will start to raise questions in people's minds about their optimal reproductive strategies, more especially if the environment is predictable enough to enable them to feel reasonably certain that their offspring are likely to survive. What determines the level of environmental unpredictability (the Ue^c)?

Such questions form a large part of the subject matter of modern human geography and while the complexities of that field are enormous it would be unwise, indeed impossible, for us to proceed without recourse to some of its central concepts. Broek and Webb (1978) have provided a useful account of many of the principal issues involved. Like

Where volcanoes occur religious rituals are often used in attempts to control the flow of lava.

Toynbee, they reject both simplistic racial and environmental determin-
isms of cultural processes, and fully acknowledge the effect of cultural
factors on the extent and ways that human groups come to grips with
their surroundings. They make a useful distinction, between the 'operational environment' which is 'the environment we live in, affecting us
in some way or other whether or not we are conscious of it' and the
'perceptual environment', which is 'the portion of the operational environment of which we are aware' 'Persons of the same culture or sub-
culture are most likely to share basic ideas about and attitudes toward
the environment; in other words the perceptual environment is the external world as culturally conceived' (Broek and Webb 1978: 33).

One major factor that can greatly decrease the unpredictability of the
human environment is the use of non-human sources of energy. The
peasant uses the ox to pull his plough, and the ass is widely used to
transport goods or to turn a machine for threshing wheat. The power
of wind or water is used to make flour from wheat. The progress of our
civilization has been dependent on ever-widening discoveries and uses
of non-human energy: steam from coal, electricity, gas, oil, nuclear
power. Today, each of us in the West has the power of a Roman
emperor. They snapped their fingers, we push our switches. It is by
such extensions of power through tapping non-human energy that we
have come to increase beyond measure the security with which we can
face the future, the predictability of our environment, and to reduce the
possibility that it will suddenly collapse around us. We are still increasing this level of security, for instance by guaranteed subsidies for
farmers in lean years, and artificially fixed shop prices for food.

No one can say we have succeeded. We run a grave risk of massive
collapse if our system were to undergo serious breakdown. We have however made enormous progress and one has only to travel to countries
that for one reason or another have been denied this progress to
realize how far we have come from lives of sheer physical toil, with
water to be carried, not piped; children who become diseased or die; food
that is both monotonous and barely adequate in quantity and quality;
famine and flood. We in the affluent countries may be heading for disaster as our energy supplies run out, but just now we are riding on the
crest of a wave of prosperity, and to deny this is to be blind to reality.

It is, then, to the subject of energy and the amount each of us can
harness that we need to direct our attention in actually measuring, or
just thinking concretely, about the level of Ue^c. The extent of unpredictability, for us, is small because in the environment as we perceive it we
have only to bring our enormous latent resources to bear on crisis situations in order to overcome them. In the Second World War nutritional
shortages in Britain were overcome by issuing the population with
dried egg powder, dried milk and other such foods. Somehow or other,
we feel, we shall not starve. For much of the world today there is no
such comfortable feeling.

Let us once again remind ourselves of what we are looking for. We
are looking for a measure, preferably a quantitative one, of the perceived predictability/unpredictability of the environment; and we have
decided that access to energy is a good way of assessing this. Since we
have in earlier parts of the book wanted to focus on the individual (e.g.
individuals' reproductive fitness) in line with our biological orientation,
we want now to find figures relating to individuals' utilization of en-

ergy. Suitable average figures are available. The consumption for an average individual of energy from coal, lignite, petroleum products, natural gas, hydroelectricity and nuclear electricity, converted into kilograms of coal equivalent is given on a country by country basis in Table 19.1 column 3 (p. 292).

Per capita consumption of energy, while a useful way of thinking of how far individuals can reduce the unpredictability of the environment, is not the only way.

Besides the energy each of us consumes there is also the 'output' side, that is how much each of us produces. The more our productivity exceeds our needs, the more we can store against the vagaries of the future environment. The subsistence farmer in many parts of India, Africa, or Indonesia, grows little more than what he needs for a living. If a little surplus can be produced, that can be used to trade for extras that he cannot produce himself. Usually subsistence farming, which is still at the present time enormously widespread, is done on a family basis, either the nuclear family or more likely some form of joint or extended family, and sometimes at the clan or village level. In such cases we need to calculate the figure for productivity *per capita*. How can this best be done? First, what unit are we to express it in? Cabbages? Equivalents to a unit weight of potatoes? This is possible, but there is a far more convenient method that is in fact used: money; for money is, in theory at least, a universal medium of exchange. A country with a highly diversified economy based on high levels of industry and commerce will have a high level of *per capita* productivity, shown quite simply by adding together the sale value of all its products and dividing by the number of people in the population. If the calculation is done in this crude way it results in the gross national product *per capita* (GNP p/c) see Table 19.1 column 4. Let us now consider this as a second useful measure for our own concerns.

We are looking for measures of the relative unpredictability of the perceptual environment. GNP p/c reflects this quite well. If the figure for a country is low, this means the majority of its population is living at subsistence level, and while this is sufficient in normal times it will not have reserves to draw on in emergencies. Thus if there is a drought or a flood or a plague of locusts, hunger and starvation will result. (We overlook here the possible occurrence of effective outside aid.) Conditions of low GNP p/c are thus conditions of high Ue^c. On the other hand, if the figure for a country is high, this means that enough food is available (either through being grown or through being imported or both) for a large percentage of the population to be able to engage in all sorts of tasks unrelated to primary food production. Indeed, it may be that 10 per cent of the population can grow or import food for the whole community, or that there is so much food around that people complain of obesity. In such conditions a drought or a flood or a massive attack by insect pests will be a temporary nuisance at most; it may go unnoticed by the majority; wealth will be directed to rectifying the situation quickly and completely. Conditions of high GNP p/c are thus conditions of low Ue^c.

The effects of low levels of energy consumption and low productivity, in other words of a high level of environmental unpredictability, are most clearly seen in the ensuing levels of diet and mortality. A survey by the Food and Agricultural Organisation of the United Nations in 1963 found that at least 60 per cent of the people in less-developed countries were undernourished. Further, in conditions of poor hygiene and in the absence of western medicine, child mortality is very high and the average life-span of those surviving infancy is far lower than in developed countries.

Conclusions

Our book has in the main been about the reproductive strategies and consequences of belonging to particular religious groups. We then formulated a theory of selection relating religions to environments. We have shown throughout the book that religions differ in the extent to which they emphasize pro-natalist or anti-natalist strategies. In this chapter we have tried to show that two measures can demonstrate the extent of environmental unpredictability that exists for man: *per capita* energy consumption, and *per capita* gross national product. These measures can provide useful environmental dimensions on a worldwide basis against which to look at world religions and their rules. This we shall do in the final chapter, but in the next chapter we will look again at the general emphases of the world's major religions in respect of reproductivity.

Religions and their emphases 18

Introduction

In this chapter, we shall attempt to summarize the ways that religious rules instruct people and lead them to act in their everyday lives, and as a result cause them to have more or less children, catch certain diseases, marry early, become celibate and so on. In short (to repeat), we are investigating matters at the individual level, not the group or population level, and indeed religions speak to individuals, and affect them in quite intimate ways. These personal matters, though of a major biological importance, are seen by individual people in terms of their conformity to or deviance from the dictates of their religions or religious scruples.

Christianity

Christianity is against premarital and extra-marital conceptions which it labels 'illegitimate' and stigmatizes. In some countries it favours chastity before marriage. It is 'good' for conception to occur within marriage but there is no compulsion to have children. Contraception is permitted in Protestantism; in Catholicism it is disapproved of except by the 'rhythm' method and abstention from intercourse.

Once a child is conceived, however, Christianity is most concerned that it should survive, although a current debate rages over the first few post-conception weeks. Concerning this earliest period of life, many societies in the Christian world are deeply divided between those who hold that the embryo may be artificially removed by abortion and those who hold that it may not. The arguments may be couched in terms of

The god Vishnu appearing at the birth of his eighth incarnation Krishna, one of the most conspicuous figures in the Hindu pantheon.

whether or not the embryo has a 'soul' or 'spirit' at this early point, or whether it can be considered a 'human being'. At a certain stage, however, it becomes increasingly the case that Christianity favours taking all possible steps to preserve the life of the foetus. There is a great deal of maternal care, with 'childbirth' classes and overall low rates of prenatal mortality from avoidable causes (i.e. in contrast with so-called 'spontaneous' abortions). The 'Hippocratic oath' comes into operation early on, this being an idea developed for and by physicians going back to pre-Christian thinking. Again, postnatal care is excellent, with Christianity giving a lot of attention to such children as are born with handicaps, or whose parents are absent or dead. There are, and have been for centuries, Christian homes for orphans or foundlings, though as we saw the mortality rates in some were once worryingly high. Adoption and fostering are widespread among Christians.

Christianity contributes in many ways to education, not only as regards moral standards of sexual abstinence, but also more recently with regard to personal hygiene. There is no emphasis on circumcision for boys, and it is unthinkable for girls. As adolescence arrives, the Christianized child will be ready to resist the powerful sex urges of that time. Sex will have been firmly identified with sin, and both boys and girls who indulge in more than the mildest flirtation will meet with religious disapproval. Sex, Christians are taught, is for reproduction within marriage, not personal pleasure; least of all is it described by the Church as a holy or sacred activity. Books on the subject tend, if allied to religion, to concern themselves with how to control the sex urge and the need to repent if there has been indulgence. All kinds of sex are included. As a result, such sex as takes place is surreptitious and tainted with shame. Books on sex, especially explicit or pictorial matter, are regarded as inappropriate reading for adolescents, even if they contain a great deal of useful information. Christians are, to an amazing extent, 'left in the dark' about sexuality, and may remain so all their lives. Recent trends to 'liberalize' sex attitudes have by and large been made in the face of Christianity, not by it.

Marriage is not encouraged during early adolescence, nor even middle or late adolescence – it is indeed forbidden by the Christian Church before the age of 16, and people are encouraged to wait until they are 'mature'. Monogamy is insisted on, polygamy being taboo. Marriage is not only monogamous, it is for life, as the marriage ceremony makes clear, and great emphasis is placed on the relationship of love and devotion between the partners themselves, far more than on the need of the wife to produce children who are not regarded as essential, though their joyful arrival is anticipated. Should a marriage be childless, however, it in no way lessens its value as a wholly complete and worthy Christian marriage; indeed, if it is childless and the parents remain a devoted couple it is often regarded as more successful than a fertile marriage in which the parents are at loggerheads with one another.

Celibacy is a well known phenomenon in Christianity, being essential, at the present time, in the Roman Catholic priesthood both for nuns and priests, as well as for a dedicated few in a number of non-Catholic denominations. Celibacy is not conceived of as a taboo on sex, but as an aid in the overriding call of service to God and to the community. In keeping with the idea that sex is tainted with sin, however, sexual abstinence is clearly related to godliness, and thus the truly celibate person is both better able to serve others than if he or she had family preoccupations, and is spiritually 'purer' than a person indulging in sex. From the biological standpoint, celibacy is frankly anti-natalist, unless it promotes the reproductive efforts of others. We saw some evidence that this might be so, but it was not wholly convincing and we would not argue that case with much conviction.

Divorce is frowned on by Protestants and prohibited by Catholicism. 'Let no man put asunder those whom God hath joined together'. It is in no way admissible because of infertility of either spouse. 'Dissolution' of a marriage can be allowed, however, if the marriage is never 'consummated', i.e. if sexual intercourse fails to take place for any reason. Not only is divorce frowned on, it is also made difficult for people in the Christian world. This can be explained on a wholly secular basis, e.g. the law relating to ownership of property as between husband and wife, and secular rules of inheritance, but when we consider the relative ease of divorce in the other major world religions (or even in the state of Nevada, where easy divorce is available at a cost for out-of-state visitors) it does seem that a good deal more is at stake than how the property shall be divided up and who will inherit what.

During 'middle' (for women, post-menopausal) and old age, Christianity provides a number of opportunities for its members that have some biological significance. It gives opportunities to engage in care of 'unwanted' children by supporting adoption homes or agencies, or actually fostering or adopting children. In general it emphasizes their usefulness for the care of specific other individuals, whose survival and reproductive chances are thereby enhanced. Such other individuals are not necessarily of the same group, race or creed; they may even be in a different country – e.g. earthquake victims in Turkey, flood victims in Pakistan, or Vietnamese 'boat people'. Such middle-aged Christians are sometimes labelled with the derogatory title 'do-gooders' by others who do not approve of this kind of activity. At this age, actual reproduction is no longer possible, by definition, for the woman; but it is also somewhat frowned on, though not forbidden, by the man. Among the wealthy, however, older men continue to divorce and take new wives, though only in a tiny minority, without real institutional support.

With the onset of real old age, Christianity seems to be at a loss. It continues to preach care; priests do indeed care for and visit the old, sick and dying, and Christian organizations exist for their welfare. But in the ageing communities of the modern Western world, where there are often as many 'over-sixties' as 'under-twenties' and a large number of people are in their late seventies, eighties and even nineties, the religion and its resources have proved quite inadequate. Despite the existence of many charities, state support has become essential. It is a cruel but true fact that the very old and senile get better care, on the whole, if they have greater wealth.

Following this stage comes the event of death, when Christianity springs into action again. It is not involved, as a rule, in body-washing or close contact of ritual kinds between the dead one and his or her relatives. Perhaps because of considerations of hygiene, it seems to emphasize a distance between the departed and those left behind. The freshly dead body is covered all over in a sheet as if it should not be looked at; when more 'presentable' it may be available for 'last respects' at a 'chapel of rest', and so the euphemisms go on. The reason for this is hard to determine, unless it be hygienic considerations; but this is curious for in Western countries, at least, death is far more likely to be due to non-infectious than infectious disease. The Christian funeral is a very controlled affair in the Western world, with its appointed time and place, its formal rituals and a general feeling that restraint from the expression of grief by the mourners is appropriate; usually there is no loud weeping or wailing even by the closest remaining relatives. Cremation and burial are both acceptable, and the funeral contains, besides a remembrance of the dead person, a clear message that he or she has now gone on to 'a better place' or to 'everlasting life', but essentially, in mainstream Christianity, that there is now a departure from the land and concerns of the living, that intervention from or contact with the dead person is not to be expected (although Masses for the dead are held in Catholic Latin America, and certain sects continue contact with the dead – notably those embracing some form of 'spiritualism').

Though the idea of Hell and Hellfire as the ultimate destination of sinners is widespread during life, it does not feature in the funeral ceremony, perhaps again reflecting the separation between the living and dead. Judgement occurs when man meets his Maker. Again, we can contrast this lack of involvement with the widespread idea, in Africa and elsewhere, that ill-disposed ancestors can affect the lives of their descendants and have to be appeased, or the Buddhist–Hindu tradition that evil-doers can expect retribution by reincarnation in forms whose suffering increases proportionately in the 'next time round'. All such ideas differ from the Christian notion that a return to this world is not possible. (Again, however, there are a few Christians who do believe that 'ghosts' can return and do damage, and a few Western Christian priests continue to enact rituals for the exorcism of places where such events have occurred; whereas in Christianized black Africa such rituals are much more readily accepted).

Another aspect of death in relation to biology concerned the matter of autopsy and organ transplants. The Christian faith does not oppose them – possibly again deriving from the clear separation of the body (which when dead, is of no further concern) and the soul or spirit that lives on in the next world.

We noted that Christianity itself was a common cause of death: occasionally through mass destruction by sects in defence of their integrity, but more often in the conduct of religious wars, notably in the past against that old enemy, Islam; but also against tribal peoples (Catholicism versus the Incas of Peru, for instance) or more latterly Christian military reaction against Fascism (though it must be admitted that the very land of Catholicism's heart, Italy, fought on the Fascist side). With such considerations, however, this book is barely concerned, for want of space rather than lack of interest.

Part 3 of our study focused on disease. Christianity here showed itself to be an active faith. The pious were among the earliest modern health and hygiene reformers, despite Darlington's claim that Christianity was and is dirty (Darlington 1969: 299–300), and have never generally (except undoubtedly in the field of animal experimentation) opposed medical progress based on secular science. Some sects, however, do just this and are highly intolerant of any interference with God's will and prayer as the roads to health and cure, or sickness and death. Jehovah's Witnesses and Christian Scientists are cases in point, and we showed that their mortality is correspondingly increased.

In view of the 'active' attitude to care and cure, it is not surprising to find hostility among most Christians to both suicide and euthanasia: both are affronts to the notion that life is God-given and should be preserved. Occasionally during history Christianity has found itself faced with enormous and immediate health dangers, notably during the Great Plague. Here we saw a series of spectacular responses. Having determined that Plague was a result of human sinfulness and a demonstration of God's wrath, the reaction produced a highly motivated group of self-scourgers, the ultra-penitent Flagellants, who took upon themselves to make up for man's past excesses by self-torture, a sort of mass martyrdom, since they moved from one plague-ridden place to another, increasing their chances of contracting the disease, and of carrying it to others. In terms of the motivation rather than the effects, however, this was an interventionist response aimed at stopping the disease.

A number of other infectious situations have been, or are, brought on themselves by Christians. A minor one, undoubtedly, is the shared communion cup, kissing of ikons or special holy wooden crucifixes. More potentially infectious, it would seem, is the self-dipping into holy water by pilgrims at Lourdes. And even more the old-style pilgrimages of Christians to Jerusalem. Missionaries, too, expose themselves to great additional risk from infectious sources. Such situations have to be investigated one by one, and no generalizations are possible. The visits to Lourdes are certainly, however, characteristic of the active Christian search for health and cure, whatever the objective outcome. Missionary risk-taking, by nuns running leprosaria for instance, or Sister Teresa in Calcutta, or US missionaries to South America, are allied to the principle of service to others, which in these cases overrides the considerations of personal health.

Lastly, regarding those with 'constitutional' diseases, we noted that, as was to be expected, Christianity would not tolerate their destruction. The mentally handicapped or physically deformed child is a child of God nonetheless, and worthy of love as such: a challenge to faith, even. To treat such children as an unacceptable 'genetic load', or to use arguments from 'eugenics' in favour of their removal, is anti-Christian. They must be cared for whatever the cost in time, effort and money.

As for the health of Christians themselves, the Anglican clergy in Western Europe were seen to have good health and good life expectancy, with low rates of cardiac disease; members of sects banning smoking had low rates of lung cancer; and nuns, while largely avoiding cervical cancer, nevertheless had a high susceptibility to cancer of the breast. These topics were, however, not pursued at great length, being somewhat on the margins of our central concerns; but they certainly demand more study, as authors such as Vaux (1976) have already pointed out.

We look next at Islam; but before passing on, it is impossible to resist the simple statement deriving from the above survey of 'Christian biology', that here, above all, we have a faith that in almost all respects conforms to what we are calling the r- end of the r spectrum.

Islam

Muslims aim at, enjoy, and take pride in large families. The family is a
lifelong unit of central attention and social interaction. The father is a
figure of great social importance, his wife or wives having lower status.
All Muslims are enjoined to pray five times daily, but the mosque is a
male preserve and women pray and talk in a separate building. The
sexes tend to hold apart during daytime, public activities. Women conceive often, but owing to prolonged nursing for two years (Koran
31:13) there may be a long between-births interval. In the earliest times,
each Muslim man was able to take up to four wives, and while this is
still the case it tends in fact to happen that only wealthier and older men
can do so since each marriage involves the full maintenance of the wife,
an expensive marriage ceremony and probably considerable 'bride-
wealth' payments to the bride's family if she is a virgin.

The faith is mildly anti-contraceptive but has no specific laws;
however the emphasis on child-bearing and the love and status of
mothers leads to the use of contraceptives after a family of·four or five
children has been produced rather than before this. There are a goodly
number of religious festivals in the annual round, at none of which sexual activity is forbidden, and indeed Muslims are encouraged to have
intercourse during the nights of Ramadan (Koran 2:183).

Female infanticide, noted in some religions, was expressly forbidden
in early days by Muhammad himself in the Koran (thus spoken by
Allah). In this respect he broke with the pre-Islamic Arabs who practised it. Abortion is not allowed in traditional Islam, though there have
been twentieth-century moves in some countries by 'liberal' modernists
to introduce it. Such moves have had limited success and with the current revival of traditional Islam in countries such as Lebanon and Iran
we cannot tell what the outcome will be. In countries such as those of
the Eastern USSR and Lebanon, there is a continuing greater growth
rate in Islamic than Christian communities.

Islamic boys are all circumcized, usually at puberty, i.e. considerably
later than in Judaism. The effects of circumcision have been thoroughly
discussed, mainly in Chapter 13, and will not be repeated here. The
custom appears to have been taken over from pre-existing Arab custom
by Muhammad, not invented by him, and is for males only, except in
some African Muslim peoples where female circumcision has continued
despite Islamization.

In many Muslim lands, education centres around learning, often by
heart, the text of the Koran. A teacher, or 'mullah', conveys the scriptures to the children gathered around, who repeat the words until
known by heart. These principles are not, therefore, so easily subject to
question later in adolescence, as they might be in cultures emphasizing
general principles and using stories to exemplify these. The Islamic
scriptures are exact statements, to be interpreted literally, rather than
generalized injunctions subject to ambiguous interpretations.

Islamic girls in particular are betrothed early, and both sexes are exhorted to marry young, though few men can afford to do so. Betrothal
is very much a family affair rather than an individual one between the
couple concerned, but they will certainly have met before the marriage
and be tolerant of one another. Premarital sex is, however, not allowed.
Sex is a holy, not at all sinful activity, within marriage, but once married

it is a great and shameful sin outside marriage, extra-marital relations bringing a variety of penalties, up to and including, in extreme circumstances, death. The virtues of sex are extolled in numerous Islamic books, the best known in the West being *The Perfumed Garden*, owing to Sir Richard Burton's translation. Nowadays freely available in 'liberal' Christian countries, it was long considered too erotic to pass the test of Christian so-called 'respectability'. In fact it is just a book on sex with advice on how to maintain its delights with advancing age, written for married Muslims.

Unlike their Christian counterparts, Muslim widows are fully expected to remarry (after a four-month interval from their husband's death to establish the paternity of any children born). Orphans are cared for by the family, and not stigmatized; this is believed to go back to Muhammad's own experience as an orphan. Black slaves, too, in the early days, were given some status in Islam and allowed to marry and have children, in contradistinction to the prior practice of turning them into eunuchs to serve in the local royal palace and entertain the family head and his harem. Out-marriage was, indeed, encouraged in early Islam, and still is, there being a number of organizations such as the Islamic Propagation League, that exist purely for the propagation, by every means available, of the words of Allah to those of other faiths.

Celibacy is not highly regarded in Islam. It has almost no place in the Koran, and is not favoured for men or even thinkable for women. It would bring ostracism, not rewards. As in all world religions, there are sects that introduce the idea and favour it, but it cannot be considered an Islamic idea.

Divorce can occur frequently in Islamic communities since husbands are not required to give any justification for divorcing their wives. Divorce requires no court procedures or witnesses and is not regarded as severely as in Christianity; it is certainly not forbidden although Muhammad in the Traditions is credited with saying: 'Among permitted things, divorce is the most hated by Allah'. The divorced woman cannot remarry for at least three months. Remarriage is not made difficult, on the contrary it is expected. In recent times in countries such as Lebanon, Egypt and Tunisia, divorce has been made rather more difficult by secular, state laws as modernization has proceeded; it remains to be seen how far Islam will move towards the complex divorce systems found in Christian countries. Divorce is exhorted in the case of barrenness by the woman; in this case she will probably remarry and attempt to have children by another husband. If she has none, her status is low.

Older men are preferred as husbands; their status is high and their wealth gives the necessary security. This, coupled with the institution of polygyny and the expectation of bridal virginity, leads to large-scale frustration for young men, as English girl visitors to Islamic countries discover.

With advancing age the Islamic woman is not faced with any special problems as long as she has a growing family. The menopause is not a life-crisis but a natural event, and older people are given due help and respect by their offspring. On death, bodies are washed by special washers who advertise their skills in mosques, and bodies are prepared for viewing before burial. Funerals are occasions for the open expression of grief, enhanced on most occasions by the hiring of wailers who follow the coffin to the burial place with much noise of crying and weeping. The funeral, like the wedding, is a protracted process and can take several days, being generally followed by a feast of some elaborateness and high cost, depending on the status of the departed. There is no expectation in Islam of continued participation by the dead in the affairs of the living. Suicide is rare in Islam.

Regarding destruction through religious wars, much the same can be said for Islam as for Christianity; the two religions were locked in combat for centuries, with great losses on both sides; we do not consider this matter in detail in this book, though Christian–Muslim wars are still occurring, as in Lebanon and southern Philippines.

Attitudes to disease have never been as closely tied up with Islamic ideology as with the Christian pietist-hygiene school. However, we did note the practice of building hospitals in ancient Islam which led the world in medical science, and gave a considerable amount of care to the sick. Western medicine has been accepted in modern Islamic communities but we have not come across a great deal of information on this topic. Probably Islam has been unable through relative poverty to maintain its progress towards hygiene at the Western rate. An absence of sufficient water may have been a contributory factor in some countries.

This is a culture where the left hand is reserved for toilet and sexual functions, while the right is for touching food, both in preparation (the exclusive domain of women) and eating. Men in general eat first, and mostly do so together in a special front room, while women eat in a back room or in the kitchen. The woman serves the food to the husband, his brother and any guests, including women of high status, and then retires in silence.

Other aspects of disease transmission involve the Koranic insistence on washing before prayer and we saw how this could be a two-edged sword, either spreading disease if the water was static and polluted, or cleansing if it was piped, clean, and well drained.

Regarding pilgrimages, the long and often hazardous pilgrimage to Mecca demanded by the Koran of all Muslims once in their lives has, in the past, contributed a high risk to life and health through infectious diseases such as cholera. Coming, often on foot and over weeks, months or even years, from all parts of the Muslim world to Mecca, in Saudi Arabia, the central act once arrived is to kiss the black Ka'aba stone which could therefore be a powerful source of infection. Recently one danger has been death from heat-stroke in the Ka'aba square.

All in all, we see that Islam, by comparison on most points, is r+ oriented when compared to Christianity. We turn next to the Hindu religion, not truly a world religion but a vast one of great interest.

Hinduism

Hinduism cannot be called a world religion. Confined to India and the countries into which Hindus have migrated, it has no missionaries nor any methods of conversion. Nevertheless it is a vast and fascinating religion, with its panoply of gods adorning in their multiple forms and colours its temples and their surroundings. Famous for its protection of the Sacred Cow, it has in addition a large literature of poetic texts, little known to most Westerners though freely available to them. Some advocate active strength and fighting, to maintain the *status quo*; others peaceful acceptance; some of its gods are ferocious, others tranquil. For Westerners its study represents a serious challenge to which few have responded. For our purposes we have been concerned, as always, only with those aspects that seemed to have been some biological importance.

Conception is desired by all but a few Hindu women and girls. This, like Islam, is a male-dominated religion, and great emphasis is put on the necessity for having male heirs, without which a man is of no earthly worth, nor has he a bright future in any further reincarnations or life after death. Contraception is not practised, or not, where known, until after the birth of a son or sons, sufficient for a feeling to develop that there is no danger of dying son-less. Daughters too are desired but less so, and until the British put a stop to the practice in the nineteenth century, female neglect or infanticide was a common occurrence. Nursing of offspring is protracted, thus spacing births, but owing to very early (often infantile) betrothal of children by their parents, the length of child-bearing years is very long for girls and women, and family size tends to be large. There are certain periods of sexual abstinence related to religious festivals, but the overall picture is pro-natalist. Abortion is probably not widespread.

At birth, because of belief in contamination from women's blood and the afterbirth, the midwife is of low-caste and uses dirty clothes and linen generally. These, thought to be appropriate within the culture, are from a Western standpoint very unacceptable for a situation in which we believe in the highest standards of hygiene. The point just mentioned has been noted in the literature but its outcome has not, as far as we can see, been quantified in terms of perinatal mortality. If such effects are or were occurring they would tend to increase birth spacing, but not necessarily to an extent that would reduce the size of family wanted by rural Hindus.

Children are soon put to use, in the fields, minding cattle, fetching food and water, helping with younger siblings and the old of the family. They lead useful lives and rather than being subject to formal education, gain a slow acquaintance with the all-pervasive caste system and their place (based on their parents') in it. They are exhorted to live according to caste dictates or risk a return to life in a lower state with greater consequent suffering. Families try, and some succeed, to arrange marriages for their daughters with men of higher sub-caste by means of dowries. Marriage can occur very early for a girl, even before puberty, and she may never have seen her husband before the ceremony. Sex does not always follow immediately upon marriage – it depends on age and feelings. As with Islam only more so, Hinduism is frank and outspoken about sex, full of sexual imagery, with sensitive erotic writing, poetry and sculpture showing and teaching the growing child and adolescent the various ways of engaging in sexual activity, treating it as a healthy activity indulged in by the gods, to be engaged in thoughtfully for the fullest sensual and spiritual enjoyment. Most famous among Hindu sex manuals is the *Kama Sutra*.

Besides early betrothal of girls, polygyny is permitted and engaged in by the wealthier and older men of the community, and we here meet the unique but once widespread phenomenon of 'Suttee' (sometimes spelt sati). Owing to the wife's low status relative to the husband and her complete dependence on him, she is thought to 'die' when he actually does so, irrespective of her age. As a result, a good wife was supposed to immolate herself on her husband's funeral pyre, and many in the past did so, though the custom is nowadays rare. Wives committing Suttee were blessed in their next incarnation and revered by their offspring, who were cared for by their joint families. The number of widows committing suttee was never very great however; in agricultural communities able-bodied women were still needed even after their husbands had died.

As a result of the beliefs underlying suttee, widows in higher castes were despised and treated badly, even to the extent of being considered 'dead'. Widow remarriage is still extremely difficult and usually involves some 'down-casteing'. There is no joy or major celebration of remarriage. Divorce is however, enjoined by Hinduism on grounds of childlessness, and a divorcee must try and find another husband; she prays for children and leaves offerings at the local temple; and it is on record that she may try to secure a child from the temple priest, but if she cannot she will probably be divorced. Like a widow, she becomes something of an 'out-caste'.

Celibacy is not a feature of Hinduism except for some grandfathers who become ascetics, and few if any young men are celibate, while the phenomenon is either not known among women, or not approved by them. Modernist moves to reduce family size by contraception and to introduce other Western ideas like Western education have been vigorous, expensive and largely ineffective, especially in rural areas.

Death and funerals have already been mentioned in connection with suttee; the death of a man, especially an important community leader, is a major event involving much ceremony over many days. Bodies are burnt on a large pyre and then disposed of; if nearby, they are dipped into holy water. Most especially the sacred river Ganges serves this purpose, to which the corpse or its remains after burning may be brought on one of the major pilgrimages which take place every year or so.

Death and disease are treated by a socio-religious search for cure within the means available, although we noted that where Western-trained physicians were available they were in fact resorted to, mainly by older (wealthier) men so that mortality from curable diseases tends to be related to age and sex. We also noted the existence, in previous centuries, of Hindu hospitals, but as in the case of Islam, we concluded that modern times had not brought the prosperity further medical advance requires, and so traditional medical methods have continued to predominate, at least in rural areas.

Infectious disease, as in Islam, is to some extent reduced in Hinduism by a sharp distinction between the uses of the left (toilet and sex) and right (eating and food preparation) hands. Again, just as Islam had the massive and risky pilgrimage to Mecca, so Hinduism has massive pilgrimages to the River Ganges, the 'holy river', at particular times. But not only to the Ganges, for religious festivals or 'fairs' are held at many other sites in which thousands of pilgrims gather, for trade, prayers and mutual parasitic infection by drinking contaminated water and consuming polluted food, resulting in cholera and other diseases on a large scale.

Overall, indeed, in view of its strongly pro-natalist orientation, we can see Hinduism as consisting of beliefs and customs resulting from r^c+ selection within castes, though we should note the effects of certain high-caste customs such as suttee and the non-remarriageability of widows which are frankly anti-natalist.

Buddhism

Buddhism is known to the West better than either Hinduism or Islam. This is perhaps because of its emphasis on calm self-contemplation. Meditation is known to us all and we are faced with such practices as, in a sense, direct challenges to our Western 'up-and-at-them', hopeful, optimistic, consumption-oriented, rat-race, competitive ethos. Many of those who opted, and continue to opt out of Western mainstream status-seeking life with its material rewards, do so after being attracted by the inner rewards, the calm self-assurance, of the practitioners of what we call 'oriental' (usually meaning a form of Buddhist) beliefs. So called Zen Buddhism developed at first in China and later in Japan; it entered the West by crossing the Pacific into California and spreading eastwards to the East Coast, USA, and hence to Europe.

Beginning with Buddhist attitudes to conception, we find a mildly pro-natalist disapproval of contraceptive practice of a mechanical kind as preventing a further re-incarnation. This attitude is not stipulated centrally, for though there are indeed wise 'high priests' in Buddhism their influence tends to be local and their interpretations of the message of the life of the Gautama Buddha, are various. Again, with regard to infanticide and abortion, Buddhism is silent, but the silence, placed against an understanding of the philosophy, appears as one of total disapproval, for life, *all* life, from that of insects to man, is worthy of respect and devotion.

Childhood is a time of learning and of hard work. The child is loved for himself. Legitimacy does not appear as an issue. Childhood is for play and for thought, for the learning of the virtues of peace and non-aggression, for the reduction of such self-regard or egoism and competitiveness as may exist, at least in Burma, Thailand and Tibet. Yet all these things can be reversed. In modern Japan, self-styled Buddhists are highly competitive with regard to school examinations; and of course abortions are on demand. In China, commune-orientation has grown on a basis of syncretistic Buddhist tradition. Indeed, it is difficult to say anything universal about the impact of Buddhist ideology on life-style variables.

Again if we try to generalize about Buddhist ideas of adolescence, we meet with a wide range of contrasts. But as a rule, sexual activity is not especially encouraged; certainly no early betrothal exists as in Hinduism, nor is there any caste system or high degree of status consciousness leading to a desire to marry upwards. There is no rigid taboo on sexual activity, though demonstrations are expected to be in private, and any body contacts of a conceivably sexual kind, such as even kissing as a greeting, are tabooed in Buddhist countries such as Japan.

Buddhist attitudes to marriage itself are, again, poorly expressed. In Ladakh and other areas of the Himalayan foothills, there still exist communities in which some families practise polyandry, while others are polygynous or monogamous. Marriage itself is not given the high esteem we see in Islam and Hinduism, and is not felt to be the normal and appropriate state as in Christianity. We see this from the sometimes enormously high levels of celibacy in Buddhist communities, where large numbers of young men, after taking the religious training which is part of the lifestyle of all adolescents, decide to opt for the monastic life and to seek wisdom and enlightenment rather than pursue the hazards of family life. Celibacy levels in some Buddhist countries are undoubtedly the highest to be found anywhere in the world. Whereas in Christianity the celibate sees himself or herself as engaged in a life of service, Buddhist monks in many areas seek nothing but their own spiritual progress. Recently, in some countries such as Ladakh, Buddhist monks in their distinctive robes wield pickaxes on road-making schemes, and engage in the full annual round of agricultural and other duties of men in general. But historically in most areas Buddhist monks simply seek alms and do no work. They do not marry and they forgo the pleasures of sex. As they grow older they do, more and more, become embroiled in monastic duties and interpretation of the scriptures which are kept in long and elaborate scrolls in the innermost parts of the local monastery. Eventually, old Buddhist priests may acquire considerable local reputations and some become hermits.

We found no special rules for care of the aged in Buddhism, yet such evidence as we have come across indicates that the aged are both hardy and self-sufficient, and well-cared for in their communities and families. Death is subject to ceremonial rituals and is of central importance in Buddhism, with its emphasis on rebirth. There are prescribed patterns of mourning, and it is expected that the dead person, unless one of the very few to have achieved *nirvana* or release from mindfulness, will return to live again, and to again experience the pain and suffering of worldly life; such is the nature of the cycle that man is heir to.

On the topic of concepts of disease, we meet in Buddhism, as in Hinduism, a strong element of fatalism. The doctrine of predetermination based on reincarnation which these religions largely share, implies that the causes of sickness and death are not to be found in this life but in the previous one; there is no point in seeking to avoid suffering, it has to be endured. At the same time there are local medicine men in both cultures who can offer palliatives and cures of many kinds, from herbs to quite severe physical manipulations including branding the skin, down to the bone, in places thought to be responsible for sickness. The overall degree of fatalism and the generally less effective medicine resulting from this shows, even in this highly philosophically sophisticated culture, a marked contrast with the practical-minded and more effective medicine of the West.

Infectious diseases are not especially prevalent in the Tibetan and other Himalayan areas because of the long, cold winters which make it difficult for disease vectors to survive. Also the isolation of Buddhist villages there makes the spread of disease difficult and the survival of lethal disease agents unlikely since any such agent needs to find new hosts in order to survive and reproduce. Nor did we find evidence of particular forms of constitutional diseases affecting Buddhists.

All in all, Buddhism shows a mixture of r^c+ and r^c- features, but tends if anything to be anti-natalist or to favour low rates of reproduction. Care, hygiene and medicine are not, however, well developed and we feel a need for more information on most points. By comparson with Christianity, Islam and Hinduism, however, we would tend to locate it after the first and before the latter two on the r^c- to r^c+ scale.

Judaism

In the case of Judaism we are, of course, rather close in many respects to Christianity and often the two are lumped together as 'the Judaeo-Christian tradition'; however we have located a number of differences, distinctive of Talmudic/Old Testament thinking, that are of biological significance and we shall highlight these here.

Regarding conception, there are no rules against contraception, in sharp contrast with Roman Catholicism. Divorce, though normally avoided as far as possible is, as in Christianity, permitted in the case of unconsummated marriages. Widows, unlike those in Christian cultures, are actively encouraged to remarry after an appropriately lengthy period of mourning.

Infanticide is not permitted for either sex, both sons and daughters being welcomed as a joyous event in the home and the community. If, however, there is a life-or-death decision to be made during childbirth, the life of the mother is doctrinally to be saved and that of the child sacrificed. Judaism is, above all others, the religion with the most clear-cut traditional rules about what must and must not be done at various stages in the life-cycle. Regarding abortion, tradition stands clearly against this, but modern 'liberal' Jews are coming to accept it; Judaism is, indeed, like Catholicism here, a religion caught in an impasse. The former, with its long-lived, well-documented rules embodied in the Pentateuch, the Talmud, and other religious works, and the latter with its Papal edicts and sacrosanct dicta from the Vatican, both render themselves secure from sudden cultural fashions and whimseys, but also slow to adapt to what are true, real and long-lasting changes in the modern world. Thus both suffer from having to deal with conflicts between traditional orthodoxy and modern liberalism, and are deeply divided as a result on such issues as contraception and abortion.

That Judaism is fundamentally pro-natalist in its birth strategies is however clear, and will become clearer as we go on to consider marriage; for the moment let us give a memorable quote from Darlington (1969: 295) where he describes one Jewish sect which, in relation to the predicted coming of the Messiah, promised that each of the righteous would at that great time 'have the opportunity of begetting 1,000 children before they die'.

Childhood and adolescence are times of learning in all cultures, and Judaism is marked with a number of ceremonies, the first and most significant being circumcision, which Judaism shares with Islam, though in the case of Judaism the operation (or rite) is obligatory and is performed in the first few days of life whereas in Islam it is performed later and seems well-nigh universal, though it is not mentioned in the Koran. Female circumcision does not occur in Judaism. We noted that circumcision was initiated, according to the Old Testament, as a central tenet of the Covenant between God and Abraham by agreement to which the Jews were given access to the Holy Land. Together with the possibility that male circumcision increases female fertility by reducing cervical carcinoma, the whole arrangement may be, as in the case of the promise of 1,000 children each to the faithful already referred to, pro-natalist in its effects.

Towards the end of a childhood in which the Jewish child is taught the virtues of family love and devotion, sobriety, punctuality, reverence for old age and the wisdom of the Book, comes, for boys, the special ceremony of the Bar Mitzvah, in which they are welcomed as full members of the synagogue. For girls there is an equivalent Bat Mitzvah but it is less prevalent. Nevertheless the status of women is high in Judaism, more especially after marriage when they become central figures in their families; for even though the man is 'patriarch' and succession and inheritance are in the male line, the wife is recognized as the home's emotional centre, and love for her by her daughters and even more by her sons is proverbial. Jewish annual ceremonies take place in the home rather than in the synagogue.

Judaism is pro-marriage for all. This includes its rabbis and there are no exceptions: all are exhorted to marry and parents to some extent bring their children into the 'right' company (i.e. suitable Jewish boys or girls) at carefully monitored parties. Sex is highly approved in marriage but disapproved before it, and in some countries early marriage is approved, though less so in the West than in Israel and the Middle East. Monogamy is implicit in marriage and polygyny, though an Old Testament phenomenon, is nowadays unheard of. Celibacy is not at all approved of; there is no concept of it as a spiritually higher state of being or way of serving the community to best advantage; here we see a sharp contrast with Christianity, and the Roman Catholic Church faith especially.

Marriage is, as stated, for life, and if a marriage weakens great steps are taken to try and prevent divorce, which in normal circumstances is considered a great tragedy. However, as in both Islam and Hinduism, and in opposition to Christianity, reproductive failure is considered adequate grounds for divorce. Widows, again in contradistinction to Christianity, were not left to fend for themselves and find new partners in olden times, but were automatically and unquestioningly taken on by a late husband's brother under the custom of the levirate; their subsequent children, if any, still thus belonged to the same patriline.

We have already mentioned that older Jews, men and women, are held in respect. Their families normally care for them in old age, and in addition the Jews, famed for their ability to attain wealth and keep it within their own community, have many ways of disbursing it to the needy of all ages. So there is less suffering from loneliness in Jewish communities than in Christian ones, and less suicide (except under the special conditions of severe persecution).

After death, Jewish bodies are cleaned and finely dressed and then, often at home, put on view for a short spell for relatives to pay their last respects, after which comes a funeral and a feast. The departed are not believed to interfere with the living after death; they are gone; they cannot be contacted and their worth is to be assessed by the love, number of offspring and both wealth and good works they are seen and known to have achieved in life. Autopsies of, and transplants from, their bodies are forbidden; they may be cremated or buried, and their deaths are mourned noisily in the East, quietly and respectfully in the West.

Regarding 'Jewish diseases', much has been written and we dealt with some of the genetic aspects in Chapter 2. Here we can remind ourselves that Judaism has always held personal hygiene in high esteem, the Old Testament book of Leviticus containing strict rules for the isolation, care and treatment of the sick (mainly lepers), and other Jewish works stipulating the quite lengthy period of abstinence from sexual intercourse for women around the time of menstruation. Among non-infectious diseases we noted the relative absence of cancers of the mouth, throat and lungs in Jews, attributable in large part, no doubt, to relatively sober habits, especially in the last case to low incidence of smoking. If we are to place the Jewish religion on a scale from $r+$ to $r-$ then we feel it has many $r+$ features, but always in moderation. It could, perhaps, be located between Buddhism, with the emphasis of that religion on celibacy, and Hinduism−Islam, both of which are more pro-natalist and less moderate in their productivity than is Judaism.

'Tribal' or small-scale societies

Throughout this book we have presented examples from tribal societies. We have noted infanticide here, abortion there, female circumcision in some cultures, puberty ceremonies in some parts of the world, adolescent sexual promiscuity in some localities and strict taboos in others; early versus late marriages; late marriage for men coupled with early for girls in some areas; ancestor cults with active ancestral intervention in human affairs; warrior men running risks to life and limb; shamans and celibate priests; the levirate (and sororate); human sacrifices in especial circumstances; uses of 'witch doctors' and the castigation of 'witches'; effects of cannibalism and of eating inadequate diets, especially when women and children are affected more than men. It would be very difficult in this section to try to summarize the data for small-scale societies *as a whole*, and we shall not therefore do so.

Conclusion

If we therefore content ourselves with the five major world religions we have looked at, we can construct a scale based on the degree to which they seem either more pro-reproductive, or less so and more concerned with limiting reproduction and emphasizing such things as care of the living, disease control and so on. We can consider these 'grades' along a selection continuum, as shown in Table 18.1.

($r+$ end)	Grade 1	Islam	
	Grade 2	Hinduism	
	Grade 3	Judaism	
	Grade 4	Buddhism	
	Grade 5a	Christianity: Roman Catholicism	
($r-$ end)	Grade 5b	Christianity: Protestantism	**Table 18.1** Religious emphases

We can proceed now to our final chapter, in which we shall put together the emphases of these religions with relevant environmental data to see how well they 'fit'. If they fit well, this will be taken as evidence of the action of cultural selection and confirmation of the theory put forward in Chapter 16.

19 Testing the theory: conclusions

In this chapter we present the final step in our analysis, which will be to put the various data already presented together in such a way as to see whether our theory of cultural selection receives support or not. We initially predicted (in Chapter 1) that if there was a process of cultural selection affecting reproductive success, and if it worked through the impact of religiously sanctioned rules on the actions of individuals, then this would be reflected in one of two ways – either by promoting rules leading to *high* rates of reproductivity (r^c+) or to low rates (r^c-). In Table 1.1 we took our chapter topics one by one and predicted in catch-phrase form what 'attitude' religious rules would take to each part of the life-cycle, and to disease, according to whether they were r^c+ or r^c- selected. In the main part of the book (Parts 2 and 3), we examined in detail a substantial quantity of documentary evidence pertaining to this theme, showing quite clearly and at very many points that religious rules and practices do have a direct bearing on survival, reproductive rates and strategies, and hence the (Darwinian) fitness of individuals.

It also became clear that a crucial determinant of whether a religion was very pro-reproductive, or more mildly so, or had a number of frankly anti-reproductive features and tended to throw itself behind care of the few who were born, was the environment. We suggested the possibility that the most important feature of the environment was the extent to which people felt it was predictable, so that crises such as sickness, food shortages, droughts and floods could be successfully overcome, as against the opposite feeling: that the environment was unpredictable and that it was therefore necessary to produce many children

Poor African families suffer from malnutrition during periods of food shortage with the result that infant mortality is high.

since some would probably die in view of the many hazards ahead. People would base their own reproductive strategies, or patterns of parental investment, on these feelings or attitudes to their own personal future. And in terms of cultural selection, a continuity of such perceptions and strategies over several generations would provide the basis for the incorporation into religions of rules about how much effort to put into child-bearing and how much into care and education of the young, together with corresponding attitudes to marriage, divorce, older folk, and death.

Cultural selection would thus, we suggested, take religious rules along an $r+$ or an $r-$ path depending on whether the environment was seen as very unpredictable (Ue^c+) or less so (Ue^c-) respectively. That was the essence of our theory, expressed in Chapter 16. To proceed further, we needed to have some clearer notion of the environmental dimension, and in Chapter 17 we tried to find measures that might demonstrate, or reasonably be expected to demonstrate, how likely individuals in any given area would be to feel that they were or were not able to find sufficient environmental resources to rear their young successfully, and we settled on two: *per capita* energy consumption: and *per capita* gross national product, as useful and readily available indicators.

Chapter 18 was a return to Parts 2 and 3, but in the form of a summary of the emphases of the major world religions, in order to bring the large and complex mass of data we had accumulated under sufficient control to be able to proceed with the analysis. What we tried to do in that chapter was 'to see the wood rather than the trees', and to be able as a result to grade our religions according to their degree of 'pro-reproductivity'. We concluded that chapter with Table 18.1, which graded the religions in this way.

In this final chapter we shall therefore put the religious grades set out in Chapter 18 together with the environmental parameters we settled on in Chapter 17. These latter were energy consumption *per capita*, and gross national product *per capita*; both were shown in their particular ways to be appropriate measures of Ue^c.

Table 19.1 gives data for these two measures on a country by country basis, and shows in addition the world religion most prevalent in that country. Indigenous religions have been excluded. Energy consumption *per capita* is shown in kg of coal equivalent, and gross national product *per capita* is shown in US dollars.

The data presented in Table 19.1 have been rearranged in Table 19.2

Country	Predominant world religion	Energy consumption per capita (kg coal equiv.) 1976	Gross national product per capita (US dollars) 1975
Nepal	Hindu	11	110
Ethiopia	Orth. Christian	27	90
Bangladesh	Muslim	32	100
Afghanistan	Muslim	41	100
Uganda	RC/Prot. Christian	48	160
Burma	Buddhist	49	90
Zaïre	RC Christian	62	150
Tanzania	RC/Prot. Christian	68	140

Table 19.1 (Cont'd overleaf)

Country	Predominant world religion	Energy consumption per capita (kg coal equiv.) 1976	Gross national product per capita (US dollars) 1975
Nigeria	RC/Prot. Christian and Muslim	94	240
Sri Lanka	Buddhist	106	230
Vietnam	Buddhist	124	150
Sudan	Muslim	143	150
Kenya	RC/Prot. Christian	152	200
Ghana	RC/Prot. Christian	157	350
Pakistan	Muslim	181	130
India	Hindu	218	130
Indonesia	Muslim	218	150
Morocco	Muslim	273	430
Thailand	Buddhist	308	300
Philippines	RC Christian	329	310
Egypt	Muslim	473	280
Malaysia	Muslim	578	660
Peru	RC Christian	642	710
Colombia	RC Christian	685	510
China	Buddhist	706	300
Iraq	Muslim	725	970
Algeria	Muslim	729	650
Brazil	RC Christian	731	900
Turkey	Muslim	743	690
Chile	RC Christian	987	820
South Korea	Buddhist	1,020	470
Mexico	RC Christian	1,227	1,000
Iran	Muslim	1,500	1,060
Argentina	RC Christian	1,804	1,900
Yugoslavia	Orth. Christian	2,016	1,250
Spain	RC Christian	2,399	1,960
Israel	Judaism	2,541	3,019
Venezuela	RC Christian	2,838	1,710
South Africa	Prot. Christian	2,985	1,200
North Korea	Buddhist	3,072	390
Italy	RC Christian	3,284	2,770
Hungary	RC Christian	3,553	2,140
Japan	Buddhist	3,679	3,880
Romania	Orth. Christian	4,036	2,000
France	RC Christian	4,380	5,190
Poland	RC Christian	5,253	2,450
Russia	Orth. Christian	5,259	2,300
United Kingdom	Prot. Christian	5,268	3,360
West Germany	Prot. Christian	5,922	5,890
Netherlands	Prot. Christian	6,224	4,880
Australia	Prot. Christian	6,657	4,760
East Germany	Prot. Christian	6,789	3,430
Czechoslovakia	RC Christian	7,397	3,220
USA	Prot. Christian	11,554	6,640
Canada	Prot. Christian	9,950	6,080

Table 19.1 Religion, energy consumption and gross national product, by countries (data for 1975 and 1976)

(From: Broek and Webb (1978); *United Nations Statistical Yearbook* (1978); Israeli Embassy)
Orth. – Orthodox
Prot. – Protestant
RC   – Roman Catholic

Religion	r^c status	Energy consumption (kg of coal equivalent)					
		< 100	100– 249	250– 999	1,000– 2,499	2,500– 4,999	5,000+
Islam	r^c+++	2	3	6	1		
Hinduism	r^c++	1	1				
Judaism	r^c+					1	
Buddhism	r^c–	1	2	2	1	2	
Christian (RC)	r^c––			5	3	4	2
Christian (Prot.)	r^c–––					1	7

* Countries where indigenous religions are prevalent excluded.
RC – Roman Catholic
Prot. – Protestant
In the above Table we have arbitrarily split the six religious groups represented so that half are r^c+ and half are r^c–.

Table 19.2 *Per capita* energy consumption of countries in relation to religious emphasis on reproductivity (see text)*

to show how many countries with a particular religion have a given level of energy consumption. Levels of energy consumption are here taken from the 6-point scale of Broek and Webb (1978: Fig. 12.4).

As we can see from Table 19.2, there is a negative correlation between the r^c+ status of countries' major religions and the *per capita* energy consumption of those countries. In other words, when the *per capita* energy consumption is at low levels, the religion emphasizes a high rate of reproductivity, and vice versa. This is illustrated in a somewhat different way in Table 19.3, where the same data are represented again: the more stable the environment is perceived to be, the less the religion emphasizes reproductivity and vice versa. For both these tables, the correlation is highly significant (p <. 001).

We can now move on to our second environmental parameter: *per capita* gross national product (see Table 19.1 for data). We present the data in the same way as in Table 19.2 and Table 19.3, so no further explanation is needed (see Table 19.4 and Table 19.5). Again, the correlation is highly significant (p <. 001).

The conclusion we can can draw is that our theory has been largely confirmed. The correlations are as we predicted they would be. We can conclude that it *is* the case that the 'instructions' religions give to indi-

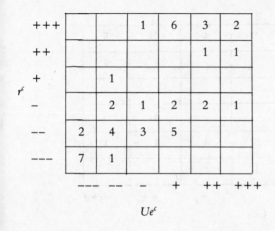

Table 19.3 Perceived environmental unpredictability (based on *per capita* energy consumption) and religious reproductivity, by countries

Religion	r^e status	Per capita GNP (US $)					
		< 250	250– 499	500– 999	1,000– 2,499	2,500– 4,999	5,000+
Islam	r^e+++	5	2	4	1		
Hinduism	r^e++	2					
Judaism	r^e+					1	
Buddhism	r^e–	3	4			1	
Christian (RC)	r^e––	1	1	4	6	1	1
Christian (Prot.)	r^e–––				1	5	3

Table 19.4 *Per capita* GNP of countries in relation to religious emphasis on reproductivity (see text)

viduals are 'adaptive'. These instructions concern people's obligations to reproduce a lot or a little; whether or not to contracept; whether or not to practise abortion or infanticide; whether to devote massive care to those who are born throughout their lives or to be more resigned to the facts of death; whether to marry young or to postpone marriage; whether to divorce easily or regard divorce as impossible; whether to regard sex as holy or sinful; whether to equate personal hygiene with religious purity and piety, or not to connect the two. These rules and the actions resulting from them are adaptive in the sense that they are found in countries where the results they produce will tend to enhance the reproductive success of individuals following them.

Religions thus act as culturally phrased biological messages. They arise from the survival strategies of past group members and continue to advise at the present time. As such, a religion is a primary set of 'reproductive rules', a kind of 'parental investment handbook'.

This is not to say that other ideas, rules, etc. cannot overrule religious ones; they not only can but often do. Thus Roman Catholics may and often do use mechanical methods of birth control in countries with Low Ue^c at the present time. But as Lévi-Strauss (1968) has put it, 'rules have their own life' and do to some extent influence action, even if only to establish the borderlines of piety and sin.

Nor is it to say that change cannot occur. As environmental factors change and some individuals, say, perceive their chances of successful child-rearing as improving if they have less children, they will try to do that, and if this means religious difficulties they will try to get round

r^e	---	--	-	+	++	+++
+++			1	4	2	5
++						2
+		1				
-		1			4	3
--	1	1	6	4	1	1
---	3	5	1			

Ue^c

Table 19.5 Perceived environmental unpredictability (based on per capita GNP) and religious reproductivity, by countries

them. A point arises when enough people have created enough pressure for public debates to occur and eventually the rules themselves are modified as a new generation of priests takes over from the old. Change is always occurring, sometimes towards increasing r sometimes towards decreasing r.

One final note. There is vastly more to religions than their adaptive dimension and how they are related to individual survival and inclusive fitness. That is just one dimension, the one we have been concerned with in this book. We have not tried to, nor would we have succeeded in encompassing all the other aspects; we have tried constantly to focus strictly on the biological dimension. This has proved rewarding, and the theory of cultural evolution presented here may, we hope, have scope for further development and modification.

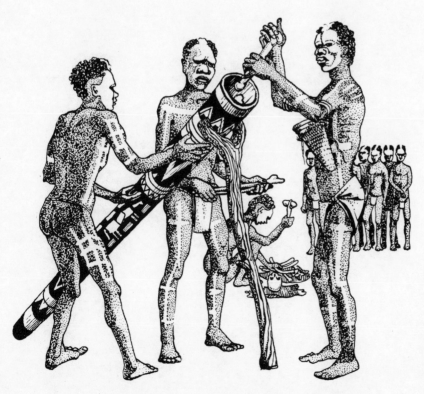

Aborigine tribesmen conducting the bone post ceremony in Arnhem Land, north-east Australia. The bones of a dead man are crushed up by his relatives and pushed into a hollow painted log, which is then erected as a permanent memorial.

References

Abou-Daoud, K. T. (1967) 'Epidemiology of carcinoma of the cervix uteri in Lebanese Christians and Moslems', *Cancer (Philadelphia)*, **20**, 1706–14.

Adam, A. (1973) 'Genetic diseases among Jews', *Israeli J. Medical Science*, **9**, 1383–92.

Adam, A., Doron, D. and Modan, R. (1967) 'Frequencies of protan deutan alleles in some Israeli communities and a note on the selection-relaxation hypothesis', *Amer. J. Physical Anthropology*, **26**, 297–305.

Ademuwagun, Z. A. (1969) 'The relevance of Yoruba medicine men in public health practice in Nigeria', *Public Health Reports*, **84**, 1085–91.

Aghababian, R. (1951) *Legislation Iranienne*, Paris.

Aitken-Swan, J. and Baird, D. (1965) 'Circumcision and cancer of the cervix', *British J. Cancer*, **19**, 217–27.

Alexander, R. D. (1979) 'Evolution and culture', in Irons, W. (ed.) *Evolutionary biology and human social behaviour*, Duxbury Press, Duxbury.

Al-Kindi (1966) *The medical formulary*, Levey, M. (trans.) University of Wisconsin Press, Madison.

Alland, A. (1964) 'Native therapists and Western medical practitioners among the Abron of the Ivory Coast', *Trans. New York Academy of Science*, Series II, **26**, 714–25.

Alphonsus (1905–12) *Praxis confessari in theologia moralis*, Rome.

Altekar, A. S. (1956) *The position of women in Hindu Civilisation*, Benarsidas, Benares.

Alther, L. (1975) 'The snake handlers', *New Society*, **34**, 532–5.

Alvirez, D. (1973) 'The effects of formal church affiliation and religiosity on the fertility patterns of Mexican–American Catholics', *Demography*, **10**, 19–36.

Amort, E. (1752) *Theologia moralis appendix ad tractatum de matrimonio*, Augustae Vindelicanum.

Anderson, S. (1904) 'The cholera epidemic in Puri town and district July 1902', *Indian Medical Gazette*, **39**, 48–51.

Antoun, R. T. (1968) 'On the modesty of women in Arab Muslim villages', *American Anthropologist*, **70**, 671–97.

Aquinas, St T. (1964) *Summa theologiae*, Blackfriars, London.

Archer, W. G. (1974) *The hill of flutes. Love, life and poetry in tribal India*, Allen and Unwin, London.

Arensberg, C. M. and Kimball, S. T. (1940) *Family and community in Ireland*, Harvard U.P. Cambridge, Mass.

Aristotle (1962) *Politics*, Sinclair, T. A. (trans), Penguin, London.

Armstrong, B., van Merwyk, A. J. and Coates, H. (1977) 'Blood pressure in Seventh Day Adventist vegetarians', *American J. Epidemiology*, **105**, 444–9.

Arregui, G. M. (1927) *Summarium theologiae moralis ad recentum codicem juris canonici accomodatum*, El Mensajero del Corazon de Jesus, Bilbao.

Ashley-Montagu, M. F. (1957) *The reproductive development of the female with* *special reference to the period of adolescent sterility*, Julian Press, New York.

Ashton, H. (1952) *The Basuto*, Oxford U.P., UK.

Askovitz, S. I. (1961) 'Distribution of malignant neoplasms with reference to the patient's religion', *J. Albert Einstein Medical Center*, **9**, 229–32.

Athenagoras (1972) *Legatio pro Christianis*, Clarendon Press, Oxford.

Augustine, St (1847) *Seventeen short treatises; Enchiridion to Laurentius*, Parker, Oxford.

Augustine, St (1884) *Short Treatises*, William Smith, London.

Augustine, St (1966) *De moribus manichaeorum*, Catholic University of America, Washington.

Avalon, A. (1963) *The great liberation*, Ganesh, Madras.

Awan, A. K. and Mobashar, M. (1975) 'Age differential between spouses and pregnancy wastage', *J. Pakistan Medical Assoc.*, **25**, 46–52.

Bacon, F. (1905) *Philosophical works*, Routledge, London.

Bagchi, P. O. (1950) *India and China; a thousand years of Sino-Indian cultural relations*, China Press, Bombay.

Baker, D. (1950) 'Etude de la dénatalité dans le Territoire d'Ikela', *Bull. du Centre d'Etudes des Problèmes Sociaux Indigènes*, **13**, 34–65.

Balakrishnan, T. R., Ross, S., Allingham, J. D. and Kanther, J. F. (1972) 'Attitudes toward abortion of married women in metropolitan Toronto', *Social Biology*, **19**, 35–42.

Bandelier, A. F. (1880) *On the social organisation and mode of government of the ancient Mexicans*, Peabody Museum Reports No. 2, Harvard.

Banerjea, A. C. (1951) 'A note on cholera in the United Provinces', *Indian J. Medical Research*, **39**, 17–40.

Barber, T. X. (1961) 'Death by suggestion; a critical note', *Psychosomatic Med.*, **23**, 153–5.

Bardet, J. P. (n.d.) Enfants abandonnés et enfants assistés à Rouen dans la seconde moitié du XIIIe siecle, in *Homage à Marcel Reinhard*, Paris.

Barr, H. M. (1970) 'Aging and religious disaffiliation', *Social Forces*, **49**, 60–71.

Barrow, M. L. (1958) 'The role of religion and religious institutions in creating the milieu of older people', in Scudder, D. (ed.), *Organised religion and the older person*, University of Florida Press, Gainesville.

Bateson, G. (1936) *Naven; a survey of the problems suggested by a composite picture of the culture of a New Guinea tribe drawn from three points of view*, Macmillan, New York.

Bell, H. M. (1938) *Youth tell their story*, American Council on Education, Washington.

Bender, L. and Spalding, M. A. (1940) 'Behaviour problems in children from the homes of followers of Father Divine', *J. Nervous Mental Diseases*, **91**, 460–72.

Benedict, R. (1935) *Patterns of Culture*, Routledge, London.

Berger, M. (1970) *Islam in Egypt today. Social and political aspects of popular religion*, Cambridge U.P, UK.

Berkman, P. L. (1969) 'Spouseless motherhood, psychological stress and physical morbidity', *J. Health and Social Behaviour*, **10**, 323–34.

Berndt, R. M. and Berndt, C. H. (1964) *The world of the first Australians*, Angus and Robertson, London.

Bhardwaj, S. M. (1973) *Hindu places of pilgrimage in India*, University of California Press, Berkeley.

Bibeau, G. (1979) 'The World Health Organisation in encounter with African traditional medicine; theoretical conceptions and practical strategies', in Ademuwagun, Z. A. *et al.* (eds) *African therapeutic systems*, Crossroads Press, Waltham.

Bieler, L. (ed.) (1963) *The Irish penitentials*, Dublin Inst. for Advanced Studies, Dublin.

Bishop, M. W. H. (1970) 'Aging and reproduction in the male', *J. Reproduction and Fertility*, **Suppl. 12**, 65–87.

Bittles, A. H. (1981) 'Genetic defects associated with human inbreeding', *Social Biology and Human Affairs*, **45**, 145–7.

Bleich, A. R. (1950) 'Prophylaxis of penile carcinoma', *J. American Medical Assoc.*, **143**, 1054–7.

Blofeld, J. (1979) *Bangkok*, Time–Life, Amsterdam.

Blood, R. O. (1969) *Marriage*, Free Press, New York.

Blurton-Jones, N. G. (1976) 'Growing points in ethology; another link between ethology and the social sciences?', in Bateson, P. P. G. and Hinde, R. A. (eds) *Growing points in ethology*, Cambridge U.P., UK.

Boas, F. (1966) *Race, language and culture*, Free Press, New York.

Bodmer, W. F. and Cavalli-Sforza, L. L. (1976) *Genetics, evolution and man*, Freeman, San Francisco.

Boelaert, E. (1947) *La situation démographique des Nkundo-Mongo*, Centre d'Etudes des Problèmes Sociaux Indigènes, Elizabethville.

Boldrini, M. and Ugge, A. (1926) *La mortalità dei missionari*, Catholic University, Milan.

Bolton, J. M. (1968) 'Medical service to the aborigines in West Malaysia', *British Medical J.*, 818–23.

Bolton, J. M. (1972) 'Food taboos among the Orang Asli in West Malaysia; a potential nutritional hazard', *American J. Clinical Nutrition*, **25**, 789–99.

Boniface (1973) *Letters*, Octagon Press, New York.

Bonnè, B. (1965) 'A preliminary report on some genetical characteristics in the Samaritan population', *American J. Physical Anthropology*, **23**, 397–400.

Bonney, M. E. (1949) 'A study of friendship choices in college in relation to church affiliation, in church preferences, family size and length of enrolment in college', *J. Social Psychology*, **29**, 153–66..

Book of the Discipline, The (1970) Horner, I. B. (trans.), Pali Text Society, London.

Borisov, V. (1976) *Perspectives of fertility*, Moscow.

Bose, K. C. (1912) 'Infantile mortality; its causes and prevention', *Proceedings of Second All-India Sanitary Conference*, Delhi.

Bowman, H. S., McKusick, V. A. and Dronamraju, K. R. (1965) 'Pyruvate kinase deficient hemolytic anemia in an Amish isolate', *American J. Human Genetics*, **17**, 1–8.

Breil, J. (1959) *La population en Algerie*, Paris.

Broek, J. O. M. and Webb, J. W. (1978) *A geography of mankind*, McGraw Hill, New York.

Bromley, D. G. and Shupe, A. D. (1979) *Moonies in America. Cult, church and crusade*, Sage, Beverly Hills.

Bumpass, L. (1970) 'The trend of interfaith marriage in USA', *Social Biology*, **4**, 253–9.

Bunnag, J. (1973) *Buddhist monk, Buddhist layman*, Cambridge U.P., UK.

Burchinal, L. G. and Chancellor, L. G. (1963) 'Survival rates among religiously homogamous and inter-religious marriages', *Social Forces*, **41**, 353–62.

Burnham, K. E. (1969) 'Religious affiliation, church attendance, religious education and student attitudes towards race', *Sociological Analysis*, **30**, 235–44.

Burton, R. (1963) *The book of a thousand nights and a night*, Allen and Unwin, London.

Burton, R. (trans.) (1963) *The perfumed garden of Shaykh Nefzawi*, Spearman, London.

Burton, R. and Arbuthnot, F. F. (trans.) (1963) *The Kamasutra of Vatsyayana*, Allen and Unwin, London.

Butler, A. (1978) 'Sexual apartheid in Saudi Arabia', *New Society*, **822**, 13–15.

Buxton, J. (1973) *Religion and healing in Mandari*, Oxford U.P., UK.

Cady, J. (1958) *A history of modern Burma*, Cornell U.P., Ithaca.

Calderone, M. S. (1958) *Abortion in the United States*, Hoeber–Harper, New York.

Campbell, D. (1975) 'On the conflicts between biological and social evolution and between psychology and moral tradition', *American Psychology*, **30**, 1103–26.

Canaan, T. (1931) 'Unwritten laws affecting the Arab women of Palestine', *J. Palestine Oriental Society*, **II**, 172–203.

Cannon, W. B. (1942) 'Voodoo death', *American Anthropologist*, **44**, 169–81.

Carr-Saunders, A. M. (1922) *The population problem. A study in human evolution*, Clarendon Press, Oxford.

Carstairs, G. M. (1961) *The twice-born*, Hogarth Press, London.

Catlin, G. (1841) *The manners, customs and conditions of the North American Indians*, London.

Chabot, C. (1827) *Encyclopedia Monastique*, LeRoy, Paris.

Chagnon, N. A. (1977) *Yanomamö; the fierce people*, Holt, Rinehart and Winston, New York.

Chagnon, N. A. and Hames, R. B. (1979) 'Protein deficiency and tribal warfare in Amazonia; new data', *Science*, **203**, 910–3.

Chagnon, N. A. and Irons, W. (eds) (1979) *Evolutionary biology and human social behaviour; an anthropological perspective*, Duxbury Press, Duxbury.

Chamie, J. (1981) *Religion and fertility. Arab Christian Muslim differentials*, Cambridge U.P., UK.

Chance, M. R. A. and Mead, A. P. (1953) 'Social behaviour and primate evolution', *Symposium. Society for Experimental Biology*, **7**, 397–438.

Chancellor, L. E. and Burchinal, L. G. (1962) 'Relations among inter-religious marriages, migratory marriages and civil marriages in Iowa', *Eugenics Q.*, **9**, 75–83.

Chadrasekaran, C. (1952) 'The cultural component of sexual abstinence in Indian life', *Proceedings Third International Conference on Planned Parenthood*, 73–9.

Chandrasekhar, S. (1959) *Infant mortality in India. 1901–55*, Allen and Unwin, London.

Chang, J. (1977) *The Tao of love and sex*, Wildweed House, London.

Chevers, N. (1870) *A manual of medical jurisprudence*, Thacker Spink, Calcutta.

Christensen, H. T. (1953) 'Studies in child spacing. I Premarital pregnancy as measured by the spacing of the first birth with marriage', *American Sociological Review*, **18**, 53–9.

Christensen, H. T. (1960) 'Cultural relativism and premarital sex norms', *American Sociological Review*, **25**, 31–9.

Christensen, H. T. and Cannon, K. L. (1964) 'Temple vs. non-temple marriage in Utah; some demographic considerations', *Social Science*, **39**, 26–33.

Christensen, H. T. and Gregg, C. F. (1970) 'Changing sex norms in America and Scandinavia', *J. Marriage and the Family*, 32, 616–27.

Christensen, H. T. and Meissner, H. M. (1953) 'Studies in child spacing. 3 Premarital pregnancy as a factor in divorce', *American Sociological Review*, **18**, 641–4.

Clark, C. (1975) 'The cannibal sign', *Royal Anth. Inst. News*, **8**, 1–3.

Clarke, E. (1957) *My mother who fathered me*, Allen and Unwin, London.

Clifford, J. J. (1942) 'The ethics of conjugal intimacy according to St Albert the Great', *Theological Studies*, **3**, 1–26.

Cohn, N. (1962) *The pursuit of the millennium. Revolutionary Messianism in the Middle Ages and its bearing on modern Totalitarian movements*, Mercury, London.

Cole, P. (1971) 'Coffee-drinking and cancer of the lower urinary tract', *Lancet*, **I**, 1335–7.

Cole, P. (1973) 'A population based study of bladder cancer', in Doll, R. and Vodopija, I. (eds) *Host environment interactions in the etiology of cancer in man*, International Agency for Research on Cancer, Lyon.

Colle, T. (1925) 'Au pays du Bashi. Ideé que nos Bashi se font de l'espouse', *Congo*, **6**, 399–404.

Collipp, P. J. (1969) 'The efficacy of prayers; a triple-blind study', *Medical Times*, **97**, 201–4.

Compton, P. A., Goldstrom, L. and Goldstrom, J. M. (1974) 'Religion and legal abortion in Northern Ireland', *J. Biosocial Science*, **6**, 493–500.

Comstock, G. W. (1971) 'Fatal arteriosclerotic heart disease, water hardness at home and socio-economic characteristics', *American J. Epidemiology*, **94**, 1–10.

Comstock, G. W. and Partridge, K. B. (1972) 'Church attendance and health', *J. Chronic Diseases*, **25**, 665–72.

Comstock, P. A., Abbey, H. and Lundin, F. E. (1970) 'The non-official census as a basic tool for epidemiologic observations in Washington County, Maryland', in Kessler, I. I. and Leven, M. L. (eds) *The community as an epidemiologic laboratory. A casebook of Community Studies*, Johns Hopkins, Baltimore.

Converse, T. A. (1973) 'Hutterite midwifery', *American J. Obstet. Gynec.*, **116**, 719–25.

Cook, S. F. (1946) 'Human sacrifice and warfare as factors in the demography of pre-colonial Mexico', *Human Biology*, **18**, 81–102.

Cooley, C. E. and Hutton, J. B. (1965) 'Adolescent response to religious appeal as related to IPAT anxiety scale', *J. Social Psychology*, **67**, 325–7.

Cory, H. (1951) *The Ntemi. Traditional rites of a Sukuma chief in Tanganyika*, Macmillan, London.

Cory, H. (1953) *Sukuma law and custom*, Oxford U.P., UK.

Cox, T. (1978) *Stress*, Macmillan, London.

Cragg, K. (1971) *The event of the Koran*, Allen and Unwin, London.

Crook, J. H. (1964) 'The evolution of social organisation and visual communication in weaver birds (Ploceinae)', *Behaviour*, Suppl., 1–178.

Crook, J. H. (1980) *The evolution of human consciousness*, Clarendon Press, Oxford.

Cross, H. E., Kennel, E. E. and Lilienfeld, A. M. (1968) 'Cancer of the cervix in an Amish population', *Cancer*, **21**, 102–8.

Cross, H. E. and McKusick, V. A. (1970) 'Amish demography', *Social Biology*, **17**, 83–101.

Cruden, A. (1769) *A complete concordance to the Old and New Testament or a dictionary and alphabetical index to the Bible*, Warne, London.

Culwick, A. T. and Culwick, G. M. (1938) 'A study of population in Ulanga, Tanganyika Territory', *Sociological R*, **30**, 365–79, **31**, 25–43.

Curran, W. J. (1977) 'Religious objection to a medico-legal autopsy', *New England J. Medicine*, **297**, 260–1.

Dalton, E. T. (1872) *Descriptive ethnology of Bengal*, Council of the Asiatic Society of Bengal, Calcutta.

Damjanovski, L., Marcekic, V. and Miletic, M. (1963) 'Circumcision and carcinoma colli uteri in Macedonia, Yugoslavia. Results from a field study. III Benign gynaecological disorders', *British J. Cancer*, **17**, 406–10.

Dandekar, K. (1959) *Demographic survey of six rural communities*, Asia Publishing House, Bombay.

Dandekar, K. (1961) 'Widow remarriage in six rural communities in western India', *International Population Union Conference*, New York.

Daniel, C. (1966) *The story of the Eyam Plague*. Privately printed, Eyam.

Darlington, C. D. (1969) *The evolution of man and society*, Allen and Unwin, London.

Das, S. K. (1978) 'Serological and biochemical investigations among five endogamous groups in Delhi, India', *Ann. Human Biology*, **1**, 25–31.

David-Neel, A. (1977) *Magic and mystery in Tibet*, Abacus, London.

Davidson, J. (1948) 'Protestant missions and marriage in the Belgian Congo', *Africa*, **18**, 120–8.

Davis, K. (1946) *Moral and pastoral theology*, Sheed and Ward, London.

Davis, K. (1951) *The population of India and Pakistan*, Princeton U.P., USA.

Davis, K. (1967) 'Population policy. Will current programs succeed?', *Science*, **158**, 730–9.

Dawkins, R. (1976) *The selfish gene*, Oxford U.P., UK.

Denzler, G. (1973–6) *Das Papsttum und der Amtszölibat*, Anton Hiersemann, Stuttgart.

de Waard, F. (1975) 'Breast cancer incidence and nutritional status with particular reference to body weight and height', *Cancer Research*, **35**, 3351–6.

Dickemann, M. (1979) 'Female infanticide, reproductive strategies and social stratification; a preliminary model' in Chagnon, N. A. and Irons, W. (eds) Evolutionary biology and human social behaviour; an anthropological perspective, Duxbury Press, Duxbury.

Dickinson, L. E., MacMahon, B., Cole, P. and Brown, J. B. (1974) 'Estrogen profiles of oriental and caucasian women in Hawaii', *New England J. Medicine*, **291**, 1211–3.

Diener, P. (1980) 'Quantum adjustment, macroevolution and the social field; some comments on evolution and culture', *Current Anthropology*, **21**, 423–31.

Dinkle, R. M. (1944) 'Attitude of children toward supporting aged parents', *American Sociological Review*, **9**, 370–9.

Diodorus Siculus (1946) *The library of history*, Heinemann, London.

Dirksen, J. D. D. (1954) 'Recent demographic changes in the Netherlands', in Lorimer, F. (ed.) *Culture and Human Fertility*, Unesco, Paris.

Dixon, R. B. (1971) 'Explaining cross-cultural variations in age at marriage and proportion never marrying', *Population Studies*, **25**, 215–33.

Dobzhansky, T. (1950) 'Evolution in the tropics', *American Science*, **38**, 209–21.

Dodge, O. G., Linsell, C. A. and Davies, J. N. P. (1963) 'Circumcision and the incidence of carcinoma of the penis and cervix', *East African Medical J.*, **40**, 440–1.

Dodwell, H. (1684) *De paucitate martyrum*, London.

Dondog, C. R. (1972) 'Lamaism and its influence on the natural growth of the population of the Mongolian Peoples' Republic', *Sov. Zdravookhr.*, **31**, 52–4.

Dorjahn, V. R. (1958) 'Fertility, polygyny and their interrelations in Temne society', *American Anthropologist*, **60**, 838–60.

Douglas, M. (1966) *Purity and danger*, Routledge and Kegan Paul, London.

Dube, S. C. (1956) *Village India*, Routledge and Kegan Paul, London.

Dublin, L. I. (1963) *Suicide. A sociological and statistical study*, Ronald Press, New York.

Dubois, J. A. (1972) *Hindu manners, customs and ceremonies*, Oxford U.P., UK.

Duguit, L. and Monnier, H. (1898) *Les constitutions de la France depuis 1789*, Paris.

Dumont, L. (1970) *Home hierarchus. The caste system and its implications*, Weidenfeld and Nicolson, London.

Duren, A. (1943) 'La situation démographique des populations indigènes de la Région de Pawa, suivent les enquêtes des docteurs Radna, Degotte and Zanetti', *Bull. de Séances de l'Institut Royal Colonial Belge*, **14**, 356–93.

Durham, W. H. (1976) 'The adaptive significance of cultural behaviour', *Human Ecology*, **4**, 89–121.

Durham, W. H. (1978) 'The co-evolution of human biology and culture', in Blurton-Jones, N. and Reynolds, V. (eds) *Human behaviour and adaptation*, Taylor and Francis, London.

Durkheim, E. (1932) *Suicide. A study in sociology*, Free Press, Chicago.

Durkheim, E. (1961) *The elementary forms of religious life*, Collier, New York.

Eaton, J. W. and Mayer, A. J. (1953) 'The sociobiology of very high fertility among the Hutterites. The demography of a unique population', *Human Biology*, **25**, 206–64.

Economist, The (1981) 'Soviet Moslems. The Kremlin's deep south'. 29 August, 54–6.

Eddy, M. B. G. (1906) *Science and health with key to the Scriptures.* Trustees under the will of M. B. G. Eddy, Boston.

Ehrlich, P. R. and Ehrlich, A. H. (1972) *Population, resources, environment; issues in human biology,* Freeman, San Francisco.

Elgood, C. (1951) *A medical history of Persia and the Eastern Caliphate,* Cambridge U.P., UK.

El Saadawi, N. (1980) *The hidden face of Eve. Women in the Arab world,* Zed, London.

El Tayeb, E. M. (1976) 'Health problems in the Sudan associated with the Mecca pilgrimage', dissertation for Diploma in Tropical Public Health, Ross Institute, London.

Elwin, V. (1947) *The Muria and their ghotul,* Oxford U.P., Bombay.

Encyclopedia Judaica (1971) Keter, Jerusalem.

Enstrom, J. E. (1975) 'Cancer mortality among the Mormons', *Cancer,* **36**, 825–41.

Erlanger, P. (1962) *St Bartholomew's Night,* Weidenfeld and Nicolson, London.

Erman, A. (1901) *Zaubersprüche für Mutter und Kind. Aus dem Papyrus 3027 des Berliner Museums,* Abhandlungen der Königlichen Akademie der Wissenschaften zu Berlin.

Eusebius (1890) *Church history,* Parker, Oxford.

Evans-Pritchard, E. E. (1937) *Witchcraft, oracles and magic among the Azande,* Oxford U.P., UK.

Evans-Pritchard, E. E. (1951) *Kinship and marriage among the Nuer,* Oxford U.P., UK.

Evans-Pritchard, E. E. (1956) *Nuer religion,* Oxford U.P., UK.

Evans-Pritchard, E. E. (1965) *The position of women in primitive societies and other essays in social anthropology,* Faber, London.

Fagley, R. M. (1965) 'Doctrines and attitudes of major religions in regard to fertility', *Ecumenical Review,* **17**, 332–44.

Farooq, M. and Mallah, M. B. (1966) 'The behavioural pattern of social and religious water-contact activities in the Egypt-49 bilharziasis project area', *Bull. World Health Org.,* **35**, 377–87.

Farrow, M. G. and Juberg, R. C. (1969) 'Genetics and laws prohibiting marriage in the United States', *J. American Medical Assoc.,* **209**, 534–8.

Faul, J. P. (1979) 'I studied the monkeys in Kathmandu', *Today's Education,* **April–May,** 48–53.

Fichter, J. H. (1966) *Religion as an occupation. A study in the sociology of professions,* University of Notre Dame, Notre Dame, U.S.A.

Finegold, S. M., Sutter, V. L., Sugihara, P. T., Elder, H. A., Lehmann, S. D. and Phillips, R. L. (1977) 'Fecal microbial flora in Seventh Day Adventist populations and control subjects', *American J. Clinical Nutrition,* **30**, 1781–92.

Finucane, R. C. (1973) 'Faith healing in mediaeval England; miracles at saints' shrines', *Psychiatry,* **36**, 341–6.

Firth, R. (1981) 'Euthanasia', *Royal Anth. Inst. News,* **45**, 1–4.

Fisher, R. A. (1930) *The genetical theory of natural selection,* Oxford U.P., UK.

Flandrin, J-L. (1979) *Families in former times. Kinship, household and sexuality,* Cambridge U.P., UK.

Flick, A. C. (1930) *Decline of the mediaeval Church,* Kegan Paul, London.

Flood, P. (1956) *New problems in medical ethics,* Mercier Press, Cork.

Ford, J. C. and Kelly, G. (1963) *Contemporary moral theology,* Mercier Press, Cork.

Fortes, M. (1949) *The web of kinship among the Tallensi,* Oxford U.P., UK.

Fortier, B. de la (1963) 'Les "enfants trouvés" à l'hôpital général de Montréal; 1754–1804', *Laval Médical,* **34**, 442–53; **35**, 335–47; **36**, 351–9.

Fouchet, M. P. (1957) *L'art amoreux des Indes,* Guilde du Livre, Lausanne.

Frame, J. D. (1968) 'Hepatitis among missionaries in Ethiopia and Sudan', *J. American Medical Assoc.,* **203**, 819–26.

Francis, W. J. A. (1970) 'Reproduction at menarche and menopause in women', *J. Reproduction and Fertility*, **Suppl. 12**, 89–98.

Friedl, J. and Ellis, W. S. (1974) 'Inbreeding, isonymy and isolation in a Swiss community', *Human Biology*, **46**, 699–712.

Friedl, J. and Ellis, W. S. (1976) 'Celibacy, late marriage and potential mates in a Swiss isolate', *Human Biology*, **48**, 23–5.

Friedman, M. and Rosenman, R. H. (1959) 'Association of specific overt behaviour pattern with blood and cardiovascular findings', *J. American Medical Assoc.*, **169**, 1286–96.

Frisch, R. E. (1974) 'Critical weight at menarche. Initiation of the adolescent growth spurt and control of puberty', in Grumbach, G. D., Grave, G. D. and Mayer, F. E. (eds) *Control of the onset of puberty*, Wiley, New York.

Fromageau, G. (1733) *Dictionnaire des cas de conscience*, Paris.

Frommer, D. J. (1964) 'Changing age of menopause', *British Medical J.*, **11**, 349–51.

Gagnon, F. (1950) 'Contribution to the study of the etiology and prevention of cancer of the cervix of the uterus', *American J. Obstet. Gynec.*, **60**, 516–22.

Gajdusek, D. C. (1973) '*Kuru* in the New Guinea Highlands', in Spillane, J. D. (ed.) *Tropical neurology*, Oxford U.P., UK.

Galton, F. (1883) *Inquiries into human faculty and its development*, Macmillan, London.

Gandhi, M. K. (1926) *Young India*, Ganesen, Triplicane.

Ganss, G. E. (1970) *The constitutions of the Society of Jesus with commentary*, Institute Jesuit Sources, St Louis.

Ganzfried, S. (1927) *Code of Jewish Law; a compilation of Jewish laws and customs*, Hebrew Publishing, New York.

Garden, M. (1970) *Lyon et les Lyonnais au xviiie siècle*, Paris.

Garner, J. (1974) 'Spontaneous regressions; scientific documentation as a basis for the declaration of miracles', *Canadian Medical Assoc. J.*, **III**, 1254–64.

Gaudefroy-Demombynes, M. (1954) *Muslim institutions*, Allen and Unwin, London.

Geertz, C. (1960) *The religion of Java*, Free Press, New York.

Gennep, A. van (1960) *The rites of passage*, Routledge, London.

German, J. L. (1979) 'The current state of Bloom's syndrome', in Goodman, R. M. and Motulsky, A. G. (eds) *Genetic diseases among Ashkenazi Jews*, Raven Press, New York.

Gibb, H. A. R. and Kramers, J. H. (1953) *Shorter Encyclopaedia of Islam*, Brill, Leiden.

Giel, R., Gezahegh, Y. and Luijk, J. N. van (1968) 'Faith-healing and spirit possession in Ghion, Ethiopia', *Social Science and Medicine*, **2**, 63–79.

Gjorgov, A. N. (1980) 'Barrier contraception and breast cancer', *Contributions Gynecology and Obstetrics*, **8**, 101–21.

Glass, B., Sacks, M. S., Jahn, E. F. and Hess, C. (1952) 'Genetic drift in a religious isolate; an analysis of the causes of variation in blood group and other gene frequencies in a small population', *American Naturalist*, **86**, 145–59.

Glass, H. B. (1953) 'The genetics of the Dunkers', *Scientific American*, **189**, 76–81.

Glass, J. C. (1972) 'Premarital sexual standards among church youth leaders', *J. Scientific Study of Religion*, **II**, 361–7.

Glasse, R. (1967) 'Cannibalism in the Kuru region of New Guinea', *Trans. New York Academy of Sciences*, **29**, 748–54.

Glubb, J. B. (1970) *The life and times of Muhammad*, History Book Club, London.

Gombrich, R. (1971) 'Food for seven grandmothers; stages in the universalism of a Sinhalese ritual', *Man*, **6**, 5–17.

Goode, W. J. (1960) 'Illegitimacy in the Caribbean social structure', *American Sociological Review*, **25**, 21–30.

Goode, W. J. (1965) *Women in divorce*, Free Press, Glencoe.

Goode, W. J. (1973) *World revolution and family patterns*, Free Press, New York.

Goodman, R. M. (1979) *Genetic disorders among the Jewish people*, Johns Hopkins, Baltimore.

Goody, E. (1970) 'Legitimate and illegitimate aggression' in Douglas, M. (Ed) *Witchcraft confessions and accusations*, Tavistock, London.

Goody, J. (1962) *Death, property and the ancestors. A study of the mortuary customs of the Lodagaa of West Africa*, Tavistock, London.

Gordon, A. I. (1964) *Intermarriage*, Beacon, Boston.

Gorer, G. (1938) *Himalayan village*, Michael Joseph, London.

Gosden, M. (1935) 'Tetanus following circumcision', *Trans. Royal Society Tropical Medicine Hygiene*, **28**, 645–8.

Gosse, E. (1970) *Father and son*, Heinemann, London.

Gould, S. J. and Eldredge, N. (1977) 'Punctuated equilibrii; the tempo and mode of evolution reconsidered', *Paleobiology*, **3**, 115–51.

Graham, J. B., Sotto, L. S. J. and Paloucek, F. P. (1962) *Carcinoma of the cervix*, Saunders, Philadelphia.

Greene, G. (1971) *The power and the glory*, Bodley Head, London.

Greenwald, P., Korns, R. F., Nasca, P. C. and Wolfgang, P. E. (1975) 'Cancer in United States Jews', *Cancer Research*, **35**, 3507–12.

Grégoire, H. (1951) *Les persécutions dans l'Empire Romain*, Royal Academy of Belgium, Brussels.

Gregory, K. F., Carpenter, J. A. and Bending, G. C. (1967) 'Infection hazards of the common communion cup, *Canadian J. Public Health*, **58**, 305–10.

Griscom, J. H. (1843) *Annual report of the interments in the city and county of New York for the year 1842 with remarks theron, and a brief view of the sanitary condition of the city*, James van Norden, New York.

Griscom, J. H. (1847) *First lessons in human physiology to which are added brief rules of health. For the use of schools*, Roe Lockwood and Son, New York.

Griscom, J. H. (1850) *The uses and abuses of air; showing its influence in sustaining life and producing disease,* Redfield, New York.

Griscom, J. H. (1857) *Improvements of the public health and the establishment of a sanitary police in the city of New York*, C. van Benthuysen, Albany.

Groen, J. J. (1964) 'De levenswijze der Trappisten en haar invloed op het ontstaan van coronaire hartziekten en het cholesterolgehalte van het bloed', *Voeding*, **25**, 310–3.

Groen, J. J., Tijong, K. B., Koster, M., Willebrands, A. F., Verdonck, G. and Pierloot, M. (1962) 'The influence of nutrition and ways of life on blood cholesterol and the prevalence of hypertension and coronary heart disease among Trappist and Benedictine monks', *American J. Clinical Nutrition*, **10**, 456–70.

Gruesser, M. J. (1950) 'Categorical valuations of Jews among Catholic parochial school children,' *Catholic University of America Studies in Sociology*, **34.**

Guha, U. M. A. (1943) 'The concepts of God and the ghosts in children', *Indian J. Psychology*, **18**, 133–7.

Guppy, N. (1958) *Wai-wai; through the forests north of the Amazon*, Murray, London.

Haenazel, W. (1961) 'Cancer mortality among the foreign-born in the United States', *J. National Cancer Institute*, **26**, 37–132.

Hair, P. E. H. (1966) 'Bridal pregnancy in rural England in earlier centuries'. *Population Studies*, **20**, 233–43.

Hallpike, C. R. (1973) 'Functionalist interpretations of primitive war', *Man*, **8**, 451–70.

Hamarneh, S. (1962) 'Development of hospitals in Islam', *J. History of Medicine*, **36**, 366–84.

Hamilton, W. D. (1975) 'Innate social aptitudes of man; an approach from evolutionary genetics', in Fox, R. (ed.) *Biosocial Anthropology*, Maleby Press, London.

Hammond, E. C. and Garfinkel, L. (1961) 'Smoking habits of men and women', *J. National Cancer Institute*, **27**, 419–42.

Handley, W. S. (1936) 'The prevention of cancer', *Lancet*, **I**, 987–91.

Haney, C. A. (1972) 'Legitimacy, illegitimacy and live birth ratios in a black population', *J. Health Social Behaviour*, **13**, 303–10.

Hanks, J. R. (1968) *Maternity and its rituals in Bang Chan*, Cornell Thailand Project Report No. 6, Cornell, New York.

Hardinge, M. G., Chambers, A. C., Crooks, H. and Stare, F. J. (1958) 'Nutritional studies of vegetarians. III Dietary levels of fiber', *American J. Clinical Nutrition*, **6**, 523–5.

Hardinge, M. G., Crooks, H. and Stare, F. J. (1962) 'Nutritional studies of vegetarians. IV Dietary fatty acids and serum cholesterol levels', *American J. Clinical Nutrition*, **10**, 516–24.

Häring, B. (1972) *Medical Ethics*, St Paul Publications, Slough.

Harris, M. (1966) 'The cultural ecology of India's sacred cattle', *Current Anthropology*, **7**, 51–66.

Harris, M. (1974) *Cows, pigs, wars and witches; the riddles of culture*, Random House, New York

Harrison, I. E. (1974) 'Traditional healers; a neglected source of health manpower', *Rural Africana*, **26**, 5–16.

Hartley, I. S. (1882) *Memorial of Robert Milham Hartley*, Privately printed, Utica.

Hathout, H. (1972) 'Abortion and Islam', *J. Medicine Libanais*, **25**, 237–9.

Hathout, H. M. (1963) 'Some aspects of female circumcision', *J. Obstet, Gynec. Brit. Comm.*, **70**, 505–7.

Hauser, G. A., Obiri, J. A., Valaer, M., Erb, H. Müller, T., Remen, V. and Vanäänen, P. (1961) 'Der Einfluss des Menarchealters auf das Menopausealter', *Gynaecologia*, **152**, 279–86.

Hebrew Encyclopedia (1953) Encyclopedia Publishing, Jerusalem.

Heer, F. (1962) *The mediaeval world. Europe 1100–1350*, New American Library, New York.

Hegel, G. W. F. (1877) *Lectures on the philosophy of history*, English and Foreign Philosophical Library, London.

Heins, H. C., Dennis, E. J. and Pratt-Thomas, H. R. (1958) 'The possible role of smegma in carcinoma of the cervix', *American J. Obstet. Gynec.*, **76**, 726–35.

Heiss, J. S. (1961) 'Interfaith marriages and marital outcome', *Marriage and Family Living*, **23**, 228–33.

Hemerijckx, F. (1948) 'Enquête sur les causes médicales et sociales de la dénatalité', *Zaire*, **2**, 471–524.

Herodotus (1952) *History*, Heinemann, London.

Hertel, B., Henderson, G. E. and Grimm, J. W. (1974) 'Religion and attitudes to abortion; a study of nurses and social workers', *J. Scientific Study of Religion*, **13**, 23–34.

Hertling, L. (1944) 'Die zahl der martyr bis 313', *Gregorianum*, **25**, 103–29.

Hiatt, L. R. (1981) 'Polyandry in Sri Lanka; a test case for parental investment theory', *Man*, **15**, 583–602.

Hinton, J. M. (1963) 'The physical and mental distress of the dying', *Q. J. Medicine*, **32**, 1–21.

Hippocrates (1957) *Oath*, Heinemann, London.

Hobbs, B. C., Knowlden, J. A. and White, A. (1967) 'Experiments on the communion cup', *J. Hygiene Cambridge*, **65**, 37–48.

Hochman, A., Ratzkowski, E. and Schreiber, H. (1955) 'Incidence of carcinoma of the cervix in Jewish women in Israel', *British J. Cancer*, **9**, 358–64.

Hoffman, L. (1956) 'The problem patient; the Christian Scientist', *Medical Economics*, **33**, 265–83.

Hollings, M. (1977) *The Living Priesthood*, Mayhew-McCrimmon, Great Wakering.

Horowitz, I. and Enterline, P. E. (1970) 'Lung cancer among Jews', *American J. Public Health*, **60**, 275–82.

Horton, P. B. (1940) 'Student interest in the church', *Religious Education*, **35**, 215–9.

Hostetler, J. A. (1970) *Amish society*, Johns Hopkins, Baltimore.

Hotchner, A. E. (1976) *Doris Day. Her own story*, W. H. Allen, London.

Huber, J. (1960) 'Uterus carcinoma and circumcision. Studies in Ethiopia', *Wiener Medizinische Wochenschrift*, **110**, 571–4.

Hudson, E. H. (1963) 'Treponematosis and pilgrimage', *American J. Medical Science*, **246**, 645–56.

Hussein, F. H. (1971) 'Endogamy in Egyptian Nubia', *J. Biosocial Science*, **3**, 251–7.

Imperato, G. (1977) *African folk medicine; beliefs and practices of the Bambara and other peoples*, York Press, Baltimore.

India, Government of (1902a) *Census of India, 1901*, Government Printing Office, Delhi.

India, Government of (1902b) *Census of India, 1901 vol 12, part I (Burma Report)*, Government Printing Office, Rangoon.

India, Government of (1948) *Report of the Committee on indigenous systems of medicine*, Ministry of Health, Delhi.

India, Government of (1964) *Reference Annual*, Ministry of Information and Broadcasting, Delhi.

Inoguchi, R. and Nakajima, T. (1960) *The divine wind; Japan's kamikazi force in World War II*, Bantam, New York.

Ishaq, Ibn, (1970) *The life of Muhammad*, Guillaume, A. (trans.) Oxford U.P., UK

Irons, W. (1979) 'Cultural and Biological Success' in Chagnon, N. A. and Irons, W. (eds). *Evolutionary Biology and Human Social Behaviour*, Duxbury Press, North Scituate, Mass.

Jackson, C. E. and Carey, J. H. (1961) 'Progressive muscular dystrophy, autosomal recessive type', *Pediatrics*, **28**, 77–84.

Jackson, C. E., Symon, W. E., Pruden, E. L., Kaehr, I. M. and Mann, J. D. (1968) 'Consanguinity and blood group distribution in an Amish isolate', *American J. Human Genetics*, **20**, 522–7.

Jahoda, G. (1968) 'Scientific training and the persistence of traditional beliefs among West African University students', *Nature*, **220**, 1356.

Jakobovits, I. (1961) 'Medical aspects of circumcision in Jewish law', *Hebrew Medical J.*, **I**, 258–70.

Jakobovits, I. (1961) 'The religious problem of autopsies in New York Jewish hospitals', *Hebrew Medical J.*, **2**, 233–8.

Jakobovits, I. (1971) 'Euthanasia', *Encyclopedia Judaica*, **6**, 978–9.

Jalal al-Din al Siyuti (1900) *The book of exposition in the science of coition*, Carrington, Paris.

Janzen, J. M. (1974) 'Pluralistic legitimation of the therapy systems in contemporary Zaïre', *Rural Africana*, **26**, 105–22.

Jarvis, G. K. (1977) 'Mormon mortality rates in Canada', *Social Biology*, **24**, 294–302.

Jenks, A. E. (1905) The Bontoc Igorot, Government Ethnographic Surveys No. 1, Manila.

Jenner, D. A., Reynolds, V. and Harrison, G. A. (1980) 'Catecholamine excretion rates and occupation', *Ergonomics*, **23**, 237–46.

Jerome, St (1893) *Letters and selected works*, Parker, Oxford.

John of Damascus (1955) *De fide orthodoxa*, Franciscan Institute, New York.

Johnson, H. M. (1964) 'The Kahuna Hawaiian sorcerer; its dermatologic implications, *Arch. Derm.* (Chicago), **90**, 530–5.

Jones, J. and Nortman, D. (1968) 'Roman Catholic fertility and family planning. A comparative review of research literature', *Studies in Family Planning*, **34**, 1–27.

Jordan, Hashemite Kingdom of (1960) *Statistical Yearbook*, Amman.

Joseph, M. (1917) 'Care of the aged', in Hastings, W. (ed.) *Encyclopedia of Religion and Ethics*, Clark, Edinburgh.

Joyce, C. R. B. and Welldon, R. M. C. (1965) 'The objective efficacy of prayer', *J. Chronic Disease*, **18**, 367–77.

Kaberry, P. M. (1939) *Aboriginal woman; sacred and profane*, Routledge, London.

Kaku, K. (1975a) 'Were girl babies sacrificed to a folk superstition in 1966 in Japan?', *Annals Human Biology*, **2**, 391–3.

Kaku, K. (1975b) 'Increased induced abortion rate in 1966; an aspect of a Japanese folk superstitution', *Annals Human Biology*, **2**, III–5.

Kane, P. V. (1946) *History of the Dharmasastra*, Bhandarkar Oriental Research Institute, Poona.

Kane, P. V. (1950) *Hindu custom and modern law*, University of Bombay Press, Bombay.

Kapadia, K. M. (1957) 'A perspective necessary for the study of social change in India', *Sociological Bulletin*, **6**, 40–9.

Karlin, S., Kenett, R. and Bonné-Tamir, B. (1979) 'Analysis of biochemical genetic data on Jewish populations. II Results and interpretations of heterogeneity and distance measures with respect to standards', *American J. Human Genetics*, **31**, 341–65.

Karve, I. (1953) *Kinship organisation in India*, Deccan College Monograph Series No. 11. Poona.

Kaye, M. M. (1979) *The Far Pavilions Picture Book*, Penguin, Harmondsworth.

Kelly, G. A., Fulkerson, B. R. and Whitford, C. F. (1943) *Modern youth and chastity*, The Queen's Work, St Louis.

Kendrick, M. A. (1974) 'Viral hepatitis in American missionaries abroad', *J. Infectious Disease*, **129**, 227–9.

Kennaway, E. L. (1948) 'The racial and social incidence of cancer of the uterus', *British J. Cancer*, **2**, 177–212.

Kenton, E. (1925) *The Jesuit relations and allied documents; travels and exploration of the Jesuit missionaries in North America (1610–1791)*, Albert and Charles Boni, New York.

Keys, A. (1961) 'Further observations on monastic cholosterol', *New England J. Medicine*, **264**, 1005.

Khanolkar, V. R. (1948) 'Cancer in India', *Acta Unio Internat. Contra Cancrum*, **6**, 880–90.

King, H. (1965) 'Cancer mortality and religious preference; a suggested method in research', *Millbank Memorial Fund Q.*, **43**, 349–58.

King, H. and Bailar, J. C. (1969) 'The health of the clergy; a review of demographic literature', *Demography*, **6**, 27–43.

Kinsey, A. C., Pomeroy, W. B. and Martin, C. E. (1949) *Sexual behaviour in the human male*, Saunders, Philadelphia.

Kinsey, A. C., Pomeroy, W. B. and Martin, C. E. (1953) *Sexual behaviour in the human female*, Saunders, Philadelphia.

Klass, M. (1966) 'Marriage rules in Bengal', *American Anthropologist*, **68**, 951–70.

Kmet, J., Damjanovski, L., Stucin, M., Bonta, S. and Cakmakov, A. (1963) 'Circumcision and carcinoma colli uteri in Macedonia, Yugoslavia. Results from a field study. I Incidence of malignant and premalignant conditions', *British J. Cancer*, **17**, 391–99.

Knutsson K. E. and Selinus, R. (1970) 'Fasting in Ethiopia. An anthropological and nutritional study', *American J. Clinical Nutrition*, **23**, 956–9.

Koran, The (1960) Bell, R. (trans.), Clark, Edinburgh.

Kottmeier, H. L. (1953) *Carcinoma of the female genitalia*, Williams and Wilkins, Baltimore.

Kralj-Cercek, L. (1956) 'The influence of food, body-build and social origin on the age of menarche', *Human Biology*, **28**, 393–406.

Kraus, A. S. and Lilienfeld, A. M. (1959) 'Some epidemiologic aspects of the high mortality rate in the young widow group', *J. Chronic Diseases*, **10**, 207–17.

Krikler, D. M. (1970) 'Diseases of Jews', *Postgraduate Medical J.*, **46**, 687–97.

Kroeber, A. L. (1952) *The nature of culture*, University of Chicago, Chicago.

Krzywicki, L. (1934) *Primitive society and its vital statistics*, Macmillan, London.

Kuhlen, R. G. and Arnold, M. (1944) 'Age differences in religious beliefs and problems during adolescence', *J. Genetic Psychology*, **65**, 291–300.

Kunin, C. M. and McCormack, R. C. (1968) 'An epidemiological study of bacteriuria and blood pressure among nuns and working women', *New England J. Medicine*, **278**, 635–42.

Kurokawa, M. (1969) 'Aculturation and mental health of Mennonite children', *Child Development*, **40**, 689–705.

Kushner, A. W. (1967) 'Two cases of auto-castration due to religious delusions', *British J. Medical Psychology*, **40**, 293–8.

Kyle-Little, S. (1957) *Whispering wind. Adventures in Arnhem Land*, Hutchinson, London.

Lachiver, M. 'Deaths in infancy at Bléré', *Annales de démographie* historique, 224.

Lachiver, M. and Dupaquier, J. (1969) 'Breast feeding and fertility', *Annales. E S C*. 1399.

Lagercrantz, S. (1941) 'Über willkommene und unwillkommene Zwillinge in Afrika', *Ethnologiska Studier*, **12/13**, Gothenburg.

Lambo, T. A. (1971) 'Problems of adjustment between traditional and modern methods of medical practice', in *The Traditional background to medical practice in Nigeria*, Occasional Publication No. 25, Institute of African Studies, Ibadan.

Lambrecht, F. (1938) *Death and death ritual*, Catholic Anthropological Conference, Washington.

Landauer, K. (1925) 'Äquivalente der Trauer', *Internationale Zeitschrift fur Psychonanlysee*, **II**, 194–205.

Landis, J. T. (1949) 'Marriages of mixed and non-mixed religious faiths', *American Sociological Review*, **14**, 401–7.

Landis, J. T. (1960) 'Religiousness, family relationships and family values in Protestant, Catholic and Jewish families', *Marriage and Family Living*, **22**, 341–7.

Lane, E. W. (1954) *Manners and customs of the modern Egyptians,* Dent, London.

Langland, W. (1935) *The vision of Piers Plowman*, Sheed and Ward, London.

Lankester, A. (1924) *Lecture on the responsibility of men in matters relating to maternity*, Govt. of India Press, Simla.

Laslett, P. (1977) *Family life and illicit love in earlier generations*, Cambridge U.P., UK.

Laws of Manu (1969) Buhler, G. (trans), Dover, New York.

Lea, H. C. (1966) *(The history of sacerdotal celibacy*, University Books, USA.

Leach, E. (1976) *Culture and communication*, Cambridge U.P., UK.

Le Bas, P. (1840–45) *Dictionnaire Encyclopedique*, Firmin-Didot, Paris.

Lecky, W. E. H. (1877) *A history of European morals*, Longman, London.

Leff, G. (1967) *Heresy in the later Middle Ages*, Manchester U.P., UK.

Le Flon, J. (1949) *Histoire de l'Église. 20. La crise révolutionnaire. 1789–1846*, Bloud and Gary, Paris.

Leighton, D. and Kluckhohn, C. (1947) *Children of the people*, Harvard U.P. Cambridge, Mass.

Lemon, F. R. and Walden, R. T. (1966) 'Death from respiratory system disease among Seventh Day Adventist men', *J. American Medical Assoc.*, **198**, 117–26.

Lemon, F. R., Walden, R. T. and Woods, R. W. (1964) 'Cancer of the lung and mouth in Seventh Day Adventists', *Cancer*, **17**, 486–97.

Leonard, A. G. (1906) *The lower Niger and its tribes*, Macmillan, London.

Lester, D. (1972) 'Voodoo death; some new thoughts on an old phenomenon', *American Anthropologist*, **74**, 386–90.

Levine, R. R. (1968) 'Judaism and some modern medical problems', *J. Medical Society New Jersey*, **65**, 638–9.

Lévi-Strauss, C. (1962) *La pensée sauvage*, Libraire Plon, Paris.

Lévi-Strauss, C. (1968) 'Discussion No. 22 (b)', in Lee, R. B. and Dvore, I. (eds) *Man the hunter*, Aldine, Chicago.

Levy, R. (1969) *The social structure of Islam*, Cambridge U.P., UK.

Lewis, I. M. (1971) *Ecstatic religion*, Penguin, Harmondsworth.

Leyden, J. (1811) 'On the language and literature of the Indo-Chinese nations', *Asiatic Researches*, **10**, 202.

Lex, B. W. (1974) 'Voodoo death; new thoughts on an old explanation', *American Anthropologist*, **76**, 818–23.

Lightman, S. L., Carr-Locke, D. L. and Pickles, H. G. (1970) 'Frequency of PTC tasters and males defective in colour vision in a Kurdish population in Iran', *Human Biology*, **42**, 665–9.

Lindblom. G (1920) *The Akamba in British East Africa*, Appelbergs Boktryckeri Aktiebolog, Uppsala.

Ling, T. O. (1969) 'Buddhist factors in population growth and control. A survey based on Thailand and Ceylon', *Population Studies*, **23**, 53–60.

Lipsett, M. B. (1975) 'Hormones, nutrition and cancer', *Cancer Research*, **35**, 3359–61.

Longmore, L. (1959) *The dispossessed. A study of the sex-life of Bantu women in and around Johannesburg*, Cape, London.

Lorimer, F. (1954) *Culture and human fertility*, Unesco, Paris.

Losito, P. (1946) 'Church hygiene; microbic content of holy water in various churches in Perugia', *Bulletin Soc. Ital. Bio. Sp.*, **22**, 463–5.

Luckmann, T. (1967) *The invisible religion*, Macmillan, New York.

Lumsden, C. J. and Wilson, E. O. (1981) *Genes, mind and culture*, Harvard U.P., Cambridge, Mass.

Lynch, J. B., Verzin, J. A. and Hassan, A. M. (1963) Cancer of the female genital tract among the Sudanese', *J. Obstet. and Gynec.*, **70**, 495–504.

Lyon, J. L., Klauber, M. R., Gardner, M. S. and Smart, C. R. (1976) 'Cancer incidence in Mormons and non-Mormons in Utah. 1966–70', *New England Medical J.*, **294**, 129–33.

MacArthur, R. H. and Wilson, E. O. (1967) *The theory of island biogeography*, Princeton U.P., USA.

Mackintosh, J. R. (1978) 'The experimental analysis of overcrowding', in Ebling, F. J. and Stoddart, D. M. (eds) *Population control by social behaviour*, Institute of Biology Publications, London.

MacMahon, B., Cole, P. and Brown, J. (1973) 'Etiology of human breast cancer; a review', *J. National Cancer Institute*, **50**, 21–42.

MacMahon, B., Hertig, A. and Ingalls, T. (1954) 'Association between maternal age and pathologic diagnosis of abortion', *Obstet. Gynec.*, **4**, 477–83.

Maddison, D. and Viola, A. (1968) 'The health of widows in the year following bereavement', *J. Psychosomatic Research*, **12**, 297–306.

Maier, W. (1964) 'Die Säuglingssterblichkeit chelich und unchelich Lebendgeborener: Todesursachen, Lebensdauer', *Archiv für Gynakologie*, **199**, 468–74.

Maimonides (1949) *Code*, Yale Judaica Series, Yale U.P., USA.

Malhotra, P. and Prasad, B. G. (1966) 'A study of morbidity among children below 5 years of age in an urban area in Delhi', *Indian J. Medical Research*, **54**, 285–314.

Malinowski, B. (1913) *The family among the Australian Aborigines*, University of London Press, London.

Malinowski, B. (1935) *Coral gardens and their magic*, Allen and Unwin, London.

Malinowski, B. (1944) *The scientific theory of culture*, Oxford U.P., New York.

Marnham, P. (1980) *Lourdes. A modern pilgrimage*, Heinemann, London.

Marris, P. (1959) *Widows and their families*, Institute of Community Studies, London.

Marsden, A. T. H. (1958) 'The geographical pathology of cancer in Malaya', *Brit. J. Cancer*, **12**, 161–76.

Martin, C. E. (1967) 'Marital and coital factors in cervical cancer', *American J. Public Health*, **57**, 803–14.

Marx, K. (1970) *Capital*, Lawrence and Wishart, London.

Mather, C. (1853) *Magnalia Christi Americana*, Hartford.

Mather, I. (1685) *A discourse concerning the danger of apostasy. A call to heaven*, Boston.

Mathieu, Cardinal. (1904) *Le Concordat de 1801*, Paris.

May, G. (1931) *Social control of sex expression*, Morrow, New York.

Maycock, A. L. (1927) *The Inquisition*, Constable, London.

Mayer, A. C. (1965) *Caste and kinship in Central India*, Routledge, London.

Mboria, L. (1938) *La population de l'Egypte*, Procaccia, Cairo.

McAuliffe, M. F. (1954) *Catholic moral teaching on the nature and object of conjugal love*, Catholic University of America, Washington.

McCullagh, E. P. and Cervis, L. A. (1960) 'A study of diet, blood lipids and vascular disease in Trappist monks', *New England J. Medicine*, **263**, 569.

McKusick, V. A. (1973) 'Genetic studies in American inbred populations with particular reference to the Old Order Amish', *Israeli J. Medical Science*, **9**, 1276–84.

McKusick, V. A., Egeland, J. A., Eldridge, R. and Krusen, D. E. (1964a) 'Dwarfism in the Amish. I The Ellis–van Creveld syndrome', *Bull. Johns Hopkins Hosp.*, **115**, 306–36.

McKusick, V. A., Eldridge, R., Hostetler, J. A., Ruangwit, U. and Egeland, J. A. (1965) 'Dwarfism in the Amish. II Cartilage-hair hypoplasia', *Bull. Johns Hopkins Hosp.*, **116**, 285–326.

McKusick, V. A., Hostetler, J. A., Egeland, J. A. and Eldridge, R. (1964b) 'The distribution of certain genes in the Old Order Amish', *Cold Spring Harbor Symp. Quant. Bio.*, **29**, 99–114.

McNeill, J. T. and Gamer, H. M. (eds) (1938) *Mediaeval Handbooks of Penance*, Columbia U.P., New York.

McQuay, R. M. (1967) 'Parasitologic studies in a group of furloughed missionaries. I Intestinal protozoa. II Helminth findings', *American J. Tropical Medicine*, **16**, 154–66.

Mead, G. H. (1934) *Mind, self and society*, University of Chicago Press, Chicago.

Mead, M. (1971) *Coming of age in Samoa*, Penguin, Harmondsworth.

Meals, R. A. (1971) 'Paradoxical frequencies of recessive disorders in Ashkenazi Jews', *Chronic Diseases*, **23**, 547–58.

Meer, F. (1976) *Race and suicide in South Africa*, Routledge and Kegan Paul, London.

Meggitt, M. J. (1965) *The desert people*, Chicago U.P., USA.

Merton, R. K. and Nisbet, R. (1976) *Contemporary social problems*, Harcourt Brace Jovanovich, New York.

Middleton, J. (1971) *Lugbara religion*, Oxford U.P., UK.

Millroth, B. (1965) *Lyuba. Traditional religion of the Sukuma*, Studia Ethnographica Upsaliensia No. 22, Uppsala.

Miner, H. (1953) *The primitive city of Timbuctoo*, Princeton U.P., USA.

Minuck, M. and Lambie, R. S. (1961) 'Anaesthesia and surgery for Jehovah's Witnesses', *Canadian Medical Association J.*, **54**, 1187–91.

Mirone, L. (1954) 'Nutrient intake and blood findings of men on a diet devoid of meat', *American J. Clinical Nutrition*, **2**, 246.

Mishkat al-Masabih or A collection of the most authentic Traditions regarding the actions and sayings of Muhammed (1963) Robson, J. (trans.) Ashraf, Lahore.

Mitra, S. (1958) 'Cancer of the cervix', *Cancer*, **11**, 1190–4.

Moberg, D. O. (1965) 'Religiosity in old age', *Gerontologist*, **5**, 78–87.

Momeni, D. A. (1972) 'The difficulties of changing the age at marriage in Iran', *J. Marriage and Family*, **34**, 545–51.

Momeni, D. A. (1976) 'Husband–wife differentials in Iran', *Social Biology*, **23**, 341–6.

Monahan, T. P. (1973) 'Some dimensions of interreligious marriages in Indiana. 1962–7', *Social Forces*, **52**, 195–203.

Monpin, R. (1918) *L' avortement provoque dans l'antiquité*, Vigot, Paris.

Monteil. V. (1952) *Revue des Études Islamique*, **20**.

Moore, J. L. (1964) 'Religion and blood transfusions', *J. Medical Assoc. Georgia*, **53**, 304.

More, Thomas. (1965) *Utopia*, Yale U.P., USA.

Moreton, F. E. (1944) 'Attitude to religion among adolescents and adults', *British, J. Educ. Psychology*, **14**, 69–79.

Morgan, E. S. (1966) *The Puritan family. Religion and domestic relations in 17th century New England*, Harper and Row, New York.

Morgan, J. N., Meyers, N. and Baldwin, G. (1962) *Income and welfare in the USA*, McGraw-Hill, New York.

Morris, I. (1975) *The nobility of failure*, Secker and Warburg, London.

Mourant, A. E. (1954) *The distribution of human blood groups*, Blackwell, Oxford.

Mourant, A. E., Kopec, A. C. and Domaniewska-Sobczak, K. (1978) *The genetics of the Jews*, Oxford U.P., UK.

Murdock, G. P. (1949) *Social structure*, Macmillan, London.

Murphy, D. P. (1947) *Congenital malformations*, Lippincott, Philadelphia.

Mustafa, A. (1966) 'Female circumcision and infibulation in the Sudan', *J. Obstet. Gynaec. British Commonwealth*, **73**, 302–6.

Myrdal, G. (1968) *Asian drama*, Twentieth Century Fund, New York.

Nadel, S. F. (1954) *Nupe religion*, Routledge, London.

Nag, M. (1962) *Factors affecting human fertility in non-industrial societies*, Yale University Publications in Anthropology No. 66, New Haven.

Naguib, S. M., Comstock, G. W. and Davis, H. D. (1966a) 'Epidemiologic study of trichomoniasis in normal women', *Obstet. Gynec.*, **27**, 607–16.

Naguib, S. M., Lundin, F. E. and Davis, H. J. (1966b) 'Epidemiologic factors related to cervical cancer detected by a screening program in Washington', *Obstet. Gynec.*, **28**, 451–9.

Nansen, F. (1893) *Eskimo life*, Longmans, London.

Nash, J. and Nash. M. (1963) 'Marriage, family and population growth in Upper Burma', *South-Western J. Anthropology*, **19**, 251–66.

Nath, V. and Grewal, K. S. (1935) 'Cancer in India', *Indian J. Medical Research*, **23**, 149–90.

Nath, V. and Grewal, K. S. (1937) 'Cancer in India', *Indian J. Medical Research*, **24**, 633–66.

Needham, J. (1954) *Science and Civilisation in China*, Cambridge U.P., UK.

Neumann, A. K. and Bhatia, J. C. (1973) 'Family planning and indigenous medical practitioners', *Social Science and Medicine*, **7**, 507–16.

New Catholic Encyclopedia (1967) McGraw-Hill, New York.

Newcombe, H. B. and Tavendale, O. G. (1965) 'Effects of father's age on the risk of child handicap or death', *American J. Human Genetics*, **17**, 163–78.

Niebuhr, H. R. (1937) *The kingdom of God in America*, Harper, New York.

Nodari, R. and Pirovane, G. (1970) 'Sulla mortalita infantile. Raffronte dei dati statistici referiti ai bambini nati nel matrimonio e fuori del matrimonio', *Minerva Pediatrica*, **22**, 1254–6 and 1449–51.

Noirhomme, G. (1969) *L'image du prêtre; vu par les grands séminaristes du Congo*, Centre de Recherches Sociologiques, Kinshasha.

Noonan, J. T. (1966) *Contraception; a history of its treatment by Catholic theologians and canonists*, Harvard U.P., Cambridge, Mass.

Nordenstam, T. (1968) *Sudanese ethics*, Scandinavian Institute of African Studies, Uppsala.

Nunn, O. Z. (1964) 'Child control through a "coalition with God"', *Child Development*, **35**, 417–32.

Nurge, E. (1970) 'Birth rate and work load', *American Anthropologist*, **72**, 1434–9.

Ohsawa, G. (1956) *The philosophy of oriental medicine*, Ohsawa Foundation, New York.

Ohsawa, G. (1965) *Zen macrobiotics – The art of longevity and rejuvenation*, Ohsawa Foundation, New York.

Okumiya, M. (1980) *Kamikaze and the Japanese*, New York.

Oliver, S. (1894) *Historia Damiatana*, Bibliothek des litterarischen Vereins in Stuttgart, Tübingen.

Olivier, L. and Ansari, N. (1967) 'The epidemiology of bilharziasis', in Mostofi, F. K. (ed.) *Bilharziasis*, Springer Verlag, New York.

O'Malley, L. S. S. (1932) *Indian caste customs*, Cambridge U.P., UK.

Omar, W. (1958) 'The Mecca pilgrimage is no longer a hazard', *Medical J. Malaya*, **13**, 187–90.

Opler, M. E. (1963) 'The cultural definition of illness in village India', *Human Organisation*, **22**, 32–5.

Otterbein, C. S. and Otterbein, K. F. (1973) 'Believers and beaters; a case study of supernatural beliefs and child rearing in the Bahama Islands', *American Anthropologist*, **75**, 1670–81.

Pakrasi, K. B. (1970) *Female infanticide in India*, Editions Indian, Calcutta.

Pakter, J. (1961) 'Out of wedlock births in New York City. II Medical aspects', *American J. Public Health*, **51**, 846–55.

Paquin, J. (1967) 'Organ transplants', *New Catholic Encyc.*, **10**, 754–6.

Parkes, C. M. Benjamin, B. and Fitzgerald, R. G. (1969) 'A statistical study of increased mortality among widowers', *British Medical J.*, **1**, 740–3.

Parkes, C. M. and Brown, R. J. (1972) 'Health after bereavement. A controlled study of young Boston widows and widowers', *Psychosomatic Medicine*, **34**, 449–61.

Parsons, E. C. (1939) *Pueblo Indian religion*, University of Chicago, Chicago.

Patai, R. (1955) 'Cousin right in Middle Eastern marriage', *South-Western J. Anth.*, **II**, 371–90.

Patimokkha, 227 fundamental rules of a Bhikhu, The (1966) Maha Makut, Bangkok.

Peel, J. D. Y. (1968) *Aladura; a religious movement among the Yoruba*, Oxford U.P., UK.

Philippe, P. (1974) 'Amenorrhea, intrauterine mortality and parental consanguinity in an isolated French Canadian population', *Human Biology*, **46**, 405–24.

Phillips, R. L. (1975) 'Role of life-style and dietary habits in risk of cancer among Seventh-Day Adventists', *Cancer Research*, **35**, 3513–22.

Phillips, R. L., Kuzma, J. W. and Lemon, F. R. (1973) *Mortality from colon-rectal cancer among California Seventh-Day Adventists*, American Public Health Association, San Francisco.

Pianka, E. R. (1970) 'On r– and K– selection', *American Naturalist*, **104**, 592–7.

Pius XI (1931) *Casti connubii*, Catholic Truth Society, London.

Pius XII (1960) *Papal teachings. The human body. Christ the model of blood donors*, St Paul Press, Boston.

Plato (1953) *The Republic*, Heinemann, London.

Pollitzer, R. and Swaroop, S. (1959) *Cholera*, WHO Monograph Series No. 43, Geneva.

Population Council (1968) 'Roman Catholic fertility and family planning. A comparative review of the research literature', *Studies in Family Planning*, No. 38, New York.

Potter, R. G., New, M. L., Wyon, J. B. and Gordon, J. E. (1964) 'Application of field studies to research on the physiology of human reproduction; lactation and its effects upon birth intervals in eleven Punjab villages, India', *Symposium on research issues in public health and population change*, University of Pittsburgh, Pittsburgh.

Potts, M., Diggery, P. and Peel, J. (1973) *Abortion; a study in medical sociology*, Cambridge U.P., UK.

Price-Bonham, S., Santee, B. and Bonham, J. M. (1975) 'An analysis of clergyman's attitude toward abortion', *Review of Religious Research*, **17**, 15–27.

Putai, R. (1958) *The kingdom of Jordan*, Princeton U.P., USA.

Puzo, M. (1972) *The Godfather*, Book Club, London.

Quin, P. V. (1965) 'Critical thinking and open-mindedness in Public and Catholic Secondary Schools', *J. Social Psychol*, **66**, 23–30.

Radcliffe-Brown, A. R. (1952) *Structure and function in primitive society*, Cohen and West, London.

Radcliffe-Brown, A. R. and Forde, D. (1950) *African systems of kinship and marriage*, Oxford U.P., UK.

Rao, P. S. S., Rajamanickam, C. and Fernandez, S. R. J. (1973) 'Personal health expenses among rural communities of North Arcot district', *Indian J. Medical Research*, **61**, 1100–9.

Rappaport, A. (1968) *Pigs for ancestors*, Yale U.P, USA.

Rasmussen, K. (1931) *The Netsilik Eskimos. Report of the Fifth Thule Expedition. 1921–24*, Gylendalske Boghandel, Copenhagen.

Rawson, P. and Legeza, L. (1979) *Tao. The Chinese philosophy of time and change*, Thames and Hudson, London.

Reddy, D. V. S. (1941) 'Medical relief in medieval South India. Centres of medical aid and types of medical institutions', *Bull. History Medicine*, **9**, 385–400.

Rees, W. D. and Lutkins, S. G. (1967) 'Mortality of bereavement', *British Medical J.*, **4**, 13–6.

Remmers, H. H. (1951) 'Some personality aspects and religious values of high school youth', *Purdue Opinion Panel*, **10**, 3.

Renan, E. (1883) *Souvenirs d'enfance et de jeunesse*, Levy Bros, Paris.

Resseguie, L. J. (1974) 'Pregnancy wastage and age of mother among the Amish', *Human Biology*, **46**, 633–9.

Resseguie, L. J. (1976) 'Paternal age, stillbirths and mutation', *Annals Human Genetics*, **40**, 213–9.

Rewell, R. E. (1957) 'Ethnological factors in the aetiology of cancer of the uterine cervix', *J. Obstet. Gynec. British Empire*, **64**, 821–6.

Reynolds, V. (1980) *The biology of human action*, Freeman, Reading.

Reynolds, V., Jenner, D. A., Palmer, C. D. and Harrison, G. A. (1981) 'Catecholamine excretion rates in relation to life-styles in the male population of Otmoor, Oxfordshire', *Ann. Human Biology*, **8**, 197–209.

Rhoads, P. S. (1968) 'Moral considerations in the prolongation of life', *J. South Carolina Medical Assoc.*, **64**, 422–8.

Richards, A. I. (1956) *Chisungu; a girls' initiation ceremony among the Bemba of Northern Rhodesia*, Faber, London.

Rigoni-Stern, D. (1844) 'Nota sulle richerche del Dotter Tanchou interno la frequenza del cancro', *Ann. University Medicine*, **110**, 484–503.

Roberts, I. F., West, R. J., Ogilvie, D. and Dillon, M. J. (1979) 'Malnutrition in infants receiving cult diets; a form of child abuse', *British Medical J.*, **1**, 296–8.

Robson, J. R. K., Konlande, J. E., Larkin, F. A., O'Connor, P. A. and Liu, H.-Y. (1974) 'Zen macrobiotic dietary problems in infancy', *Pediatrics*, **53**, 326–9.

Rogers, L. (1926) 'The conditions influencing the incidence and spread of cholera in India', *Proceedings Royal Society of Medicine. Epidemic Section*, **19**, 59–91.

Rose, H. A. (1907) 'Hindu birth observances in the Punjab', *J. Royal Anthropological Institute*, **37**, 220–36.

Rosen, G. (1958) *A history of public health*, M. D. Publications, New York.

Rosenberg, C. E. and Rosenberg, C. S. (1968) 'Pietism and the origins of the American Public Health Movement; a note on John. H. Griscom and Robert M. Hartley', *J. History Medicine*, **42**, 16–35.

Rosenfeld, H.(1958) 'An analysis of marriage and marriage statistics for a Moslem and Christian Arab village', *International Archives Ethnography*, **49**, 32–62.

Rosenthal, E. (1968) 'Jewish intermarriage in Indiana', *Eugenics Q* , **15**, 277–87.

Rosner, F. (1971) 'Transplants', *Encyclopedia Judaica*, **15**, 1337–40.

Ross, A. D. (1961) *The Hindu family in its urban setting*, University of Toronto Press, Toronto.

Rotkin, I. D. (1962) 'Relation of adolescent coitus to cervical cancer risk', *J. American Medical Assoc.*, **179**, 486–91.

Rowe, J. H. (1944) 'Inca culture at the time of the Spanish conquest', in Steward, J. H. (ed.) *Handbook of the South American Indians*, Smithsonian Institution, Washington.

Rowland, B. (1954) *The art and architecture of India*, Penguin, London.

Runciman, S. (1933) *Byzantine civilization*, Arnold, London.

Rusd, Ibn (1355AH) *Bidâyat al-mujtahid wa nihâyat al muqtasid*, Cairo.

Russell, A. D. and Suhrawardy, A. A.-M. (n.d.) *A manual of the law of marriage*, Kegan Paul, London.

Russell, W. M. S. (1967) *Man, nature and history*, Aldus, London.

Russell, W. M. S. and Russell, C. (1968) *Violence, monkeys and man*, Macmillan, London.

Ryan, B. (1952) 'Institutional factors in Sinhalese fertility', *Milbank Memorial Fund Q.*, **30**, 371–2.

Ryan, B. (1953) 'Hinayana Buddhism and family planning in Ceylon', *Milbank Memorial Fund Conference*, New York.

Sakellariou, G. T. (1938) 'A study of the religious life of Greek youth', *Ereunai Psuchol Ergasteriou Thessalonika*, **2**.

Salisbury, W. S. (1962) 'Religiosity, regional sub-culture and social behaviour', *J. Scientific Study Religion*, **2**, 94–101.

Salmon, J. (1951) 'La polygamie en Chefferie Wamuzimu', *Bull. du Centre d'Etudes des Problèmes Sociaux Indigènes*, **16**, 114–50.

Sargant, W. (1957) *Battle for the mind*, Heinemann, London.

Schaller, G. B. (1972) *The Serengeti lion; a study of predatory relations*, University of Chicago Press, Chicago.

Schapera, I. (1966) *Married life in an African tribe*, Faber, London.

Schechter, D. C. (1968)' Problems relevant to major surgical operations in Jehovah's Witnesses', *American J. Surg.*, **116**, 73–80.

Schneider, G. T. (1974) 'Abortion in a predominantly Catholic community', *J. Louisiana Medical Society*, **126**, 323–5.

Schömig, G. (1953) 'Die weiblichen Genitalkarzinome bei sexueller Enthaltsamkeit', *Strahlentherapig*, **92**, 156–8.

Schull, W. J. (1953) 'The effect of Christianity on consanguinity in Nagasaki', *American Anthropologist*, **55**, 74–88.

Schull, W. J., Yanase, T. and Nemoto, H. (1962) 'Kuroshima. The impact of religion on an island's genetic heritage', *Human Biology*, **34**, 271–98.

Schwarz, B. E. (1960) 'Ordeal by serpents, fire and strychnine. A study of some provocative psychosomatic phenomena', *Psychiatry Q.*, **34**, 405–29.

Schwetz, J. (1923) 'Contribution à l'étude de la démographie Congolaise', *Congo*, **4**, 297–340.

Scribonius Largus (1887) *Compositiones Medica*, Leipzig.

Scurletis, T. D., Surles, K. and Abernathy, J. R. (1969) 'Trends in illegitimacy and associated mortality in North Carolina. 1957–66', *North Carolina Medical J.,* **10**, 214–21.

Seal, S. C. (1964) 'Morbidity survey of contributory Health Service beneficiaries. Part 2; *Indian Council Medical Research*, New Delhi.

Sears, R.R., Maccoby, E. E. and Levin, H. (1957) *Patterns of child rearing*, Row Patterson, Evanston.

Seidman, H. (1966) 'Lung cancer among Jewish, Catholic and Protestant males in New York City', *Cancer*, **19**, 185–90.

Seidman, H. (1970) 'Cancer death rates by site and sex for religious and socio-economic groups in New York City', *Environmental Research*, **3**, 234–50.

Seklawi, M. (1960) 'La fecondité dans les pays Arabes; données numerique, attitudes et comportements', *Population*, **15**, 846.

Seligman, C. G. and Seligman, B. Z. (1911) *The Vedas*, Cambridge U.P., UK.

Selvin, S. and Garfinkel, J. (1976) 'Paternal age, maternal age, birth order and the risk of fetal loss', *Human Biology*, **48**, 223–30.

Sen H. (1903) 'Cholera in the district of Puri with a special account of the epidemic during 1901', *Indian Medical Gazette*, **38**, 135–8.

Shah, J. H. (1959) 'Causes and prevention of suicide', *Indian Conference Social Work*, Hyderabad.

Sheba, C., Szeinberg, A., Ramot, B., Adam, A. and Ashkenazi, I. (1962) 'Epidemiologic surveys of deleterious genes in different population groups in Israel', *American J. Public Health*, **52**, 1101–6.

Sherlock, P. and Rothschild, E. O. (1967) 'Scurvy produced by a Zen macrobiotic diet', *J. American Medical Assoc.*, **199**, 794–8.

Sherring, M. A. (1872) *Hindu tribes and castes*, Thacker Spink, Calcutta.

Shulman, J. (1964) 'Surgical complications of circumcision', *Amer. J. Diseases of Childhood*, **107**, 149–54.

Simpson, C. (1953) *Adam with arrows*, Angus and Robertson, Sydney.

Simpson, C. G. (1944) *Tempo and mode in evolution*, Columbia U.P., New York.

Singer, P. (1981) *The expanding circle; ethics and sociobiology*, Farrar Strauss and Giroux, New York.

Singh, S., Gordon, J. E. and Wyon, J. B. (1962) 'Medical care in fatal illnesses of a rural Punjab population; some social, biological and cultural factors and their ecological implications', *Indian J. Medical Research*, **50**, 865–79.

Smith, M. (1954) *Baba of Kano. A woman of the Moslem Hausa*, Faber, London.

Smith, M. G. (1962) *West Indian family structure*, Washington U.P., USA.

Smith, W. R. (1901) *Lectures on the religion of the Semites*, Black, London.

Smyth, R. B. (1878) *The Aborigines of Victoria*, Government Printer, Melbourne.

Socrates, S. (1891) *Ecclesiastical history*, Parker, Oxford.

Sonneborn, T. M. (1960) 'The human early foetal death rate in relation to age of father', in Strehler, B. L. (ed.) *The biology of aging*, American Institute Biological Sciences, Washington.

Sorsby, M. (1931) *Cancer and race. The incidence of cancer among Jews*, Bales, London.

Spencer, A. (1968) 'Religious census of Bishops Stortford', in Martin, D. (ed.) *Sociological yearbook of religion in Britain*, SCM Press, London.

Spengler, O. (1954) *The decline of the west*, Allen and Unwin, London.

Spiegal, Y. (1977) *The grief process*, SCM Press, London.

Spiro, M. E. (1967) *Burmese supernaturalism*, Prentice Hall, New Jersey.

Spiro, M. E. (1971) *Buddhism and society*, Allen and Unwin, London.

Srinivas, M. N. (1962) *Caste in modern India*, Asia Publishing House, London.

Stearns, S. C. (1977) 'The evolution of life history traits; a critique of the theory and a review of the data', *Ann. Rev. Ecological Systems*, **8**, 145–71.

Steichele, D. F. and Herschlein, H. J. (1964) 'Die Bedeutung der Proteolyse bei geburtshilflichen Defribrininierungsblutungen und die Therapie mit Trasyel', *Archiv für Gynäkologie*, **199**, 475–95.

Stern, C. (1960) *The principles of human genetics*, Freeman, San Francisco.

Stevenson, A. C., Johnston, H. A., Stewart, M. I. P. and Golding, D. R. (1966) 'Congenital malformations', *Bull. World Health Organisation*, **34** Suppl., Geneva.

Stiles, H. R. (1869) *Bundling; its origins, progress and decline in America*, Munsell, Albany.

Stone, J. H. (1969) *Crisis fleeting. Original reports on military medicine in India and Burma in the Second World War*, Office of the Surgeon General, Dept of the Army, Washington.

Strabo (1950) *Geography*, Heinemann, London.

Struhsaker, T. T. (1969) 'Correlates of ecology and social organisation among African Cercopithecines', *Folia. Primat.*, **11**, 80–118.

Sudhoff, K. (1926) *Essays in the history of medicine*, Medical File Press, New York.

Sugiyama, Y. (1965) 'On the social change of Hanuman langurs (*Presbytis entellus*) in their natural condition', *Primates*, **6**, 381–418.

Suriyabongse, L. (1954) 'Human nature in the light of the Buddha's teachings', *J. Siam Society*, **42**, 11–22.

Sutker, P. B. Sutker, L. W. and Kilpatrick, D. G. (1970) 'Religious preference, practice and personal sexual attitudes and behaviour', *Psychological Reports*, **26**, 835–4.

Swantz, M.-L. (1970) *Ritual and symbol in transitional Zaramo society*, Gleerup, Uppsala.

Swaroop, S. and Raman, M. V. (1951) 'Endemicity of cholera in relation to fairs and festivals', *Indian J. Medical Research*, **39**, 41–9.

Tabari, Muhammad ibn Jarir (1879) *Annales*, Leiden.

Tak, J. van der (1974) *Abortion, fertility and changing legislation; an international review*, Lexington Books, Lexington.

Talmud, The (1968) Cohen, A. (trans.) Dent, London.

Tamiya, Ibn (1950) '*Iqtidâ' al-sirât al-mustaqim, muhâlafat 'ashâb al-jahîm*, Cairo.

Tanner, R. E. S. (1957) 'The magician in northern Sukumaland, Tanganyika', *South Western J. Anthropology*, **13**, 344–51.

Tanner, R. E. S. (1958) 'Sukuma ancestor worship and its relationship to social structure', *Tanganyika Notes and Records*, **50**, 52–62.

Tanner, R. E. S. (1964) 'Cousin marriage in the Afro-Arab community of Mombasa, Kenya', *Africa*, **34**, 127–38.

Tanner, R. E. S. (1970) *The witch murders in Sukumaland; a sociological commentary*, Scandinavian Institute of African Studies, Uppsala.

Tapia, A. de (1866) 'Relacion sobre la Conquista de Mexico', in Icazbalceta, J. G. (ed.) *Coleccion de documentos para la historia de Mexico*, Mexico City.

Terris, T. and Oalmann, C. (1960) 'Carcinoma of the cervix', *J. American Medical Assoc.*, **174**, 1874–51.

Tertullian (1884) *Writings*, Clark, Edinburgh.

Thapar, R. (1961) *Asoka and the decline of the Mauryas*, Oxford U.P., UK.

Thompson, J. E. (1933) *Mexico before Cortes; an account of the daily life, religion and ritual of the Aztecs and kindred people*, Scribner, New York.

Thompson, W. S. and Lewis, D. T. (1965) *Population problems*, McGraw-Hill, New York.

Tiwari, S. C. and Bhasin, M. K. (1968) 'The blood groups of the Brahmins and Rajputs of Garhwal', *Human Biology*, **40**, 386–95.

Toland, J. (1971) *The Rising Sun. The decline and fall of the Japanese Empire. 1936–45*; Cassell, London.

Towne, J. E. (1955) 'Carcinoma of the cervix in nulliparous and celibate women', *American J. Obstet. Gynec.*, **69**, 606–13.

Toynbee, A. (1935) *A study of history*, Oxford U.P., UK.

Trimingham, J. S. (1949) *Islam in the Sudan*, Oxford U.P., UK.

Trivers, R. L. (1972) 'Parental investment and sexual selection', in Campbell, B. G. (ed.) *Sexual selection and the descent of man. 1871–1971*, Aldine, Chicago.

Trivers, R. L. and Willard, D. E. (1973) 'Natural selection of parental ability to vary sex ratio of offspring', *Science*, **179**, 90–2.

Turnbull, C. M. (1966) *Wayward servants. The two worlds of the African pygmies*, Eyre and Spottiswoode, London.

Turner, H. W. (1967) *African Independent Church*, Oxford U.P., UK.

Ukaegbu, A. O. (1977) 'Fertility of women in polygynous unions in rural Eastern Nigeria', *J. Marriage and Family*, **39**, 397–404.

Underwood, P. and Underwood, Z. (1980) 'Expectations and realities of Western medicine in a remote tribal society in Yemen, Arabia', in Stanley, N. F. and Joshe, R. A. (eds) *Changing disease patterns and human behaviour*, Academic Press, London.

United Nations Secretariat (1949) *Annual Report* , Department of Social Affairs, New York.

United States, Department of Commerce (1979) *Statistical Abstract*, Government Printing Office, Washington.

United States, Department of Health, Education and Welfare (1960) *Monthly vital statistics report. Annual summary for 1959*, Government Printing Office, Washington.

Vacandard, E. (1908) *The Inquisition*, Longman, New York.

Vatican II Council (1966) *Constitution on the Church in the modern world*, Secretariat of the Council, Vatican.

Vaux, K. (1976) 'Religion and health', *Preventative Medicine*, **5**, 522–36.

Vayda, A. (1976) *War in ecological perspective. Perspective, change and adaptive processes in three Oceanic societies*, Plenum Press, New York.

Vayda, A. P. (1969) 'Expansion and warfare among swidden agriculturalists', in Vayda, A. P. (ed.) *Environment and cultural behaviour*, Doubleday, Garden City.

Versluys, J. J. (1949) 'Cancer and occupation in the Netherlands', *British J. Cancer*, **3**, 161–85.

Waddell, L. A. (1967) *The Buddhism of Tibet*, Heffer, Cambridge.

Wagner, G. (1949) *The Bantu of north Kavirondo*, Oxford U.P., UK.

Wahi, P. N. (1972) 'Religion and cervical carcinoma in Agra', *Indian J. Cancer*, **9**, 210–5.

Wall, R. L., McConnell, J., Moore, D., Macpherson, C. R. and Marston, A. (1967) 'Christmas disease, color blindness and blood group Xg^A' *American J. Medicine*, **43**, 214–26.

Walsh, J. J. (1928) *The Catholic Church and healing*, Burns Oates and Washbourne, London.

Ward, C. D. (1973) 'Anti-semitism at College; changes since Vatican II', *J. Scientific Study Religion*, **12**, 85–8.

Watt, W. M. (1967) *Companion to the Qur'an*, Allen and Unwin, London.

Watt, W. M. (1968) *Muhammad at Medina*, Oxford U.P., UK.

Watt, W. M. (1970a) *Bell's Introduction to the Qur'an*, Edinburgh U.P., Edinburgh.

Watt, W. M. (1970b) *The faith and practice of Al-Ghazali*, Allen and Unwin, London.

Weeks, H. A. (1943) 'Differential divorce rates by occupation', *Social Forces*, **21**, 334–7.

Weindling, P. (1981) 'Theories of the Cell State in Imperial Germany', in Webster, C. (ed.) *Biology, medicine and society, 1840–1940*, Cambridge U.P., UK.

Weiner, I., Burke, L. and Goldberger, M. A. (1951) 'Carcinoma of the cervix in Jewish women', *American J. Obstet. Gynec.*, **61**, 418–22.

Weiss, C. (1962) 'Ritual circumcision. Comments on current practice in American hospitals', *Clin. Pediat. (Phila)*, **1**, 65–72.

Weiss, C. (1964) 'Routine non-ritual cicumcision in infancy', *Clinical Pediatrics (Philadelphia)*, **3**, 560–3.

Weiss, N. (1888) 'La Seine et le nombre des victimes parisiennes de la Saint Barthélemy', *Bulletin Société de l'histoire du Protestantisme Française*, **36**, 374.

Welbourn, E. M. (1955) 'The danger period during weaning; a study of Baganda children who were attending Child Welfare Clinics near Kampala, Uganda', *J. Tropical Pediatrics*, **I**, 34–46, 98–111 and 161–73.

Wendt, H. W. (1965) 'Points of origin for infant ecologies. Religion and purchase of devices affecting pre-verbal mobility', *Psychol Reps.*, **16**, 209–10.

Westermarck, E. (1912) *The origin and development of moral ideas*, Macmillan, London.

Westermarck, E. (1914) *Marriage ceremonies in Morocco*, Macmillan, London.

Westermarck, E. (1921) *The history of human marriage*, Macmillan, New York.

Westoff, C. F., Moore, E. C. and Ryder, N. B. (1969) 'The structure of attitudes to abortion', *Milbank Memorial Fund Q.*, **47**, 11–37.

Westoff, C. F. and Ryder, N. B. (1977) *The contraceptive revolution*, Princeton U.P., USA.

Weyl, N. (1968) 'Some possible genetic implications of Carthaginian child sacrifice', *Perspectives Biology Medicine*, **12**, 69–78.

Whelpton, P. K. and Kiser, C. V. (1943) 'Social and psychological factors affecting fertility. I Differential fertility among 41,498 native white couples in Indianapolis', *Milbank Memorial Fund Q.*, **21**, 221–80.

Wieger, L. (1929) *Textes historiques*, Mission Press, Hsienhsien.

Wilbois, J. (1934) *Le Cameroun; les indigènes, les colons, les missions, l'Administration Française*, Payot, Paris.

Wilkins, W. J. (1975) *Modern Hinduism*, B.R. Publishing, Delhi.

Williams, G. C. (1966) *Adaptation and natural selection*, Princeton U.P., USA.

Williams, R. H. (1969) 'Our role in the generation, modification and termination of life', *Archives International Medicine*, **124**, 215–37.

Willshire, W. H. (1895) 'On the manners etc. of the natives of Central Australia', *J. Anthropological Institute*, **24**, 183–5.

Wilson, B. (1970) *Religious sects*, Weidenfeld and Nicolson, London.

Wilson, E. O. (1975) *Sociobiology*, Harvard U.P. Cambridge, Mass.

Wilson, G. E. (1956) 'Christian Science and longevity', *J. Forensic Science*, **1**, 43–60.

Wingrove, C. R. and Alston, J. P. (1971) 'Age, aging and church attendance', *Gerontologist*, **11**, 356–8.

Wolbarst, A. L. (1932) 'Circumcision and penile cancer', *Lancet*, **1**, 150–3.

Wolf, A. J. (1976) 'Judaism on medicine', *Yale J. Biology Medicine*, **49**, 385–9.

Woodburn, J. (1968) 'Stability and flexibility in Hadza residential groupings', in Blee, R. and DeVere, I. (eds) *Man the Hunter*, Aldine, Chicago.

Woolf, C. M. (1965) 'Stillbirths and parental age', *Obstet. Gynec.*, **26**, 1–8.

Workneh, F. and Giel, R. (1975) 'Medical dilemma; a survey of the healing practice of a Coptic priest and an Ethiopian sheikh', *Tropical and Geographical Medicine*, **27**, 431–9.

Worswick, C. (1980) *Japan: photographs 1854–1905*, Hamish Hamilton, London.

Wynder, E. L., Cornfield, J., Schroff, P. D. and Doraiswami, K. R. (1954) 'A study of environmental factors in carcinoma of the cervix', *American J. Obstet. Gynec.*, **68**, 1016–52.

Wynder, E. L., Lemon, F. R. and Bross, I. J. (1959) 'Cancer and coronary artery disease among Seventh Day Adventists', *Cancer*, **12**, 1016–28.

Wynder, E. L. and Mantel, N. (1966) 'Some epidemiological features of lung cancer among Jewish males', *Cancer*, **19**, 191–5.

Wynder, E. L., Mantel, N. and Licklider, S. D. (1960) 'Statistical considerations on circumcision and cervical cancer', *American J. Obstet. Gynec.,* **79**, 1026–30.

Yadin, Y. (1970) *Masada*, Weidenfeld and Nicolson, London.

Yaukey, D. (1961) *Fertility differentials in a modernising country*, Princeton U.P., USA.

Yerushalmy, J. (1939) 'Age of father and survival of offspring', *Human Biology*, **11**, 342–56.

Yoke, H. P. (1973) 'Elixer plants; pharmaceutical manual of Lü Ch'un-yang', in Nakayama, S. and Sivin, S. (eds) *Chinese Science. Explorations of an ancient tradition*, MIT Press, Cambridge, Mass.

Young, M., Benjamin B. and Wallis, C. (1963) 'Mortality of widowers', *Lancet*, **2**, 454–6.

Zaenglein, M. M., Vener, A. M. and Stewart, C. S. (1975) 'The adolescent and his religion; beliefs in transition', *Review Religious Research*, **17**, 51–60.

Ziegler, P. (1970) *The Black Death*, Penguin, Harmondsworth.

Zimmerman, C. C. and Cervantes, L. F. (1960) *Successful American families*, Pageant, New York.

Zuk, G. H., Miller, R. L., Bartram, J. B. and Kling, F. (1961) 'Maternal acceptance of retarded children; a questionnaire study of attitudes and religious background', *Child Development*, **32**, 525–40.

Author Index

Subject Index